Between Tsar and People

Between Tsar and People

EDUCATED SOCIETY AND THE QUEST
FOR PUBLIC IDENTITY
IN LATE IMPERIAL RUSSIA

Edited by Edith W. Clowes,
Samuel D. Kassow, and
James L. West

PRINCETON UNIVERSITY PRESS

PRINCETON, NEW JERSEY

Copyright © 1991 by Princeton University Press
Published by Princeton University Press, 41 William Street,
Princeton, New Jersey 08540
In the United Kingdom: Princeton University Press, Oxford

Library of Congress Cataloging-in-Publication Data

Between tsar and people : educated society and the quest for
public identity in late imperial Russia / edited by Edith W. Clowes,
Samuel D. Kassow, and James L. West.
p.   cm.
Includes index.
1. Soviet Union—History—Alexander II, 1855–1881. 2. Soviet
Union—History—Alexander II, 1881–1894. 3. Soviet Union—
History—Nicholas II, 1894–1917. 4. Intellectuals—Soviet Union—
History—19th century. 5. Middle classes—Soviet Union—History—
19th century. 6. Soviet Union—Intellectual life—19th century.
I. Clowes, Edith W. II. Kassow, Samuel D. III. West,
James L., 1944–   .
DK220.B48   1991   947.08′1—dc20   90-9079

ISBN 0-691-03153-3 (cloth)—ISBN 0-691-00851-5 (pbk.)

This book has been composed in Times Roman

Princeton University Press books are printed on acid-free paper,
and meet the guidelines for permanence and durability of the
Committee on Production Guidelines for Book Longevity of the
Council on Library Resources

Printed in the United States of America by Princeton University Press,
Princeton, New Jersey

1   3   5   7   9   10   8   6   4   2

1   3   5   7   9   10   8   6   4   2
(Pbk.)

To our teachers

Robert L. Jackson and the late Cyril E. Black

CONTENTS

LIST OF ILLUSTRATIONS

ACKNOWLEDGMENTS

MANY PEOPLE and institutions have helped us as we developed this project. The National Endowment for the Humanities was very generous in its support of our research conference on Russian *Obshchestvennost'*, held at Purdue University, West Lafayette, Indiana, in September 1987. Trinity College of Hartford, Connecticut, and Indiana University's Russian and East European Institute as well as Purdue's Department of Foreign Languages and Literatures, Department of History, and the Office of the Dean of the School of Humanities, Social Sciences, and Education provided additional supporting funds.

For their help in running the conference and preparing the manuscript we especially thank Diane Lasic, Carol Gog, Karen Knight, and Rhonda Woods of Purdue's Department of Foreign Languages and Literatures.

Abbott Gleason and Sidney Monas gave us valuable comments on the first drafts of the papers. At a later stage, Bernice Rosenthal and Thomas Owen gave generously of their time to read and comment on the volume as a whole.

ABBREVIATIONS

GIIsk	Gosudarstvennoe izdatel'stvo iskusstva
GIKhL	Gosudarstvennoe isdatel'stvo khudozhestvennoi literatury
GIPL	Gosudarstvennoe izdatel'stvo politicheskoi literatury
ROBIL	Rukopisnyi otdel biblioteki imeni V. I. Lenina
TsGALI	Tsentral'nyi gosudarstvennyi arkhiv literatury i iskusstva
TsGAOR	Tsentral'nyi gosudarstvennyi arkhiv Oktiabr'skoi revoliutsii
TsGIA	Tsentral'nyi gosudarstvennyi istoricheskii arkhiv
VTO	Vserossiiskoe teatral'noe obshchestvo

PART ONE

The Problem

Chapter 1

INTRODUCTION: THE PROBLEM OF THE MIDDLE IN LATE IMPERIAL RUSSIAN SOCIETY

SAMUEL D. KASSOW, JAMES L. WEST, AND EDITH W. CLOWES

OBSHCHESTVENNOST' AS CIVIL SOCIETY

The central theme of this collection of essays is the interrelationship between social change—specifically the rise of an urban Russia in the late nineteenth century—and the search for new patterns of social identity that could define and perhaps unite emerging "middling" groups in Russian society. Defining a "middle class" is notoriously difficult, especially when one is dealing with Russian terms, such as *obshchestvennost'*, that have no exact equivalents in English. From these essays emerges an emphasis on process rather than result, an awareness of a nagging problem rather than its clear resolution.

Instead of starting from the assertion that a middle class actually existed, this collection focuses on the way that disparate groups in Russian society, groups that previously had little mutual contact, confronted both the possibility of achieving national renewal and the creation of new coalitions using political symbolism, cultural institutions, education, and professionalization. The contributors examine the assertion that the idea of a middle class was a basic element of this political symbolism, a term connoting the transcendence of traditional estate loyalties in favor of wider class identities. Merely confronting the problem of middle-class identity is quite different from saying that such an identity actually developed. But by the end of the nineteenth century, economic, political, and social pressures had forced serious consideration of how and on what terms various groups could find a new vocabulary of self-definition and how this vocabulary would affect their relationship to the state and the peasant masses. In short, we examine the interrelationship of language, politics, social class, and culture while remaining conscious of the clear differences in connotation between terms like middle class and Russian semi-equivalents such as obshchestvennost' and *burzhuaziia*.

Obshchestvennost' connoted an "educated society" whose sense of identity rested on a keen perception that the Russian "nation" differed from the Russian "state"; that is, Russia's future depended on achieving a proper and harmonious balance between autonomous social initiative and state power. Obshchestvennost' implied not so much a class, possessing a consciousness based on economic self-interest, as an informal yet authoritative presence of educated Russians determined to work for the common good, for "progress." The Great Reforms and, more important, the Liberation Movement just prior to the Revolution of 1905 imbued the concept of obshchestvennost' with force and legitimacy. The aftermath of the 1905 Revolution, however, exposed the precariousness of its ideology of social unity. Hopes that political parties like the Kadets would craft the vision of obshchestvennost' into an effective lever for political and cultural transformation foundered on the hard realities of the social and cultural gaps that not only divided middling groups from the masses but also exposed the fragile self-image and lack of unity of the groups themselves.

If obshchestvennost' provided a frail foundation for anchoring middle-class identity, then burzhuaziia was even less suitable. With the conspicuous exception of a few industrialists who took pride in the term, this was a pejorative label, for not only Marxists but also professionals and intellectuals in general. It implied the fact of class, the presence of class conflict, and the need to admit social division rather than social unity. Moreover, burzhuaziia legitimized self-seeking behavior—the pursuit of material gain—as a proper goal of human enterprise. The traditional guilt felt by relatively more fortunate members of Russian society when confronted with the vast sufferings of the masses did not yield easily to new notions about individual initiative and legitimate profit. Nonetheless, as these essays show, coming to terms with the problem of legitimizing individual initiative was basic to the social and cultural history of Late Imperial Russia.

The problem is both complex and clear. How can one speak of middle-class identity when many of those whom historians are tempted to push into the middle class resisted the very notion of class? Until the mid-nineteenth century, Russian social identity had been largely defined by traditional categories: nobility, clergy, merchantry, and peasantry. These identities rested on the uneasy but crucial legal concept of *soslovie*, created by the tsarist state for its own administrative and fiscal purposes. But then urbanization, the growth of educational opportunities, the rise of institutions of self-administration such as the zemstvo, and general economic transformation created many new social groups—professionals, industrialists, artists—who did not fit the traditional categories but who derived social position and self-conception from a fundamental premise of negative definition. In short, they were defined by what they were not: They were not gentry, not *chinovniki* (bureaucrats), not peasants. Their place meshed poorly, if at all, with traditional soslovie categories. As time went on, these emerging, primarily urban groups could not easily identify with another traditional category: the intelligentsia. Intelligentsia implied a basic contradiction between self-interest and the common good. The traditions of the intelligentsia came under increasing attack for many reasons: lack of patriotism; intolerance; failure to recognize the importance of the private life; an implausible, monistic approach to reality that left little room for artistic creativity and experimentation; a rejection of the self-discipline necessary for individual expression.

To say that traditional labels like soslovie and intelligentsia fit poorly is not the same thing as asserting their unimportance or minimizing their persistent power to shape perceptions. The resurgent political power of the landed gentry after 1905, or Lenin's role in 1917 underscore the folly of briskly burying traditional labels in order to proceed to new categories. Important here, as we see, is the questioning of these labels, a crucial step in the search for a new personal and social identity. Could these groups then reach out to each other and find common ground, either under the ideological umbrella of obshchestvennost' or, less plausible, within an emerging structure of classes as a burzhuaziia? And if neither concept was entirely suitable, then is there a workable framework within which one can pursue the question of middle-class identity in tsarist Russia?

If the problem were simply another gloss on the theme of an emerging "society" confronting a restrictive "state," then its dynamics would be essentially political, and matters would be simpler. The challenge of this book is to seek a new and more appropriate balance between the political dimension, of crucial importance, and those aspects of middle-class formation that proceeded without explicit reference to political factors. There was a goodly dose of disaggregation as well as aggregation here. Building coalitions to achieve political ends was one side of the coin; exercising individual choices and searching for a legitimate private sphere formed the other. Changing attitudes toward privacy, stricter delineation of the religious and the private spheres, new notions of property law and contracts were just as significant as the development of political parties or internecine ideological conflicts. And we argue that precisely in the intersection of law and society facile assumptions about the chasm between state and society break down.

In his article on the American middle class—admittedly a different historical case—Stuart Blumin suggested a "central paradox in the concept of middle class formation": "the building of a class which binds itself as a social group in part through the common embrace of an ideology of social atomism! Only if this is indeed a paradox, and not an outright contradiction, does it help explain how the middle class could come to exist without manifesting itself in politics."[1] In defining this paradox, Blumin stipulates an essential precondition: a political system already structured to meet the demands of the middle class. Such a system did not exist in Russia. But as this collection shows, Blumin's remarks give vital clues to understanding the formation of the "middle" of tsarist Russian society. For if there was much unique in the tsarist political system, it was nevertheless not as far from Blumin's precondition as

[1] Stuart Blumin, "The Hypothesis of Middle-Class Formation in Nineteenth-Century America: A Critique and Some Proposals," *American Historical Review* 2 (1985): 299–338.

one might think. Under tsarist authoritarianism, in contrast to Stalin's reign of terror, there was just enough interplay between repression and freedom, obscurantism and liberty, arbitrariness and legal order, to create the preconditions for what we commonly call a "civil society."

The elusive concept of civil society implies a critical mass of educated individuals, voluntary associations, journalistic media, professional societies, universities, patronage networks, cultural organizations, and other structures that establish intermediate identities between the family and the state. Central to the notion of civil society is the assumption of a basic legal framework that protects freedom of organization and choice. One might also assume values that protect the idea of a "civic sphere," a sense of a "public culture" that legitimizes social collaboration as an indispensable adjunct to family life, on the one hand, and the realm of state and administrative power, on the other.

One can readily admit that any society must have some structure. What emerges, however, is the decisive importance of how a structure of autonomous social, professional, and cultural organizations and options creates a sense of difference as well as a keen awareness of both the necessary functions of and the inherent limitations of the state. Civil society reflects some sense, however amorphous, that one must avoid both the extremes of excessive individualism, where pursuit of private gain outweighs any public obligation, and excessive state power, where monistic force crushes the public sphere.

The question of civil society raises vital and interrelated issues concerning, for example, public identity, civic responsibility, and professional ethics. An obvious challenge is to delineate two complementary but different concepts: civil society and middle class. Civil society implies not so much a specific complex of ideas, institutions, and identities; rather, it connotes, through the presence of organizational and cultural networks, a basic attitude about power. The presence of the civil society implies agreement on two things: the state should not and cannot do everything, and people are public as well as private creatures.

Relating middle class to the concept of civil society is not easy. These essays do so in the only possible way: by tracing an interactive process between these new civil institutions and relations and those groups in Russian society that did not fit, or were not satisfied with, traditional legal, social, or cultural categories. Emerging networks of voluntary associations or professional groups forged new possibilities for defining identity and exercising choice. They also raised the likelihood that a growing number of individuals affected by these new opportunities would develop or at least seek new associations having articulate common concerns. Part of this effort might involve the indispensable search for adequate language to buttress these new identities, as well as the conscious rejection of some traditional labels we have already mentioned. This interplay of aggregation and rejection, based on an emerging civil society, underlay the emergence of a "middle" in tsarist Russia.

It is hard to conceive of a civil society without the large-scale urbanization that occurred in the second half of the nineteenth century. Indeed, the rise of an urban landscape in tsarist Russia is another vital theme of this collection. City spaces, and their seeming promise for the future, provided the essential setting for creating a new social sensibility. Urban living more clearly distinguished between public and private spheres and allowed a personal life that included leisure and enjoyment. Along with this impulse came a new idea of "service": a desire to improve and embellish the city environment by defining a presence in the urban landscape, through asserting private visions of an alternative social or aesthetic order. This complex gave birth to a social consciousness altogether distinct from the ascetic gentry-*raznochinets* ideal of self-lessness in the name of society or service to the *narod*.

This sensibility in part reflected the growing influence of professionalization and the professional ideal. To serve required not just moral fervor but skill, knowledge, autonomy, and respect. The professional served the public good not by debasing himself before the people, but by perfecting his own expertise and creative powers. If along the way he earned enough for a comfortable life, then that was not something to feel guilty about.

The process of professionalization was yet another reminder of the complex issues surrounding the formation of a middle in tsarist Russia. For professionals, two particular sources of ambivalence persisted: first, the relationship between the "free" professions and the state was tenuous; and second, egalitarian impulses were strained while recognizing the inherent need for hierarchy and authority. Although professionals wanted autonomy from the state, much of their professional work would be useless without the government's active cooperation. Many wanted a democratic political system yet rejected the notion of nonhierarchial, egalitarian organization demanded by colleagues below them in status. A new nexus of values, emerging from the professional ideal, strove to integrate the imperatives of personal achievement with service to the greater good.

In trying to integrate these imperatives, Russia's professional groups tended to espouse values that questioned not only the prerogatives of the bureaucracy but also the emerging claims of Russia's entrepreneurial elite. In his work on the development of the middle class in nineteenth-century Britain, Harold Perkin suggested an interplay between two competing ideals: the entrepreneurial and the professional.[2] The professional, to follow Perkin, stressed the central role of informed expertise in mediating social progress and overcoming tensions generated by economic development. The entrepreneur, however, relied on the driving force of hard work, courage, and the free market. Both ideals

[2] Harold Perkin, *The Origins of Modern English Society, 1780–1880* (London: Routledge and Kegan Paul, 1969).

converged in their assault on the traditional aristocracy's claims to leadership and the entitlements of tradition and birth.

In Russia, these ideals diverged. The new professionals tended to share the old intelligentsia's distaste for things bourgeois. For their part, Russian industrialists found themselves even more isolated from the cultural elites and even more divided along regional, ethnic, and economic lines than their continental counterparts. Nor was it clear that private enterprise and free-market capitalism, on their own, could conceive coherent economic and investment strategies to solve Russia's various developmental problems. Even if such strategies were feasible, from the time of Herzen in the 1840s, there remained the formidable obstacles posed by Russia's intellectual and cultural traditions, which were largely hostile to the idea of laissez-faire capitalism and the profit motive. One well-known result of Russia's underdevelopment was the luxury of observing—and rejecting—the bourgeois West. The last years of the nineteenth century exposed the disunity and diffidence of the European bourgeoisie; this did little to displace these perceptions. Marxist and Populist ideology rejected the vision of a bourgeois future, and writers and artists of all political stripes typically portrayed the merchant in an unflattering light.

A central theme of this collection is the effort of a few leading industrialists to defend not just the traditional merchant estate but, more importantly, to articulate an ideology that justified a work-oriented, capitalist Russia under the leadership of a burzhuaziia. These industrialists were not alone. Intellectuals emerged to argue for an "Orthodox work ethic," a kind of public religion capable of encouraging creativity and diligence and countering the traditional stigmatization of profit and the marketplace. Neither industrialists nor intellectuals relied primarily on Western models, preferring instead to reach into Russia's Orthodox and—more suggestively—Old Believer traditions. One cannot pretend that these stirrings changed the course of history, but they do provide more than just vital clues to the formation of a middle in tsarist Russia. Through patronage and civic leadership, merchants were central to the process of forming the new urban landscape.

Experimentation in the arts played a crucial role in creating and exploring the new world of the city. A vibrant and innovative culture was emerging, supported by and addressed to an expanding and increasingly educated urban audience. This culture suggested a definition of the "self" quite distinct from the earlier gentry and raznochinets notion of *lichnost'*. With their new industrial wealth patrons endowed cultural institutions at the heart of the new civil sensibility: educational facilities, theaters, museums, conservatories, professional organizations, publishing houses, newspapers, and journals. Such ventures helped move the city to the center of Russian life and make it more than just the large village it had been in the pre-Reform era.

A new conception of how one functions as a private individual and citizen was appearing in artistic and musical circles, in the theater, and in urban architecture. Here, as elsewhere, deep ambiguities emerged as new styles and attitudes jostled with old ones. At the heart of the varied-artistic trends of the age could be found an ambiguous sense of self. At the same time, as individual identity, private experience, personal will, and self-motivation fueled the creativity of this period, images of self-doubt and lost self-assurance abounded. Whether expressed in solitary creativity, social elitism, or new cultural movements, the search for individual consciousness conflicted with the lingering attraction to collective forms of identity: the yearning to blend with the narod or with a new national community.

Cultural expressions of Russia's place in the world were also growing more ambiguous. The old dichotomy of Russia and the West was no longer so clear as it had been for previous generations. This culture possessed a strong cosmopolitan quality: for the first time in history, Russian theater, art, music, and dance entered into a dialogue of equals with contemporary Europe. Russian creativity was beginning to have a significant impact on developments in the West, and Russian artists traversed national and aesthetic boundaries as never before, The sense of cultural inferiority that had haunted Russian artists and intellectuals for generations now faded; it was replaced by a more subtle anxiety about Russia's place between East and West. This anxiety was expressed in an artistic and intellectual flux between modernist experimentation and nostalgic nationalism.

The new sense of time that characterizes this culture of the middle was as difficult to define as the new sense of place. A strong impulse toward the future was mixed with retrospective moods. The perception of the present was fleeting and uncertain. There was a marked ambiguity between liberating aesthetic experimentation and a persistent need for ritual and tradition, between modernist innovation and the reanimation of archaic forms. The nostalgic attempt to recapture the past jostled with the parodic impulse to undermine previous patterns and to press for new forms of artistic statement.

Together these patterns represented varied expression of a new social and cultural consciousness and pointed suggestively toward the creation of social myth that might have legitimized change and sanctified an emerging social and economic order. This attempt to create a culture based on private wealth, private institutions, and private perceptions should be understood as belonging to a century-long effort on the part of the urban middle in Russia to assert its own distinctive identity against both the state and the traditional and revolutionary forms of collectivism.

The Problem of Middle-Class Society in European Historiography

In the last twenty years, historians, raising new questions, have devoted more attention to the problematic of the bourgeoisie. Although Eric Hobsbawm has eloquently defended the popular paradigm of the "bourgeois century" in his

Age of Capitalism, most scholars would now lean toward Arno Mayer's thesis of late nineteenth-century bourgeois failure to become a "class for itself"; the bourgeoisie was unable to gain political power or social preeminence over entrenched aristocratic elites.[3] One important reason for the fragile bourgeois identity, as the works of Phil Nord and Jürgen Kocka illustrate, is the specific problem of the "lower middle classes" and "shopkeepers" and the constant tensions that complicated the relationships between them and other middling groups.[4] In other words, the closer one gets to the bourgeoisie, the less united and more elusive it appears.

Nonetheless, it would be absurd to throw out the term and pretend that the idea of the bourgeoisie is irrelevant. Recent work by Blumin on the United States Eley and Blackbourne on Germany suggest promising new directions of research.[5] While supporting Arno Mayer's argument that the bourgeoisie failed to win political preeminence, Eley and Blackbourne nonetheless try to recast the debate by making a powerful (albeit unconvincing) argument that the Bismarckian Reich was in fact a bourgeois system. In other words, they assert that historians like Wehler and Mayer were asking the wrong questions.[6] Who controlled the apparent levers of political power in pre-1914 Germany was less important than the bourgeoisie's success in molding and defining social, legal, and cultural structures.

In the end, we find this argument unpersuasive. It takes more than voluntary associations and property laws to make a bourgeois society. But we recognize the vital importance of exploring the interrelationship between the development of a civil society and the search for bourgeois identity in tsarist Russia. And although the focus of this book is on process rather than result, the thrust of the essays tends toward a pessimistic appraisal of the social cohesion of Russia's middling groups on the eve of World War I.

These essays further contribute to the questions raised by Hobsbawm, Blumin, Eley, Blackbourne, Perkin, Mayer, and others. Although there are several excellent studies of Russian liberalism and key bourgeois elites—for example, those by Emmons, Rosenberg, Rieber, Ruckman, Owen, and Frieden—there is much less work on the relationship between language, civic structures, and social definition.[7] Recent articles by Freeze in the *American*

---

[3] Arno Mayer, *The Persistence of the Old Regime: Europe to the Great War* (New York: Pantheon, 1981).

[4] Phil Nord and Jürgen Kocka, *Paris Shopkeepers and the Politics of Resentment* (Princeton: Princeton University Press, 1986); Jürgen Kocka, ed., *Angestellte im europäischen Verleich* (Göttingen: Vandenhoeck and Ruprecht, 1981); Kocka, *White Collar Workers in America* (London: Sage, 1980).

[5] Blumin "Middle-Class Formation"; Robert Eley and David Blackbourne, *The Peculiarities of German History* (Oxford: Oxford University Press, 1984).

[6] See Hans-Ulrich Wehler, *Das deutsche Kaiserreich, 1871–1918* (Göttingen: Vandenhoeck und Ruprecht, 1973).

[7] See, for example, Terrence Emmons, *The Formation of Political Parties and the First Na-*

Historical Review and Haimson in the *Slavic Review* provide a promising beginning.[8] We hope these essays will offer additional thoughts in this direction.

SOCIETY AND CULTURE

This volume's essays on art, philosophy, literature, journalism, and theater all take as a point of departure the notion that cultural life in prerevolutionary Russia played a vital role in developing and elaborating new public identities. This approach to the problem of culture supports a long-standing assumption in Russian, but emphatically nonparty, theories of sociology of culture that has only recently received attention in Western scholarly circles. Traditional thinking, as different as Gramsci, Lukàcs, or Goldmann, that operates on the determinist Marxian "base-superstructure" model is quite unsuitable to the Russian case and, we may speculate, to other "eccentric" cases of developing, non-Western countries in which there was ample time to evaluate and modify the Western experience.[9] In attempting to construct a theory of sociocultural interrelations, critics such as Lukàcs tend to cling to concepts, such as "class," which give the impression of cohesive social hierarchies suitable for use as a point of departure for cultural analysis. The highest art, in this view, is "realist" in style and performs the relatively passive aesthetic function of "mirroring" social reality. Such theories insist on the predominance of socioeconomic conditions over the creative process and link aesthetic forms and categories in too direct a way to prevailing social structures.

In a society such as Russia's that evolved throughout the nineteenth century in the presence of an influential "other" in the form of the Western social and cultural experience, it would indeed be misguided to argue that socioeconomic conditions determined social and cultural consciousness. Of course, such politically motivated theorists as Plekhanov, Lenin, and Gorky and their adherents in the "official" Soviet critical establishment had compelling political reasons for insisting on the deterministic Marxian model. As Bakhtin and

---

tional Elections in Russia (London: Harvard University Press, 1983); William Rosenberg, *Liberals in the Russian Revolution* (Princeton: Princeton University Press, 1974); Alfred Rieber, *Merchants and Entrepreneurs in Imperial Russia* (Chapel Hill: University of North Carolina Press, 1982); Jo Ann Ruckman, *The Moscow Business Elite* (DeKalb: Northern Illinois University Press, 1984); Thomas Owen, *Capitalism and Politics in Russia: A Social History of the Moscow Merchants* (Cambridge: Cambridge University Press, 1981); Nancy Mandelker Frieden, *Russian Physicians in an Era of Reform and Revolution, 1856–1905* (Princeton: Princeton University Press, 1981).

[8] Gregory Freeze, "The Soslovie (Estate) Paradigm and Russian Social History," *American Historical Review* 91, no. 1 (1986): 11–36; Leopold Haimson, "The Problem of Social Identities in Early Twentieth-Century Russia," *Slavic Review* 2 (Spring 1988): 1–21.

[9] Antonio Gramsci, *The Prison Notebooks* (New York: International Publishers, 1971). For a good review of the problem, see Raymond Williams, "Literature and Sociology," in *Problems in Materialism and Culture* (London: Verso, 1980), 11–30.

Medvedev noted as early as 1928, the base-superstructure model as a mode of understanding the interaction of society and culture is prone to oversimplification and schematization when applied to real situations, thus shortchanging the actualities of either cultural production or socio-economic institutions.[10] Since the 1960s, Western Russianists have similarly dispensed with deterministic orthodoxies and argued for the active and creative role of the arts in shaping social consciousness. In his work, William Mills Todd examines the interaction of forms of social behavior in polite society and the evolution of creative forms.[11] Victor Ripp's study, *Turgenev's Russia*, argues that Turgenev in his early works contributed to formulating a gentry consciousness by creating a palpable sense of time and place in which the gentry could feel they belonged.[12] In his book, *When Russia Learned to Read*, Jeffrey Brooks has gone even further to study social values as they were shaped in popular literature at the turn of the century.[13] Finally, perhaps the most useful theoretical contribution has been made by Iury Lotman and Boris Uspensky in their work on semiotics of culture.[14] They emphasize the ways in which cultural activity can influence social behavior through their concept of the "semiosphere"—a dynamic cultural system of symbols, stereotypes, and rituals that provide mechanisms of interpretation to members within a cultural community. For Lotman and Uspensky, the semiosphere embraces every kind of utterance, intentional or not, in every area of human activity, but the implications for the sociology of culture are obvious.

In this volume the essays on culture focus on the ways in which cultural production formulated and shaped public consciousness. They examine the sociocultural codes embedded in various cultural artifacts or modes of discourse and the kinds of public responses to these codes; together they suggest how socioeconomic relations and human behavior interacted in prerevolutionary Russia. The tension between artistic production and social structure emerges as each essay attempts to define the difference between formal, intentional statements of social identity and other only partially conscious patterns of behavior and expression that informed emerging identities. Two crucial questions implicit in these essays concern the vitality of the semiosphere of Late Imperial Russia: Did it work as a coherent system that allowed some measure of communication between disparate social groups? Or did it become

[10] M. M. Bakhtin and P. N. Medvedev, *The Formal Method in Literary Scholarship: A Critical Introduction to Sociological Poetics*, trans. A. J. Wehrle (Cambridge: Harvard University Press, 1985).

[11] William Mills Todd III, *Fiction and Society in the Age of Pushkin: Ideology, Institutions, and Narrative* (Cambridge: Harvard University Press, 1986).

[12] Victor Ripp, *Turgenev's Russia* (Ithaca: Cornell University Press, 1980).

[13] Jeffrey Brooks, *When Russia Learned to Read* (Princeton: Princeton University Press, 1985).

[14] Jurij Lotman and Boris Uspenskij, *The Semiotics of Russian Culture* (Ann Arbor: Ardis, 1984), xii.

so fragmented and stagnant as to hinder the production of commonly held symbols and vehicles for their interpretation.

APPROACHES TO *OBSHCHESTVENNOST'*

This volume is divided into seven parts, each approaching the problem of obshchestvennost' from a different point of view. In Part One, Abbott Gleason and Sidney Monas discuss the evolution of various concepts of the middle in Russian society as reflected in language and intellectual discourse from the eighteenth to the twentieth centuries.

Part Two focuses on the native entrepreneurial elites and their efforts to find identity, organization, and legitimization. James L. West analyzes an attempt of the entrepreneurs, headed by the Riabushinskys, to articulate their vision of Russia's future, a peculiar amalgam of aggressive capitalism and Old Believer piety. Bernice Glatzer Rosenthal discusses the efforts of certain early twentieth-century intellectuals, most notably economist Sergei Bulgakov, to elaborate a philosophical-moral defense of free enterprise and entrepreneurship on the basis of Orthodox theology. Thomas C. Owen examines the many historical obstacles to forming a unified entrepreneurial bourgeoisie in Russia.

Part Three documents the efforts of the Moscow merchants and entrepreneurs to achieve social status and acceptance through art patronage. John O. Norman examines the first merchant patron of Russian art, Pavel Tretiakov, and his attempt to create a national artistic tradition through cultivating indigenous talent. John E. Bowlt focuses on the role of Moscow merchants, especially the flamboyant Nikolai Riabushinsky, in the birth of Russian Modernism. Both studies emphasize the way in which new patterns of exhibition, publication, and marketing, sponsored by the merchant community, contributed to the social identity and self-esteem of Russia's entrepreneurial stratum.

Part Four focuses on the emergence of public and private institutions that undergird a civil society in Russia. Joseph Bradley treats the rapid proliferation of voluntary associations in Moscow at the turn of the century. In his study of divorce law William Wagner shows the growing impact of public opinion on evolving legal norms and codes. Charles E. Timerlake analyzes the rural zemstvo as an alternative to state service for Russia's emerging professionals. These articles document the development of autonomous institutions and private attitudes as vehicles for the creation of a "public" consciousness in Russia.

The central issue of Part Five is the intelligentsia's evolution toward modern professional organization and consciousness. In his overview of the professions, Harley Balzer distinguishes the emerging new professionals from their spiritual forebears of the nineteenth-century intelligentsia. Christine Ruane and Ben Eklof examine what is perhaps the canonical example of profession-alization in Russia, the schoolteachers.

The authors of Part Six explore the development of social consciousness among the broader strata of the emerging lower middle class. Gregory L. Freeze examines the efforts of the Orthodox Church to maintain the allegiance of its constituencies under conditions of rapid urbanization and secularization. Louise McReynolds discusses the popular press and traces the career of its most popular exponent, V. Doroshevich, who shaped the tastes and expecta-tions of Russia's growing mass-reading public. Daniel T. Orlovsky studies the increasing radicalization of the lower middle strata and the eventual success of the Bolsheviks in garnering their allegiance.

Part Seven addresses the emergence of cultural myths and symbols around which new social identities could crystallize. Edith W. Clowes examines the attempt of playwrights such as Chekhov and Gorky to move their audiences beyond traditional forms of social identity on the stage of the Moscow Art Theater. Mary Louise Loe deals with the Sreda circle around Maksim Gorky to show the crisis of the socially "engaged" literary intelligentsia in their traditional role as mediator between state and people. In a discussion of Fedor Shekhtel, William C. Brumfield illuminates the changing social attitudes be-hind the transformed urban landscapes of Moscow and St. Petersburg. James M. Curtis explores the new notions of privacy and individual worth implicit in the art of Konstantin Korovin.

Each essay examines some element of late imperial social dynamics, insti-tutional structure, or cultural and artistic creativity that either symbolized or presaged the development in Russia of a stable and prosperous middle, yet each demonstrates the precariousness and fragility of that process. These stud-ies convey the impression of a widening gulf between the possible forming of a cohesive urban public and a real growing discord, faltering communication, and difficult definition of common political and economic ground. Rapid strides in literacy, accelerating economic growth, expanding educational op-portunities, a vibrant cultural renaissance, and the continued development of Russia's cities all provided the structural basis for the development of a civil society in Russia. Despite these promising signs of progress, the political and social foundations upon which these new structures were being erected were not sufficiently solid. The formation of educated, autonomous, and stable middle in Russian society thus remained an incomplete process, one whose very inconclusiveness still haunts the Soviet leadership as it encourages its own version of obshchestvennost' and civil society in the Gorbachev era.

Chapter 2

THE TERMS OF RUSSIAN SOCIAL HISTORY

Abbott Gleason

IT IS WELL to stress the duality about our efforts to define terms at the outset. Our principal focus, of course, is the changing social reality in Russia, and our vocabulary is intended to help us understand that change. The terminology we employ, however, is far from timeless and objective, but crucially related to changing cultural systems, which in Russia means, in part, to Westernization. When we speak of moving from an estate paradigm to one of class, we are speaking about not only social change in Russia but also the arrival of an intellectual tradition, new to Russia, involving Ricardo, Hegel, and Marx. When the crucial, active elements in Russia begin to be called *obshchestven- nost'* instead of *obshchestvo*, we face changes in both the social composition of the elite and its political attitudes and the public's consciousness of those changes. The terms we employ shape social reality, even as they describe and define it.

Before introducing some social categories that we must use in our discussion of obshchestvennost', I want to speak briefly and generally about certain aspects of Imperial Russia's inheritance and condition as we approach the last twenty-five or thirty years of its existence. These features of Russia's past are well-known. But despite their familiarity, it may be helpful to call attention to them as we begin because they underlay so many particularities of Russian history, perhaps its social history most of all.

Numerous historians have called attention to a whole cluster of physical characteristics that when considered together suggest a strikingly inhospitable milieu for the evolution of the Great Russian society and state.[1] I have in mind, of course, aspects and consequences of the ferocious climate of Great Russia: the extremities of heat and (especially) cold, the poor soil, the irregular rainfall and brief growing season, the lack of a useful access to the sea, and so on. Any society centered upon this part of northern Eurasia—the heart of Moscovy and Imperial Russia—was bound to be poor, operating almost invariably out of insufficiency and scarcity.

The various social groups that together made up Imperial Russia, especially the peasant society that dominated it demographically, were always struggling

[1] From relatively recent work discussing these factors, let me mention only Richard Pipes, *Russia under the Old Regime* (New York: Scribners, 1974), 1–24, and Edward L. Keenan, "Muscovite Political Folkways," *Russian Review* 45, no. 2 (1986): 115–81.

to survive. If Russian peasant society was as collective as the Slavophiles said it was, the fundamental reason was surely that collective solutions were necessary for survival. If Russian peasant society was as brutal as the Westernizers said it was, that brutality must have been heavily conditioned by the struggle to stay alive, to reproduce oneself and one's society.

Because the subjects of the Russian state were so poor, it is at least understandable that the state became more callous and more single-mindedly extractive in its attitude toward them than was usual in Europe and perhaps more grandiose in its claims on them. As the state became hardened to what it had to do to acquire the resources it needed, its leaders understood that—as was also the case in the peasant society below them—outsiders ought not be allowed to see the struggles within the walls, and Russia's leaders became the specialists in concealment and facades, in *pokazukha*, that we know them to have been. Everywhere in Europe, states and monarchs interacted with the "estates" of premodern society, but in Russia the role of the state was unusually great, the role of society unusually small.

We must also remember, as we start out, how extremely rural and agrarian this society remained right into the time period to which this volume is devoted. Of course, the "two capitals," Moscow and St. Petersburg, were world-class cities, at least in size, even in the nineteenth century; they were also, as many scholars have suggested, deeply emblematic of the great rift and struggle of Russian cultural history, stemming from Westernization. In 1856, the population of St. Petersburg was approaching half a million and that of Moscow was just under 370,000;[2] only Odessa and Warsaw, of the other cities of the Russian Empire, had more than 70,000 inhabitants in 1856. About 6 percent of the population of Russia lived in cities.[3]

These cities themselves had hardly played a central role in Russia's history. Since fabled Novgorod lost its liberty to Ivan III of Moscow in the 1470s and 1480s, no city had been notable for its commercial vitality; a large percentage of Russian cities owed their origin to the state's need for defense and/or administration. They had neither corporate or patrician traditions nor any libertarian ones: town air in Russia never "made free." The tiny elite of upper merchants wore livery tailored by the autocracy.[4] A cohesive urban community was weak and late in developing; the line of socioeconomic demarcation between the lower orders inside and outside the Russian town or city was

[2] Michael Hamm, ed., *The City in Late Imperial Russia* (Bloomington: Indiana University Press, 1986), 3.

[3] Gilbert Rozman believes it to have been more than 8 percent. See his "Comparative Approaches to Modernization: Russia, 1750–1800," in *The City in Russian History*, ed. Michael Hamm (Lexington: University of Kentucky Press, 1976), 80.

[4] On the premodern city in Russia, see Aleksandr Kizevetter, *Posadskaia obshchina v Rossii XVIII st.* (Moscow: Universitetskaia tipografiia, 1903), and J. Michael Hittle, *The Service City: State and Townsmen in Russia, 1600–1800* (Cambridge: Harvard University Press, 1979).

indistinct. Often the majority of those who lived in a town or a city was not made up of local urban dwellers but of peasants ascribed to various far away places. The state, through the Law Code of 1649, had tried to bind the inhabitants to their locale and local society, but it succeeded far better in theory than in practice.

Prior to the 1860s, neither Moscow nor St. Petersburg had yet been much marked by the industrial revolution; the most recent historian of industrializing Moscow refers to the city in that period as still a "big village," lacking the physical artifacts of modernity—"museums, galleries, clinics, hospitals, charitable and educational institutions."[5] No cities or larger towns much leavened the peasantness of the society and the traditional relations between gentry and peasant. During the approximately sixty years between the Emancipation and World War I this ancient, rural Russia of landlord and peasant erupted into explosive change—economically, socially, demographically, and politically. It was the real beginning of the Russian Revolution, which accelerated after 1890.

Peasant attitudes toward those breaking away from the collectivity to do well for themselves seem to have been negative, at least when one judges by moral and cultural values.[6] Gentry hostility toward the systematic pursuit of financial success was also strong. Of course there were those who braved the opprobrium, and we should probably distinguish between the publicly sanctioned attitudes of the culture (what sociologists sometimes call "values for others") and the more complex, private attitudes toward one's *own* gain. Just because it was bad to be a kulak did not mean that *kulachestvo* was not widespread. Certainly any household or community was involved in a zero-sum game with others: that was life.

Finally, the culture of the intellectuals, whether of the left or the right, must have been among the most antibourgeois in Europe. Economists early turned away from Adam Smith toward Friedrich List and the *Kathedersozialisten*.[7] Both radical and romantic intellectuals hated social rationalism and individualism; it was virtually all they could agree on. So if the *burzhuaziia* was missing in Russia, it was easy to find the *burzhui*, as well as the kulak and other negative stereotypes of combined greed, cruelty, and calculating rationality.

Both within and outside Russia's borders Russian development produced powerful national, racial, and social hostilities. The communities and groups involved in industrialization tended to keep to themselves; Jewish, Polish,

[5] Joseph Bradley, "Moscow," in Hamm, *City in Late Imperial Russia*, 9–11; the quotation is on p. 11. Also see Bradley, *Muzhik and Muscovite* (Berkeley: University of California Press, 1985), 1–69.

[6] See, for example, "Success," in Jeffrey Brooks, *When Russia Learned to Read* (Princeton: Princeton University Press, 1985), 269–94.

[7] See Esther Kingston Mann, "In Search of the True West: Problems of Russian Rural Development" (unpublished paper), for the views of the economists.

Russian, and German merchants and industrialists had surprisingly little to do with each other, although total isolation was not possible. Across Russia's borders, industrialization was also taking off in the United States and Germany. Both cultures already had a dubious reputation in Russia for self-discipline, coldness, and the lust for gain. As Russian industrialization developed and the attention of Russians was focused on these negative qualities, the reputations of Germans and Americans in Russian culture further declined, and the symbolic meanings of Germany and America became more negative. Within the Russian Empire, much of the industrialization was in the hands of non-Russians. So stereotypes of Jews and Poles became similarly linked with the bad values of capitalism and thus were perceived and often portrayed as anti-Russian. Russian industrialization was a terrible struggle in cultural as well as social, political, and economic terms. The state led that struggle, but many elements within the state were opposed to doing so, as were many of the most influential elite.

In the pre-1860s Russia that we have been discussing, the classic division involved "society" and "people," obshchestvo and *narod*. This was the working vocabulary of the elite of the Old Regime; through their writings and their presence they subsequently transmitted the term obshchestvo to foreign historians who first wore it proudly as a badge of their familiarity with Russia and then dropped it as unscholarly. Recently it has undergone a mild revival, together with its later permutation, obshchestvennost'.

Of the terms that we will consider, these are perhaps the most peculiar to Russia—peculiar not in the sense that comparable terms do not exist elsewhere in Europe, but in that nowhere other than in Russia do they assume so much importance or are they forced to bear so much weight.[8] Obshchestvo is comparable to what the English meant in the seventeenth and eighteenth centuries by "society" and to what the French meant by *le monde*. In Russia, too, these aristocratic terms offer the deepest layer of meaning.

But obshchestvo differs from its French and English analogues (and I daresay there are other national analogues of which I am not aware) in several ways. Most important, obshchestvo came into existence as a binary opposite to narod, the common people, those not touched by the Westernization process. Notions of high society in England or France had no such global and stark opposite. No matter how nuanced or specific the term later became in

[8] A number of recent publications have used the term *obshchestvo* to frame their analyses of nineteenth-century Russia. Among the more significant are Anthony Graham Netting, *Russian Liberalism: The Years of Promise, 1842–1855* (Ph.D. diss., Columbia University, 1967); Nicholas Riasanovsky, *A Parting of Ways: Government and the Educated Public in Russia, 1801–1855* (Oxford: Oxford University Press, 1977); Victor Ripp, *Turgenev's Russia* (Ithaca: Cornell University Press, 1980); Abbott Gleason, *Young Russia* (New York: Viking, 1980); and William Mills Todd, *Fiction and Society in the Age of Pushkin* (Cambridge: Harvard University Press, 1986).

Russian culture, it could be used, should the occasion warrant it, in this global fashion, even until 1917.

There is another important difference. In both England and France the idea of high society was not—or at least no longer—coeval in the late eighteenth and early nineteenth centuries with the world of either politics or culture. In Russia, membership in obshchestvo came to mean, over the course of the eighteenth century, not only that you were a person who could be "received" by the best people but also that you were part of the small group that created Russia's literary culture, thought Russia's great thoughts, governed the country, represented it abroad, and so on. In its origins, the world of obshchestvo was the world of the Petrine gentry, aristocratic (but with a certain meritocratic possibility), and culture-bearing (although that culture was the new Western-type culture sponsored by Peter and the dynasty), with its profound social isolation and its ambiguous commitment to service. In England and France high society, which had long since ceased to have such cultural and political significance, had been replaced or diluted by other social elements.

In the late eighteenth and early nineteenth centuries the boundaries of obshchestvo were shifting and a bit blurred. It might be used to mean *ne narod*. But specifically aristocratic usage was far more common. Although many upper bureaucrats of established family were surely considered part of obshchestvo by nearly everybody, as the bureaucracy and the gentry began to diverge sociologically in the nineteenth century, a certain hostility to bureaucrats began to develop in obshchestvo culture. With the rise of the grandees of the eighteenth century, many of the old nobility felt keenly the reduction in their status to that of "middle gentry," measured in strictly economic terms; the peculiar blend of exacerbated aristocratism and commitment to meritocracy that one finds in Pushkin's politics owes much to this phenomenon.[9] It is not clear whether men like Pushkin would admit that *arriviste* families of the eighteenth century were truly part of obshchestvo; to some extent they sought an obshchestvo that defined truly good families as pre-Petrine, as "ancient." At the same time, however, men like Pushkin and Prince Petr Viazemsky insisted that all Russian cultural creativity derived from obshchestvo, and this insistence heightened its meritocratic aura. I hope even this impressionistic sketch suggests the degree to which the boundaries of obshchestvo—and to some extent its central assumptions—were not absolutely agreed upon by its most secure members. There were those who saw leadership in obshchestvo connected with pre-Petrine families, or with success in the court politics in the eighteenth century, or simply with imperial favor. Most saw one's position in obshchestvo as connected, at least weakly, with political or cultural achievement; some few would have denied that connection altogether.

[9] Todd, *Fiction and Society*, 51–136. The most recent study is Sam Driver's *Puškin: Literature and Social Ideas* (New York: Columbia University Press, 1989).

By the time of Pushkin's death in 1837, I have the impression that obshchestvo was already becoming less socially exclusive and perhaps more defined by both the creation of culture and the developing rift with the autocracy.
Anthony Netting explicitly and others implicitly treat obshchestvo in the
1840s as crucially defined by its "liberalism," which means much less a political doctrine than a more general opposition to autocratic government derived in great part from Western cultural values. In Pushkin's time, by contrast, the anti-autocratic Decembrists were very much part of obshchestvo but
did not define it in any absolute way.[10]

It has been recognized that under the stable surface of Russian life during
the reign of Nicholas I were being prepared the radical ideas that would ultimately play so important a role in destroying the Old Regime. Many of them,
of course, were articulated and developed by obvious members of obshchestvo, such as Aleksandr Herzen. But the spread of Western liberal and
radical ideas in Russia during the 1840s and early 1850s went beyond those
who could or would have thought of themselves as members of obshchestvo
except in the very most general sense of the term, to marginal and impoverished members of the provincial gentry or the children of lesser bureaucrats
and lower army officers. Many of these people were attempting to engage in
journalism or teaching in one of the newly opened Russian secondary schools.
Many of them were not members of obshchestvo by anybody's definition;
moreover, some were not even members of the gentry itself, falling into another anomalous and very Russian category, the so-called *raznochintsy* or
"people of various ranks."[11] At the same time, as Lincoln, Wortman, and
others have shown, both society and bureaucracy were becoming better educated and more professional.[12] The bureaucrats and professionals, who would
increasingly control the administration of Russia after Nicholas's death, were
being prepared for their task while he was still on the throne.

These social changes were accompanied by cultural ones. As those elements in Russian society committed to Western, "liberal," or even radical
ideas became more numerous and more socially diverse, the aristocratic and
elitist sense of obshchestvo lost its central shaping power. No doubt many
traditionally minded gentry families thought of their social world as com-

---

[10] For an interesting sense of the special way in which the Decembrists affected the shape and
direction of obshchestvo culture, see Iurii Lotman's already classic essay, "The Decembrist in
Everyday Life." It is readily available in Lotman and Boris Uspenskij, *The Semiotics of Russian
Culture* (Ann Arbor: Ardis, 1984), 71–123.

[11] Netting, *Russian Liberalism*; J. H. Seddon, *The Petrashevtsy: A Study of the Russian Revolutionaries of 1848* (Manchester: Manchester University Press, 1985). V. R. Leikina-Svirskaia,
"Formirovanie raznochinskoi intelligentsii v Rossii v 40-kh godakh xix v.," *Istoriia SSSR* 1
(1958): 83–104.

[12] W. Bruce Lincoln, *In the Vanguard of Reform* (DeKalb: Northern Illinois University Press,
1981); Richard S. Wortman, *The Development of a Russian Legal Consciousness* (Chicago: University of Chicago Press, 1976).

pletely unchanged, but new arrivals began to think of themselves as connected in some ways to obshchestvo and thus began to define obshchestvo in different terms from those of the earlier period. In Belinsky's *Letter to Gogol*, for example, obshchestvo is used simply to mean the Westernized educated elite of the nation, opposed to obscurantism. Netting, in his study of Russian liberalism in the 1840s, clearly understood obshchestvo to be the social group that produced the vaguely liberal, Western opposition to Nicholas that was developing during the period. Obshchestvo, to use Nicholas Riasanovsky's phrase, was coming to "a parting of the ways" with *gosudarstvo*, the state.

As in so many other areas, the Great Reforms are our watershed. In the period following the Crimean War, we find the meanings of obshchestvo further changing and developing, away from the aristocratic sense of Pushkin's time toward more modern and politically challenging notions of a social elite, devoted to changing the stagnant society around them. Having seen how steeped in aristocratic values obshchestvo was at the outset, we can now see how important the Westernizing element, also an essential inheritance from Peter the Great, is becoming.

The challenge to aristocratic values was a great theme of the 1860s; it is hardly surprising to find writers and critics of the period developing the notion that Russia's development had come to be at least partly in the hands of a critical elite of intellectuals. This group, created by Westernization, was now cut off from the dynasty that originally sponsored Westernization but lost its progressive mandate in the course of the nineteenth century.[13] At this point we can see how close one version of obshchestvo is coming to the most mainstream idea of the Russian intelligentsia, with its developing assault on the autocratic order.

The process of social diversification, which I have already mentioned, intensified in the wake of the Great Reforms. Purely snobbish notions of the Russian elite now had to compete with radical and political ones.[14] Any generally agreed upon meaning of obshchestvo became increasingly difficult to find. The Russian gentry began its long, slow, complex retreat from social dominance while, as the reforms developed, Russia began to acquire more lawyers, more medical personnel, more professors, more agronomists, more veterinarians, with increased professional training for all of them. A new term emerges: obshchestvennost'.[15] What does it mean?

In some basic way, obshchestvennost' has some sense of the English word

[13] For one version of this idea, see Aleksandr Herzen, *Du développement des idées révolutionnaires en Russie. Sobranie sochinenii* (Moscow: Izd. Akademii Nauk, 1956), 5–132.

[14] See Baron Wrangel's aristocratic lament about the passing of *his* idea of obshchestvo in Roberta Thompson Manning, *The Crisis of the Old Order in Russia* (Princeton: Princeton University Press, 1982), 37.

[15] *Obshchestvennost'* is such a new term that it is not included in the great dictionary of V. I. Dal, the three-volume *Tolkovyi Slovar'*, first published between 1863 and 1866.

"public." From society to the public undoubtedly gets at some of the change from obshchestvo to obshchestvennost'. From a lexicographical point of view, the transition is far from simple: The term obshchestvo continues to be used, but with less and less of a precise and unified meaning; alongside it we increasingly find the new phrase *obshchestvennoe dvizhenie*, originally derived from obshchestvo, but with a meaning closer to obshchestvennost'.

In the writings of the younger critics of the 1860s, such as Aleksandr Pypin, one first finds extensive historical scholarly development of the idea of a Russian "public opinion" (*obshchestvennoe mnenie*), opposed to the autocracy, activist and reform-minded, and above all independent in its intellectual formation and moral-political judgments. In numerous journal articles dating mostly from the 1870s and 1880s, Pypin began to write the history of the movement of educated public opinion in Russia.[16] This idea of the educated public is actually much closer to obshchestvennost' than to any older conception of obshchestvo. It has lost much of its connection with the upper gentry world of Pushkin's time, although it retains the sense of Westernization and culture-bearing; it is still a term that defines an elite (however more modern and variegated) as opposed to the peasantry. In Pypin's influential version, this self-created elite's critique of the autocracy, in the name of the best values of European civilization, was already beginning to be evident in the time of Novikov and Freemasonry.

Note too the new spirit of activism: obshchestvennoe dvizhenie is a social movement, implying purposive reform over time, a notion far removed from the old idea of obshchestvo and its aristocratic creativity that had still been largely intact in the 1830s. The pervasive influence of Hegel, in a rather left interpretation, is clear in the new concept; society is developing, due in large part to this vanguard, toward a better future that could be either revolutionary or evolutionary, according to one's political preference. If one were touched with Slavophile or Populist ideas, one would want to reserve a large role for the creativity of the narod. If one were a more straightforward and elitist "enlightener," one could vest the leadership of the obshchestvennoe dvizhenie more entirely in the intelligentsia.

At this point, one might also observe in conclusion, the stage was set for the emergence of a Marxist version of this Hegelian Westernizer model. The general outlines of the struggle between the Populist and the Marxist versions are well known. Here I only point out that the insistence of Marxism on a class-based model had an important effect on the Russian debate: all intelligentsia political-cultural leadership since Novikov and Radishchev now had to be understood as bourgeois in character. The obshchestvennoe dvizhenie,

---

[16] These were later collected and published under the title of *Moskovskoe masonstvo* (Petrograd: Izd. "Ogni," 1916) and *Obshchestvennoe dvizhenie v Rossii pri Aleksandre I* (St. Petersburg: M. M. Stasiulevich, 1885).

as it had developed in Russia, and obshchestvennost' itself up to that point at least had to be understood as middle class. And as all students of Russian intellectual history know, a great deal—far too much, in my opinion—of the energy of Soviet historical scholarship has gone into an elaborate and intricate set of Marxist categories to differentiate the class character of intelligentsia thought.

Let us turn now to another term that requires discussion: *soslovie*, the Russian variant of the general European category of estate, and its replacement by a more modern social paradigm, usually conceived in terms of a class society. Let me say at the outset that the development of soslovie is much more obscure to me than that of obshchestvo; fortunately we have some excellent signposts at hand (to introduce accidently another important period reference), one old and several new. I am referring to Vasily Kliuchevsky's classic study of the origins of the Russian estates and to Gregory Freeze's recent article on the *soslovie* paradigm as well as to his earlier study of the Russian parish clergy, which is the only serious account of the creation of a clerical soslovie in the eighteenth century.[17]

Historians of Europe have generally assumed that estates, the "estate order," and even the "estate constitution" are characteristic of Europe as a whole.[18] But recognition seems to be equally general that estates and their evolution are identical in no two nations, regions, or cities, that the number of estates found in estate structures, their makeup, and their legal-constitutional importance varied widely from place to place. Everyone seems to agree that the estate was primarily a juridical rather than an economic category, but there is surprising disagreement about how comprehensive this kind of juridical category must for definition as an estate.[19]

If estates are common to Europe as a whole, the Russian version is surely an extreme and eccentric one. In much of Europe, one can speak of one or

---

[17] Vasilii Kliuchevskii, *Istoriia soslovii v Rossii* in: *Sochineniia* (Moscow: GIPL, 1959), 6: 276–466. Gregory Freeze, "The *Soslovie* (Estate) Paradigm and Russian Social History," *The American Historical Review* 91, no. 1 (1986): 11–36; Freeze, *The Russian Levites: Parish Clergy in the Eighteenth Century* (Cambridge: Harvard University Press, 1977).

[18] A good introduction to the problem is A. R. Meyers, *Parliaments and Estates in Europe to 1789* (New York: Harcourt, Brace, Jovanovich, 1975). See also Peter Calvert, *The Concept of Class* (London: St. Martin's, 1982), 45–55; Kliuchevskii, *Istoriia soslovii*, 285; Otto Hintze, "Typologie der ständischen Verfassung des Abendlandes," *Staat und Verfassung: Gesammelte Abhandlungen zur all gemeinen Verfassungs geschichte* (Göttingen: 1962), 1: 120–39. An historically important, but highly romantic, discussion is Ferdinand Tönnies, *Stände und Klassen*, a portion of which is reprinted in Reinhard Bendix and Seymour M. Lipset, eds., *Class, Status and Power* (Glencoe: Free Press, 1953), 49–63.

[19] In Russia, Kliuchevskii believed, there were four periods of juridically distinct soslovie formation: the Kievan, the appanage, the Moscovite, and the imperial periods, each of which could be distinguished in terms of the legal documents that made up its "soslovie law." In the Kievan period, he asserts, we can distinguish two sosloviia—the conquerors and the conquered—so one can see Kliuchevskii's broad definition of *soslovie*.

another kind of "estate constitution." This really means that whether created primarily by the monarch or by social elements trying to force acceptance of their principles, the estates achieved some relationship to each other, some regular procedure for congregation, a defined relationship to the crown, and the ability to extract concessions from it. But neither Kliuchevsky nor Freeze thought it plausible to discuss the *Zemskii sobor* in relation to the development of sosloviia in Russia. By the eighteenth century, when the numerous smaller social categories of the Muscovite period are coming to be defined in four primary soslovie groups, the Zemskii sobor had long ceased to be a living social institution, if indeed it could ever have been so described. For it never really transcended the status of a convenient sounding board for the ratification of policy by the tsars. The strength of the autocracy easily prevented anything like an estate constitution from coming into existence; Russian estates were nothing like the kind of entities that can be imagined banding together and challenging the monarch.

The Russian estates, extremely late in developing (between the seventeenth and nineteenth centuries), were of no constitutional significance. Their creation resulted from a complicated interplay of interests involving autocratic legislation and a kind of lobbying by the groups involved; they aimed at ensuring and extending their privileges, preventing others from gaining access to them, and lightening their obligations. (It goes without saying that the peasants, without privileges or access, could not engage in such lobbying.) Only rather late in this process were analogies drawn to the estates of Western Europe.

Freeze demonstrates that the germ, as opposed to the reality it was supposed to describe, became established later than the conventional wisdom has it, really not before the early nineteenth century. And he maintains that the regular use of the term soslovie added an element of corporateness and cultural distinctiveness, thus affecting the reality it described.[20]

The Russian state, Freeze asserts, did not deliberately establish a "four-estate model" for Russia.[21] And yet it is hard to deny that laws promulgated by the autocracy in the seventeenth and eighteenth centuries—to be sure, for other purposes—played a central role in amalgamating the numerous ranks and social categories of Muscovy into the four large "hereditary social strata" that were to become sosloviia. This "estate law," as Kliuchevsky calls it, created lines of demarcation that became harder and harder to cross: between serving people and townspeople, between townspeople and peasants. The autocracy intended, in promulgating these laws, to ensure that these groups acquitted their obligations to the state. Subsequently, usually in response to intensive lobbying by the groups themselves, certain rewards or perquisites were specified for the performance of these obligations: No one but the man who

---

[20] Freeze, "*Soslovie* Paradigm," 14–19.
[21] Ibid., 20.

serves can own land. No one but the townsman can conduct "manufacturing" in the town or city.

In the face of such legislation to ensure the performance of obligation, the difference between the various ranks and categories within these larger divisions diminished.[22] The creation of these sosloviia can thus be attributed to a dialectical process that involved the state acting to ensure its needs were met; leading members of the affected groups attempted to get a *quid* for themselves while accepting the *quo* the state was imposing. By vesting landowning or serfowning rights within a certain large category, the importance of the categorical boundaries grew.

Freeze's account of the creation of a closed clerical (*dukhovnoe*) soslovie in the eighteenth century is not dissimilar, although he stresses the activities of the clergy themselves more and those of the state less.[23] He confirms the traditional view that the Russian gentry seldom wished to enter the clergy and very rarely did. Townsmen and peasants, who often had entered the clergy in the past and continued to do so in the early eighteenth century, were almost completely excluded by the 1780s "primarily as a result of three processes: the clergy's efforts to reserve positions for relatives; the new restrictions of the poll tax registry; and the establishment of formal educational requirements which only clerical children could satisfy."[24] That is, every time a state peasant or a townsman entered the clergy, whom Peter the Great had exempted from the poll tax, the state suffered a loss in revenue. Small wonder that the Senate regularly rejected the Holy Synod's efforts to authorize the ordination of townsmen, state peasants, and serfs.

By the late eighteenth century, then, there were indeed four hereditary, castelike social strata in Russia—gentry, merchants, clergy, and peasants.[25] But this order was not a purposeful, self-conscious creation by the Russian autocracy, and it was quite different from the older estate order of Western Europe. Freeze warns us that if the term soslovie, which came into general use only in the 1820s, is "applied retroactively to the hereditary social strata

[22] Kliuchevskii, *Istoriia soslovii*, 437–38.

[23] Freeze, *Russian Levites*, esp. 184–217.

[24] Ibid., 187.

[25] But the government vacillated on how to make urban dwellers into an estate. Catherine's Charter of 1775 was only to the top group of wealthy merchants; their poorer brethren were relegated to the status of meshchanstvo (petty townspeople). But in the 1892 Collection of Laws we find an estate of town dwellers, subdivided into four sostoianiia (status groups): "honored citizens," merchants (kupechestvo), petty townspeople (meshchanstvo), and artisans. Thomas Owen, in *Capitalism and Politics in Russia* (Cambridge: Cambridge University Press, 1981), 2, considers these categories to be estates. Government usage could be extraordinarily confusing. Nancy Frieden has noted that the medical oath of a graduating physician, according to this same 1892 Collection of Laws, described the medical profession, into which the young doctor was entering, as a soslovie. See Nancy Mandelker Frieden, *Russian Physicians in an Era of Reform and Revolution* (Princeton: Princeton University Press, 1981), 5, 326–27.

of the late eighteenth century, [it] must be . . . carefully distinguished from the later phenomenon of a 'constituted body' with a distinctive culture, status and social identity.''[26]

The question of whether or to what extent estates were still able, in the last thirty years of the imperial period, to provide a social identity for Russians is a question for the participants in this volume to consider. Still, a few general remarks may be in order. The attitude of the state, as revealed in its actions, toward the estate order was fundamentally incoherent. On the one hand, the reforms of Alexander II began to undermine the estate idea, accelerating the growth of the professions and professional organizations as well as proto-classes like the proletariat. On the other hand, as Freeze has pointed out, in the resurgent conservatism of the post-1870 period, the Russian state's com-mitment to the soslovie system actually became stronger and much more ideo-logical, although irregularly so.[27] In the course of the reign of Nicholas II, the monarchy developed an increasingly archaic view of itself and the society over which it ruled. Unable actually to reverse social and economic development, the court and segments of the upper bureaucracy nevertheless substituted re-ligious, seventeenth-century dynastic myths for the Petrine vision of Europe-anizing Russia that had never been repudiated, even by Nicholas I.

The reassertion of the soslroviia became one of the several important weap-ons of Russian statesmen in their struggle against modernity. After 1905 the struggle became even more intense and complex, with statesmen like Witte and Stolypin clearly committed to the development in Russia of a unified civil society, antithetical to an estate system. The radical parties and the Kadets were determined enemies of an estate society.[28] Prominent representatives of privileged groups, however, still asserted *soslovnost'* as a weapon against so-cial change, although most of them recognized that they were somewhere near the last ditch. It seems clear that soslovnost' became far more important to both government and gentry after it had already been fatally undermined by the Great Reforms than ever before.

In a brief discussion paper presented at the World Congress in 1985, Alfred J. Rieber coined the term ''sedimentary society'' to characterize the social

---

[26] Freeze, "*Soslovie* Paradigm," 19. Alfred J. Rieber is similarly negative. "In the absence of any generally recognized term," he writes, "the word *soslovie* may be used to describe the social situation of the merchantry after 1785, as long as it is taken to connote an intermediate social form possessing a legal identity and collective privileges but no inviolate corporate rights." Rieber, *Merchants and Entrepreneurs in Imperial Russia* (Chapel Hill: University of North Carolina Press, 1982), xxii.

[27] Freeze, "*Soslovie* Paradigm," 27. For a somewhat different view, which attributes greater vitality and importance to the estates, see Neil B. Weissman, *Reform in Tsarist Russia* (New Brunswick: Rutgers University Press, 1985), especially 7–20.

[28] Weissman, *Reform*, 103–4, 108, 142–44. See also Francis W. Wcislo, "Soslovie or Class? Bureaucratic Reformers and Provincial Nobility in Conflict, 1906–1908," *Russian Review* 47, no. 1 (1988): 1–24.

complexity of the later Imperial period; let me revive the term for such heuristic benefits as it may provide. "What I mean to suggest," wrote Rieber,

> is the result of a process in which a successive series of social forms was laid down one overlapping the other in the course of the more than two hundred years between the Ulozhenie of 1649 and the Revolution of 1917. . . . Because of the massive discontinuities of Russian history, the imposition of new layers of social forms did not displace or destroy the previous ones. Thus the soslovie organization of society . . . covered over the multiplicity of Muscovite social categories, leaving many of the smaller urban ones . . . untouched, which is how they remained for centuries.[29]

"Subsequently," Rieber continues, "the *dvorianstvo* silted in to cover the whole," and he treats the creation of estates as part of this long, drawn-out layering process, which was continuing at the end of the Old Regime, with the creation of classes providing the newest archaeological layer.

It seems to me that the notion of an archaeological layer of postestate forms, obscuring but scarcely destroying the still changing lines of estate thinking and estate consciousness, is a plausible notion on which to end. It presents a picture of the social complexity that confronts us; at the same time—archaeology being a science—it suggests that this social complexity may eventually be intelligible to sober-minded, undogmatic, hard-working scholars.

---

[29] See Rieber, "The Sedimentary Society," in this present volume. Daniel Brower's view seems similar; he directs us to study "the process by which groups dissolved and others emerged under particular constraints and possibilities." Brower sees that process as frequently discontinuous and catastrophic, and he regards urbanization as a central aspect of it. See " 'In the World': Urbanization and the History of Russian Society in the Late Tsarist Period" (Paper delivered at the AAASS convention, November 22, 1986); the quotation is from pp. 8–9. Teodor Shanin takes Imperial Russia to be the world's first developing nation, in the context of the "dependency theory" developed by Peter Evans and others to understand Latin American development. Shanin's account has the virtue of paying attention to the world economy and Russia's place in it, but it does not reveal much that is new about Late Imperial Russian social structure per se. See Shanin, *Russia as a Developing Society*, Vol. 1 of *The Roots of Otherness: Russia's Turn of Century* (London: Macmillan, 1985), especially 196–206; unfortunately the book is poorly and hastily written, full of typographical and other errors.

Chapter 3

THE TWILIT MIDDLE CLASS OF NINETEENTH-CENTURY RUSSIA

SIDNEY MONAS

UNTIL THE 1890s in Russia almost nobody wanted a bourgeoisie. For Nicholas I, and for that matter for his son as well, the third estate and its heir the middle class conjured up shades of the French Revolution. The political instability—the restless element, the ever-unsatisfied and corrosive disrespecter of tradition, stability, authority—of most of nineteenth-century Western Europe was placed at its feet. *Embourgeoisement* was equivalent to desacralization. Poets disliked it because it took the magic out of the world and steeped it in *poshlost'* instead. Rulers disliked it because it took away their halos.

Marx so eloquently described the dynamics of capitalism with words by which he intended, if not entirely in a positive sense at least positively in part, to send shivers up the spine of the Russian autocrat:

> The bourgeoisie cannot exist without constantly revolutionizing the instruments of production, and with them the relations of production, and with them all the relations of society. . . . Constant revolutionizing of production, uninterrupted disturbance of all social relations, everlasting uncertainty and agitation, distinguish the bourgeois epoch from all earlier ones. All fixed, fast-frozen relations, with their train of ancient and venerable prejudices and opinions, are swept away, all new-formed ones become antiquated before they can ossify. All that is solid melts into air, all that is holy is profaned, and men at last are forced to face . . . the real conditions of their lives and their relations with their fellow men.[1]

To the state, the bourgeoisie was the revolutionary class.

Those who opposed autocracy in Russia, however, took an equally dim view of the bourgeoisie. "Russia will never be Protestant," Herzen wrote. "Russia will never be *juste milieu!*"[2] He saw embourgeoisement as the fatal flaw of the so-called "radical" European intellectual. The presence and pressure of a numerous, prosperous, and self-conscious bourgeoisie not only cor-

---

[1] The passage is, of course, from Karl Marx and Friedrich Engels, "The Communist Manifesto." I have used Marshall Berman's translation for its eloquence: Marshall Berman, *All That is Solid Melts in Airs* (New York: Simon and Schuster, 1982), 21.

[2] Alexander Herzen, "The Russian People and Socialism: Letter to Jules Michelet," in *The Memoirs of Alexander Herzen*, 4 vols. (London: Chatto and Windus, 1968), 4: 1674.

rupted the Western radical, led him into temptation, blazed a pathway of be-
trayal that broke the course of revolutionary action, but even at best it filled
him with a respect for the past, for the monuments of former accomplishment,
that unnerved his revolutionary will and made him an uncertain and insecure
partisan of the revolutionary cause. The revolutions of 1848 failed, according
to Herzen, in spite of the heroism of the French workers and the Italian car-
bonari because the leaders of the radical political parties were too hopelessly
tied to an overrespect for the past, too superstitiously attached to law-and-
order and to property. The young Russian intelligent suffered from no such
devotion to the past. His gift for self-sacrifice, unencumbered by a pious orientation to property, along with the sense of communal responsibility of the
Russian peasant, nurtured and preserved by the institution of the *mir* and the
obshchina, would yet save Europe from the moral and political stagnation in
which the failure of the revolutions of 1848 had left it.[3]

In spite of his respect for English liberties, Herzen thought the middle
classes lived, "like worms in a cheese."[4] It was not his ideal. During his long
sojourn in England, Herzen never ceased to think of the native country to
which he would never return. He lacked the appreciation shown by his friends
Belinsky and Botkin for the role of an entrepreneurial class in solving the
problem of productivity, for an awareness of the urgency of such a solution as
the prerequisite to forming a civil society. Herzen was interested in the full
development of the individual and, in a negative way, in the state and the
obstacles it posed to such development. The finer intermediate articulations of
society were not where he lavished his keenest thought. Belinsky was aware,
from the 1840s, of the importance of a middle-class role in *sotsial'nost'* and
saw something of the cultural as well as the economic implications of the
growth of modern industry.[5] Botkin, of merchant origin himself, resisted the
antibourgeois tendencies of the intelligentsia of the 1860s.[6] Yet Herzen was
the first really effective champion of a free public opinion in Russia. His influence on the course of the great reforms was considerable; likewise it was great
on the creation of journalistic-publicistic standards of honesty and truth telling. Not only was the Free Russian Press a mine of information, read even by
those who feared it, it was as well a kind of anthology of suppressed Russian
intellectual and social history, publishing many key essays, poems, and studies the censor had banned—Catherine the Great's memoirs, Dolgorukov's ge-

[3] Ibid., 1647–79; also *"Du développement des idées révolutionnaires en Russie,"* *Polnoe sobranie sochinenii* (Moscow: Akademia Nauk, 1956), 7: 5–132.

[4] *Memoirs of Alexander Herzen,* 3: 1025. See, however, in the same volume his essay on Mill,
1075–86.

[5] For an interesting passage concerning the debate in Herzen's former circle about the bourgeoisie in 1847, see Martin Malia, *Alexander Herzen and the Birth of Russian Socialism* (Cambridge: Harvard University Press, 1961), 353–58.

[6] *P. V. Annenkov i ego druz'ia,* 3 vols. (St. Petersburg: Suvorin, 1892), 1: 540, 550–51.

nealogy of the Russian nobility, Chaadaev's "First Philosophical Letter," Belinsky's letter to Gogol, Lermontov's poem on the death of Pushkin, and many others. Nor was he unaware of the need to increase productivity; he preferred, however, to promote such increase through the support of a "liberated" peasant commune rather than through the agency of a rapacious bourgeoisie. Unfortunately, the subsequent two generations of the Russian intelligentsia, so profoundly influenced by Herzen's ideas, did not take with them his willingness to compromise, his respect for circumstance and individual idiosyncrasy, and his distaste for violence. With the great reforms that Herzen supported, a revolutionary movement also began that, for all its changes and ramifications, nevertheless followed a continuous historical development to 1917.[7]

What constitutes a bourgeoisie? The term is so slippery that the 1968 edition of the *Encyclopedia of Social Sciences* skips it entirely. The standard Marxist definition—"owners of the means of production along with their dependents and hangers-on"—simply displaces the difficulty to "dependents" and "hangers-on." The 1931 edition of the *Encyclopedia of Social Sciences* however, is helpful. It centers its discussion on the political rights that accompanied the ownership of urban property and distinguished the possessors of those rights from the feudal aristocracy on the one hand and the "disenfranchised" on the other, and the explanation emphasizes the dynamic, historically changing nature of such a grouping.[8] "Bourgeoisie" may therefore be taken, if we do not press the matter for more precision than it can offer, as vaguely equivalent to "civil society" or "public" or the Russian *obshchestvo*. Its members could be seen as characterized by their "accumulative thrift" (or "avarice") and by an acquisitive and organizing genius (or "exploiting rapacity"), and "bourgeois" tastes in the arts may be seen neutrally as showing a concern for material interests and respectability and negatively as so bound to the material and the respectable as to embrace mediocrity. Bourgeosie has been associated with a dynamism of social change, with capitalism and its attendant expansion of productive capacity and accelerating technological innovation; it has also been concerned with personal and property "rights," legal bulwarks against the encroachments of the state on the one hand and a well-organized and disciplined police on the other.

A purely local or parochial or merely regional bourgeoisie appears as either a fleeting temporality or a contradiction in terms. Its dynamics, its political and economic interests, have propelled it in the direction of national unification and beyond. Marx accused it of identifying its own interests with the

---

[7] Franco Venturi, *Roots of Revolution: A History of the Populist and Socialist Movement in 19th Century Russia* (London: Weidenfeld and Nicholson, 1960). See also Abbott Gleason, *Young Russia: The Genesis of Russian Radicalism in the 1860s* (Chicago: University of Chicago Press, 1980).

[8] "Bourgeoisie," *Encyclopedia of the Social Sciences* (New York: Macmillan, 1931), 2: 654–56.

interests of everyone, with the national interest. He also pointed out, however, that this perhaps imaginary universalizing was typical of any ruling class worthy of the name. One might add that to achieve any degree of stability the image had to be persuasive enough to garner the allegiance of other classes and groups.

Autocracy as a political institution in Russia tended to be chary, and at worst even hostile, not only to the formation of a bourgeoisie but also to any social formation of potentially national scope outside its own direct sponsorship and control. There was something of a paradox in this because at the same time the autocracy tended to deal with the rights of private property in a punctiliously correct and even legalistic manner, during both the era of the reforms and the reign of Nicholas I.[9] Herzen, for instance, though under threat of instant arrest if he ever set foot within the Russian Empire, continued to receive income from the estates he had inherited. In his eloquently judicious manner, Hans Rogger has written:

> To examine the materials of Russian history for the years 1881 to 1917 for purposes of a general study is to come away with a sense of the extraordinary influence the character and conduct of government had on the way Russia's problems were treated or perceived. This is not to suggest that autocracy was the source of all problems or that a more liberal polity and more enlightened rulers would have assured their solution. It is difficult, however, not to share the feeling of most articulate Russians—including those who were not committed revolutionaries—that their country's multiple crisis was exacerbated and its resolution complicated by the absoluteness of power claimed by their rulers.[10]

Even as it launched the vast program of social transformation that began with emancipating the peasantry, even as it proclaimed "the all-class principle" in legislation, the autocracy insisted that its own power and authority remain undiminished and unlimited and retained in that very legislation the old social categories of *soslovie* and *sostoianie* that an all-class principle might be presumed to eliminate. Although they ceased to be fixed by heredity, taxes were collected, censuses taken, legal judgments rendered, and civic obligations enforced on their basis. In granting official awards and honors, the autocracy continued to favor the landowning nobility long after that class had lost its economic dominance and even its prevalence in the upper reaches of the bureaucracy. Alexander II and his successors preferred to deal with individuals rather than institutions; it might almost seem a concomitant of their conception of the sacred personal nature of autocracy. In his *Merchants and Entrepreneurs in Imperial Russia*, Alfred Rieber has suggested that the so-

[9] In addition to the account in *My Past and Thoughts*, see Malia, *Alexander Herzen*, 389–90.
[10] Hans Rogger, *Russia in the Age of Modernisation and Revolution, 1881–1917* (London: Longman, 1983), 2.

slovie system forged by the autocracy in the eighteenth century as a means of
mobilizing the human and fiscal resources of a vast and disparate empire, became in the nineteenth and early twentieth centuries a means for retarding
change.[11]

The imperial regime refused to countenance even the formation of
"proper" ministerial government and consistently opposed the all-national
structuring of even the most utilitarian professional organizations, to say nothing of its determined stand against a union of *zemstva*. Curiously enough the
most energetic exponents of the positive historical role of capitalism and the
bourgeoisie were the Marxists. Arguing respectfully against his former populist cohorts, Plekhanov pointed out that social differentiation and class struggle had already begun in the countryside and corrupted the workings of the
village commune, that the already intense dynamics of capitalism were destroying the institution on which populist hopes centered, and that only the
effective action of the industrial working class, introduced by capitalism,
could save the bulk of the peasantry from its impending impoverishment.
Lenin, still the disciple of Plekhanov, in his first and only published "scholarly" work, *The Development of Capitalism in Russia*, showed himself already as a man of strong hope by exaggerating and accelerating that development. As Rieber aptly remarks, each from his own point of view was right:
"In Russia social groups that normally composed the bourgeoisie in Western
Europe moved into [that social space between the immobility of caste and the
dynamism of class] separately without giving any indication of joining together or moving forward at any future time."[12]

Between 1881 and 1917 Russia underwent great change. Slowly the effects
of the reforms became felt. Large-scale social and geographical mobility occurred. The urban population grew, and there was a considerable migration to
the Siberian lands. The merchant soslovie appeared to give a new focal point
to social, economic, and cultural growth. Although its ranks had been severely
depleted in the first half of the nineteenth century, in the later nineteenth and
early twentieth centuries it was reinvigorated by an influx of newcomers.
Trading peasants joined it from below, and an increasing number of nobles—
engaged in commerce, finance, and industry—joined it in this sense from
above. A new class of entrepreneurs emerged, daring and innovative, highly
cultivated and technologically sophisticated; they were in the process of formulating and projecting a genuinely national ideology. These, unfortunately,
were all too few (Rieber estimates two thousand at most in 1910), and they
seemed to be located preponderantly in Moscow. Yet they were a dynamic and
promising force. Their patronage and their taste formed an essential back-

[11] Alfred Rieber, *Merchants and Entrepreneurs in Imperial Russia* (Chapel Hill: University of
North Carolina Press, 1982).
[12] Ibid., 416.

ground to the great cultural flowering commonly known as the Silver Age. During this period the Russian railroad network was essentially built, facilitating both geographical mobility and industrial expansion. Although state subsidies and guarantees as well as the large-scale investment of foreign capital promoted by the state played a crucial role in building the Russian railroads, these very factors encouraged the expansion and intensification of Russian entrepreneurship and the growth of a technocratic elite. Two first-rate civil engineering academies established in St. Petersburg produced a group of highly competent engineers and managers. A petroleum industry was created using the United States model. By world standards, Russian science and all the arts, including architecture, took a distinguished place. Both higher and secondary education expanded, and there was an impressive increase in literacy. As Jeffrey Brooks has pointed out, a mass colportage publishing industry responded to the changing values and ambitions of the rural masses. The Russian peasant discovered that literacy was no longer a liability in the countryside, and he wanted to learn and began to read.[13] Henry Adams, touring Russia at the turn of the century, saw it as the coming rival of the United States and projected a future in which the two great powers—the United States representing the energy of "tension" and intensity and Russia representing the accumulating massive force of "inertia"—would confront each other on the global scene.[14]

Crisis followed crisis, almost as in a novel by Dostoevsky. Two unnecessary wars, ineptly conducted, were followed by two devastating revolutions. Somehow the social fabric never quite became whole cloth. Increasingly isolated, the autocracy lost whatever social base it had, while the autocrats all along insisted that the "people," particularly the peasants, were behind it. At the same time, these putatively loyal people were denied institutional representation on any scale beyond the local or regional. The autocracy's most gifted ministers—Witte and Stolypin particularly—were circumscribed, limited, and radically undermined by the very autocracy they were attempting to preserve.

The ethnic problems of a multinational empire not only went unsolved but were also severely exacerbated by impositing disabilities on the more "advanced" minorities and by ill-advised, sporadic, and ineffective attempts at russification. The landowning nobility was well on the road to bankruptcy and dissolution. Its more talented members went into industry, finance, or the learned professions. Yet the autocracy, symbolically at least, continued to associate itself with this class. The intelligentsia, by no means all radicals and

[13] Jeffrey Brooks, *When Russia Learned to Read* (Princeton: Princeton University Press, 1985), 101–8.

[14] For Adams's account of his trip through Russia, see his letters and, above all, the essay by R. P. Blackmur, "Lancelot on Knife's Edge," *Henry Adams* (New York: Harcourt Brace, 1980), 152–59.

revolutionaries, became increasingly alienated from the state and state service. Publicistic writing tended strongly to distinguish between service to the state *(gosudarstvo)* and "public" institutions, representative bodies like the zemstva, the "free" professions, and publicistic and cultural activity (obshchestvo). (In this dichotomy, the universities were in an anomalous position: professors were technically civil servants *(chinovniki)*, holding governmental rank; at the same time the universities enjoyed a certain chartered independence, and professors were generally considered *obshchestvennye deiateli* rather than chinovniki).[15] As the rule, not the exception, public institutions were interlaced with bureaucratic entanglements, and whether an institutional position was obshchestvo or gosudarstvo probably depended more on its prevailing spirit than its actual line of command. Even the clergy, so long servile to the autocracy and *dvorianstvo*, tried to move in the direction of independence. In the twentieth century, there was a significant movement within the Church, as Gregory Freeze points out, toward a separation of church and state. There was no real middle class, only a growing conglomeration of middling groups, divided by regional and ethnic and cultural differences that were bridged only rarely and with difficulty. The most promising of these groups were those whom Rieber calls the Moscow entrepreneurs, among whom old merchant families and newer Old Believer merchants were prominent. They were few in number and generally regarded with a jaundiced eye by officialdom.

Mass political parties appeared for the first time within a few years after 1900. The largest of these, the Socialist Revolutionaries, contained a genuinely revolutionary nucleus, committed to both the overthrow of autocracy and radical change. Marxism, originally supportive of the forming a bourgeoisie and encouraging capitalist development, split into two parties and a number of factions. Among these an increasing number argued that the Russian middle class was too weak and too cowardly to make a bourgeois revolution and that the working class would have to make "its" revolution for it. The Constitutional Democrats *(Kadets)*, nominally a liberal party, were more representative of the liberal landowners and the zemstva than of the industrialist entrepreneurs. Certainly they were divided on such issues as industrial tariffs and subsidies. The only real entrepreneurial party was the relatively small Octobrist Union.

Increasing participation in political and public life by wider and wider segments of the population created a vital and energetic public atmosphere, only ineffectually stifled by continued censorship, surveillance, and tutelage and punctuated by outbursts of terrorism and political assassination. Broader par-

---

[15] There is no good English equivalent for the phrase, *obshchestvennyi deiatel'*. "Civic employee" will not quite do, and "social activist" is even farther off. The phrase denotes someone who works in the public arena without occupying a position or "rank" in the central or provincial bureaucracy.

ticipation also created pogroms, political strikes, mass demonstrations, and riots. A revolutionary movement that practiced political terror took a high toll of government officials and finally resulted in the assassination of the autocracy's most talented minister, Stolypin; his reforms had created a small but growing class of prosperous peasants, but at the same time they helped to impoverish many more and drove a large mass of uprooted and impoverished former peasants into the increasing turmoil of the urban centers where the radically proselytizing intelligentsia found them all too accessible. Even the formation of a large, competent, "conscious" working class is more doubtful than has commonly been assumed. Orlovsky shows in his highly original paper that much of the structure and organization of civil war institutions accredited by the Bolsheviks to "workers" were in fact accomplished by people who clearly belonged to the "lower middle strata," in other words, the petite-bourgeoisie. Rieber believes that social fragmentation was a more pronounced tendency during this period than social coherence and that the days of the autocracy were clearly numbered, yet the social basis for a representative constitutional regime (as Max Weber pointed out after 1905) scarcely existed.[16] By the 1880s it was late even for a more flexible and liberal policy on the part of the autocracy. The time for flexibility—at least so it seems to me— had been the reign of Nicholas I, who instead attempted to "freeze" Russia in its autocratic mold, to the admiration of such later autocratic ideologues as Leontiev and Pobedonostsev.

I do not wish to belittle the accomplishments of the Silver Age of Russian culture. Indeed, in terms of achievement, in terms of the richness of fulfilled talent in all branches of culture, it might well have been called a golden age, comparable even to the great flowerings of Periclean Athens and Renaissance England. Although there was no Pushkin and no novelist of the stature of the great ones of the 1850s, 1860s, and 1870s, the arts and sciences—lyric poetry and lyric prose, and even the novel, to say nothing of drama, opera, the visual arts, architecture, the revival of native folk arts, medicine, science, music, mathematics, agronomy and engineering—flourished with a kind of renaissance richness that has few equals for such a brief period of time. Many chapters in this volume chronicle and analyze that richness and the promise for the future that richness seemed to imply. Yet most of them seem to conclude or to stop just short of concluding that all this was fragile and foredoomed and that although doom in fact took the shape of the Bolshevik revolution, even without that, the fate of this great flowering could go no further than permitted by the thinness of the social soil in which it grew. The beautiful purple twilight was evening, not morning; and the night was coming on.

[16] For Max Weber on Russia after the Revolution of 1905, see *Archiv fur Sozialwissenschaft und Sozialpolitik* (Tubingen: J. C. Mohr, 1906), 22: 234–354; 23: 165–402. For a trenchant critique of Weber's analysis, see Meyer Schapiro, "A Note on Max Weber's Politics," *Politics* 1–2 (February, 1945): 44–48.

That is the prevailing mood of the great literature of this period and of much of its easel painting as well. Blok, the great lyricist, was the poet of doom. He sang of the "black waters of oblivion." Chekhov, the great playwright, cast a gentle if sardonic melancholy over his world of helpless and doomed people. Gorky's Nietzschean Prometheanism was the least convincing thing about him as a writer; his Nietzschean bandits and tramps ring hollow as an empty drum, whereas his melancholy river landscapes, his unmanned, alcoholic, dissolute heroes, his reminiscences of his powerful, long-suffering grandmother and of his sad self-contradictory writer-friends like Blok and Andreev, live on with a plastic vividness. Sologub's self-asserted "joy of life" is a complete fraud, whereas his tormented, pathological Peredonov will live forever. Belyi, who might be considered a great novelist if he were not so clearly haunted by the ghosts of Gogol and Dostoevsky, wrote appallingly bad short stories, brilliant and highly anticipatory if uneven and eccentric criticism, a few marvelous poems, some interesting prose experiments, and three fine novels. The issue is not so much his stature as a novelist as the escape to anthroposophy as a way of resolving the conflicts that his life and work engendered. His greatest novel, *Petersburg*, which manages to parade almost all classic Russian literature allusively through its pages, has a curiously irresolute ending, permeated by an intense irony, another way, albeit modernist, of evading resolution. Belyi's own vision of Russia's future seemed to deteriorate to a kind of Scythian primitivism that linked him fraternally to Ivanov-Razumnik. Vrubel's greatest paintings breathe the same twilight atmosphere that seemed to hover over all intellectual Russia. It was a time when even the least decadent writers imitated to some extent the decadent manner.

More than any other single figure, Blok was the spokesman for his intellectual generation. A great poet Bloc bridged the nineteenth and the twentieth centuries. In his unfinished long autobiographical poem, "Retribution," he rejects himself, educated Russian society, and indeed the high European post-Renaissance culture that society and Blok himself had so successfully absorbed. He echoed and elaborated that rejection of "his own" in the essays he wrote during the revolutionary and civil war periods—for example, "The Revolution and the Intelligentsia" and the essay "Cataline"—and in his poetic concept of "music." His poem "The Twelve" treats "the people," however, with a certain contempt; he sees them as chaotic, ignorant, and barbaric. Nevertheless, he sees God on their side. The end-of-an-era, fall-of-the-Roman-Empire atmosphere was pervasive. It prevailed in the literary cabarets of Petrograd, like the "Stray Dog," and it even infected some late poems of Gumilev and some poems of Akhmatova. A promising young poet and disciple of Gumilev, Konstantin Vaginov, enjoyed seeing himself as a civilized Roman, like Petronius, say, witnessing the "last days."

Although that is the prevailing impression, one cannot rest entirely easily with it. In literature and thought not all was decadent or mournfully elegaic.

There were, especially in the antiSymbolist revolt after 1909, distinct signs of a new energy and, without silly sentimentalism or Pollyannaish hopes, a certain optimism. Pasternak and Mandelshtam, Khlebnikov and Tsvetaeva were not part of the "violet hour." Nor was Babel, nor Pilniak, nor Zamiatin. Neither was Malevich nor Kandinsky nor Filonov. Mikhail Bakhtin, the son of a landless nobleman turned banker, demonstrated that original Russian thought was by no means dead. But these figures, great as they were, were more a part of the revolutionary upsurge against civil society than an organic outgrowth of the old order. In a broad sense, they belonged to the revolution. All identified themselves in some sense as revolutionary. Even in Pasternak's distinctly anti-Marxist *Doctor Zhivago*, the February Revolution and the provisional government are given short shrift, and the Bolshevik Revolution, though seen as a disaster in the long run, nevertheless speaks with the voice of destiny. Uncle Nikolai Vedeniapin in his didactic passages sounds perilously close to Uncle Nikolai Berdiaev. Mandelshtam identified himself with the "fourth estate" and his "classicism" with revolution. In his intertextual polemics with Blok, he defended the intelligentsia and its heritage. His Marxism, if he ever had any, was that of the Erfurt Program in a distinctly late nineteenth-century German setting. Yet the idea of a civil society free of the trammels of the state was foreign to him, as is clear, for example, in his essay "The State and Rhythm." Tsvetaeva, with her passion for the underdog, Babel and Malevich, with their self-imposed bolshevism, and the others I have mentioned, thought of themselves as revolutionary artists, and their revolution was directed against the bourgeoisie.

Unfortunately, the revolution devoured its children. If the cultural developments that survived into the 1920s and to some degree (of course, it is a mixed picture) flourished had been allowed to grow into the 1930s as well, our present perspective might well be different. We might then speak of a twilight that turned to brilliant day. But it was not to be.

PART TWO

The Search for
the ''Russian Bourgeoisie''

THE RIABUSHINSKY CIRCLE: *BURZHUAZIIA* AND *OBSHCHESTVENNOST'* IN LATE IMPERIAL RUSSIA

James L. West

ONE OF THE most striking characteristics of social development in Imperial Russia was the historic divorce between the entrepreneurial stratum and educated society. The *kupecheskoe soslovie* (merchant estate) was long excluded from intercourse with polite society by its notoriously low level of culture and by deeply ingrained agrarian and aristocratic prejudices against self-regarding, profit-oriented, entrepreneurial activity. Merchants and industrialists, who operated largely as clients of the autocratic state, were accorded semiprivileged status only through their purchased soslovie membership. As with many other groups, however, the soslovie structure was little more than a legal fiction that concealed beneath it numerous competing regional oligarchies, themselves further divided by differences of sector, scale, and ethnic identity (see the Owen essay in this volume). Little united these groupings beyond the hostility of the surrounding society and the rituals of a fading soslovie order.[1]

The Revolution of 1905 profoundly altered these traditional relationships. The eclipse of autocratic power raised hopes among the opponents of the old order that educated society (*obshchestvennost'*) could claim both legitimacy and political power from the faltering autocracy. At the same time, however, a multiplicity of hitherto invisible or inchoate constituencies emerged to make their claims against both the autocracy and educated society, portending the creation of new tensions and divisions in the social and political structure.

The constitutional experiment of the post-1905 period seemed to open the way for the formation of broad new social and political coalitions, and indeed the terminology of class, interest group, and profession emerged alongside the archaic language of soslovie and "humble petition." It remained to be seen, however, whether post-1905 social realities would in fact conform to these new concepts. More important, it was still an open question how Russian obshchestvennost', based on a coalition of elite social groups sharing a common dedication to Western, predominantly liberal values, would recognize and accommodate the claims of new groups.

---

[1] For background on the *kupechestvo*, see Alfred J. Rieber, *Merchants and Entrepreneurs in Imperial Russia* (Chapel Hill, 1982); Thomas J. Owen, *Capitalism and Politics in Russia* (Cambridge, 1981); P. A. Berlin, *Russkaia burzhuaziia v staroe i novoe vremia* (Moscow, 1922).

The *kupechestvo* represented one such challenge. The rapid progress the industrialists and merchants made during 1905 in defining and defending their common interests signaled the emergence of a new and potentially influential force in Russia. Contemporary observers began to speak of the advent in Russia of an industrial *burzhuaziia*.[2] The possibility was thus raised that the cultural and political sophistication of the entrepreneurs had reached a level sufficient to permit their inclusion in the obshchestvennost' coalition.

Although the majority of entrepreneurs eschewed oppositional activity after 1905, new contenders for leadership of the bourgeoisie did emerge to demand a place beside the intelligentsia and gentry in the leadership of the anti-autocratic movement. The compatibility of their ideas with those of the older elites, the unity of the forces they represented, and the degree of acceptance they encountered are all important indicators of the flexibility and cohesiveness of Russian obshchestvennost' on the eve of the First World War.

The most vocal and audacious entrepreneurial group in Russia, in terms of both its advocacy of class solidarity and its determination to be taken seriously by obshchestvennost', was the Riabushinsky circle of Moscow. Pavel P. Riabushinsky, his brother Vladimir P. Riabushinsky, and his colleagues Alexander I. Konovalov, Sergei N. Tretiakov, Nikolai D. Morozov, and Sergei I. Chetverikov are best known as the leaders of Russia's liberal entrepreneurs.[3] Called by contemporaries the "young" industrialists, or "young group," they became after 1905 the most active proponents of the transformation of the old *kupechestvo* into a modern entrepreneurial burzhuaziia. Riabushinsky's ringing assertion "*Kupets idët!*" ("The merchant is on the move!") announced the advent of the progressist movement on the national political stage in 1912. In the ensuing years, he and his colleagues came to personify the effort to create the ideological and organizational basis of a modern entrepreneurial class.[4]

While Riabushinsky's activism was rooted in his desire to lead his *klass* to find "its place in the sun" in Russia, he and his collaborators represented far more than narrow advocates of a single constituency. They seemed painfully aware of the fragility of Russia's nascent civic culture and the brittleness of its

---

[2] On the entrepreneurs in 1905, see S. E. Sef, *Burzhuaziia v 1905 godu* (Moscow, 1926); and E. D. Chermensky, Burzhuaziia i tsarism v pervoi russkoi revolutsii (Moscow, 1970).

[3] This core group is defined by the participation of its members in a variety of joint activities, extending through the war and revolution to emigre organizations in Paris and elsewhere. To this list might be added D. V. Sirotkin, an Old Believer shipbuilder from Nizhny-Novgorod, Riabushinsky's principal collaborator in schismatic affairs, and lesser figures such as P. A. Buryshkin, A. I. Kuznetsov, S. A. Smirnov, and M. N. Bardygin. Some notion of the extent of their support in Moscow might be gleaned from the list of those who signed the "Protest of the Sixty-Six" in 1911. See *Utro Rossii* (henceforth UR), Feb. 11, 1911, 3.

[4] On the activities of the Riabushinsky circle, see James L. West, "The Rjabusinskij Circle: Russian Industrialists in Search of a Bourgeoisie," *Jahrbücher für Geschichte Ost Europas* 32 (1984), Heft 3, 358–77.

evolving social structures. It was their oft-stated intention to foster coherence and collaboration among disparate social and political groupings both within and beyond the entrepreneurial stratum.

Their incentive to do this arose from their position as outsiders. Riabushinsky was an Old Believer who worked for the unification of all dissident sects, urging his coreligionists to shed their ancient indifference to secular affairs and join in the struggle for political and religious freedom. As *nouveaux arrivés* in Duma politics, he and his associates bent their efforts to build a broad coalition of liberal forces through their Progressist party. And as strangers to the intellectual salons of Moscow, they mounted a number of initiatives designed to reach out to the liberal intelligentsia, including the Economic Discussions (1909–1912), the Protest of the Sixty-Six (1911), and the Information Committee (1914). Finally, as the owner of a publishing house, Riabushinsky propagated his views to a wide public in such periodicals as *Narodnaia Gazeta* (People's Newspaper, 1906), *Utro Rossii* (The Russian Morn, 1907, 1909–1917), and the Old Believer paper *Tserkov'* (Church, 1908–1914), and the *Velikaia Rossiia* (Great Russia) symposium (1910–1911).[5]

Representatives of the new generation of Moscow industrialists, Riabushinsky and his collaborators were particularly anxious to gain entrée into and acceptance from educated society, not only to assuage their own sense of self-esteem and professional pride but also because they believed they possessed knowledge and experience without which the forces of obshchestvennost' could not succeed in their effort to lead the nation. Yet as newcomers to intellectual and political circles, they were by cultural provenance and personal inclination very different people from those with whom they sought to work. They brought to the debates ideas often at variance with the prevailing notions of the educated elites, and while they offered their help to "society," they also undertook to challenge certain of its most cherished beliefs and assumptions. The record of these activities between 1905 and 1914 provides a window into the mental world of men who aspired to become members of Russian obshchestvennost', but whose experience and concerns reached well beyond the charmed circle of nineteenth-century educated society.

The views of the young industrialists evolved from three sources: their private entrepreneurial experience, Riabushinsky's association with Old Belief, and their contacts after 1905 with the liberal professoriate of Moscow. They came of age in the world of merchant Moscow, and they absorbed from this background the slavophile patriotism of the old *kupechestvo*. They inherited its slavophilic animosities toward "bureaucratic" Petersburg as well as the

[5] On the Progressist party, see *Fraktsiia progressistov v IV gosudarstvennoi dume*, 1–4, St. Petersburg, 1913–1914. See also V. N. Seletskii, "Obrazovanie partii progressistov," *Vestnik Moskovskovo universiteta: Istoriia* 5 (1970): 32–48. On Riabushinsky's publishing work, see A. P. Bokhanov, "Iz istorii burzhuaznoi pechati," *Istoricheskie zapiski* 97 (1976): 263–89.

Moscow merchants' pretensions of standing closer to the narod than did the denizens of the northern capital.[6] Their animus toward St. Petersburg was reinforced by the independent economic position they occupied as heads of family textile firms founded by serf and schismatic ancestors and by their commercial contacts with the peasantry of the Great Russian heartland, on which they depended for their market.[7]

While they came of age in the world of *soslovnost'*, the younger generation of entrepreneurs was moving rapidly beyond the factory and warehouse walls that had encompassed the world of their fathers. They gained in professional confidence as they modernized their enterprises, which were among the largest manufacturing operations in the empire. They enjoyed the accumulated wealth of generations of effort and received the best education that wealth could buy, as well as extensive foreign travel. They participated in the vibrant cultural life of Silver-Age Moscow, patronizing the *style moderne* creativity of men like Vrubel and Shekhtel.

The Revolution of 1905 catalyzed these forward-looking impulses into political action. Riabushinsky and his associates took the lead in urging the kupechestvo to end its alliance with the autocracy and raise its voice with that of the rest of society in demanding an end to the arbitrary authority of the unreformed tsarist regime. The more cautious business majority reluctantly declared its opposition to the regime, but then it beat a hasty retreat back into the government camp after the October Manifesto. In the post-1905 period, the entrepreneurial establishments of Moscow and St. Petersburg attempted to reach a new modus vivendi with the bureaucracy, through the Association of Industry and Trade and the Octobrist party.[8] The Riabushinsky group, in contrast, persisted in its liberal oppositional stance and gained a following in Moscow as disillusionment set in over the results of this collaborationist effort.

The second pillar of Riabushinsky's outlook was his association with Old Belief, shared by Morozov, and Konovalov. The world of the *staroobriadtsy* was even further removed from the main currents of educated society than that of the Russian Orthodox kupechstvo. Branded ''schismatics'' and persecuted for 250 years, the Old Believers had evolved an autonomous religious subculture hermetically sealed off from the Orthodox mainstream. Geographically dis-

---

[6] On the nineteenth-century merchant-Slavophile alliance, see Owen, *Capitalism and Politics* chap. 2.

[7] On the Moscow industrial families, see P. A. Buryshkin, *Moskva kupecheskoe* (New York, 1954); Jo Ann Ruckman, *The Moscow Business Elite, 1840–1905* (DeKalb, 1984). See also the lavish family histories of the Riabushinskys, Konovalovs, and others, published to celebrate the centennials of their firms; for example, *Torgovo-promyshlennoe delo Riabushinskikh* (Moscow, 1913).

[8] The best sources on what I have called the ''Octobrist compromise'' remain: Ruth A. Roosa, ''The Association of Industry and Trade'' (Ph.D. diss., Columbia University, 1967); and Louis Menashe, ''Alexander Guchkov and the Origins of the Octobrist Party'' (Ph.D. diss., Columbia University, 1966).

persed and threatened with imprisonment, torture, and execution by the authorities, they turned in on themselves to become the most energetic and literate element of the Russian peasantry. From their ranks the merchant cadres of Moscow were replenished in the nineteenth century, a process of renewal that was the genesis of industrial "dynasties" to which the "young group" belonged.[9]

The Riabushinskys adhered to the Belokrinitsa hierarchy of Priested Old Believers, the most developed and least seditious of the dissident sects.[10] Yet even this Old Believer elite, classified by the authorities as a "harmful sect," was subject to periodic repressions. Thus when the coercive machinery of church and state was weakened in 1905, Riabushinsky stepped forward with a passion born of persecution to demand an end to religious intolerance and guarantees of freedom of thought, conscience, and speech in religious and civil affairs.

When Riabushinsky succeeded in organizing a massive Old Believer Peasant Congress in 1906, he found that the majority of his coreligionists were even more reluctant to follow his political lead than were the *kuptsy*.[11] Yet his activism did provide the nucleus around which a small but dedicated Old Believer intelligentsia could coalesce. With the help of these "Neo–Old Believers," Riabushinksy reanimated the All-Russian Congress of Old Believers and through it worked to unify and politicize the scattered forces of the schismatics. His efforts on behalf of his coreligionists were often frustrating, but Riabushinsky never lost his abiding faith in the narod or his identification with what he believed to be their values and their welfare.[12]

If the liberal impulses of the young industrialists had crystallized in 1905, the revolution had also provided them painful reminders that they were still not taken seriously by the forces of obshchestvennost'. In the thick of the struggle, they had been forced to operate in isolation from the Zemstvo Congress, which had rebuffed their offers of cooperation. The Constitutional Democrats also had warned them away, as Kadet leader Miliukov declared that there was no room for "narrow class interests" in his "above-class" party.[13] As proud as they were of their status as "men of practical experi-

---

[9] For the classic source on the Old Believers, see A. S. Prugavin, *Staroobriadchestvo vo vtoroi polovine XIX veka* (Moscow, 1904). See also V. P. Riabushinsky, *Staroobriadchestvo i russkoe religioznoe chuvstvo* (Joinville-le-pont, 1936). On the schismatic role in economic development, see William L. Blackwell, "Old Believers and the Rise of Private Enterprise in Early Nineteenth Century Russia," *Slavic Review* 24, no. 3 (September 1965): 406–24.

[10] For information on the Belokrinitsa Hierarchy, see J. S. Curtiss, *Church and State in Russia* (New York, 1972).

[11] On Riabushinsky's Peasant Congress, see *Vserossiiskii s''ezd krest'ian staroobriadtsev: Materialy po voprosam zemelnomu i krest'ianskomu* (Moscow, 1906).

[12] On the Congress of Old Believers, see *Trudy: Vserossiiskii s'ezd staroobriadtsev*, nos. 6–12 (Nizhny-Novgorod, 1905–1912).

[13] TsGIA, f. 150, op. 1, l. 20; Chermensky, *Burzhuaziia*, 134.

ence,'' Riabushinsky and his people concluded that they could not continue to function in a vacuum; they sorely needed support and assistance from ''men of science'' to sharpen and broaden their ideas.

Fortunately for them, the convulsions of 1905–1907 had provoked a reassessment of the attitudes of the intelligentsia among members of the Moscow professoriate. The Right Kadets around Peter B. Struve had come to question the long-standing anticapitalist and antibourgeois prejudices implicit in the radical and liberal traditions. On their way to producing the famous *Vekhi* (Landmarks) symposium, Struve, Berdiaev, Bulgakov, and others were now willing to explore contacts with the liberal industrialists. Riabushinsky and Konovalov established social contact with the Moscow professors by inviting them to ''take tea'' in their private salons. Thus were born the Economic Discussions, one of the few sustained collaborations between entrepreneurs and intellectuals in Russian history.[14]

These gatherings, which lasted from 1909 to 1912, served as a kind of graduate education for the industrialists. While listening to lectures on such technical topics as the role of syndicates and trusts and foreign capital, they were also exposed to Struve's liberal nationalism, Berdiaev's theology, Bulgakov's Orthodox work ethic (see Rosenthal's essay in this volume), and Ozerov's views on labor policy. For their part, the industrialists viewed these symposia as a ''nascent political club,'' a forerunner of new and powerful coalitions they hoped to build in the future.[15]

By 1912 they felt confident enough to leave the tutelage of the professors to launch their own ''national-liberal'' vehicle, the Progressist party. They owed much to the professors and still stood somewhat in awe of their intellectual prowess. But it was on their own convictions that they hung the intellectual structure erected for them by Struve and his associates. As they prepared to enter national politics in their own right, they did not conceal their belief that they were more important to the nation, more in tune with its traditions, and closer to the narod than those elites who hitherto comprised Russian obshchestvennost'.

The young industrialists existed simultaneously in two worlds, a duality architectonically symbolized by the Shekhtel house of Riabushinsky's brother Stepan: its style moderne living quarters concealed behind them a meticulously recreated Byzantine chapel meant for private worship according to pre-Nikonian rites (see the Brumfield essay in this volume). They admired the advanced cultures of the West, and they embraced the values of science, technology, and reason. At the same time, they also cultivated a nostalgic reverence for the values and rituals of Pre-Petrine Rus. They were determined that

---

[14] On the Economic Discussions, see Richard Pipes, *Struve: Liberal on the Right* (Cambridge, 1980), 174–86.

[15] TsGAOR, f. 4047, op. 1, d. 18. On the views of the professors, see Samuel D. Kassow, *Students, Professors, and the State in Tsarist Russia* (Berkeley, 1989).

Russia's transformation must go forward but not at the expense of national stability, identity, or sovereignty. In a synthesis of seventeenth-century tradition and the institutions of modern capitalism they sought solutions to the problems of the twentieth century.

The oppositional views of the industrialists were deeply felt, for they judged the autocracy to have failed the nation on many counts. For centuries the self-appointed engine of Russia's development, the tsarist state now stood ponderously astride the economy, impeding the emergence of new productive forces with its bureaucratic inertia and police controls. The government had also forfeited its political legitimacy by resisting and undermining the development of democratic forms and by allowing itself to become captive of "the agrarians," powerful landed elites hostile to "all things that were not themselves."[16] Finally, the regime endangered the sovereignty, perhaps even the existence, of the nation by its military incompetence.

The government's difficulty in maintaining control of the country in 1905 and after evidenced the bankruptcy of the ancien régime. Forced on the defensive, the authorities reverted to their oldest and worst expedient: rule by force and coercion.[17] Whatever liberal reforms the government had been compelled to make in 1905, the industrialists feared, it would rescind as soon as the forces of order were strong enough to prevail. This reactionary resurgence, however, would, in Riabushinsky's view, soon call forth "its own 1905" and a new "struggle, coming perhaps tomorrow, between the old and new foundations of Russian life."[18] For this new round of conflict he and his collaborators were constantly preparing.

Legitimacy was now passing to obshchestvennost', to educated society, which possessed the scientific knowledge and the professional expertise to place the institutions of the nation on a firm scientific and technological foundation. The concept of obshchestvennost' for the young industrialists was imbued with political meaning: to them the coalition of all educated groups, united to disarm the forces of order and transform the autocracy into a constitutional monarchy, could serve as a unifying symbol without impeding progress. But they insisted that to be successful this alliance would have to include the "serious *obshchestvennyi* force" represented by the "young, energetic bourgeoisie," which alone could provide the "practical experience" and "material power" to impart dynamicism to the nation's economy.[19]

The values that educated society had long nurtured would also have to undergo change. The "powerless altruism" and "service idea" of the gentry and the "abstract" outlook of the intelligentsia would have to give way before the virtues of productivity and initiative cultivated by the new "creators of

[16] *UR*, June 23, 1910, 1; July 5, 1911, 1.

[17] *UR*, June 6, 1910, 1; Oct. 2, 1911, 2; Feb. 23, 1911, 1.

[18] *UR*, Jan. 1, 1912; May 18, 1910, 1.

[19] *UR*, May 23, 1910, 1; Jan. 8, 1911, 3.

material value."[20] Society would also have to accept the fundamental premise of the industrialists' activity: that, as Riabushinsky often asserted, "capitalism [is] the only vital and practical system for the conduct of economics."[21]

The young industrialists insisted, against prevailing opinion, that self-sustaining capitalist development in Russia was not only possible, but essential. It was possible because the narod possess the innate capacity to make it so, given adequate freedom, incentive, and leadership. It was necessary because only capitalism could act as the rapid economic accelerator that Russia so desperately needed to keep pace with her Western competitors. Continued reliance on a paternalistic state, they argued, would stunt social development and retard economic growth.

Capitalism was the great "steam engine" needed to drive the economy forward at top speed, and while it would require popular acceptance of competitive mechanisms and self-regarding effort, its Russian variant would be more "enlightened" than in the West. Riabushinsky's motto, "*bogatstvo obiazyvaet*" (*richesse oblige*), suggested the kind of moral tone with which the industrialists wished to invest their activities.[22] In their capitalist vision, employer and employee would be bound by mutual obligations within a religious and nationalist ethos unique to Russia.

The priority of the moment was the struggle with the autocracy and the retrograde forces it sheltered. Riabushinsky always insisted that "economic freedom is indissolubly linked with political freedom," and hence the immediate task of the bourgeoisie was to bring its "material power" to bear on the side of obshchestvennost'.[23] Even after the political battle had been won, however, the bourgeoisie would remain the prime mover in Russia's transformation. The "service classes," the gentry and intelligentsia, would fade from prominence as vestiges of Russia's preindustrial past, and "those forces capable of demonstrating authority" would supersede them. In place of the "beautiful altruism" of earlier elites, the entrepreneur would emerge animated by a "creative egoism" that would promote "the material construction by each of us of our own personal lives." In postautocratic Russia, the bourgeoisie would claim its rightful place as "the dominant political force."[24]

Capitalism, in turn, would reshape the social structure of the country. A revolution in economic relations would "speed the collapse of the *soslovie*

[20] *UR*, May 18, 1910, 1.

[21] From a 1922 speech of Riabushinsky, see "Protokol zasedaniia soveta rossiiskovo finansovo-promyshlenno-torgovogo soiuza," Columbia University Archive, M. M. Zolotarev Collection, Box 4.

[22] V. P. Riabushinsky, "Kupecheskoe moskovskoe," *Den' russkovo rebenka* (San Francisco), 18 (April 1951): 180.

[23] From Riabushinsky's 1922 speech; see note 21. Their views on the political role of the "rising bourgeoisie" were drawn from the political mythology of Britain and France, the countries they most admired.

[24] *UR*, Jan. 1, 1912, 1.

structure" and encourage the creation of modern social classes. The industrialists welcomed the advent of a class society, for they felt the realignment of interests it entailed would end the volatile transitional stage of inchoate resentments and anarchic violence. A period of more conscious and organized social competition would follow. The further this process progressed, the more stable the society would become. Parliamentary democracy would provide the political flexibility necessary to absorb and attenuate social antagonisms, as the rule of law would establish the "legal conditions for the free struggle" of classes, interests, and nationalities. Distinctions between city and country would begin to disappear; society would become culturally and educationally homogeneous; newly created wealth would become more evenly distributed; and the "psychology of the bourgeois" would become universal.[25]

Social cohesion during this period of transformation would be guaranteed by the cement of nationalism, a force that the industrialists charged obshchestvennost' had abandoned by default to the anti-Semitic, reactionary right in Russia. Borrowing from the professors' "Neo-Slavophile" conceptions, Riabushinsky's group envisioned a "great mission of Slavic unification," a crusade to create a free commonwealth of nations and nationalities capable of demonstrating "the tribal genius of the Slavs."[26] The interests of all groups and classes would be subordinated to the goal of building this Slavonic condominium. Labor and enterprise would cease to be exclusively self-regarding; instead, they would be understood as social service in the interests of the nation. The narod, always deeply and instinctively patriotic, according to the Riabushinskys, would be imbued with a "healthy militarism," a "heroic world view" which would galvanize free Russia, its power and identity restored, to face "the ancient oppressors of Slavdom," "the Teutons."[27]

This transition could not come soon enough, the industrialists argued, for in the arena of great power rivalry, Russia's industrial backwardness and its governing elites' incompetence had already undermined the nation's status and prestige to an alarming degree. Imperial Germany stood ready to exploit internal difficulties and weaknesses, either by military aggression or more insidiously by economic penetration. The autocracy's incapacity to manage military affairs and its inability to mobilize the elites and the narod to meet this threat portended to them an accelerated erosion of Russia's status as a great power, leading to eventual subversion or defeat by the "hand of German imperialism."[28]

If nationalism were to cement the nation, then the industrialists understood

[25] *UR*, May 30, 1910, 1.

[26] *UR*, Jan. 30, 1910, 1.

[27] V. P. Riabushinsky, ed., *Velikaia Rossiia: Sbornik statei po voennym i obshchestvennym Voprosam*, Book II (Moscow, 1911), 5; *UR*, Jan. 30, 1910, 1; Feb. 4, 1911, 1.

[28] *UR*, Jan. 12, 1922, 1.

it had to be recast and reshaped. Nationalist appeals, long the monopoly of the right, had been used to bolster the autocratic and nativistic principles espoused by the forces of order. Liberal Russian nationalism, in Struve's words, was "still in the making."[29] The industrialists thus set forth what they saw as a more "authentic" response to the German challenge than the programs of the autocracy or obshchestvennost'. They sought to clothe Russia's modernization in "native" costume and to demonstrate that the skills and values necessary for this transformation were implicit in the ancient culture of Rus. Had capitalism triumphed in Russia under the leadership of the Riabushinskys it might well have been draped in the strange vestments of the seventeenth century.

Riabushinsky's unique cultural vantage point enabled him and his Neo–Old Believer collaborators to develop a novel conception of Russia's history and national character. They resurrected slavophile myths of the merchant subculture, infused them with schismatic intensity, and shaped them to sustain their capitalist, democratic, and nationalistic aspirations. These myths formed the emotional subsoil beneath their progressist views on vlast, obshchestvennost', and narod.

Their point of departure was a classic slavophilic idyl, a mythic vision of "the free and independent Rus" of pre-Petrine, pre-Nikonian time, in which vlast' (authority) and *zemlia* (land) existed in separate but not antagonistic spheres. Riabushinsky insisted that the term *samoderzhavie* (autocracy) in its original meaning referred to the sovereignty of the Russian tsars vis-à-vis foreign rulers and implied no autocratic powers over the Russian people.[30] The people and the elites shared the same religious culture, and the narod exercised indigenous democratic rights, through "*zemskii* self-government" and the *sobornyi* (conciliary) principle of local election of religious authorities. Vlast' defended the zemlia and thus upheld the "democratic principle in church and in life." This balance, and the religious culture and rites that sanctified it, "worked out over centuries," "corresponded to the psycho-religious feelings in the soul of the Russian people."[31]

The Church Schism of 1667, however, represented a "great psychological rupture" in the "organic" course of Russian history. In its wake, both church and state adopted new and illegitimate concepts of rulership: arbitrary power was extended over the zemlia, the ancient rights of the narod were unilaterally abrogated, and the people were enserfed to the authority of the "Moloch state." Patriarch Nikon replaced "free Christian *obshchestvennost'* " with "hierarchical arbitrariness." In turn, the Nikonian church paid for its hubris by being reduced to a "bureaucratic and lifeless mechanism" within the administrative machinery of the Petrine state.[32]

[29] *UR*, June 1, 1910, 1.

[30] Riabushinsky quoted in *Golos staroobriadchestva* (Feb. 19, 1906), no. 11, p. 1.

[31] *Tserkov'* (henceforth *Ts*) (Oct. 19, 1914; Dec. 20, 1909).

[32] *UR*, June 19, 1911, 2; *Ts* (Aug. 28, 1911; Feb. 2, 1914).

"The epoch of the destruction of the rights of the *zemlia* corresponded to the so-called *raskol*." For Riabushinsky, the centuries-long resistance of the Old Believers represented a popular struggle against this subjugation, carried on by "the most highly developed part of the Russian people." The issue at stake was one of not only rites and vestments but also freedom to live a cherished way of life. Indeed, *Tserkov'* argued that to call the Old Believers *raskolniki* was a misnomer, for the Old Believers did not break with the church; rather, the church and state broke faith with the people and their culture. The follower of the old rites intuitively understood that the new bureaucracy and "religious police" of the tsarist regime were "not organic" but "alien to the Russian spirit."[33] They saw that the autocratic state was erected "at the expense of all that was local, individual and personal" in the ancient traditions of the narod and entailed "the renunciation of our freedom and our culture."[34] They thus fled beyond the state's control and cultivated their way of life in the face of its "savage persecution."

Old Belief represented for Riabushinsky the ideology of Russia's dispossessed and disinherited masses. It rejected a process of state building based on alien models, carried on by elite to the exclusion of the narod, and built at the cost of suppressing its indigenous freedom and cultural identity. Deprived of its national essence, the Russian people "stood before the western peoples in the pitiful rags of a Holy Fool," their true creativity and productivity concealed under the weight of autocracy, serfdom, and poverty.[35]

Authentic Russia withdrew into the remote schismatic communities of the far north and Siberia. There the "followers of the ancient piety," who "retained the religious faith, national appearance and characteristic way of life," of Old Russia "in the secrecy of their souls . . . preserved the memory of the past ancient free Rus."[36] For all their inquisitional efforts, the authorities could not stamp out this heresy. Indeed, Old Belief spread among the common people and even penetrated into the elites through the "native" kupechstvo.

The surviving schismatics, the most "deprived, beaten and forgotten part of the *narod*," represented for Riabushinsky the best and truest representatives of "great masses of the indigenous Russian people."[37] Unlike the Nikonian Orthodox peasantry, whose spiritual and economic independence was crushed by the weight of authority, the dissidents "held firmly to the path which ancient Rus had followed."[38] They embodied in their culture the traditions of *zemskii* self-government and *sobornyi* democracy long since extinguished in the general population. The schismatics also demonstrated the true economic

[33] *Ts* (Feb. 2, 1914; March 28, 1910).
[34] *UR*, June 19, 1911, 2.
[35] *Ts* (Aug. 17, 1914).
[36] *Ts* (Feb. 6, 1911; Oct. 3, 1910).
[37] *Ts* (Feb. 1, 1909; Aug. 23, 1909).
[38] *Ts* (Oct. 19, 1914).

capacities of the narod: they were "harder, more energetic" than others and displayed their "love of work and sobriety" in all their endeavors.[39] Within Old Belief, it was argued, "there are no class divisions," for believers of all stations were united by their work ethic and shared reverence for "the ancient piety."[40]

To Riabushinsky, the Revolution of 1905 represented an extension to the whole population of the ancient anti-autocratic struggle for freedom of the Old Believers. It had been violent and anarchic because the narod struck out blindly and instinctively against authority. At this stage in their development, the people lacked both the class and national identities that would organize and focus their resistance in the future. For all its incoherence, however, the revolution signaled "the end of the Petersburg period of Russian history," of building the state by autocratic means, and it opened the way for the "recovery of all that was lost." Henceforth, Moscow, "the city of the Russian bourgeoisie" would "speak in the name of the Russian *zemlia*."[41]

The industrialists clearly understood that there was no going back, no possibility of a return to the forest communes of the schismatic past. Rapid modernization of the state and society was the order of the day. Even while the country moved forward, however, the liberation of this hidden Russia would make possible the "renunciation of alien principles" of bureaucracy, police, and arbitrary authority and the "rediscovery of our own indigenous way of life."[42] The fall of autocracy would mean the end of "*Nikonianstvo*," for under conditions of true religious freedom, the Neo-Old Believers hinted, the Nikonian church would collapse of its own bureaucratic weight. Old Belief would once again become "a living popular cause"; the ethos of its 10 to 20 million followers would spread to the rest of the population through mass reconversion.[43] In this way the narod would regain its true cultural identity.

The defeat of autocracy would represent "the victory of self-government over absolutism, and the destruction of the absolutist principle in the popular consciousness." The centralized bureaucratic apparatus of autocracy would be dismantled, and the rights of the zemlia would be restored under the auspices of a "strong, sovereign (*derzhavnyi*) parliament," while cultural diversity and economic decentralization would be protected and encouraged.[44]

Postautocratic Russia would be built by new men, "able to demonstrate

[39] *Ts* (Feb. 6, 1911; April 1, 1912).

[40] *Ts* (March 23, 1914).

[41] *UR*, April 3, 1911, 5; June 19, 1911, 2.

[42] *UR*, June 19, 1911, 2; *Ts* (Oct. 19, 1914).

[43] *Ts* (Jan. 11, 1910). The idea of mass conversions may not have been as outlandish as it seems. Gregory Freeze documents the abiding fear of church officials of mass defections to the "schismatic wolves." See Gregory L. Freeze, *The Parish Clergy in Nineteenth-Century Russia* (Princeton, 1983).

[44] *UR*, Sept. 18, 1911; March 11, 1910, 2.

authority" and dedicated to the principle of "cultural freedom," the concept that Riabushinsky identified as "the bourgeois idea."[45] The "native" bourgeoisie, "linked by a thousand unseen threads" to the narod, would act simultaneously as agent of change and guardian of national values. In this it would also win popular support that no other elite could hope to muster. The Old Believer masses, already in their "work habits and sobriety thoroughly bourgeois," would "follow their bourgeoisie" toward building a free and more productive society.[46]

Old Belief, in its origins an act of negation, would now reemerge as a force of affirmation. Together the "native bourgeoisie" and the "followers of the ancient piety" would constitute "the independent living nucleus" of an awakening nation, based on native traditions of democracy, labor, and "free Christian community (obshchestvennost')."[47] Russian capitalism would be infused with "the principles of the enlightened raskol," and worker and employer would come to realize that they were, in Riabushinsky's words, "laboring in a single cause, linked by common aims" of "raising the productive forces of the nation." In contrast to the "abstract chaos" of the West, free Russia would be guided by "the religious-ethical ideas of the native Russian people."[48] Industry would be harnessed to national ends and religious values, and the class conflict and exploitation so characteristic of Western capitalism would be attenuated by a shared consciousness that "workers and employers are parts of the same body."[49]

Riabushinsky's nostaligic modernism, with its evocations of aggressive capitalism and schismatic piety, demonstrates vividly his desire to mediate between the indigenous and foreign streams of Russian historical experience. His Neo-Old Believer and the Progressist appeals were, to be sure, broadcast through different organs—Tserkov' and Utro Rossii, respectively—to different constituencies. But the voice and inspiration of Riabushinsky and his colleagues echo authentically in both.[50] Essentially they created two social myths, one of a utopian religious past and the other of a visionary capitalist future. When juxtaposed, these elements constitute a world view laced with contradictions: "creative egoism" versus a longing for community; devotion to science and technology versus mystical piety; admiration for the West versus assertion of Slavic exceptionalism; exuberant liberalism versus incipient nativism.

[45] UR, May 18, 1910, 1.
[46] Ts (May 24, 1909).
[47] Ts (Aug. 28, 1911).
[48] Ts (Dec. 20, 1909).
[49] UR, May 10, 1912, 1.
[50] Riabushinsky's writings in emigration and his service as a "pillar" of Old Belief in France, related in interviews with descendents, together suggest that he retained his beliefs and affiliations until his death in 1924.

The key to reconciling these apparent contradictions was an unshakable faith in the narod, to which the industrialists felt bound by ties of blood and culture. They tended to look beyond the workers, about whom they said surprisingly little (as if not to waken the sleeping dragon), to the peasant masses from which their ancestors had come. V. P. Riabushinsky retrospectively observed that the industrialists considered themselves "nothing more than enterprising peasants, the highest stratum of Russian trading peasants."[51]

Unlike those before them who had looked to the peasantry, the industrialists did not wish to preserve the rural way of life; they actively applauded the triumph of individual values over collective ones in the countryside. They did, however, wish to retain the moral community and self-reliance of the schismatic commune, even while capitalism dismantled the peasant culture as a whole. Because they considered themselves "of the people," the Riabushinskys seemed convinced that the masses could replicate their own experience and be brought into the modern secular world without losing their "national face."

To their credit, the young industrialists seem to have been sincerely committed to liberal values: democratic freedoms, the rule of law, civil rights, and cultural pluralism. Nowhere in their action or rhetoric does one discern the kind of anti-modern resentments, cultural and political intolerance, anti-Semitism, or predilection for violence that were the precursors of the fascist movements to come.[52] Yet in their haste to make democracy, capitalism, and nationhood comprehensible to the masses, they verged close to those appeals to "blood and soil," national community, and heroic vitalism that elsewhere were being used to undermine the liberal faith.

Riabushinsky thought he had discovered what might be called a usable past, one independent of and antithetical to the traditions of the autocracy. Old Belief for him was a cultural template through which modern skills and values could be recast as ancient and indigenous, the primordial components of a hidden cultural heritage. The capacity of the people for self-government and productive labor had not been tested for centuries. Freedom would bring that test, and the industrialists were confident the narod, if properly tutored and led, would pass it. For this reason, they were less disturbed by the possibility of popular revolution than by the prospect of continued stagnation and decline under the senescent ancien régime.

---

[51] V. P. Riabushinsky, "Kupechestvo moskovskoe," 189. The Riabushinskys may well have tended to glide over the differences between peasant and worker because he gave preference in hiring in the family's enterprises to their coreligionists. Interview with M. I. Chuvanov, apprentice in the *Tipografiia br. Riabushinskikh*, Moscow, 1978.

[52] Police reports, as well as published editorials, confirm an absence of anti-Semitic bias in the industrialists' thinking. On the contrary, they consistently demanded full civil rights for Jews, along with all other nationalities. See ROBIL, f. 4047, op. 1, d. 15; TsGAOR, f. DPOO, d. 343, op. 4, 1915, ll. 120–23; f. D-4, d. 42 1911, l. 22; *Ts* (Oct. 20, 1913).

The industrialists also had faith in themselves, in their own moral superiority, charismatic personalities, and ability to address the narod and command its respect. Yet their rhetoric consistently outran their organizational capacities. The Old Believers and the bourgeoisie they evoked were more myth than substance. In reality, in the prewar period both groups showed clearly accelerated fragmentation rather than the "crystallization" the industrialists sought. The religious community, historically fractured by theological disputes as arcane as they were numerous, was spawning still more splinter sects over the issue of how to respond to the new freedoms offered it in 1905.[53] Similarly, the merchants and manufacturers of many localities were frenetically organizing themselves but doing so in such a haphazard fashion as to threaten, according to *Utro Rossii*, "the total disorganization of the commercial-industrial class."[54] One can only conclude that these constituencies were experiencing severe difficulty in negotiating the transition from soslovie and sectarian identity to more modern forms. In a moment of rare candor, *Utro Rossii* was compelled to concede: "The *soslovnyi* structure, despite all supports, is collapsing rather than consolidating, yet class groupings are just beginning to form; [they] still exist more as theoretical constructs than as living reality."[55]

The Riabushinsky group may actually have contributed to these centrifugal forces. Its tendency to demand cooperation on its own terms suggests a thinly veiled contempt for its opponents within as well as outside its constituencies. The group members insisted that the way to unify Old Belief was to subsume all sects under their own, and their arrogation of entrepreneurial leadership to the "native Moscow bourgeoisie" left little scope for the largely non-Russian entrepreneurs who controlled the industries of St. Petersburg and the periphery of the empire. Beneath their liberal rhetoric, one senses only a weakly developed capacity for cooperation and compromise, skills essential to a well-functioning democratic order.[56]

It is difficult to conclude that the activities of the young industrialists before the war strengthened the forces of obshchestvennost'. On the face of it, the arrival of such articulate and active figures, professing a sincere desire to help, would seem to promise the awakening of the heretofore somnolent Russian entrepreneurial stratum. But it is also possible that their strange vision and their determination to realize that vision, represented a disruptive force. Their

[53] There were indications in *Tserkov'*, for example, that among the priestless Old Believers a schism arose over the issue of whether to register communities as the new law permitted. The resulting factions were called *obshchiniki* and *protivoobshchiniki*. Other issues of compliance with new civil regulations were causing similar disagreements. See *Ts* (June 21, 1909).

[54] *UR*, Feb. 10, 1911, 1; Sept. 23, 1911, 1.

[55] *UR*, March 11, 1910, 1.

[56] *Utro Rossii* often spoke in disparaging terms of the tendencies toward compromise with the government among its opponents. See *UR*, Jan. 9, 1911, 2.

assertive self-certainty and their combative style may well have undermined and weakened the very forces they sought to consolidate.

The industrialists mounted a formidable challenge to the principles of obshchestvennost'. They demanded a broader criteria for membership in elite society, an end to the monopoly of those with education and culture, and the inclusion of "productive" groups formerly excluded. They persistently pointed out the weaknesses and vulnerabilities of educated society—its foreign cultural orientation, its isolation from the popular culture, its indifference to economic questions. They demanded that the elites end their fixation with the struggle between vlast' and obshchestvennost' and turn instead to face the narod beneath them. When they did this, the industrialists seemed to warn, they had best have something to say. Finally, they even questioned the future role of the gentry and intelligentsia in building postautocratic Russia. In the age of classes and class interests, they predicted, the "above-class" and "service" traditions of obshchestvennost' would rapidly become obsolete.

It is hardly surprising that these "new men" encountered resistance; even those willing to collaborate with them had difficulty concealing their distaste for these "creative egoists." And the feeling seemed mutual. The industrialists' own attitude toward obshchestvennost' was colored by their disdain for those who either had "a poor idea of work" or were "organically incapable of experiencing patriotism," code words for denatured state of Russia's educated elites.[57]

In a deeper sense, the Riabushinsky group questioned the very foundations on which both obshchestvennost' and the autocratic state had been built. They offered nothing less than an alternative path of national development, one that rejected the Petrine tradition of state-centered modernization managed by a Westernized service elite. Despite the modernism of their educational and professional background, the industrialists represented in a very literal sense a schismatic force aggressively seeking entry into the culturally homogeneous ranks of obshchestvennost'.

In its essence, the activism of the Riabushinsky circle represented perhaps the last of many efforts on the part of elements claiming to embody "native" values to wrest control of the nation's future from both the autocracy and the Westernized elites. Although they saw themselves as pioneers of Russia's capitalist revolution, they were actually carrying on a cultural struggle that began in the seventeenth century. The injection of these ancient and bitter disputes into the volatile prewar atmosphere only created new tensions in the already fragile coalition of Russian obshchestvennost'.

[57] *UR*, Aug. 17, 1910, 1; March 6, 1911, 2.

Chapter 5

THE SEARCH FOR A RUSSIAN ORTHODOX
WORK ETHIC

BERNICE GLATZER ROSENTHAL

THE WORK ETHIC is often considered the prime value of middle-class culture. Max Weber called it the "Protestant ethic" and maintained, in his famous book by that title (1904–1905) that Protestantism, especially Calvinism, motivated and facilitated the shift from a feudal to a capitalist economy by giving religious sanction to the pursuit of wealth and by treating as virtues the traits of hard work, self-discipline, and thrift needed for capitalist development. By the early twentieth century, some Russian intellectuals—Petr Struve, Nikolai Berdiaev, Simeon Frank, and Sergei Bulgakov—were advocating a kind of work ethic that left out Western individualism and materialism. But they did want to abolish poverty and argued that this entailed placing production before consumption and increasing the national wealth. Thus, they advocated hard work and self-discipline to be directed toward social or national, not personal, goals. This chapter discusses the issue of work in the intellectuals thought and then focuses on Bulgakov's attempt to create a specifically Russian Orthodox work ethic.

These intellectuals—all former Legal Marxists who had returned to religion by way of Kant—were heirs to an older Russian tradition based on Genesis that emphasized work as God's commandment and man's punishment for original sin: "In the sweat of thy face shalt thou eat bread" (Gen. 3:19); "And therefore the Lord God sent him from the Garden of Eden to till the ground from whence he was taken" (Gen. 3:23). The emphasis was on the work, or task, itself, rather than on the goal. Peter the Great constantly reminded his subjects, and his son Alexis, that work was God's commandment and condemned the idle monks as parasites. Ivan Pososhkov's *Book of Poverty and Wealth* (1725) emphasized hard work and argued the usefulness to the nation of trade and industry. Nikolai Gogol's statement, "Do your job as though it were an order from God," expressed the Orthodox sense of work as a divinely ordained task.[1] The Old Believers developed their own ethos of work and

Research for this paper was done in part with the support of a Von Mises Fellowship. I would like to thank Jeffrey Brooks and James Billington for their helpful comments. A version of this paper was presented at the Kennan Institute, February 18, 1988.

[1] Yuri Liubimov as quoted by Margaret Croyden, in "A Drama of Exile," *New York Times Magazine*, Dec. 21, 1986, p. 59.

thrift. Moscow merchant P. A. Buryshkin, for example, saw in his enterprise "the fulfillment of a task, his own type of mission entrusted to him by God or by fate."[2] In the 1880s Nikita Giliarov-Platonov, a priest's son, developed an apologia for capitalism that stressed the "psychological-moral element" in production and exchange but subsumed this to spiritual/religious goals. The highest good in production, he wrote, is to nourish the spiritual, for "material wealth is not an autonomous good."[3] Ivantsov-Platonov in his book *On Our Obligations* (O nashikh obiazatel'stvakh, 1889) argued a kind of social gospel, the creation of wealth to benefit the poor.[4]

The rudiments of a work ethic can be seen in Russian literature as well. Tolstoi preached the blessedness of physical labor. According to Richard Gustafson, "Tolstoi's theology of perfection is a theology of work. He speaks of life in terms of a 'task' to be done, and 'to accomplish' is one of his most common verbs and major values. 'The entire life of all people is work'."[5] Goncharov's character, Oblomov (1859), a lazy and totally passive aristocrat, became the very symbol of the indolent nobility. Dobroliubov's essay, "What Is Oblomovism?" (1859), lambasted *oblomovshchina* as the curse of Russia. The word became part of the language as the radical intelligentsia, many of them sons of priests, advocated working for the people, instead of for God. Lenin himself frequently alluded to Oblomov: "The Old Oblomov has remained, and for a long while yet he will have to be washed, cleaned, shaken, and thrashed if something is to come of him."[6] One of Chekhov's *Three Sisters*, Irina, also refers to Genesis: "Man must labor, work in the sweat of his face, whoever he is, and here lies the meaning and goal of his life, his happiness, his delights." "A person needs to work, work. That is why we are so dour, and we look at life in such a gloomy way; because we don't know labor. We were born from people who scorned labor." At the end of the play, Irina repeats her emphasis on work, but this time as an escape from despair. Not one of these writers advocated work as a means to achieve personal material goals. Work was always subordinated to a higher ideal: the fulfillment of a divinely ordained task for some, service to the state or to the people for others. A work for personal success ethos did develop in popular literature, but the intelligentsia was extremely hostile to it.[7]

[2] Thomas Owen, *Capitalism and Politics in Russia* (Cambridge: Cambridge University Press, 1981), 150.

[3] Alfred Rieber, *Merchants and Entrepreneurs in Imperial Russia* (Chapel Hill: University of North Carolina Press, 1982), 216.

[4] I am indebted to Adele Lindenmayer for this information.

[5] Richard Gustafson, *Leo Tolstoy: Resident and Stranger* (Princeton: Princeton University Press, 1986), 434.

[6] Thomas Riha, *Readings in Russian Civilization*, Vol. 2 (Chicago: University of Chicago Press, 1969), 332.

[7] Jeffrey Brooks, *When Russia Learned to Read* (Princeton: Princeton University Press, 1985), chaps. 8 and 9.

The Russian Orthodox Church preached hard work and personal discipline to the peasants and workers. During the Revolution of 1905 a few liberal and radical priests condemned the idleness of the rich as well and advocated a universal obligation to labor based on Geneis and on St. Paul's statement in II Thessalonians 3:10.: "If any would not work, neither should he eat." But even they viewed work in the traditional way as a religious obligation or task. Some priests recommended work as a means of overcoming poverty, of earning enough for one's needs, simply defined, but invariably they coupled this with both warnings against amassing wealth for its own sake and condemnations of materialism, hedonism, and luxury. Trying to foster the traditional Christian virtues, they did not allude to the newer issues—increasing the productive powers of Russia, augmenting the national wealth.

Struve, Berdiaev, Frank, and Bulgakov stressed these goals. In the early twentieth century they became major figures in the attempt to revitalize Orthodoxy by reinterpreting it. Frightened by the Revolution of 1905, they looked to economic growth to abolish poverty and thereby restore the social peace; thus, they emphasized productivity, the creation of new wealth. They considered hard work and personal discipline universal rather than class values and, except for Struve, defended them on religious grounds. Bulgakov, however, was the only one who consciously tried to apply Max Weber's views on the Protestant ethic to Russia and tried to develop a specifically Orthodox work ethic.

Struve was personally religious but philosophically positivist; he adamantly opposed all attempts to link economics or politics with religion, for he regarded mysticism in politics as dangerous. He accused the intelligentsia of economic irresponsibility and constantly invoked the need for labor discipline. Insisting that raising the cultural level of the people—he meant both material and spiritual wealth—was the precondition for a new and free Russia, he believed that industrial capitalism was a civilizing force and a necessity for a great power. "The question of the economic rebirth of Russia," he stated, "is above all a question of creating the new economic man." Yet even Struve did not advocate self-interest or class interest alone; rather he viewed entrepreneurship as national service, "the accomplishment of a certain function in having creative significance for the society as a whole."[8] He maintained that individuals must direct their efforts to some sort of higher goal. For him, this was nationalism, the creation of a Great Russia, a mystique of the state. In a sense nationalism was his religion.

Berdiaev's pronouncements on economic issues were made in 1905–1907 as reactions to the revolution, which terrified him. Forced to acknowledge the horror of poverty, he wrote, "after death, the strongest manifestation of world

[8] Rieber, *Merchants and Entrepreneurs*, 321. See also Richard Pipes, *Struve: Liberal on the Right* (Cambridge: Harvard University Press, 1980), 97–185.

depravity, of metaphysical evil on earth, is the burden of the struggle for survival, of need and poverty, of earning one's bread from the accursed earth'' (alluding to Genesis 3:17). Recognizing that ''poverty and excessive material oppression do not ennoble but rather embitter and brutalize,'' he advocated rapid improvement in ''the material position of the oppressed classes . . . so that they do not become wild and do develop.'' The ''elimination of economic exploitation, the erection of economic prosperity for the whole human mass,'' he said, entailed an emphasis on production, on the creation of national wealth. Berdiaev's hostility to capitalism stemmed from his antibourgeois rather than proworker or propeasant orientation. An aristocrat, he disdained materialism and insisted that the purpose of labor was religious not utilitarian: ''In humanity's past economic life, labor was linked to religion, and in one way or another was sanctified by religion. . . . Economic materialists are perfectly correct in establishing a connection between the productive economic process and the people's religious beliefs . . . but it is . . . economic relations that depend on religion.'' He and Bulgakov favored a ''neutral socialism,'' which he defined as the ''organization of the nourishment of humanity and a purposeful economic life,'' but he opposed what he called ''socialism as religion,'' the promise of a materialistic kingdom of God on earth.[9] As the revolutionary threat receded, Berdiaev returned to his true interests—religion, philosophy, and aesthetics. He still preached hard work, self-discipline, and overcoming poverty, but he did not pursue these subjects further.

Simeon Frank, a Marxist in the early 1890s, left the revolutionary Marxist milieu in the autumn of 1896 and spent the last two years of his student life at the University of Moscow studying political economy. In 1900, he published *Marx's Theory of Value and Its Significance*, a critique of Marx's theory of surplus value, which was influenced by the Austrian economists, especially Eugen Boehm-Bawerk. After 1901 his interest turned to epistemological, psychological, cultural, and moral-ethical issues. His advocacy of natural law and natural right specifically excluded property rights. He condemned ''Americanism'' as ''Genghis Khan with a telegraph'' because of the egoism, positivism, and utilitarianism he perceived in American culture.[10] Influenced by Nietzsche, he hoped to create a new culture. In his *Vekhi* essay, ''The Ethic of Nihilism,'' he stated, ''it is time to move beyond distribution and the struggle for it to cultural creation, to the creation of wealth.'' To him, material and spiritual wealth was a metaphysical ideal; he associated it with culture, ''the totality of ideal values embodied in historical life.''[11] Although he maintained

[9] Nikolai Berdiaev, ''Sotsialism kak religiia,'' in *Voprosy filosofii i psikhologii* 5 (1905): 508–45; English translation in *A Revolution of the Spirit*, ed. B. G. Rosenthal and M. B. Chomiak (Newtonville, Mass.: Oriental Research Partners, 1982), 116–38; see esp. 113–15, 126.

[10] Simeon Frank, ''Kapitalism i kul'tura,'' *Moskovskii ezhenedel'nik* 16 (1910): 39.

[11] Boris Shragin and Albert Todd, eds., *Landmarks*, trans. Marian Schwartz (New York: Karz Howard, 1977), 176.

that popular welfare is inconceivable without national wealth, formulating an Orthodox work ethic was not one of his priorities.

Bulgakov tried to develop a specifically Russian Orthodox work ethic. Except for Struve, he was the only one of the group who sustained interest in economic issues. Part of the reason for this was personal. Unlike the wealthy Berdiaev and the comfortable Struve and Frank, Bulgakov was raised in an extremely poor priestly family. In his autobiography, he testifies to the "yoke of poverty" or "at least of constant inadequacy" and to family quarrels over money. His father had a chronic nervous eczema from the constant worry about feeding his family; his mother had hardly anything for herself; two of his brothers became alcoholics, and Bulgakov strongly hints that he himself narrowly escaped alcoholism.[12] When he wrote, as he often did, of the moral dangers of poverty, he had specific experiences in mind. After taking a degree in law, he obtained advanced training in economics and statistics and taught economics at the Kiev Polytechnical Institute and at Kiev University until 1906.[13] He then became professor of political economy at the Moscow Commercial Institute and privat dotsent at Moscow University. In 1912 he defended his doctoral dissertation ("The Philosophy of Economy") at Moscow University. His early Marxism as well as his decision to study economics may have been motivated, at least partly, by his desire to abolish poverty. His attempt to supplement Marx with Kant in the early twentieth century and his return to Russian orthodoxy is well known. Certain elements of Marxist economic and social analysis, however, remained with him: the Marxist stress on production as the means of overcoming scarcity, the centrality of labor, the hostility to individualism and capitalism, and the Hegelian and Marxist emphasis on the categories of freedom and necessity. His search for a Russian Orthodox work ethic involved subsuming them in a Christian metaphysic. This effort had a double purpose: he could refute both Marxist materialism and the apostolic communism preached by Christian radicals. He detested all philosophies based on "economic man," capitalism as well as Marxism, and favored a kind of Christian socialism. His ideal was a modern industrialized Christian society and Christian economy based on love of neighbor and the mystical unity of all humankind, a society in which the material necessities of life were available to all.

As a Kantian, he rejected the materialist aspect of Marxism but endorsed its "social ideal" and viewed the struggle with poverty as a moral obligation.[14]

[12] Sergei Bulgakov, *Avtobiografischeskie zametki* (Paris: YMCA, 1946), 17.

[13] For Bulgakov's early economic views, see *O rynkakh pri kapitalisticheskom proizvodsvtve* (Moscow: M. I. Vodovozov, 1897), and *Kapitalizm i zemledelie*, 2 vols. (St. Petersburg: V. A. Tikhanov, 1900); the latter shows his increasing doubts on applying Marxist economics to Russia.

[14] Sergei Bulgakov, *Ot marksizma k idealizmu* (St. Petersburg: Obshchestvennaia pol'za, 1903), 132–35; see esp. the essays "Ob ekonomicheskom ideale," "O sotsial'nom ideale," and "Zadachi politicheskoi ekonomii."

The Revolution of 1905 spurred him to reinterpret Christianity so that it would sanction economic growth. A new Christian economics was needed, he said, for advances in the social sciences require a new view of poverty and wealth. The economics of the Gospels imply the "liquidation" of the economy rather than its organization; hence they cannot be followed literally. "The Jerusalem commune of the apostles was founded in union in love, primarily as regards consumption; production occurred outside it. . . . The task of production was not even posed to the consciousness of the time." Ironically, Rosa Luxemburg made the same point in her essay "Socialism and the Churches" (1905). Distinguishing between the eternal ethics and the temporal economics of the Gospels, Bulgakov argued that, although "community of property must be recognized as the norm in property relations," there is an essential difference between a Christian community of love and present-day socialism, an external and impersonal union of people based on common interests and devoid of regenerative significance. Lambasting utopian visions of a society of consumption without production as a "social plague," he opposed the immediate abolition of private property in land as harmful to production and insisted that the "feeling" of property rather than the institution is harmful. He lauded socialism for its enunciation of the universal obligation of labor for the able-bodied and its declaration of war on idlers and parasites. In this sense, he said, socialism is the apotheosis of labor as a moral principle; it places the "sacred object of labor" at the base of its economic order.[15] He considered the success of socialism a punishment for the sins of historical Christianity, ignoring the problems of life on this earth. By proclaiming that the demands of collectivism be absorbed entirely in the tasks of Christian politics, in 1906 he tried unsuccessfully to form a Christian political party.

In subsequent essays, Bulgakov continued to reinterpret early Christian religious-ethical ideas and their modern relevance.[16] He maintained that Christianity created a new kind of person and a new social ideal, inner union in love, and he opposed external forced unions, rejected contemporary versions of Christian communism, and argued that the Sermon on the Mount neither mandated a particular political system nor endorsed revolution. Responding to Christian radicals such as D. S. Merezhkovsky, who proclaimed that "Jesus was a revolutionary," Bulgakov emphasized the quiescence and passivity of the first Christians, their refusal to enter into direct conflict with the Roman state on the issue of slavery. Slavery, he said, was the economic base of the ancient world. The first Christians "recognized it as a historic fact as we recognize the fact of capitalism"; they treated slavery as a religious-ethical rather than a sociopolitical issue and did not even require Christian slave owners to

[15] Sergei Bulgakov, "Khristianstvo i sotsial'nyi vopros," in *Dva grada*, Vol. 1 (1906; reprint, Moscow: Put', 1911), 206–33; esp. 216–17, 219, 221, 227.

[16] "O pervom khristianstve," *Dva grada* 1: 234–303; "Pervoe Khristianstvo i noveishii sotsializm," *Dva grada* 2: 1–50.

free their slaves. Within the church, however, slaves were equal. Gradually a sense that slavery was sinful permeated society and led to its eventual abolition. The same moral process led to the emancipation of the serfs and will in time end the exploitation of labor. In other words, capitalism is historically necessary, just as slavery and serfdom were in their time; the proletariat should not revolt.

Bulgakov argued that the contemporary struggle against poverty stemmed from the Christian principle of love of neighbor (he ignored Old Testament social legislation) and stressed the voluntary nature of apostolic communism. To the apostles, sharing with others according to need was a matter of personal conscience; their voluntary poverty was moral and religious rather than compulsory and political in nature, and they did not prohibit private property. Their loving family turned into an institution with planned economic tasks. Community of property led to other forms of early Christian benevolence and social policy—for example, support of widows, orphans, and people unable to work. Some Christian communities shared their property; others took care of their poor by different voluntary means. Bulgakov considered modern socialism merely a means to fulfill Christian ethics. In opposition to Karl Kautsky, who interpreted early Christianity as a class struggle, and Nietzsche, who viewed it as a slave morality, Bulgakov emphasized the diverse class origins of the first Christians, some of whom were wealthy.

Positing a distinction within Christianity between a suprahistorical, purely religious ethic, which defines exclusively life in God, and a Christian morality of the earth, Bulgakov argued that Christians are not morally obligated to disregard economic matters. The suprahistorical ideal is exemplified by Jesus' advice to be like the birds of heaven, without worrying about tomorrow, and by the ideals of St. Francis; the freedom they exalt is a higher freedom, freedom from the economy. But implicit in Christianity is a historical ethic that recognizes economic necessity—the sanctification of economic labor.[17] The ancient world disdained physical labor; but Jesus was a carpenter, and all the apostles worked. Thus the first Christians accomplished a revaluation of attitudes toward labor. Bulgakov believed that the labor theory of value derived from Christianity's positive attitude to labor.

Bulgakov's "The National Economy and the Religious Person" (1909) marks the beginning of his search for a specifically Russian Orthodox rather than generally Christian work ethic. Although this is his first published reference to Weber, he may already have heard about Weber's ideas from Bogdan Kistiakovsky.[18] The essay summarizes and interprets the writings of Max

---

[17] "Prostota i oproshchenie," in *Sbornik vtoroi: o religii Tolstogo* (Moscow, 1912), 132. See also note 16.

[18] On Kistiakovskii and Weber, see Susan Heumann, "Bogdan Kistiakovsky and the Problem of Human Rights in the Russian Empire" (Ph.D. diss., Columbia University, 1977), 32; Richard Pipes, "Max Weber and Russia," *World Politics* (April 1955): 371–401.

Weber, Werner Sombart, and Schulze-Gåvernitz on the religious sources of English capitalism. Weber, especially, inspired Bulgakov to focus his search for a new Christian economics on the formulation of a Russian Orthodox work ethic.

As far as Bulgakov was concerned, Weber had proven that the economy is not the result of blind economic forces but of the creative initiative and free interaction of individuals. The German writers had demonstrated that the human person is an independent factor in the economy. He now proclaimed that "the economy is ruled by the proprietor" (*khoziaistvo vedet khoziain*).[19] Khoziaistvo can also be translated as the household, but because Bulgakov believed that the national economy grew out of the household economy the distinction is not crucial. It does, however, reflect his attempt to develop a new terminology for a new Orthodox economics. For him the crucial question was "What motivates the proprietor?" his answer, of course, was religion. Repeating his assertion that Christianity dignifies and sanctifies labor as God's commandment, he emphasized that the early monasteries were places of work and prayer where monks cleared the forests and tamed the wilderness; thus, by their ascetic self-discipline, they created the material basis for subsequent economic development. Every religion, he asserted, has its own characteristic economic attitude. Medieval Catholicism, for example, upheld an otherworldly ideal and preached contempt for wealth.

By contrast, the Protestant Reformation legitimized the pursuit of wealth for the sake of God; it created an ethic of worldly life. By teaching people not to shun the world but how to act in it, Protestantism stimulated personal energy and made initiative psychologically possible. Bulgakov admired Protestantism's focus on "rational, professional, methodical labor," not for itself, but as the means to a goal. After noting the Puritan maxim "God blessed the trade," he explained that to the Puritan "to want to be poor was like wanting to be sick" and praised the Puritan view of one's business or profession as a calling from God. "The Merchant sitting at his counter, was at the place where God had called him and none other''; he felt himself an important wheel in the economic cosmos and served the interest of the monarchy as well.[20] Methodic discipline of life was Puritanism's first result. Puritan asceticism was the cradle of "economic man," the stock exchange, and the market; it stemmed from the need to account to God for every penny. Slowly accumulation became a capitalist fetish. Bulgakov did not endorse the Protestant virtue of thrift. A specific bourgeois professional ethic arose, dedicated to labor as a goal of life, and created the national and social discipline that led to national wealth and political power. The new Protestant religious spirit became a powerful means

[19] Bulgakov, "Narodnoe khoziaistvo i religioznaia lichnost,' " in *Dva grada* 1: 183.

[20] In his discussion of the merchant (p. 195) Weber is citing Schulze-Gåwernitz, who maintained that the British fleet developed to defend Protestant England against Catholic Spain.

for educating the person; it engendered feelings of personal responsibility, duty, and social service, which permeated all areas of life and enabled capitalism to achieve its historic mission—industrialization.

Bulgakov then called for studies of the spiritual sources of Russian industrial life. He attributed the economic achievements of the Old Believers to the ascetic self-discipline demanded by their religious beliefs, but he rejected their religious conservatism. He also sought to clarify the economic potential of Russian Orthodoxy. Recognizing that Protestantism led to individualism and capitalism, both of which he disliked, he hoped to find in Orthodoxy a different set of economic attitudes, communal and loving, that would lead to a different path of modernization, one consonant with Russia's historical roots, faithful to her national and cultural identity, and conducive to sobornost' (a spiritually unified body in which the elements retain their individuality). For this reason, he urged that Russian Orthodox attitudes to the world, "its discipline of 'ascetic obedience' and 'going before God,' " be clearly distinguished from their Protestant counterparts.[21] Observing that contemporary capitalism had become detached from its religious roots, that increasing wealth had become a goal in itself, he predicted that economic stagnation would soon result because a "healthy national economy demands a spiritually healthy populace."[22]

> The social progress of our time is inseparably connected with the growth of the person and consequently with the raising of personal responsibility and self-discipline. That which in political economy is designated the transition from a low-wage to a high-wage economy is actually the raising of the productivity and intensity of labor [which] is inseparably connected with the self-discipline of the representatives of labor. But this self-discipline cannot be attained on the soil of naked interests alone; it presumes the recognition of higher ethical and in the last analysis, religious values, moral obligations in the sphere of professional labor.[23]

Arguing against the Marxist apotheosis of the proletariat, Bulgakov maintained that in the productive process every class has its place, its duties, and its responsibilities. He attacked "Social Benthamism" (the "greatest good of the greatest number") for fostering class antagonism and retarding the development of productive forces. While he insisted on the importance of economic growth, he also lamented the "lordly condescension of Russians to the prose of life" and the intelligentsia's tendency to label any stress on productivity as bourgeois. He urged the intelligentsia to foster a climate of opinion conducive to economic development and social progress and believed that "social opinion belongs to the imponderable spiritual factors in the historical development

---

[21] Bulgakov, "Narodnoe khoziaistvo," 198–99.
[22] Ibid., 201.
[23] Ibid., 203.

of economic life.'' The national economy is not a mechanism but a complex activity of human persons; social life is not just class struggle but a complex system of duties of all classes. Civic consciousness—that is, ethical and religious convictions—is necessary for the economic recovery and renewal of Russia.[24] A socialist society also needs personal responsibility, self-discipline, and a highly ethical culture; without them Russia will be conquered economically by foreigners.

To Bulgakov, asceticism meant self-discipline and personal responsibility; it was a means of curbing the appetites and of regulating egoism, not a goal. He regarded early Christian asceticism as a reaction to the debauchery of the Roman Empire, a means for rising above the material world, rather than an absolute value. He had always hated the mandatory asceticism imposed by poverty. Attacking Tolstoi's asceticism as an aristocrat's affectation, he wrote: ''Buddha was an Emperor's son. Francis Assisi was the son of a rich merchant.''[25] Bulgakov objected to emulating the involuntary fasts of the poor, the vegetarianism of those who cannot afford meat, people who walk beside the railroad because they cannot afford the fare. A firm believer in industrialization, he maintained that economic progress frees man from the tyranny of nature and considered its opponents—for example, Tolstoi, Carlyle, Ruskin— socially reactionary. He also denied their view that the ''natural labor'' of the farmer or artisan was morally superior to that of the educated agronomist, doctor, or factory worker.

Bulgakov's most extensive attempt to create a Russian Orthodox economics is his doctoral dissertation, published as *The Philosophy of Economy Part I* (Filosofiia khoziaistva, 1912). This philosophical and theological discussion studies the meaning and significance of the economy, including its epistemology, ontology, and phenomenology.[26] He wished to reveal an inherent cosmic meaning in the most prosaic human actions: production and consumption, the intrinsic kinship of man and the cosmos, and an ideal basis in God and the creative spirit that permeates the entire creation. His purpose was both to refute ''economism'' (the view of life as an economic process), not by denying or ignoring material needs, but by subsuming them in a religious framework, and to understand the world as an object of labor and a product of labor. By going beyond mere criticism of secular liberal and Marxist economics, Bulgakov hoped to develop a metaphysical base for a Russian Orthodox economics as part of an elaborated and modernized Russian Orthodox cosmology. His book constitutes the fullest expression of Bulgakov's own call for clarifying of Russian Orthodox attitudes to the world, especially to the economy, and

[24] Ibid., 204–5.
[25] ''Ob ekonomicheskom ideale'' (1903) in Bulgakov, *Ot marksizma k idealizmu*, 281; similar sentiments are repeated in subsequent essays on Ruskin, Carlyle, and Tolstoi.
[26] *Filosofiia khoziaistva; Mir kak khoziaistvo, chast' pervaia* (Moscow: Put', 1912).

includes his attempt to create a Russian Orthodox work ethic—a theology of labor as a creative task.

The theology of labor put forth in *Philosophy of Economy* is based on Sophia, an Orthodox principle of divine wisdom understood by Bulgakov as a creative force.[27] Human labor, that which creates material and spiritual wealth, has cosmic and metaphysical significance. Through purposeful creative human labor, Sophia permeates and transfigures the world. Thus, Bulgakov regarded economic activity as the path to fulfilling God's plan and attaining the world's eventual reunion with God—what he called the "Sophianization" of the world. Incidentally, Bulgakov's use of terms derived from Orthodoxy, such as Sophia and *sobornost'*, was an intrinsic part of his attempt to develop an economics counter to that of secular liberalism and Marxism.

Although Bulgakov opposed the very concept of "economic man," motivated by material considerations, he admired labor that creates knowledge and cultural values. He criticized Marxists for valuing only manual labor and promoting their determinist view of the economy. But he also rejected individualism and maintained that egoism, whether individual or group or class, is destructive and must be regulated externally by laws and internally by self-discipline.

According to Bulgakov, the economy combines the elements of necessity and freedom. He associated necessity with slavery and freedom with creativity. Using Kantian terminology, he maintained that man is both subject and object of the economy. He defined the economy as "the laboring defense and broadening of life" and viewed economic labor—that is, labor motivated by necessity—in the traditional way as God's punishment for sin.[28] Before the Fall, labor was disinterested and loving, but then "nature, damned by God, became a hostile force, armed with the powers of hunger and death." Economic activity became a struggle for survival; economic necessity concealed the Sophian (cosmically creative) significance of labor and engendered the ideology of economic materialism. "Economic man" is the slave of necessity. Although a believer in economic planning, Bulgakov wanted human beings to control the economy rather than being controlled by it, and he objected to the rule of impersonal market forces. He looked forward to a new era when the tyranny of nature would be overcome, when man would rule the economy and labor would again be voluntary and creative. Referring to the eschatology of the economy, he believed that the "leap from necessity to freedom" would be accomplished, not by materialism, but by Christianity.

Bulgakov perceived the economy as Sophian (creative) in its roots, anti-

---

[27] Sophia became the basis of Bulgakov's theology. A complete definition of its meaning for him, which changed over time, requires a separate paper.

[28] Bulgakov, *Filosofiia khoziaistva*, 308, 42–43, 156–57.

Sophian in its existence (*bytie*), and therefore complex in its entirety, embody-
ing freedom and necessity. He spiritualized (some would say mystified) the
basic economic functions of consumption and production. Eating, the basic
consumption function, is the epitome of necessity; as Bulgakov put it, "we
are not free not to eat."[29] But in the act of eating, the person absorbs part of
the material universe into himself; eating, therefore, has cosmological significance as a "natural Eucharist." Christianity sanctifies it in the Eucharist ritual. Similarly, production is utilitarian, but it is also creative. Note Bulgakov's use of a Marxist, or Hegelian, mode of analysis; other adaptations of
Marxist concepts or terms are likewise evident in his economic and philosophical writings.

Bulgakov distinguished between civilization and culture; he viewed civilization as a product of necessity, of man's adaptation to nature, and hence it is
inferior to culture that represents man's creative approach to the world and to
himself. In cultural creativity, the blind instinctive labor of nature becomes
the conscious labor of man. Human beings struggle with the elemental forces
of nature, subjugate and humanize them, and turn the inert matter that exists
in mechanical necessity into a living organic body.

> Man creates nothing anew that did not already exist in nature, in hidden or poten-
> tial form, but he reveals these forces of life and realizes their possibilities only by
> labor, and this labor, directed equally to the eternal world, and to his very self, is
> expended on the production of both material goods and spiritual values, and cre-
> ates that which in opposition to nature, i.e. to the primordial, given, and gratui-
> tous, carries the name of culture. Culture is only the labor of humanity, hewn
> from nature, and in this sense, one can say together with economic materialism,
> that all culture is economy.[30]

Bulgakov regarded human labor as special, a new force in nature, a new
world-forming cosmological factor, fundamentally different from all the impersonal forces of nature. He insisted that man is the subject, more than the
object, of the economy: "The ability to labor consciously, deliberately, crea-
tively, belongs only to a free essence, i.e. only to man. The machine only
transforms strength; the animal works most of all by need and without goals,
or is ruled by instinct. Only man works fully consciously."[31]

Stressing the role of the person in the economy, Bulgakov maintained that
economic activity is the creative activity of a reasoning essence, necessarily
realizing in itself its own individual principles. By equating individuality with
freedom and freedom with creativity, he asserted that "individuality is the
authentically creative principle in us, which is unextinguishable and irremov-

[29] Ibid., 84.
[30] Ibid., 308.
[31] Ibid., 235.

able even in the economy.''[32] From Adam Smith through Karl Marx, he said, political economists have stressed the objective side of production and ignored the human subjective side. He wanted to restore the subjective, to give it its proper due, for he considered economic creativity a primarily psychological phenomenon, "*a phenomenon of spiritual life.*" He believed that every economic epoch has its own spirit, its own special type of economc man, which engenders the spirit of the entire economy and expresses the human response to a given economic situation. "The economy, i.e. the spirit of capitalism, on which many are now writing is neither a fiction nor an image but a historical reality.''[33] The economy is created by persons, not by impersonal economic forces. Again and again he stressed the economy's Sophian aspect—free, creative activity. For example, he wrote, "Possessing the forces of nature, [man] creates something that he wishes. he creates . . . new worlds, new wealth, new knowledge, new feelings, new beauty—*he creates culture.* . . . Together with the 'natural' world he creates an artificial world and this world of new strengths and new values increases from generation to generation.''[34] He even implied that eventually a new man, a superman, would be formed, an allusion to Nietzsche, of course, but also to Soloviev's concept of Godmanhood.[35] His ideal of man controlling nature and directing the economy, however, derives more from Marx and modern Western thought in general, though there are indirect links to the Orthodox concept of transfiguring nature. His emphasis on Sophia reflects Pavel Florensky's Sophiology and the influence of Vladimir Soloviev.

Like Soloviev and like the Slavophiles, Bulgakov advocated sobornost'; he even argued that the economy is *sobornyi*, composed of separate acts of separate individuals who remain part of the mystical whole. There is no exact English equivalent to sobornost'; the closest would be "choral" or "chorus," a unified entity in which individuality is retained. In the economy, individual acts of humanity receive transcendental significance because the economy is a living organism tied to the World-Soul. "Alongside materialist economism one can affirm spiritual or mystical [economism] because economism can be united with a mystical and religious world view. (At least Philosophy of Economy strives to demonstrate the inner possibility of such ties).''[36]

Bulgakov viewed nature not in the spirit of "mechanical materialism" but in the tradition of the World-Soul as taught by Plato, Plotinus, the seventeenth-century mystic Boehme, Schelling, Baader, and Soloviev.[37] Bulgakov was

---

[32] Bulgakov's doctoral defense was published as "Filosofiia khoziaistva" in *Russkaia Mysl'* 5 (1913): 75. See also his *Filosofii khoziaistva*, 239.

[33] Bulgakov, "Filosofia khoziaistva," 238.

[34] *Filosofiia khoziaistva*, 134.

[35] Ibid., 136.

[36] "Filosofiia khoziaistva," 74.

[37] Ibid., 75.

particularly influenced by Schelling's *Naturphilosophie*, which held that the cosmos was the potential body of man and that man was a piece of the universal, a microcosm with a central role in the macrocosm. He did recognize, however, that the sobornost' of the economy is not always apparent, that the economy sometimes appears as the war of all against all. However, he regarded the apparent discord as the workings of a suprapersonal force, similar to Hegel's "cunning of reason," which he called "Sophianess" (*sofiinost'*).[38]

Bulgakov described his economic philosophy as an attempt to interpret "Marx in the spirit of Boehme" and "Kant in the spirit of Marx"; hence it had "two faces—one turned to philosophy and the other to social science."[39] He considered social science as well as physical science a social labor process, a branch of the common economic activity of humanity, directed to the support, defence, and broadening of life, including its organic part (collective humanity or the World-Soul). Born in the course of man's struggle with nature, science constitutes the creative response to the problems of life. Combining freedom and necessity, Sophia and anti-Sophia, its roots are in Sophia, which enters the dark chaos of inert matter and organizes the world as an object. Physical science, Bulgakov maintained, creates tangible wealth and material culture, but social science is necessary to regulate them and plan for the future. It produces "ideal values, knowledge, for various purposes necessary and useful to man" and of great economic importance. "No economy," Bulgakov wrote, "can be purely mechanical, without any plan and advisable action, any element of knowable, scientific relation to the world." Social science provides the statistics needed for planning; its findings lead to a "definite stern plan." Political economy, a branch of social science, creates "the science of the reality that must become." Bulgakov considered the concepts or laws developed by social scientists as important as the accumulation of capital in production.[40] His stress on industrial planning recalls, in some respects, the views of the Association of Industry and Trade that emphasized the role of private enterprise and opposed "state socialism."[41]

A believer in the power of ideas to change reality, Bulgakov emphasized the importance of mental labor, brain power, in the modern economy. Opposing the centrality of physical labor in classic economics, Bulgakov rejected as incomplete Adam Smith's definition of labor as the creation of a tangible product and counterposed nerve-brain energy to Karl Marx's attempt to quantify labor as nerve-muscular energy.

Science, Bulgakov concluded, liberates man from his age-old slavery to "Tsar Nature." Freedom is power; dependence on the blind and hostile forces

[38] *Filosofiia khoziaistva*, 157.

[39] "Filosofiia khoziaistva," 77

[40] *Filosofiia khoziaistva*, 173–75.

[41] See Ruth Amende Roosa, "Russian Industrialists and State Socialism," *Soviet Studies* 22, no. 31 (1972): 395–417.

of nature is impotence. Through science, man frees himself from economic slavery, from necessity. No longer nature's object, he now becomes its subject; he creates a new world alongside the natural world. The growth of wealth and the development of productive forces means power, a plus on the side of the subject, the proprietor (*khoziain*). Human striving makes the world the object of the economy, transparent for the subject and given over to its will; from mechanism the world becomes organism. Quoting the Renaissance thinker Pico della Mirandola, Bulgakov stated, "man can be what he wishes."[42]

A loose combination of economics and mysticism, *Philosophy of Economy* clearly advocates the growth of productive forces and personal initiative by sanctifying labor as a creative task. Unlike Protestantism, with its clear injunction to follow one's calling, Bulgakov's theology of labor as a creative task offered no concrete guidance on desired, permissible, and prohibited actions. He promised to treat in Part II ethics and eschatology that were linked in his mind, the means to realize eschatological goals.

Part II, however, was never published. Bulgakov's next book, *Unfading Light*, contains articles written between 1911 and 1916; its different tone reflects Florensky's theology and the disillusioning impact of the war. Bulgakov did not retract his earlier views on labor and economic activity but submerged them in an even more mystical and Sophialogical approach. The Promethean elements of Part I, especially the idea of man controlling the economy, disappeared, and economics per se was downplayed. Although Bulgakov claimed (in a footnote) to consider *Unfading Light* the continuation of *Philosophy of Economy*, the promised treatment of the ethics of the economy is couched in such mystical terminology that it is nearly unrecognizable.[43] There is no attempt to draw the boundaries between, for example, ethical and nonethical pursuit of self-interest, fair and unfair competition; they are simply condemned. In this it differed markedly from the Jewish ethical tradition, especially the Talmud, where discussions always revolve around concrete situations and particular problems.[44] From this perspective *Unfading Light* offers no ethical guidance at all.

Unfading Light reasserts Bulgakov's earlier view that labor is God's punishment for sin, obligatory for all, and that "lordly contempt" for labor has nothing in common with the Gospels. This book repeats his warnings that economic activity, the creation of wealth, must not be a goal in itself; it is only a means for the dignity of life. He again pointed out the contradictory nature of labor—Sophian in its roots, anti-Sophian in its existence—and maintained that profit and self-interest are incompatible with creativity and inspiration.

[42] *Filosofiia khoziaistva*, 241.

[43] *Svet nevechernyi* (Moscow: Put', 1917), 354 (in the section on human history).

[44] For a contemporary treatment, see Meir Tamari, *With All Your Possessions: Jewish Ethics and Economic Life* (New York: Free Press, 1987).

But *Unfading Light* is far more hostile to individualism and Protestantism than *Philosophy of Economy*. He lambasted "religious individualism" (Protestantism) as a sign of immaturity or decadence, an old slavophile idea, and insisted that "religion is a tie not only of man with God but of man with man."[45] This intensified anti-individualism resulted in reformulating the tasks of economic activity; to the primary task of overcoming material poverty by developing Russia's productive forces he added a second task of overcoming "social poverty," which Bulgakov defined as the "somnolent egoism in human relations." He questioned whether both tasks could be solved—whether humanity could triumph over poverty and attain social reform at the same time—and concluded that the second depends on the first and cannot be solved alone.[46] In a similar vein, he declared, "humanity is an organism." Man must struggle against egoistic self-affirmation. The separate human individual is not a microcosm but a part of the whole, part of the mystical human organism; the Kabbala called the whole Adam Kadmon, and Auguste Comte called it "The Great Being," but to Bulgakov the whole was the absolute human and divine organism of Jesus Christ through the church, which is his body.[47]

Bulgakov condemned Marxism as a variant of Jewish "false messianism," the "dream of an earthly paradise." Intending to refute Marxist eschatology—the leap from necessity to freedom through operating economic laws—Bulgakov stated that "the economy as connected with the accursed earth does not contain in itself an eschatological task." The economy epitomizes endlessness, for economic labor is never completed. Nevertheless through the economy the historical body of humanity is created. "Labor realizes for itself this world, constructs its own world body, really senses it, embodies the power present in it from the beginning." As a consequence of his fall, man became a captive of materiality; even so, in the role of proprietor, man preserves a gleam of the glory of the reigning Adam. The Gospels proclaim not freedom in and through the economy but from the economy. "Economism" is the economic captivity of man, but Christianity proclaims a higher freedom: it preaches not power, but impotence; not wealth, but poverty; not wisdom in this century of "economic magic," but the holy fool. Christianity has an ideal other than wealth. Even now world war is destroying "economism's Tower of Babel." Hoping to transcend "economism," to create a "supra-economy," he lauded Nikolai Fedorov's project, humanity's common task of regulating nature and resurrecting the dead, as one of great spiritual importance despite his earlier criticism of certain aspects.[48] Bulgakov's retreat from practical economic goals was paralleled by the industrialists' retreat from the Progressives and their return to the Old Belief (discussed by James West) and the architects'

---

[45] *Svet nevechernyi*, 54.
[46] Ibid., 360.
[47] Ibid., 402.
[48] Ibid., 368–69.

rejection of modernism for neo-slavophilism (discussed by William Brumfield). In different ways, they were abandoning their previous search for new solutions and returning to the past.

Bulgakov's search for a Russian Orthodox work ethic was based on the assumption that the intellectual and artistic elite, to whom his writings were addressed, could consciously and deliberately create new values and a new culture. Rejecting the West as a model, he believed that Russians could not simply restore the past but must rework and reinterpret their Orthodox legacy. He tried to steer between religious conservatives who opposed all change and religious radicals who preached apostolic communism. His emphasis on Sophia was part of his attempt to define the distinctive features of Russian Orthodoxy. A proponent of industrialization, he emphasized the primacy of knowledge and creativity over physical strength and asserted the need for expert economic and social planning. Recognizing that rank (*chin*) and estate (soslovie) were anachronisms, he did not discuss them. Buried in the mysticism was a solid core of economic realism.

Bulgakov's attempt to develop a theology of labor failed to influence his contemporaries. The very basis of his theology, Sophia, was by no means conventional Russian Orthodoxy. Indeed, in emigration he was accused of heresy because of his unconventional views. In terms of more immediate economic goals, his invocations of Sophia were simply too vague and diffuse to lend themselves to simplification and sloganeering, too unfamiliar to most Russians to counter traditional ideas on the goals of economic activity or the profit motive. His talk of Sophia probably confused the businessmen of the Riabushinsky circle, which he attended regularly. These people found Struve's nationalism far more appealing. Mystics such as Berdiaev, however, condemned *Philosophy of Economy* as too materialistic, evidence of a Hebraic rather than an Hellenic religiosity.[49] Berdiaev's statement and Bulgakov's position on "Jewish false messianism" epitomize the stereotypical view of Jews as materialists, a view specifically repudiated by Soloviev in his "Tale of Antichrist" (1900). Rather than Bulgakov trying to counter Marxism by developing an ideology of the middle class, based on either a "national bourgeoisie" of industrialists or middle-class businessmen and professionals, he hoped to transcend class consciousness altogether. Unwilling to appeal to self-interest, he lacked a natural "carrier" for his ideas. (Whether such an appeal would have worked is another issue). The seeds of a pro-middle-class ideology based on entrepreneurship, knowledge, and skill are evident in Bulgakov's writing, but they never sprouted and, in the changed climate of the war years, virtually died.

Nevertheless, elements of Bulgakov's theology of labor as a creative task

---

[49] Berdiaev, "Tipy religioznoi mysli v Rossii," *Russkaia mysl'* (June 1916): 1–32, esp. 28 (second pagination).

are surprisingly compatible with Bolshevism. This is not to argue that Bulgakov influenced Bolshevism. In fact, Bulgakov, Frank, and Berdiaev were expelled in 1923, and Struve had emigrated earlier. Rather, their respective work
ethics emanated from a common Orthodox view of work as a religious obligation, secularized by Chernyshevsky and Dobroliubov in the mid-nineteenth
century, that is specifically Russian Orthodox rather than generally Christian.
(A comparison of the attitudes to work and wealth of various Christian denom-
inations, which varied at different times of their respective histories, is beyond
the scope of this paper.) The nihilist Bazarov, in Turgenev's *Fathers and Sons*
(1862), was actually quoting Chernyshevsky's *The Aesthetic Relation of Art
to Reality* (1855) when he stated, ''Nature is not a temple but a workshop and
man is the workman in it.'' Chernyshevsky was a major influence on all Russian revolutionaries, including Lenin. Despite Bulgakov's theoretical stress on
the role of the person in the economy, he offered an underlying message: work
hard, be creative, but not for the purpose of amassing wealth or living in luxury. Work is a universal value; all must work, mentally or physically, according to their abilities. When separated from their religious context, Bulgakov's
apotheosis of labor as a creative task, his emphasis on production rather than
consumption, his condemnation of capitalism, self-interest, and the profit motive, and his advocacy of a planned economy presumably directed by social
scientists can be adapted to the secular goal of building socialism. Indeed, all
Soviet constitutions except that of 1977 contain the phrase from St. Paul, ''he
who does not work shall not eat.''

I should also note, however, that strategies linking modernization to the
nation's cultural identity and historic roots, including its distinctive religious
traditions, have been successful in other parts of the world. The rapid economic development of Japan, South Korea, Taiwan, and Singapore (Hong
Kong is different) is not the product of capitalism as understood in the Western
sense, but of conscious planning and direction by industry and government
working together; the progress includes the now famous Confucian (Shinto
plus Confucian in the case of Japan) work ethic. The general thrust, if not the
specific details, of Bulgakov's strategy of modernization—namely reinterpreting Orthodox theology to sanctify labor—was not as far-fetched and impractical as his mystical terminology makes it appear.

Chapter 6

IMPEDIMENTS TO A BOURGEOIS CONSCIOUSNESS IN RUSSIA, 1880–1905: THE ESTATE STRUCTURE, ETHNIC DIVERSITY, AND ECONOMIC REGIONALISM

Thomas C. Owen

Studies in social history have identified the core of the "middle class" in Western Europe and the United States as the prosperous merchants, manufacturers, and financiers whose attitudes and activities in public life from the late Middle Ages onward can be read as clearly as their well-preserved account books. On the periphery of the world capitalist system, however, the social types that were engaged in trade and industry varied considerably according to the nature of local cultural traditions; thus, the very concept of a middle class or bourgeoisie in Africa, Asia, and Latin America owes more to the subjective concerns of ethnocentric European or American observers than to any objective process of social development.

For example, the unique features of Japanese capitalism included the role of the Meiji bureaucracy as a catalyst of industrial development, the prominence of entrepreneurs from samurai social origins, the growth of the four great combines (*zaibatsu*), and the use of paternalistic mechanisms, borrowed from agrarian life, to ensure the docility of the industrial labor force. Although it can be argued that the logic of modern capitalism demanded certain modifications of Japanese cultural traditions in the past century, no serious historian would maintain that the Tokyo merchants in 1900 were essentially similar in cultural, political, or even economic attitudes to their counterparts in Hamburg or Boston.[1]

The case of Russia presents special conceptual problems in this regard. One major impediment to historical understanding is the very ease with which European definitions and categories can be applied to Russian realities. The current conceptual muddle owes much to Soviet historians, determined to write the history of Russian commerce, manufacturing, and banking in terms of "finance capital" and "monopoly." These familiar Leninist notions form part

[1] Johannes Hirschmeier and Tsunehiko Yui, *The Development of Japanese Business. 1600–1973*, 2d ed. (Boston: Allen and Unwin, 1981); Rodney Clark, *The Japanese Company* (New Haven: Yale University Press, 1979).

of a larger Marxist conception of world history that implicitly assumes the universal applicability of European capitalist and socialist ideas and instititutions. Insofar as concepts like ''modernization'' and ''economic backwardness'' imply that Russia would someday resemble Britain once the quantitative gaps in steel production and railroad density were closed, they obscure essential institutional and cultural peculiarities of the Russian experience.

Several investigations of founders and managers of capitalist institutions under the tsars have endeavored to distinguish the universal and particular features of Russian capitalism, but much remains to be done. A raven's-eye view of the broad terrain cannot do justice to regional variations, especially when analysis is written without the benefit of solid monographic studies of each area within the empire, and the few books devoted to a single region, although useful in their vivid detail, fail to convey the variety of capitalist experience in the empire as a whole.[2]

The complexities of this problem can hardly be resolved in a short essay such as this, but I can at least identify and clarify them in light of existing evidence on the small but increasingly influential group of men and women who founded and managed the several thousand corporations (*aktsionernye obshchestva* or *tovarishchestva na paiakh*) in the Russian Empire between 1880 and 1905. The main point is that, despite the superficial resemblance of some leaders of this group to prominent capitalists of fin-de-siècle Europe and the United States, the Russian corporate elite failed to achieve even a semblance of unity in formulating economic strategies and political attitudes, much less a mature class consciousness. The fissures that divided various elements of this group not only followed the borders of the various economic regions in this largest country in the world, but they also proceeded along quite different lines, namely those of social and cultural association and of ethnic identification. These impediments to unity, when seen in their mutual interrelation, in turn shed new light on perennial issues of Russian economic and political history, such as the state's role in promoting or hindering industrial development and the strengths and weaknesses of the liberal movement.

The concept of bourgeois class consciousness requires a brief definition. A social class is more than just an agglomeration of individuals who share roughly the same culture, status, income, and economic role within a region or nation. Such individuals cannot act as a class unless they share certain beliefs and attitudes, communicate these ideas among themselves, and organize group action in pursuit of common goals, using permanent mechanisms such

---

[2] Alfred J. Rieber, *Merchants and Entrepreneurs in Imperial Russia* (Chapel Hill: University of North Carolina Press, 1982); Jo Ann Ruckman, *The Moscow Business Elite* (De Kalb, Ill.: Northern Illinois University Press, 1984); on the Ural region, see Iu. A. Buranov, *Aktsionirovanie gornozavodskoi promyshlennosti Urala (1861–1917 gg.)* (Moscow: Nauka, 1982); on the Persian Discount and Loan Bank, see Boris V. Anan'ich, *Rossiiskoe samoderzhavie i vyvoz kapitala (po materialam uchetno-ssudnogo banka Persii)* (Leningrad: Nauka, 1975).

as membership organizations based on economic or professional function. At a higher stage of development, political parties and a whole array of cultural institutions, including schools, newspapers, and publishing houses, buttress the edifice. The crucial point is that consciousness constitutes an essential element in defining social class. Moreover, such a consciousness exists only when the feeling of solidarity within the group reaches the point of identifying opposing social groups.[3] In the course of the Revolution of 1905, some business leaders in Russia attained such a degree of class consciousness: They displayed antipathy to their traditional sponsor, the autocratic state, showed a marked hostility toward the gentry, and embraced the concept of a protracted struggle with the workers over wages, working conditions, and disciplinary regulations in the factory. Evidence at our disposal, however, strongly suggests that such bourgeois attitudes were nonexistent or weak within the Russian corporate elite prior to 1905; they scarcely influenced the political and economic institutions of the tsarist empire in the decade before World War I.

In an attempt to understand the estate system, the first impediment to forming a bourgeois consciousness in the Russian Empire, we must pay grudging tribute to the energy with which the autocratic state under the last two tsars perpetuated policies inherited from the pre-Petrine bureaucracy. The recent article of Gregory L. Freeze, an encyclopedic survey of the history of the social estates (*sosloviia*) and its precursors, complements several fine studies of the urban estates—merchants, petty townspeople, and artisans—and their evolution within the rigid social hierarchy in Russia, a system created by the Muscovite bureaucracy for its own, primarily fiscal, purposes.[4]

The principal beneficiary of the estate system was the gentry. Its great advantages of wealth, education, and preferential entry into the upper strata of the state bureaucracy multiplied its opportunities for lucrative careers when industrial processes began to be applied to agriculture, as in beet sugar production and flour milling in the decades following the Crimean War. In his discussion of "gentry entrepreneurship," Soviet historian Avenir P. Korelin noted that in 1901–1902 a total of 1,894 individuals holding hereditary gentry status or high rank owned 2,092 industrial enterprises with at least fifteen employees or machinery in European Russia (excluding Poland and Finland). Korelin's tables did not include the number of nobles who occupied managerial positions in the many corporations that proliferated in these decades—

[3] Robert A. Feldmesser, "Social Classes and Political Structure," in *The Transformation of Russian Society*, edited by Cyril E. Black (Cambridge: Harvard University Press, 1960), 235–52; J.-B. Bergier, "The Industrial Bourgeoisie and the Rise of the Working Class, 1700–1914," in *The Fontana Economic History of Europe*, ed. Carlo M. Cipolla, 4 vols. (New York: Barnes and Noble, 1976), 3: 397–451.

[4] Gregory Freeze, "The *Soslovie* (Estate) Paradigm and Russian Social History," *American Historical Review* 91 (1986): 11–36; Manfred Hildermeier, *Bürgertum und Stadt in Russland 1760–1870* (Cologne: Böhlau, 1986).

these data from the corporate charters and various reference works have yet to be tabulated—but the memoir literature makes it clear that immense fortunes were to be made in constructing and managing railroads, steamship lines, iron and steel plants, and chemical factories owned by corporations. Among the gentry entrepreneurs in these new companies were several competent and honest businessmen, exemplified by Baron Nikolai E. Wrangel, who founded a four-million-ruble hydroelectric power station in the Caucasus in 1899 and criticized the bureaucracy's irrational restrictions on Jews and foreigners.[5]

Far more numerous, however, were men from the aristocracy or gentry who simply took advantage of their powerful positions to milk the new corporations without much competent management. Three examples suffice. Vladimir M. Vonliarliarsky, a former colonel of the guards, used his connections at the imperial court to obtain lucrative mining and timber concessions in eastern Siberia. He is best remembered for his participation, with another former guards officer, A. M. Bezobrazov, in the plan to extend Russian political influence into Korea by means of a timber concession, an ill-fated scheme that helped precipitate the war with Japan in 1904.[6]

Even so brilliant a mining engineer and proponent of industrial development as Konstantin A. Skalkovsky played the arrogant gentry bureaucrat. In one of his many books about the Russian economy, he blamed the failure of the consultative Council of Trade and Manufacturing, created in 1872, on "the apathy and crass ignorance of our merchants." As director (1891–1896) of the Department of Mines in the Ministry of State Domains, he gained fame as much for his chronic bribe taking as for his rationalization of the legislation governing the mining of coal and iron. After he resigned in 1896 Skalkovsky served on the boards of several mining corporations and benefited from his close ties to the Paris Rothschilds, to whom he apparently passed secret information on governmental economic policies in return for generous "gifts."[7]

Perhaps the most skilled practitioner in the new field of corporate law was Nikolai N. Sushchov (or Sushchev). After his dismissal from the staff of the Senate for impropriety—he had represented both the prosecution and the defense in a lawsuit—he grew wealthy as a corporate director. For his skill in spinning out precise legal formulations, he collected fees amounting to tens of

[5] Avenir P. Korelin, *Dvorianstvo v poreformennoi Rossii. 1861–1904 gg.* (Moscow: Nauka, 1979), 106–22; data from 110–12 (tables 10 and 11); Nikolai E. Vrangel', *Vospominaniia (ot krepostnogo prava do bol'shevikov)* (Berlin: Slovo, 1924), esp. 132–33, 158–59, 180; corporate data from Thomas C. Owen, "RUSCORP: A Database of Corporations in the Russian Empire, 1700–1914," distributed by Inter-University Consortium for Political and Social Research, 1990.

[6] Vladimir M. Vonliarliarskii, *Moi vospominaniia. 1852–1939 gg.* (Berlin: Russkoe natsional'noe izdatel'stvo, 1939), 108–13, 119, 123–24, 191, 194; Vrangel', *Vospominaniia*, 174.

[7] Thomas C. Owen, "Skal'kovskii, K. A.," in *The Modern Encyclopedia of Russian and Soviet History* (Gulf Breeze, Fla.: Academic International Press, 1976–present), 35: 157–160; quotation from C. Skalkovsky, *Les ministres des finances de la Russie. 1802–1890*, trans. P. de Nevsky (Paris: Guillaumin, 1891), 170.

thousands of rubles. For years he sat on the board of the lavishly subsidized Russian Steamship and Trade Company and earned an oversized salary as a director of the Petersburg Water Company. He failed, however, to create any lasting enterprises of his own, led a life of gluttony and debauchery, and died penniless. Immortalized in fiction as the obese and venal corporate director Salamatov (from *salo*: fat, lard, or tallow) in Petr D. Boborykin's novel *The Wheeler-Dealers* (Del'tsy, 1872), the dissolute Sushchov behaved as the very antithesis of the frugal European bourgeois.[8]

In contrast to gentry entrepreneurs, who brought to corporate enterprise various hallmarks of their precapitalist traditions, merchants in the major cities of the empire appeared to enjoy better preparation for the advent of the steam engine, the steel mill, and the automobile. Here too the influence of the estate system in previous centuries proved debilitating in a way unknown in Europe. Because the Russian state had lavished on the gentry such economic privileges as the exclusive right to own serfs and various preferences in education and bureaucratic careers, the merchants remained closer in their cultural traditions—speech, religion, and family life—to the simple peasantry (*narod*) than to the gentry or to the European merchants who settled in the major port cities of the empire. A close examination of corporate charters issued by the tsarist government reveals the merchants' penchant for relatively uncomplicated businesses, such as textile manufacturing, leather tanning, vodka production, and the timber trade. Real innovations, for example, installing modern machinery imported from Manchester or Brussels, were largely the work of foreigners like Ludwig Knoop and William Mather.[9]

The business and political career of Nikolai A. Naidenov, the undisputed leader of the Moscow merchants, exemplified Freeze's contention that the estate system enjoyed a certain support from those who lived under its essentially artificial provisions. Naidenov, who occupied the presidency of the Moscow Exchange Committee from 1877 until his death in 1905, staunchly defended the prerogatives of the merchants under the estate system. His many forays into the political arena on behalf of greater state support for Russian industry are best understood as the efforts of a loyal subject of the tsar to seek a more honored position in an essentially hierarchical society. As Boris N. Chicherin recalled, Naidenov loved the tsar, Russian industry, and the Moscow Municipal Duma, but the merchant leader, for all his talents as a textile manufacturer and banker, remained essentially "a cunning person who pur-

[8] Vrangel', *Vospominaniia*, 139–41; Aleksandr N. Vitmer, "Otryvochnye vospominaniia," *Istoricheskii vestnik*, 125 (1911): 861–64, 869–70 (p. 870 on the accuracy of Boborykin's portrait); Boborykin, *Del'tsy* in his *Sochineniia* (Moscow: M. O. Vol'f, 1885–1886), vols. 7 and 8.

[9] *Neue Deutsche Biografie* 12 (1979): 212–13; Adele Wolde [née Knoop], *Ludwig Knoop: Erinnerungsbilder aus seinem Leben* (Bremen: C. Schünemann, 1928). On Mather, see John F. Baddeley, "Russia," in *The Right Honourable Sir William Mather . . . 1838–1920*, ed. Loris E. Mather (London: R. Cobden-Sanderson, 1925), 32–88.

sued his own personal goals; it was absolutely impossible to rely on him. For him, the interests of the merchant estate were incomparably higher than those of the city, and his own personal importance stood highest of all."[10]

Vasily A. Kokorev, perhaps the most flamboyant merchant in the new railroads, petroleum refineries, banks, and steamship lines, expressed this estate pride with special zest. Proud of his Old Believer heritage, he warned that the "rank-fever" (*chinobesie*) of merchants eager to attain gentry status through philanthropic or other public activity drew them away from their businesses and thereby weakened the Russian economy; however, Kokorev's several spectacular business failures weakened his case for the economic abilities of merchants. Perhaps Ivan S. Aksakov referred to the pride of Naidenov and Kokorev when, in 1884, he wrote that "the merchants and petty townspeople cling fervently to their estate identity (*soslovnost'*)." Years later, in emigration, the Old Believer merchant Vladimir P. Riabushinsky reiterated this disdain: "It was better to be first among the merchants than last among the gentry."[11]

The tension between the estates appears to have undergone a slight amelioration in the final decades of the tsarist period as technical experts rose to positions of leadership in Russian corporations. Engineers from various social backgrounds—trained in mining, rail and water transport, construction, electrical power generation, and chemical production—often moved from one region to another and, by virtue of their abstract education, felt relatively little devotion to a particular estate as they pursued the ideal of economic efficiency. At the same time, this process proceeded slowly against the cultural resistance of centuries. The weakness of "professional solidarity" among Russian engineers stemmed from not only the tsarist government's refusal to allow a national organization before 1917 but also differences in "social origins, reference identities, and career goals" among engineers in academic, managerial, and technical positions.[12] Furthermore, to the extent that engineers overcame these centrifugal tendencies within their own ranks, they constituted yet another separate group within the corporate elite. For example, they showed little patience with the merchants' estate pride and clashed openly with the

[10] Thomas C. Owen, "Naidenov, N. A.," in *MERSH* 24: 41–44; Boris N. Chicherin, *Vospominaniia*, 4 vols. (1929–1934; reprint, Cambridge, Eng.: Oriental Research Partners, 1973), 4: 181.

[11] For the only detailed study, see Paula Lieberman, "V. A. Kokorev: An Industrial Entrepreneur in Nineteenth Century Russia" (Ph.D. diss., Yale University, 1981). Aksakov to G. P. Galagan, Nov. 22, 1884, quoted in Nikolai I. Tsimbaev, *I. S. Aksakov v obshchestvennoi zhizni poreformennoi Rossii* (Moscow: Izdatel'stvo Moskovskogo universiteta, 1978), 254. Riabushinskii, "Kupechestvo moskovskoe," *Den' russkogo rebenka* 18 (1951): 186.

[12] Donald W. Green, "Industrialization and the Engineering Ascendancy: A Comparative Study of American and Russian Engineering Elites, 1870–1920" (Ph.D. diss., University of California, Berkeley, 1972), 233–39 (quotations from 234, 239), 252.

gentry over the issue of zemstvo taxation of mining and manufacturing enterprises.

The high degree of ethnic diversity constituted the second major impediment to forming a strong class identity. The ethnic prejudices that prevented a spirit of trust and loyalty from uniting corporate managers raised as Russians, Ukrainians, Poles, Germans, Jews, and Armenians—to name only the most important ethnic groups represented in the corporate elite—owed much to memories of conflicts in the past, but such discord received additional impetus from the state's own policies.

Two groups, the Jews and the Baltic Germans, fell under special disabilities. The tsarist government appeared unaware of the economic irrationality of its restrictions on Jewish entrepreneurship. The state rewarded such outstanding individuals as Jan Bloch (Ivan S. Bliokh) and Samuil S. Poliakov among the pioneers of Russian railroad construction in the 1860s and 1870s; the bankers Lazar and Iakov S. Poliakov and Goratsy O. Gintsburg; the sugar producers Lazar and Lev I. Brodsky in Kiev; and the president of the Flour Association (*Sovet s''ezdov mukomolov*), G. E. Veinshtein, who, as one of twelve elected representatives of business organizations, became in 1915 the first Jew to be admitted to the State Council. Less prominent Jewish corporate directors, however, encountered numerous obstacles; the most important of these was the maintenance of the Pale of Settlement in the western provinces of the empire, outside of which only selected individuals of the Jewish faith, such as university graduates and first-guild merchants, could reside.[13]

It is essential to note that the government's policies toward the non-Russian minorities and their corporations grew more repressive under the last three tsars. Decrees promulgated in 1864 and 1865, which prohibited Poles and Jews from owning or leasing rural property in the western provinces, were designed to shore up the economic position of Russian peasants. A law dated December 12, 1884, imposed similar restrictions on corporations active in that area by limiting corporate landholding to 200 desiatinas (approximately 540 acres); in 1887, foreigners and companies with foreign stockholders lost the right to own any land in this region. Although they kept Jews, Poles, and foreigners from establishing corporations with which to circumvent the restrictive laws of the 1860s, the decrees of Alexander III had the negative effect of perpetuating ethnic divisions within the population; in addition, they created opportunities for corruption, favoritism, and arbitrary administrative action by the local officialdom. In 1891 the tsarist government, with the apparent approval of Russian merchants in Moscow, expelled thousands of Jews from that city. Ironically, this action strengthened Moscow's industrial rival, Lodz,

---

[13] *Evreiskaia entsiklopediia*, 16 vols. (1906–1913; reprint, The Hague: Mouton, 1969–1971); on Veinshtein, see Valentin S. Diakin, *Russkaia burzhuaziia i tsarizm v gody pervoi mirovoi voiny, 1914–1917 gg.* (Leningrad: Nauka, 1967), 124.

where the percentage of Jews among manufacturers rose sharply, from 16.6 percent in 1885 to 68 percent in 1900.[14]

In Riga, Reval, and other port cities of the Baltic provinces, the major import-export firms and banks remained securely in the hands of German merchants, heirs to the illustrious mercantile tradition of the Hanseatic League. The Riga Exchange Committee, perhaps the most active body of its kind in the empire, was composed almost exclusively of Germans. Of the many banks in the city, Germans controlled all but two mutual credit societies, one managed by Russians, the other by Letts. To judge from the memoirs of leading political figures of Riga, the policy of Russification exacerbated tensions between Germans and Russians in the city, imposed irrational constraints on economic development, and weakened the loyalty of the Baltic German merchants toward the tsar.[15]

Such attacks proved capable of rallying the Russian population to the banner of economic nationalism, but in the end it weakened, rather than strengthened, unity within the capitalist elite. In the mid-1880s, Sergei F. Sharapov, secretary of the Moscow branch of the Russian Industrial Society (*Obshchestvo dlia sodeistviia russkoi promyshlennosti i torgovle*), warned that the growing influence of German and Jewish textile manufacturers in Lodz threatened the economic integrity of the Russian Empire. The recently established branches of the society in Lodz and Warsaw promptly responded with charges of unfair competition by Moscow. The ensuing debate destroyed the internal cohesion of this society, the only national business organization in the empire before 1906. In St. Petersburg itself, leaders of the Russian Industrial Society resorted to xenophobic rhetoric in their attacks against the economic power of the Germans and the English in the northern capital. Only one of twelve merchants on the Petersburg Exchange Committee had a Russian name, complained one member of the society in 1888, because none but first-guild merchants were allowed to vote in elections of the committee and foreigners outnumbered Russians in the first guild.[16]

[14] *Polnoe sobranie zakonov*, series 2, 55 vols. (St. Petersburg, 1830–1884), and series 3, 33 vols. (1882–1916): 2-41039 of July 10, 1864; 2-42759 of Dec. 10, 1865; 3-2633 (Art. 3) of Dec. 27, 1884; 3-4286 of Mar. 14, 1887. Kazimierz Badziak, "Burżuazja łódzka w rewolucji 1905–1907," in *Rewolucja 1905–1907 w Łodzi i okręgu: Studia i materiały*, ed. Barbara Wachowska (Łódź: Wydawnictwo Łódzkie, 1975), 51–52.

[15] Wilhelm von Bulmerincq, *Lebenserinnerungen des letzten deutschen Stadthauptes von Riga* (Wolfenbüttel: E. Fischer, 1952), 9–13, 28–29, 44; on banks, see Wilhelm Lenz, *Die Entwicklung Rigas zur Grosstadt* (Kitzingen am Main: Holzner-Verlag, 1954), 68; on major firms in Reval, see Walter Dehio, *Erhard Dehio: Lebensbild eines baltischen Hanseaten, 1855–1940* (Stuttgart: E. Salzer, 1970); Anders Henriksson, *The Tsar's Loyal Germans: The Riga German Community . . . 1855–1905* (Boulder, Colo.: East European Monographs, 1983).

[16] Thomas C. Owen, "The Russian Industrial Society and Tsarist Economic Policy, 1867–1905," *Journal of Economic History* 45 (1985): 587–606, esp. 601–2; Muriel Joffe, "Regional Rivalry and Economic Nationalism: The Central Industrial Region Industrialists' Strategy for the

In the Ukraine, ethnic tensions pervaded many economic sectors. Ukrainians in the coal and iron industry complained of unfair competition from foreign and Russian corporations, which enjoyed preferential state subsidies, loans, and sales contracts. In Odessa, the major grain port of the empire, Jewish exporters gradually displaced the Greek merchants who had long dominated the grain trade there.[17]

In vain the few Europeans in the Baku petroleum industry, such as the Nobels and representatives of the Rothschilds, endeavored to contain the deep-seated ethnic antagonisms that separated Armenians and Azeris. The Baku Petroleum Association (*Sovet s''ezdov bakinskikh neftepromyshlennikov*), created in 1884, became one of the most influential business organizations in the empire, notably because of the high quality of its statistical reports and semimonthly newspaper, *Neftianoe delo* (The Petroleum Industry). But a close examination of the corporations headquartered in Baku reveals a clear pattern of ethnic divisions. In thirteen of the twenty-two petroleum drilling and refining companies founded in Baku between 1881 and 1900, all the founders belonged to a single ethnic group (Armenians in twelve and a Russian in one). The need for a local financial institution led prominent Azeri and Armenian petroleum interests to cooperate in founding the lone joint-stock bank in that city: the Baku Merchant Bank (1899). However, in only one charter of the nine petroleum companies with a mixed ethnic composition did Armenian and Azeri names appear together.[18]

A third factor tended to fragment the Russian corporate elite before 1905: regional economic rivalries. This feature of Russian economic history is poorly illuminated in the recent scholarly literature except in Poland, where since 1956 highly skilled researchers have told, with obvious relish, of the struggle of Polish coal and textile producers against their "South Russian" (i.e., Ukrainian) and Muscovite competitors in the domestic market.[19]

Development of the Russian Economy, 1880s–1914," *Russian History* 11 (Winter 1984): 389–421, esp. 399–408; on Sharapov, see Thomas R. Trice, "Sergei F. Sharapov, A Reactionary Russian Journalist, 1855–1911," (M.A. thesis, Louisiana State University, 1987); on Petersburg, see A. P. Panov, "O neobkhodimosti reformy birzhevogo ustava 1832 goda," in *Birzha i gil'dii*, ed. M. Slavianinov (St. Petersburg, 1894), 35–57, esp. 48.

[17] Patricia Herlihy, "Greek Merchants in Odessa in the Nineteenth Century," *Harvard Ukrainian Studies* 3–4 (1979–1980): part 1, 399–420.

[18] John P. McKay, "Baku Oil and Transcaucasian Pipelines, 1883–1891: A Study in Tsarist Economic Policy," *Slavic Review* 43 (Winter 1984): 603–23; S''ezd bakinskikh neftepromyshlennikov, *Trudy: Alfavitnyi ukazatel' k trudam s''ezda bakinskikh neftepromyshlennikov (I–XXIV)* (Baku: S''ezd bakinskikh neftepromyshlennikov, 1908), an index all of 111 pages long; on Hajji Zeinal Abdin Tagiev, the illiterate but highly intelligent camel driver who became the most influential Moslem industrialist in Russia, see Georg Spies, *Erinnerungen eines Ausland-Deutschen*. Beilageband 2 of *Spiess'sche Familien-Zeitung* (Marburg: Moritz Spieses, 1926), 180–82, and Karl V. Khagelin [Karl Wilhelm Hagelin], *Moi trudovoi put'* (New York: Grenich Printing Corp., 1945), 247–49; Owen, "RUSCORP."

[19] Irena Pietrzak-Pawłowska, ed., *Uprzemysłowanie ziem polskich w XIX i XX wieku: Studia i*

The first attempts at a comprehensive analysis of disputes among business interests in the empire, namely those of Ermansky and Lure on the eve of the Great War, listed not only national organizations but also dozens of local and sectoral ones as well.[20] Besides the regional branches of the Russian Industrial Society, whose mutual vilifications had fatally weakened the organization in the 1880s, these institutions included numerous exchange committees. Despite the predominance of merchants in the exchange committees, the logic of business ties in each region occasionally ameliorated traditional estate and ethnic antagonisms.

For example, the St. Petersburg manufacturers insisted on a modicum of tariff protection for the local textile and metallurgical industries. Their cosmopolitan leadership reflected the diverse manufacturers of that region. Franz Friedrich San-Galli, son of an Italian-born customs official in Stettin, arrived in St. Petersburg as a nineteen-year-old orphan, built a metal fabricating business, married the daughter of a Russian merchant, and played a prominent role in the Petersburg Municipal Duma before helping to found the organization of manufacturers. In his memoirs, written to celebrate fifty years of successful business activity, he displayed a delightfully cosmopolitan wit and studded his Russian text with aphorisms in French, English, German, and Latin. The Polish engineer Stanislaw P. Glezmer likewise distinguished himself as an energetic manufacturer and able spokesman for the interests of this group, particularly in its resistance to mandatory accident insurance for factory workers.[21]

The largest single category of companies founded in 1881–1900 (127 of 1,636, or almost 8 percent) was that of beet sugar companies, which for reasons of climate were located primarily in the Right-Bank Ukraine. Although founded primarily by gentry landlords, these companies often hired as supervisors Jewish, German, or Austrian foremen trained in organic chemistry. Leaders of the Society of Russian Sugar Producers (*Vserossiiskoe obshchestvo sakharozavodchikov*, founded in 1897 as the successor of *Biuro predstavitelei sakharozavodchikov*, established in 1887) overlooked their ethnic and social

materiały (Warsaw: Zakład narodowy im. Ossolińskich, 1970); Ryszard Kołgodziejczyk, ed., *Dzieje burżuazji w Polsce* (Wrocław: Akademia nauk, 1974, 1980, 1983); and Wiesław Puś, *Przemysł włókienniczy w Królestwie Polskim w latach 1870–1900* (Łódź: Uniwersytet Łódzki, 1976).

[20] A. Gushka [Osip A. Ermanskii, né Kogan], *Predstavitel'nye organizatsii torgovo-promyshlennogo klassa v Rossii* (St. Petersburg: Izd. imperatorskogo tekhnicheskogo obshchestva, 1912); E. G. Lur'e, *Organizatsiia i organizatsii torgovo-promyshlennykh interesov v Rossii* (St. Petersburg: Izd. S.-Peterburgskogo politekhnicheskogo instituta, 1913).

[21] Victoria King, "The Emergence of the St. Petersburg Industrialist Community, 1870–1905: The Origins and Early Years of the Petersburg Society of Manufacturers" (Ph.D. diss., University of California, Berkeley, 1982); *Curriculum vitae zavodchika i fabrikanta Frantsa Karlovicha San-Galli* (St. Petersburg: P. O. Iablonskii, 1903); for Glezmer's speeches in the State Council, see Peterburgskoe obshchestvo zavodchikov i fabrikantov, *Materialy* (St. Petersburg, n.d. [1912]).

differences for the sake of effective negotiations with the government on the all-important issues of domestic price supports and subsidies for exports to Turkish and Persian markets. The diversity is evident from a glance at the names of both the leaders of this organization and the Kiev Exchange Committee, which supervised the major sugar market in the empire: Count Vladimir Alekseevich Bobrinskoi (descended from an illegitimate son of Catherine the Great); Lazar I. Brodsky, a Jew; the Austrian sugar expert Karl V. Fishman; Count A. A. Potocki, of Polish extraction; and the Ukrainians Fedor A. Tereshchenko and his cousin Ivan N., father of the finance minister in Kerensky's government.[22]

The textile manufacturers of Lodz developed similar feelings of regional loyalty. By 1904, many third-generation Germans had lost their devotion to Germany; "they have found their [new] fatherland in Lodz, . . . have grown attached to the city, and today are very patriotic: *Lodzmenschen.*" Although some Jewish manufacturers held to religious tradition or gravitated toward the new Zionist conviction, many there favored Polish autonomy, as did most Poles, and some leading Jewish manufacturers—Poznanski, Silberstein, and Jarocinski—had adopted German culture in Lodz.[23]

Even in Moscow, the home of the merchant-Slavophile alliance against foreigners in general and low tariffs in particular, foreigners who played essential economic roles apparently disregarded the vitriolic rhetoric of Ivan Aksakov and Sergei Sharapov. These "Moscow Germans," as they were called by one merchant, included Conrad Bansa (Banza), Mauritz Marc (Mark), Maximilian von Wogau (Vogau), and other members of the Wogau partnership. This remarkable family firm not only maintained extensive interests in Russian insurance, banking, paper, copper, and cement companies but also because of its ties to solid firms in Germany and England enjoyed the confidence of the Moscow merchants, who chose no less than five of its partners to serve on the all-powerful Exchange Committee for a total of eight terms between 1842 and 1890. A similar group of expatriate entrepreneurs whom we might call "Moscow Frenchmen," led by the Russian-born Jules Goujon (Iuly P. Guzhon, killed in Ialta in 1919), manufactured perfumes, cotton textiles, and ferrous metals.[24]

---

[22] The society's *Vestnik sakharnoi promyshlennosti* (weekly, 1900–1917); *Dvadtsatipiatiletie Kievskoi birzhi* (Kiev: S. V. Kul'zhenko, 1895), 13–15, 56–74, 91, 108–14, on production and price controls; 66 on ethnic heterogeneity. Rieber, *Merchants and Entrepreneurs*, 106–7 noted the cooperation among sugar men from various ethnic groups in the Kiev exchange.

[23] Stefan Gorski, *Łódź spółczesna* (Łódź: Rychliński i Wegner, 1904), 21–22, quoted in Badziak, "Rewolucja," 52; on Jews, see Badziak, "Rewolucja," 52–53.

[24] Erik Amburger, "Das Haus Wogau & Co. in Moskau und der Wogau-Konzern," in Amburger, *Fremde und Einheimische in Wirtschafts- und Kulturleben des neuzeitlichen Russland: Ausgewählte Aufsätze,* ed. Klaus Zernack (Wiesbaden: F. Steiner, 1982), 78–82; I. F. Gindin and K. N. Tarnovskii, eds., "Istoriia monopolii Vogau (torgovogo doma 'Vogau i Ko.')," in *Dokumenty po istorii monopolisticheskogo kapitalizma v Rossii,* ed. A. L. Sidorov (Moscow: Akade-

Even as social and ethnic antagonisms gave way in some cities to a spirit of economic cooperation, rivalries among regions increased in severity. Quarrels over the customs tariff pitted importers of raw materials such as cotton and coal against producers of such goods; manufacturers of cotton yarn and pig iron cried out for protection, but they were in turn opposed by producers of chintz and machinery, who sought cheaper yarn and iron from abroad. The triangular squabble among Moscow, Lodz, and St. Petersburg textile interests found an analogy in the acrimonious debates among the producers of iron and machinery in the Ural mountains, the Ukraine, and St. Petersburg. By 1906, each region had its own sectoral organization, such as the South Russian Coal and Iron Association (*Sovet s''ezdov gornopromyshlennikov Iuga Rossii*, founded in 1874), the Ural Coal and Iron Association (*Sovet s''ezdov gorno-promyshlennikov Urala*, 1880), and the Polish Coal and Iron Association (*Rada Zjazdu Przemysłowców Górniczych Królestwa Polskiego.* 1883). No less than fourteen gold mining associations existed in Siberia. Besides their disagreements over the tariff, manufacturers in different regions clashed over the proper length of the workday.[25]

Any comprehensive history of the Revolution of 1905 must include not only an account of the well-known outbursts of workers and peasants but also an examination of the activities of the corporate elite, which mounted its first sustained critique of the tsarist regime at this time. The most striking feature of the statements of business leaders in 1905 is the high degree of factionalism among the various business organizations. Perhaps because of the prominent role of Poles and Jews in the beet sugar industry, by far the most liberal statements in 1905 came from the Society of Russian Sugar Producers: it demanded an end to the persecution of Poles and Jews; called for "freedom of speech, press, assembly, and union—these inalienable rights of every citizen in every cultured land"; advocated the creation of zemstvos in the Kingdom of Poland; and proposed that individuals of all "estates, conditions, nationalities, and

---

miia nauk SSSR, 1959), vol. 6 of *Materialy po istorii SSSR*, 641–738; on 697–737 is reprinted the firm's own historical review of its activities in Russia (1915); electoral data from Nikolai A. Naidenov, ed., *Moskovskaia birzha. 1839–1889* (Moscow: I. N. Kushnerev, 1889), 19–22; on Frenchmen, see Maurice Verstraëte, "Sur les routes de mon passé" (typescript, 1949), Hoover Institution Archives, Verstraëte papers, Stanford University, 2 vols., chap. 8; information on Goujon's death courtesy of Erik Amburger, letter to the author, Jan. 4, 1982.

[25] See note 20. On the Ural iron manufacturers, a competent Soviet treatment is Iu. A. Buranov, "S''ezdy ural'skikh gornopromyshlennikov v kontse XIX-nachala XX vv.," in *Voprosy istorii kapitalisticheskoi Rossii: problema mnogoukladnosti*, ed. V. V. Adamov (Sverdlovsk: Ural'skii gosudarstvennyi universitet, 1972), 268–82. For a brief account of the SRCIA, see Petr I. Fomin, *Kratkii ocherk istorii s''ezdov gornopromyshlennikov Iuga Rossii* (Khar'kov: Sovet s''ezda gornopromyshlennikov Iuga Rossii, 1908). See Rieber, *Merchants and Entrepreneurs*, 222–43 (236–38 on regional conflicts over the tariff), and Susan P. McCaffray, "The Association of Southern Coal and Steel Producers and the Problems of Industrial Progress in Tsarist Russia," *Slavic Review* 47 (Fall 1988): 464–82.

religions'' be allowed equal participation in the zemstvos. This liberal tendency proved too weak, however, to prevail against ingrained pro-autocratic sentiments of other business groups in the empire. At the first meeting of business representatives from all major regions of the empire, held in July 1905 in Moscow, the aged Naidenov denounced the liberals to the police.[26]

Ethnic divisions within the corporate elite also erupted in the political arena as soon as relatively free elections were held. In Lodz in 1906, for example, ethnicity proved more powerful than economic interest, as Polish, Jewish, and German manufacturers tended to support their respective parties: the National Democrats, the Jewish bloc, and the German Constitutional-Liberal party. In St. Petersburg, Moscow, and Odessa, there arose ''special German groups of the Union of October 17,'' the moderately conservative party whose Russian members tended to disparage the rights of minorities to local autonomy. Moslem representatives from throughout the empire in 1906 resolved to establish a separate party and allied with the Kadets to promote the election of Moslem candidates to the State Duma. Ethnic animosities raged with special fury in Baku. The mutual massacres of Armenians and Azeris so seriously damaged petroleum wells and refineries in 1905 that the United States surpassed Russia as the world's leading producer of petroleum. This violence foreshadowed the even bloodier butchery of 1918–1920.[27]

The disarray of the Russian corporate elite appears to have redounded to the benefit of the autocratic state. Finance ministers Bunge, Vyshnegradsky, and Witte could pose as impartial mediators among the various business interests because each group looked to the state for essential favors to parry the threat of competition from Europe and the United States as well as from domestic rivals. Absent a vigorous liberal movement supported by a large contingent of wealthy industrialists and financiers, even the most dynamic of tsarist officials, namely Witte and his talented bureaucrats, felt free to administer the economic institutions of the empire by the well-tested methods of bureaucratic

[26] ''Polozhenie sakharnoi promyshlennosti . . . (zapiska sakharozavodchikov),'' *Pravo*, 1905, no. 12 (Mar. 27), col. 918. On discord in 1905, see Thomas C. Owen, *Capitalism and Politics in Russia: A Social History of the Moscow Merchants, 1855–1905* (Cambridge: Cambridge University Press, 1981), chap. 7; Rieber, *Merchants and Entrepreneurs*, chaps. 7–8 (silent on the sugar men's liberalism); Ruth A. Roosa, ''Russian Industrialists, Politics, and the Labor Reform in 1905,'' *Russian History* 34 (1975): 410–52.

[27] Badziak, ''Rewolucja,'' 76–80; Terence Emmons, *The Formation of Political Parties and the First National Elections in Russia* (Cambridge: Harvard University Press, 1983), 210, 217 (quoted); Henriksson, *Germans*, 111–12; resolution of the Second General Moslem Congress (Jan. 1906), in *Die russischen politischen Parteien von 1905 bis 1917: Ein Dokumentationsband*, ed. Peter Scheibert (Darmstadt: Wissenschaftliche Buchgesellschaft, 1983), 92; on demands for autonomy by merchants from minority groups, whether Poles or Moslems, see Rieber, *Merchants and Entrepreneurs*, 275. On Baku in 1905, see James Dodd Henry, *Baku: An Eventful History* (1905; reprint New York: Arno Press, 1977); Ronald G. Suny, *The Baku Commune, 1917–1918* (Princeton: Princeton University Press, 1972).

tutelage and arbitrariness. To the extent that tsarist ministers implanted modern factories by autocratic modes of behavior incompatible with the nature of modern capitalism—through subsidies to favorites, arbitrary restrictions on minority ethnic groups, prohibition of elective chambers of commerce and industry, preferential credit for the gentry, and the like—the state in fact hindered the development of capitalist industry in Russia.

In the early twentieth century, the concept of class consciousness finally arrived in Russia, but in a fully mature form, as an axiom of the Marxian left. As one student of the liberal movement wryly commented: "Perhaps the tragedy of Russia was that this country was caught by the Western doctrine of class war before the traditional estate system and the attitudes engendered by it had fully disintegrated and before the concept of the autonomous individual had been firmly established. This was probably the fatal combination that gave the Russian revolutionary process and subsequent Soviet development their special brutality."[28] To the rivalry among the estates must be added the strong ethnic and regional antagonisms within the corporate elite and the essentially apolitical role of most foreign entrepreneurs in Russia.[29]

In light of all these influences, the prospects for political action by corporate leaders on any program, whether liberal or conservative, appeared small. Semantics reveal much in this regard. The word "class" (*klass*) appeared rarely, if at all, in statements of the numerous business organizations in the Russian Empire before 1905. The official estate terminology persisted in the form of the collective noun "merchants" (kupechestvo), which applied to both traders and manufacturers, although in Moscow that term gradually yielded to Naidenov's favorite term, "the commercial-industrial estate" (*torgovo-promyshlennoe soslovie*). Likewise, the major regional and sectoral groups preferred such identifications as "producers" or "industrialists" (as in *gornopromyshlenniki* and *sakharozavodchiki*). "Class" attained prominence no earlier than 1905, and even then only in the larger cities. The bold appeals of the Riabushinsky brothers for a new class consciousness appropriate to an era of constitutional politics proved remarkably unsuccessful.

At the present stage of our historical understanding, we can perceive the importance of estate, ethnic, and regional loyalties in preventing the transformation of the corporate elite into a Russian bourgeoisie. However, until we have detailed studies of the various business organizations and their leaders in

[28] Stephen J. Bensman, "The Constitutional Ideas of the Russian Liberation Movement: The Struggle for Human Rights during the Revolution of 1905" (Ph.D. diss., University of Wisconsin, Madison, 1977), 846.

[29] The finance ministry noted in 1899 that foreign citizens comprised fully 24 percent of corporate managers in Moscow and 39 percent in St. Petersburg: King, "Emergence," 95, citing a report in TsGADA f. 560. For the best recent work on this enormously complex subject, see Amburger's books and articles; see also Urs Rauber, *Schweizer Industrie in Russland . . . (1760–1917)* (Zurich: H. Rohr, 1985).

the Russian Empire—Timofei S. Morozov, Emmanuil Nobel, Lazar I. Brodsky, Stanislaw P. Glezmer, Count Vladimir A. Bobrinskoi, and others—we shall be left with more questions and hypotheses than answers to the issues raised here. At every turn, basic issues of fact remain to be uncovered by vigorous empirical spadework.

A detailed and nuanced view of the the imperial corporate elite in each provincial capital, in addition to a definitive analysis of the relative strength of centrifugal and unifying forces throughout the empire, will be difficult to accomplish, but the task is relatively clear. The best examples of business history in the United States and Europe illuminate the evolution of capitalist institutions in their legal, political, and cultural environment.[30] The nascent field of Russian business history faces great new opportunities as its practitioners seek to emulate the most creative scholarship on European, American, and Japanese capitalism. Whether in the form of careful monographic works on Russian businesses and their managers or in theoretical and comparative studies built on the empirical base, the field offers the prospect of substantial future dividends. Unlike Witte's controversial program of forced industrialization, such a scholarly enterprise promises tangible benefits for all concerned, not only foreigners but also the subjects of the multinational state who seek to discover new visions of their own past.

[30] See Norbert Horn and Jürgen Kocka, eds., *Recht und Entwicklung der Grossunternehmen, 1860–1920* (Göttingen: Vandenhoeck und Ruprecht, 1979) [articles in German and English]; David M. Gordon, *Merchants and Capitalists: Industrialization and Provincial Politics in Mid-Nineteenth-Century France* (University: University of Alabama Press, 1985); and Charles Dellheim, "The Creation of a Company Culture: *Cadburys* 1861–1913," *American Historical Review* 92 (1987): 13–44.

PART THREE

Merchant Patronage and Social Consciousness

Chapter 7

PAVEL TRETIAKOV AND MERCHANT ART PATRONAGE, 1850–1900

JOHN O. NORMAN

THE HALF CENTURY from 1850 to 1900, the period in which Pavel Mikhailo-vich Tretiakov (1832–1898) amassed his remarkable art collection, witnessed the birth, triumph, and decline of Russian Realist art, the gradual recognition of Russian artists as professionals, and the emergence of a private art market dominated by wealthy merchant-patrons and hence far less dependent upon the traditional sources of art patronage—the state and the aristocracy. The second half of the nineteenth century was also the era in which Russians began to attend school in large numbers and read newspapers and periodicals on a regular basis. These developments created an urban public culture in which literate and even semiliterate Russians came to identify certain literary and pictorial works of art as quintessentially Russian, belonging to a common re-pository of modern national classics that have not been displaced to this day.[1] Tretiakov and the gallery he created in Moscow were pioneers in establishing the canon of Russian artistic culture and presenting these works to the public in an impressive museum open to the public from 1881. From 1871 to 1897, the years in which Tretiakov accumulated the majority of his collection, he spent over one million rubles on art purchases. In 1892, when he presented this unrivaled aggregation of Russian art to the city of Moscow, the collection comprised 1,362 oil paintings, 526 sketches, and 14 pieces of sculpture.[2] Indeed, as S. Frederick Starr has observed, "the Tretiakov legacy was nothing less than to mold the public and private taste of the Russian and Soviet middle class" (Fig. 1).[3]

The advent of merchant patronage following the Crimean War was marked by a pronounced interest in contemporary Russian art. "Buying Russian" was

---

[1] See Jeffrey Brooks, "Russian Nationalism and Russian Literature: The Canonization of the Classics," in *Nation and Ideology: Essays in Honor of Wayne S. Vucinich*, ed. Ivo Banac et al. (Boulder, Colo.: East European Monographs, 1981), 315–34.

[2] A. P. Botkina, *Pavel Mikhailovich Tret'iakov v zhizni i iskusstve* (Moscow: Iskusstvo, 1951), 242. For a guide to the Tretiakov Gallery at the time of its transfer to the city of Moscow, see *Opis' khudozhestvennykh proizvedenii Gorodskoi galerei Pavla i Sergeia Tret'iakovykh* (Moscow: Tovarishchestvo tipografiia A. I. Mamontova, 1893).

[3] S. Frederick Starr, "Introduction," *Russian Avant-Garde Art: The George Costakis Collection* (New York: Harry N. Abrams, 1981), 23.

Fig. 1. Ivan Kramskoi, *Portrait of P. M. Tretiakov* (1876). The only portrait Tretiakov ever commissioned of himself. Tretiakov Gallery.

a policy adopted by Moscow's merchant elite, and it extended to their new-found interest in art. Lacking formal education and decidedly ethnocentric, the merchant-patron found a perfect complement to his taste in the readily accessible, recognizably Russian subject matter of the burgeoning Realist school. Youthful enthusiasts of Realism, such as Ivan Kramskoi (1837–1887), who had led the secession from the Petersburg Academy of Arts in 1863 and helped organize the Society of Travelling Art Exhibitions (*Tovarishchestvo peredvizhnykh khudozhestvennykh vystavok)* in 1870, were in need of economic support because they had largely forfeited both imperial patronage and state support by rejecting the *cursus honorum* of the Academy of Arts and its aesthetic tutelage.

In the 1860s and 1870s the most prominent so-called merchant Maecenases (*kuptsy-metsenaty*) were Tretiakov, textile magnate and publisher K. T. Sol-datenkov (1829–1889), pioneering oil tycoon V. A. Kokorev (1817–1889), and railroad entrepreneur Savva Mamontov (1841–1918). They were joined by a dozen or so fellow merchants who collected on a somewhat smaller scale. The very act of collecting art represented a giant step in the cultural evolution of the Moscow merchant elite. Prior to Tretiakov's generation, the merchantry's acquaintance with secular pictorial art was limited to the obligatory acquisition of family portraits or the casual purchase of a few pictures or prints for interior decoration. By venturing into the art world, these patrons advanced the Moscow merchant elite's claim to participate more fully in the city's cultural life and expand its horizons beyond the narrow limits of Zamoskvoreche, the merchant quarter of Moscow. Although merchant patronage continued until the October Revolution, it exerted its greatest impact on the domestic art market during the second half of the nineteenth century; the best known merchant connoisseurs of the early twentieth century, Ivan Morozov and Sergei Shchukin, collected primarily post-Realist modern art from Western Europe.[4]

In 1854 Tretiakov bought his first oil paintings, nine of which were purported to be the work of old Dutch masters. Having acquired them, the novice collector began to doubt their authenticity and realized he lacked the expertise to distinguish originals from copies. He refrained from purchasing new works until 1856 or early 1857, when he resumed collecting but resolved to limit himself to Russian art whose authenticity he could verify. Of course, the merchant-entrepreneur had reasons for collecting exclusively Russian art weightier than the fear of being hoodwinked. A Neo-Slavophile and economic nationalist, Tretiakov responded enthusiastically to the call for a new art that depicted discrete Russian reality, sought to expand the indigenous art market, and offered the potential of winning a more honored place for the nation in the world of art. In 1856, even as Tretiakov was making his historic decision to collect Russian art, the nation's first widely known art critic, Vladimir Stasov (1826–1904), published a seminal essay in the leading journal, *Sovremennik*, in which he argued that the future of Russian art lay in genre painting dealing with contemporary subjects rather than in imitations of classicism or the latest trends in Western European art. Stasov found a sympathetic reader in Pavel Tretiakov.[5]

The precursor of the Tretiakov collection was, ironically, the gallery of St. Petersburg bureaucrat F. I. Prianishnikov (1793–1867), director of the Posts and active member of the Imperial Society for the Promotion of Art. Tretiakov first viewed the collection in the late 1850s when it consisted of some one hundred and fifty paintings. The Prianishnikov Gallery offered an overview of Russian artistic development from the mid-eighteenth century, with outstanding selections by Borovikovsky, Levitsky, and Fedotov. After viewing the

---

[4] See Ia. V. Bruk, "Iz istorii khudozhestvennogo sobiratel'stva v Peterburge i Moskve v XIX veke," in *Gosudarstvennaia Tret'iakovskaia galereia: Ocherki istorii, 1856–1917*, ed. Brük (Leningrad: Khudozhnik RSFSR, 1981), 11–55.

[5] V. V. Stasov, "O gollandskoi zhivopisi," *Sovremennik*, otd. 2, no. 12 (1856): 93–100.

Prianishnikov collection in the late 1850s, Tretiakov was inspired to emulate and surpass Prianishnikov by amassing a truly representative collection of contemporary Russian art that would provide historical perspective on the development of Russian secular art from its earliest manifestations. Unlike Prianishnikov, who had purchased art in accordance with his personal preferences and, not infrequently, to encourage Russia's fledgling artists, Tretiakov had in mind a broad pedagogical purpose: to familiarize the Russian public with the national artistic heritage and, via the portrait collection he began in the 1860s, to celebrate the nation's creative and scientific genius.[6]

Tretiakov's vision therefore extended far beyond the largesse of a bureaucrat such as Prianishnikov or the conspicuous consumption and transparent dilettantism of his fellow merchants. On May 17, 1860, Tretiakov composed an extraordinary testamentary letter whereby, in the event of his death, he bequeathed 150,000 silver rubles for the construction of a museum of Russian art accessible to the general public with an admission price of not more than ten to fifteen kopecks. This document also provided for the purchase of the aforementioned Prianishnikov collection and the merger of its contents with Tretiakov's own modest holdings. The remaining capital he designated for construction of a gallery to be administered by an art society composed of persons "without government ties and, in the main, without a bureaucracy (*chinovnichestvo*)."[7] In the ensuing decades this unprecedented Russian institution was established; it opened its doors to the public in 1881 with much the same salutary effect upon Russian art as Savva Mamontov's Private Opera, founded in 1885, had upon Russian theatrical culture. Despite the best intentions of both merchant-patrons, however, the institutions they founded reached primarily the better educated and more prosperous residents of Moscow rather than the general public. The Russian state, despite its immense resources, was slow to provide a public forum dedicated exclusively to Russian art. In 1898, well over a decade after the Tretiakov Gallery opened its doors, the Museum of Alexander III, now called the Russian Museum, came into being.[8]

[6] F. F. Lvov, "Obshchestvo pooshchreniia khudozhnikov v 1850–1862 godakh," *Russkaia starina* 31, no. 8 (1881): 20–24. See also A. Ivanovskii, *Fedor Ivanovich Prianishnikov i ego kartinnaia galereia* (St. Petersburg: Tipografiia F. S. Sushchinskii, 1870), 16–26.

[7] "Zaveshchatel'noe pis'mo P. M. Tret'iakova," in *Gosudarstvennaia Tret'iakovskaia galereia* ed. Bruk, 301–3. Tretiakov helped found the art society he envisioned, the Moscow Society of Lovers of Art, which received official approval in May 1860. See *Ustav Obshchestva liubitelei khudozhestv* (Moscow: Universitetskaia tipografiia, 1868).

[8] In 1825 Alexander I created the Russian Gallery of the Hermitage. Forty-one years later his successor, Alexander II, opened the collection to the public but neglected its upkeep thereafter. During the remainder of his long reign the Tsar Liberator added less than a dozen paintings to the Russian Gallery of the Hermitage; in 1865, however, the Tsar paid seventy thousand rubles for the greater part of the aforementioned Prianishnikov collection and presented it as a gift to Moscow's Rumiantsev Museum in 1867. The presence of the Prianishnikov and Tretiakov collections

Because neither the state nor the aristocracy welcomed Russian Realist art in its formative years, why did Tretiakov champion its cause? In addition to the factors previously mentioned, the Moscow merchant-entrepreneurs, as Jo Ann Ruckman has noted, adopted the service ideal from Russia's preexisting elites, the nobility, and the intelligentsia.[9] A believer in the Great Reforms of Alexander II and an opponent of the St. Petersburg bureaucracy, Tretiakov, like the Russian artists he championed, shared the intelligentsia's implicit goal of serving the people (*narod*) as opposed to the nobility's role of serving the state. Toward the end of his life he wrote to his daughter: "My idea from my earliest years was to make money so that what had been accumulated by society should be returned to society, to the people (*narod*), in some sort of beneficial institutions. This thought has never deserted me during my entire life."[10] This declaration, which calls to mind Andrew Carnegie's notion of stewardship of wealth, indicates that Tretiakov saw himself as a public-spirited man with a cause (*obshchestvennyi deiatel'*), not an aesthete or a Russian Maecenas. Tretiakov felt most comfortable in this role, and that is how he wished to be remembered. He succeeded in this, for on the tenth anniversary of his death the painter Viktor Vasnetsov wrote: "In building his collection, he could not have failed to realize that he was engaged in a historic national enterprise. . . . He was not so much a Maecenas as a serious public figure."[11] In both word and deed during the fifty years he collected art, Tretiakov did everything he could to establish his credentials as a legitimate obshchestvennyi deiatel' and to convince Russian society that he was not just another Moscow moneybags seeking to gratify his own ego by associating himself with the arts.[12] Tretiakov's impenetrable reserve and his horror of publicity stemmed

---

made Moscow a rich repository of contemporary Russian painting. Moreover, imperial subsidies, augmented by private support from the Moscow Art Society (founded 1850), permitted the Moscow School of Art, Sculpture, and Architecture (founded 1843) to function as the pedagogical center and functional alma mater of the Tovarishchestvo. In this way His Majesty's Own Chancellery actually contributed to the rivalry between St. Petersburg and Moscow and played no small role in the emergence of Russian Realist art. See *Kratkoe istoricheskoe obozrenie deistvii Moskovskogo khudozhestvennogo obshchestva* (Moscow: Tipografiia I. Chuksin, 1868) and N. A. Dmitrieva, *Moskovskoe uchilishche zhivopisi, vaianiia i zodchestva* (Moscow: Iskusstvo, 1951).

[9] Jo Ann Ruckman, *The Moscow Business Elite: A Social and Cultural Portrait of Two Generations, 1840–1905* (DeKalb: Northern Illinois University Press, 1984), 96–97.

[10] Botkina, *Tret'iakov*, 240.

[11] V. M. Vasnetsov to I. E. Evseev (president of the Society of Teachers of Graphic Arts), Dec. 9, 1908, in "Tret'iakovskii vecher," *Izvestiia Obshchestva prepodavatelei graficheskikh iskusstv*, no. 10 (1908): 347.

[12] For example, in a letter of March 1874 to Vasilii Vereshchagin, Tretiakov took pains to establish his altruistic motives in purchasing the artist's Turkestan collection in collaboration with his fellow merchant-collector D. P. Botkin (1829–1889): "[Our common endeavor] is not speculative, since we won't sell a thing; nor is it arrogance or egoism, since we won't claim [even] a sketch for ourselves." *Perepiska V. V. Vereshchagina i P. M. Tret'iakova. 1874–1898*, compiled and annotated by N. G. Galkina (Moscow: Iskusstvo, 1963), 19–20.

largely from his fears of having both his motives for collecting art questioned and his lack of formal education exposed to public ridicule.[13]

The advent of Russian industrialization following the Crimean War made possible the accumulation of capital needed to realize Tretiakov's dream of a privately funded national gallery of Russian art. At mid-century the Tretiakov family's flax-spinning enterprise had been quite modest with hand looms and a small number of employees. In 1866, however, Tretiakov, his younger brother Sergei (1834–1892), later mayor of Moscow, and their brother-in-law V. D. Konshin (d. 1918) founded the New Kostroma Linen Company and equipped it with the latest European technology. By 1914 it contained the largest number of spindles under one roof anywhere in Europe. In 1870 the completion of Savva Mamontov's Moscow-Iaroslavl Railway permitted Tretiakov to ship goods by rail as far as Iaroslavl and supplemented the Volga River route to the factory. By 1890 rail service directly linked Moscow and Kostroma.[14]

Tretiakov's personal impact on Russian art was great indeed due to the undeveloped nature of the domestic private art market in the second half of the nineteenth century. In Russia prior to the turn of the century, the absence of both an effective dealer network and a central auction house, such as the Hôtel Drouot in Paris, meant that the Russian artist dealt much more directly with his patron than did his European counterpart. Moreover, for at least the first decade of the Tovarishchestvo's existence (1870–1880), the Peredvizhniki largely depended upon the patronage of a few merchant collectors, among whom Tretiakov was clearly preeminent. Ilia Repin, Russia's most illustrious Realist artist, hardly overstated the case when he wrote, "the survival of the entire Russian School [of art] rested on Tretiakov's shoulders."[15]

Certainly Tretiakov had much in common with the Peredvizhniki. Having reached maturity during the era of the Great Reforms—Tretiakov and Perov

[13] An incident that occurred in 1893 confirms that Tretiakov had cause to fear censure for his lack of formal education. A newly appointed inspector at the Moscow School of Art, N. A. Filosofov (1838–1895), incurred the vigorous opposition of the teaching staff and the student body by trying to push through substantial changes in the school's curriculum. Instructors and students appealed to Tretiakov as a senior member of the school's executive committee and treasurer of its affiliate, the Moscow Art Society, to present their case to Grand Duke Sergei Aleksandrovich, director of the school's executive committee and governor-general of Moscow. When Tretiakov obtained an audience with him however, the grand duke cut him off in midsentence, barking out: "I know Filosofov well—he's an *educated man* with great tact, and I will not tolerate any unsubstantiated accusations against him" [my emphasis]. Tretiakov was cut to the quick. He immediately resigned from the school's executive board and from the Moscow Art Society. See N. V. Polenova to V. D. Polenov, Feb. 10, 1893, cited in S. N. Goldshtein, "P. M. Tret'iakov i ego sobiratel'skaia deiatel'nost'," *Tret'iakovskaia galereia*, ed. Bruk, 120, n.106.

[14] Ch. M. Ioksimovich, *Manufakturnaia promyshlennost' v proshlom i nastoiashchem* (Moscow: Izdanie Knizhnogo magazina "Vestnik manufakturnoi promyshlennosti," 1915), pt. 2, 1–2.

[15] Repin, *Dalekoe i blizkoe* (Moscow: Akademiia khudozhestv SSSR, 1964), 162.

were born in 1832, Savrasov in 1830, Kramskoy in 1837, Repin and Savitsky in 1844—patron and artists shared the epoch's comparatively democratic impulses. Indeed, Russia's artists and her budding entrepreneurial class were both seeking a more secure place in post-Emancipation society. Both groups resented the built-in privileges of the nobility and the high-handedness of the state bureaucracy. More specifically, each sought social recognition as creative forces and more secure guarantees of their professional status. Yet in Russia the persistence of key Old Regime features, in particular retention of the soslovie system, retarded fulfillment of these aspirations.

Although Tretiakov and the Realists had a great deal in common, social and economic tensions were nevertheless present. Along with the appreciation and gratitude so well chronicled by Soviet art historians, the Peredvizhniki sometimes resented their economic dependence upon Tretiakov. Many painters were indignant at the "concessions in price" expected from artists on the grounds that Tretiakov was engaged in building a national gallery of art for the benefit of future generations. The formation of the Tovarishchestvo in 1870 had been in part a dramatic bid by Russian artists for economic independence from the state and for recognition as professionals. Yet, during the 1870s, instead of having to kowtow to the court and the nobility, the Realists found themselves dependent upon the patronage of "merchant freaks."[16]

Moreover, the traditional Russian animus toward the merchantry was also present among the Peredvizhniki. Hence in 1874 we find the great Realist pioneer Vassily Perov complaining to Stasov that the "millionaires several times over" who dominated the Moscow Society of Lovers of Art had categorically refused to provide a mere 15,000 rubles for a gallery to display V. V. Vereshchagin's Turkestan paintings.[17] Perhaps because of his gentry birth and his international reputation, Vereshchagin himself felt little need to conceal his resentment at having to deal with a merchant. In 1876 he told Stasov that he considered Tretiakov "a merchant first and foremost." Nor did he always prove susceptible to Tretiakov's appeal for special discount prices: "[My painting] *The Dressing Station* (1881) cost me two years of labor, and you want to get it virtually as a gift—let other artists make still more concessions, but I cannot." Eventually, Tretiakov defended himself, retorting that he was neither a concessionaire nor a middle-man (*poriadchik*) engaged in making a profit from the sale of art works but an individual dedicated to building a fully representative collection of Russian painting.[18] In Tretiakov's view,

[16] Kramskoi to Repin, Dec. 26, 1877, in *Ivan Nikolaevich Kramskoi. Pis'ma. Stat'i*, ed. S. N. Gol'dshtein, 2 vols. (Moscow: Iskusstvo, 1965–1966), 1: 435–36.

[17] Botkina, *Tret'iakov*, 134–35.

[18] Vereshchagin to Stasov, Aug. 11/23, 1876, *Perepiska V. V. Vereshchagina i V. V. Stasova*, 2 vols. (Moscow: Iskusstvo, 1949), 1: 131; Vereshchagin to Tretiakov, June 28/July 9, 1887, in *Vereshchagin-Tretiakov*, 76; Tretiakov to Stasov, April 2, 1879, in *Perepiska P. M. Tret'iakova i V. V. Stasova* (Moscow: Iskusstvo, 1949), 42.

his limited means, the grand scale of his collection, and its eventual transfer to the public sector required him to seek the lowest possible price for each new acquisition. Therefore, if the appeal to conscience and national pride failed to move an artist to generosity, he was willing to employ all the skill he had acquired in a lifetime of business dealings to achieve the lowest price the market would bear.

Tretiakov exhibited many characteristics of the milieu from which he sprang, the Moscow merchantry. With his patriarchal beard, old-fashioned long black frockcoat, and high-topped, square-toed boots, Tretiakov appeared the archetypal *kupets*. Yet his simple personal tastes and habitual frugality also strongly resemble the virtuous bourgeois. Because the Tretiakovs were repelled by the conspicuous consumption of Russia's nouveaux riches, their home never featured the opulence so characteristic of the merchant-princes of Russia's Gilded Age. Tretiakov insisted that the picture galleries be sparsely appointed and without the luxurious furnishings and clutter then typical of private art collections.

Tretiakov's unpretentious tastes extended to art. For example, in the area of landscape painting, a genre to which he was especially devoted, Tretiakov expressed quite succinctly his basic preferences in 1861 when he wrote the Russian landscape painter A. G. Goravsky (1833–1900): "As for me, [I want] neither bounteous nature, magnificent composition, dramatic lighting, nor any kind of wonders—give me a muddy pool if you like, as long as there is truth [and] poetry in it."[19] *The Rooks Have Returned* (Grachi prileteli, 1871), Savrasov's realistic yet lyrical evocation of rural Russia in the early spring thaw, seemed to fulfill literally Tretiakov's injunction of ten years previous and became one of his favorite landscape paintings (Fig. 2).

The artists Tretiakov admired above all others were not the Russian Realists of his own day but the great precursors of Realism—Holbein, Titian, Vandyke, Rubens, and Rembrandt. Among contemporary Western European artists, Tretiakov greatly revered the work of Mariano Fortuny (1833–1874), whose historical canvases were celebrated for their virtuoso technique and masterful use of color. The greatest artist of the Russian School, according to Tretiakov, was Repin. Writing to Lev Tolstoi in 1890, Tretiakov declared flatly that Repin would "take first place" when the history of Russian Realist art was written. He also took issue with Tolstoi's proto-Socialist Realist view that art must be judged first and foremost by its content, declaring: "My opinion is that in the art of painting one cannot but recognize the painting (*zhivopis'*) itself as of paramount importance; . . . of course it would be all the better if [a painting] had a lofty content."[20]

[19] Tretiakov to Goravskii, undated, in *Pis'ma khudozhnikov Pavlu Mikhailovichu Tret'iakovu, 1856–1869* (Moscow: Iskusstvo, 1960), letter 82, n. 6, 302.

[20] Kramskoi to Tret'iakov, June 18, 1890, in Botkina, *Tret'iakov*, 207.

Fig. 2. Aleksei Savrasov, *The Rooks Have Returned* (1871). Tretiakov Gallery.

Though Russian artists and his fellow collectors recognized him as a great connoisseur, Tretiakov maintained he was nothing of the sort. Put to work in the family business as a small boy, he always felt keenly his lack of formal education. Among Russia's cultured elite in which the command of several foreign languages was common, Tretiakov's restriction to Russian was a real handicap. Although he read voraciously and traveled abroad extensively, making a particular point of viewing the great international exhibitions of commerce and art, he never overcame a certain inferiority complex. In a revealing exchange of letters with V. V. Vereshchagin, who had made a flattering allusion to his patron's highly developed appreciation of art, Tretiakov denied that he had "even for a minute fallen into the mistaken notion of seeing myself as a connoisseur," maintaining that he was a "devoted amateur" whose judgments were highly subjective. Hence, he concluded, "no article or opinion, whether indigenous or foreign could have any influence on me what-soever—I see according to the limits of my understanding."[21]

Both Perov and Kramskoi testified as to the independence and incorrupti-bility of Tretiakov's artistic judgments.[22] Despite their private and public af-firmations of Tretiakov's connoisseurship, however, rumors persisted that the wealthy merchant was merely following the directives of some artist or well-educated intelligentsia savant.[23] Tretiakov himself was painfully unsure of his long-term contribution to Russian art. He revealed these doubts to Tolstoi and shared with him his personal view of the gallery as a haven and refuge from the world of commerce that surrounded him: "In my short time on earth, views [on art] have already changed so much that I've lost track of who is right and simply continue to build my collection without certainty of its use-fulness. And so I will carry on, uncertain of [the collection's ultimate] useful-ness but with love, because I truly love museums and collections in which one may find rest from the persistent cares of daily life, and [because] I wish to make accessible to others that which I myself love."[24]

Yet personal taste was not the only criterion by which Tretiakov selected works for the gallery. To "provide a full picture of our art," Tretiakov pur-chased many paintings and sketches from earlier periods.[25] For example, he first acquired works by Aleksandr Ivanov (1806–1858), creator of the epic work *Appearance of Christ to the People* (Iavlenie Khrista narodu, 1837–1857), in 1858, the year of the artist's death. Tretiakov continued collecting Ivanov and other pre-Realist painters until his own demise in 1898. A pioneer in the acquisition and study of sketches, watercolors, and engravings by Rus-sian artists, in the last decade of his life, the merchant-patron purchased a splendid collection of icons that entered the gallery only after his death.[26]

[21] For Vereshchagin's comments, see V. V. Vereshchagin to V. M. Zhemchuzhnikov, March 4, 1880, and for Tretiakov's remarks, see Tretiakov to Zhemchuzhnikov, March 8, 1880, in *Vereshchagin-Tretiakov*, 4, 113.

[22] See V. V. Stasov, "Pavel Tretiakov i ego kartinnaia galereia," *Russkaia starina* 80 (1893): 600.

[23] In autumn 1875, for example, Kramskoi revealed to Tret'iakov that D. V. Grigorovich (1822–1899), secretary of the Imperial Society for the Encouragement of the Arts from 1864 to 1884, had asked him to advise the merchant-patron to purchase a watercolor by Briullov based on the assumption that Tretiakov followed Kramskoi's instructions. See Kranskoi to Tret'iakov, No-vember 19, 1875, *Perepiska I. N. Kramskogo: I. N. Kramskoi i P. M. Tret'iakov, 1869–1887* (Moscow: Iskusstvo, 1953), 128.

[24] Kramskoi to Tret'iakov, June 18, 1890, in Botkina, *Tret'iakov*, 206–7.

[25] Ibid., 207.

[26] See N. P. Likhachev, *Kratkoe opisanie ikonov sobraniia P. M. Tret'iakova* (Moscow: Sino-dal'naia tipografiia, 1905).

Tretiakov's portrait commissions resulted in a veritable hall of fame of the nation's men of letters, art, and science. From the 1862 acquisition of N. V. Nevrev's portrait of the famous actor born a serf, M. S. Shchepkin (1788–1863), to the 1898 commission of I. E. Braz's portrait of the playwright Anton Chekhov, Tretiakov gave pictorial expression to his personal view of Russia's best men. He found no place in his gallery for either the statesmen of Imperial Russia or the leaders of the revolutionary intelligentsia. Realist painters such as Perov and Kramskoi were pleased to accept commissions for portraits of Dostoevsky, Tolstoi, Ostrovsky, Dal, and Chaikovsky (Fig. 3). In at least one

Fig. 3. Vasily Perov, *Portrait of F. M. Dostoevsky* (1872), an early commission for Tretiakov's gallery of notables. Tretiakov Gallery.

instance, however, Tretiakov's conservative political views led him to solicit a portrait of the ultranationalistic publicist Mikhail Katkov (1818–1887). Not a single reputable Russian artist would accept the commission, and in 1881 Ilia Repin wrote Tretiakov an indignant plea not to spoil his gallery of Russian notables by adding a portrait of the notorious Katkov.[27]

Not infrequently, Tretiakov bought works he was not entirely satisfied with—usually the early efforts of promising young artists. If, after due consideration, Tretiakov decided that such an apprentice work was not worthy of the gallery, he would either sell it, exchange it for something he liked better, or simply give it to a fellow collector. But Tretiakov never purchased a work of art simply for purposes of investment or speculation. He sharply distinguished between his persona as merchant-entrepreneur and as merchant-patron.

Although Tretiakov alone made the final decision to purchase a work of art, he actively solicited the aid and advice of leading Russian artists, who frequently acted as informants regarding works in progress and even as his purchasing agents. Over the forty years he collected art, his closest advisers were all artists—Perov in the 1860s, Kramskoi in the 1870s, Repin in the 1880s, and after 1880 Pavel Chistiakov and the merchant-born Ilia Ostroukhov. Tretiakov rarely dealt with art dealers and refused to purchase works sight unseen. The seriousness with which he regarded the advice of his artist-mentors may be judged from an urgent entreaty to Repin, asking him "for God's sake" to continue offering criticism of his purchases because he found himself so "easily mistaken."[28] Nor was Tretiakov entirely candid when he wrote Vereshchagin that he could not be influenced by anyone else's opinion in selecting a work of art for his collection. One such instance occurred when Lev Tolstoi wrote Tretiakov criticizing him for not buying Nikolai Ge's controversial "*What Is Truth?*" (Chto est' istina, 1890) depicting an all too mortal looking Christ standing before Pontius Pilate. Tretiakov responded that he did not understand the painting and felt that in any case the authorities would prohibit him from exhibiting the picture. He nevertheless bought the work in question, admitting that he had done so only out of respect for the great Tolstoi.[29]

Tretiakov's contribution to the propagation of Russian Realist art extended, of course, beyond outright purchases. By placing the Peredvizhniki's works in his gallery, he gave them a permanent exhibition hall in the heart of Moscow; the prestige of the gallery grew, and so did the reputations of the artists whose works were exhibited there. As Elizabeth Valkenier has magisterially chronicled, thanks to the tireless efforts of Vladimir Stasov and other late nineteenth-century critics, a renewal of state patronage under Alexander III, and the acceptance by senior Peredvizhniki of teaching positions in the renovated

[27] Tret'iakov to Tolstoi, April 8, 1881, *I. E. Repin: Perepiska s P. M. Tret'iakovym, 1873–1898* (Moscow-Leningrad: Iskusstvo, 1946), 48.

[28] Ibid., April 18, 1883, 68.

[29] Botkina, *Tret'iakov*, 206–7.

Academy of Arts in the early 1890s, Russian Realist art underwent a conservative transformation and became identified with Russian national art in the mind of the public long before the advent of Social Realism under Stalin.[30]

Although the vast scale of Tretiakov's patronage and the prestige achieved by the gallery permitted him to play a decisive role in the reputation of the Russian Realists, the Russian art world was never Tretiakov's exclusive preserve. After 1880 the emergence of collectors who were wealthier and less frugal than Tretiakov provided the Realists with alternative sources of private patronage. The Tereshchenkos, Kiev's sugar beet magnates, for example, not only outbid Tretiakov at auctions, but they also emulated him by endowing their native city with a fine collection of Russian art. Moreover, even in the heyday of the Peredvizhniki, easel painting in the tradition of the Academy continued to flourish. After 1870, as a result of the efforts of Savva Mamontov, Princess Tenisheva, and others, decorative and theatrical art blossomed as never before. Simultaneously, the middlebrow and lowbrow art market of urban and provincial Russia expanded greatly, providing employment for the graduates of Russia's expanding network of provincial art schools.[31]

After 1880 the Peredvizhniki themselves began to receive commissions from both the imperial family and the nobility. For example, in the years 1880 to 1881, Kramskoi executed commissioned portraits of two members of the imperial family and other prominent personages such as Moscow Mayor Prince A. A. Shcherbatov, Senator I. M. Gedeonov, banker and art collector Baron G. O. Gintsburg, leading Slavophile Prince V. A. Cherkassky, State Council member N. V. Isakov, former Minister of the Interior P. A. Valuev, and conservative editor of the newspaper *Novoe vremia* (New Times) A. S. Suvorin. A balanced assessment of the Russian art market in the second half of the nineteenth century requires sustained inquiry into the nature and extent of state and aristocratic patronage, far from negligible in this period.

In September 1892 Tretiakov fulfilled the dream he had conceived over thirty years earlier by donating the Tretiakov Gallery to the city of Moscow with the proviso that he remain its director and chief purchasing agent until his death. During the first year of municipal administration, the Moscow City Duma provided the munificent sum of five thousand rubles for new acquisitions. Seven years earlier Tretiakov had paid more than four times this amount for one major work of art, Repins history painting *Ivan the Terrible and His*

---

[30] See Elizabeth Valkenier, "The Decline of an Ethos," *Russian Realist Art* (Ann Arbor, Michigan: Ardis, 1977), 115–34.

[31] See Boris Lossky, "The Popular Arts in Russia and Their Revival," *Apollo* 98 (December 1973): 354–59; Wendy Salmond, "The Solomenko Embroidery Workshops," *Journal of Decorative and Propaganda Arts*, no. 5 (Summer 1987): 126–43; G. Iu. Sternin, *Khudozhestvennaia zhizn' Rossii na rubezhe XIX-XX vekov* (Moscow: Iskusstvo, 1970) and *Khudozhestvennaia zhizn' Rossii nachala XX veka* (Moscow: Iskusstvo, 1976); V. R. Leikina-Svirskaia, "Khudozhniki," *Russkaia intelligentsiia v 1900–1917 godakh* (Moscow: Mysl', 1981), 147–77.

Son (Ivan Groznyi i syn ego Ivan 16 noiabria 1581 goda, 1885). Hence Tretiakov found it necessary to go on spending his own money in order to develop the collection.

During the last decade of his life, Tretiakov faced opposition from some of the very artists he had helped establish. Tretiakov never intended the gallery to be a museum devoted entirely to the Peredvizhniki, yet, had Stasov and the senior Russian Realists prevailed, by 1890 the Tretiakov Gallery would have systematically excluded all that was new and fresh in Russian art. For example, in 1888 when Tretiakov acquired Valentin Serov's ravishing impressionist portrait *Girl in Sunlight* (Devushka, osveshchennaia solntsem, 1888), he was severely criticized by the elder realists. Indeed, Vladimir Makovsky (1846–1920) boldly accused Tretiakov of infecting the Tretiakov Gallery with syphilis.[32] Two years later, when Tretiakov bought Mikhail Nesterov's lyrical and mystical evocation, *Vision of the Youth Bartholomew* (Videnie otroku Varfolomeiu, 1889–1890), he encountered even more formidable opposition. Tretiakov's friends V. V. Stasov, D. V. Grigorovich, A. S. Suvorin, and G. G. Miasoedov all condemned the painting, but Tretiakov purchased it anyway.[33] By acquiring the early work of the luminaries of the Silver Age, not infrequently paintings done while they were still in the classroom, Tretiakov helped establish the reputations of such artists as Aleksandr Benois, Leonid Pasternak, Konstantin Somov, and Nikolai Roerich. As Pasternak attested, even in fin-de-siècle Russia, a young artist's career could still be made by having a work in the Tretiakov Gallery. In 1889 Tretiakov purchased Pasternak's *Letter from Home* (Vesti s rodiny, 1889) for two thousand gold rubles, and the young artist promptly received invitations to become the art editor for the Moscow journal *Artist* and design the set for Antony Arensky's opera *Raphael*.[34]

In the last years of his life, however, Tretiakov had clearly reached the limits of his adaptability to the newer trends in Russian art. Although unenthusiastic about the twilight effusions of the Peredvizhniki, he was also quite out of sympathy with the aestheticism of the Silver Age of Russian culture. Tretiakov lived long enough to see the first number of the journal *Mir iskusstva* (World of Art) and found it pretentious and poorly edited, as he noted in a letter to his son-in-law S. S. Botkin (1859–1911), a collector in his own right and an enthusiastic supporter of the journal.[35] He was susceptible to neither the exquisite, aristocratic nostalgia of the World of Art group nor the power-

[32] Quoted in P. I. Neradovskii, *Iz zhizni khudozhnika* (Leningrad: Khudozhnik RSFSR, 1965), 32.

[33] M. V. Nesterov, *Davnie dni* (Moscow-Leningrad: Iskusstvo, 1959), 159.

[34] Leonid Pasternak, *Zapisi raznykh let* (Moscow: Sovetskii khudozhnik, 1975), 38–41, 45–51.

[35] Tretiakov to S. S. Botkin, November 1898, in Botkina, *Tret'iakov*. 262.

ful, unconventional style of Mikhail Vrubel, the greatest and most original talent of Late Imperial Russia.

Tretiakov must have had very morose thoughts about the future of Russian art and his gallery because he added a codicil to his will in May 1898, expressly forbidding the gallery to use the sum of 125,000 rubles he had bequeathed to it for the acquisition of new paintings. His explanation that the gallery was already quite large and might become tiring to the viewer seems disingenuous. More at issue was his concern that the character of the collection should remain unchanged.[36] Fortunately for Russian art, this codicil was set aside with his family's approval, and the gallery used these funds for new acquisitions.

In many ways Tretiakov was a lonely figure. As a private man, he was to a great extent the child of merchant Moscow, an old-fashioned, authoritarian, antifeminist husband and father with proprietorial control over his family and domestic milieu.[37] As an industrialist and entrepreneur, though by no means an enlightened employer, he made important contributions both to the expansion and modernization of the Russian textile industry and to the economic institutions that allowed the remarkable independent development of Moscow and the central industrial region of the Russian Empire.[38] In contrast to his outgoing brother Sergei, mayor of Moscow from 1876 to 1881, Tretiakov avoided public office. He also spurned the offer of Alexander III to elevate him to the nobility by affirming that he was born and would die a simple merchant.[39] Only in his role as a public figure (*obshchestvennyi deiatel'*) dedicated to providing Russia with a national gallery of art was Tretiakov able to transcend his social limitations and discrete economic ties. Like Savva Mamontov, his wife's cousin, he found in art patronage the means whereby tradition and innovation could be blended. True to his merchant heritage, he served as a cultural go-between (*posrednik*), bringing art, the traditional domain of the Russian elite, to a wider public. For more than half a century Pavel Tretiakov cast a giant shadow over the Russian art market, and both Russian and Soviet artistic culture continues to bear the deep imprint of this great merchant-patron.

[36] See "Dukhovnoe zaveshchanie P. M. Tret'iakova," in *Tret'iakovskaia galereia*, ed. Bruk, 307.

[37] For a more substantive discussion of Tretiakov's background, character, public life, and art patronage, see John O. Norman, "Pavel Tret'iakov (1830–1898), Merchant-Patron of the Russian Realists" (Ph.D. diss., Indiana University, 1989).

[38] See Alfred J. Rieber, "The Moscow Entrepreneurial Group: The Emergence of a New Form in Autocratic Politics," *Jahrbücher für Geschichte Osteuropas* 25, no. 1 (1977): 1–20 and no. 2 (1977): 174–99.

[39] N. A. Mudrogel', "58 let v Tret'iakovskoi galeree," *Novyi mir* 16, no. 7 (1940): 148, 162.

Chapter 8

THE MOSCOW ART MARKET

John E. Bowlt

THE POETRY, philosophy, and painting of Russian Modernism owed much to the organizational talents and aesthetic sensitivity of a group of entrepreneurs often referred to as the Moscow merchants. Distinguished patrons of the arts, they came to the fore in the decade before the First World War by acquiring works of art, subsidizing art books and magazines, arranging exhibitions, and in general constituting a principal clientele for the growing art market in Moscow. It should be stressed, however, that the title ''Moscow art market'' here is provisional: by art market we might understand that complex—or conspiracy—of methods whereby artifacts are bought and sold. In contemporary terms, the art market presupposes the presence of the manufacturer or supplier of the work of art (e.g., the painter, the archaeologist, the faker), the dealer or merchant who offers the piece for sale in the marketplace, and the buyer (private collector, museum, average consumer). This series of interactions is stimulated and facilitated by the ancillary system of galleries, auctions, exhibition facilities, publications (e.g., catalogs), appraisers, and attributors who sell their expertise, auctions, and so on. The art market, therefore, is an intricate mechanism that functions efficiently and advantageously when all or nearly all these elements are operative.

As the capitalist boom and embourgeoisement of Imperial Russia proceeded, Moscow and St. Petersburg society at the turn of the century began to adopt certain cultural rituals and customs generally identifiable with ''middle-class values'': an aspiration toward and claim to intellectual awareness, an increased desire to attend scholarly meetings devoted to the arts, and, not least, a vigorous interest in connoisseurship in collecting works of art both antique and modern, Russian and non-Russian. Of course, there were many regal and common precedents to these activities, but perhaps the figure most emulated by Moscow's Modernist collectors was Savva Mamontov[1] After all, during the 1880s and 1890s Mamontov and his wife Elizaveta not only turned their estate Abramtsevo (thirty kilometers from Moscow) into an art colony,

---

[1] For information on the Mamontovs and Abramtsevo, see D. Kogan, *Mamontovskii krushok* (Moscow: Izobrazitelnoe iskusstvo, 1970), O. Arzumanova et al., *Muzei-zapovednik Abramtsevo* (Moscow: Izobrazitelnoe iskusstvo, 1980). For comparative data, see also W. Salmond, ''The Solomenko Embroidery Workshops,'' *Journal of Decorative and Propaganda Arts* 5 (1987): 126–43.

encouraging prominent or promising artists such as Vasily Polenov, Ilia Repin, and Valentin Serov to share in their neonationalist revival, but they also established their own art market. They trained peasants to create specimens of popular arts and crafts such as toys, icons, and embroideries; then they advertised these products, exhibited them, and sold them at their Moscow outlet. In other words, Abramtsevo, contrary to what Soviet historians tell us, was not altogether a philantrhopic venture; rather, it was an entire program of commercial investment. If it had not been for Mamontov's untimely imprisonment in 1899 and the collapse of his industrial empire, Abramtsevo might have proven to be a major force in the packaging, disseminating, and marketing of the new Russian art.

Mamontov, like Pavel Tretiakov, was a member of an economic or social group that might loosely be associated with the notion of "middle class," although it is a middle class that cannot be easily categorized or described. The real problem is that Moscow's merchants of the Modernist period, from about 1900 until the October Revolution, did not form a cohesive, integrated unit. True, Vladimir and Genrietta Girshman, Ivan Morozov, Nikolai Riabushinsky, and Sergei Shchukin owed much of their wealth and power to their support of the capitalist system; that is, they bought and sold, juggled with stocks and shares, and established and disbanded companies to suit the shifting patterns of the Russian and international economies. In this sense, they shared the same economic base, but, by their very nature, the fiercely individual Moscow merchants commercially and artistically distrusted each other. Nikolai Riabushinsky, for example, came from a family of Old Believers, while the Girshmans were Jewish, and even though neither party manifested particular interest in their religions, they were distant from each other. Morozov and Shchukin, also Old Believers, had little time for each other. And Ilia Ostroukhov and Stepan Riabushinsky, the great icon collectors, were hardly on speaking terms. In other words, it is misleading to regard the Moscow merchants and patrons of the Silver Age as a single cohesive class united in their aspirations and endeavors, even though they all took considerable pride in their newfound fortunes and supported similar types of art.

As far as artistic preference is concerned, for example, it is important to realize that the merchant patrons of Moscow were contemporary rather than retrospective in their taste, despite their general interest in their national past. They did not try to duplicate the aesthetic preferences of the old aristocracy by amassing Italian Renaissance and Old Dutch Masters, as the Demidovs and the Stroganovs had done. Rather, they concentrated on the new art—Impressionism, Post-Impressionism, Symbolism. Certainly, members of the old Moscow *dvorianstvo*—the Gagarins, the Golitsyns, and the Tolstois—were still active as patrons and collectors during the Silver Age, but their traditional role as the arbiters of taste was rapidly assumed by the new representative middle class. Unlike the Moscow and St. Petersburg aristocracy, with their

nostalgia for more classical and more tranquil eras, the Moscow merchants—
when it came to studio or "high" art—looked forward, not backward, recognizing precisely those artistic trends that questioned and rejected artistic convention, just as their own social position was also to some extent presumptu-
ous and avant-garde. Perhaps that is why so many paintings by the early
Moscow Modernists such as Pavel Kuznetsov and Nikolai Milioti were acquired by Genrietta Girshman, Nikolai Riabushinsky, and their colleagues.
These collectors were not impervious to the ceremonies of aristocratic life;
they were flattered by imperial attention. Nikolai Riabushinsky was received
by Tsar Nicholas for his services as publisher of the lavish journal *Zolotoe
runo*. They sat for court painters (both the Girshmans and Morozov were portrayed by Valentin Serov, Russia's painter laureate), and, of course, they built
themselves palatial residences in town and country. Indeed, they realized that,
by the early 1900s, their influence on the development of artistic taste and the
market was as decisive as that of kings and queens. Indicative of this is the
impressive exhibition of Russian portraits, furniture, and icons—the "Exhibition of Art Works from Antiquity"—held at the Stroganov Institute of Technical Drawing in Moscow in 1901. Merchant families (for example, the Morozovs) lent just as many pieces as the old *dvoriane* (for example, the
Golitsyns).[2]

Those qualities of private initiative and rugged self-assurance that we associate with Moscow's business interests in the prerevolutionary era also
helped them operate in a cultural environment where the slightest deviation
still caused condemnation and reprehension and where, as the poet Benedikt
Livshits later recalled "atrophy of artistic taste had become a general phenomenon. While continuing to pay official tribute to the great shadows of the past,
the bourgeoisie, firmly ensconced in power, created few idols for itself, ones
that incarnated its esthetic canon."[3]   Actually, Livshits had in mind the petit-
bourgeois here that regarded the historical potboilers by Konstantin Makovsky
and Genrikh Semiradsky as the modern transcriptions of Titian and Louis David. Moscow merchants rejected precisely this kind of salon painting in favor
of Gauguin, Kuznetsov, Natalia Goncharova, Matisse, and Martiros Sarian—
another reason we should hesitate to identify them too readily with the general
category of middle class or bourgeoisie. How, then, did the Moscow merchants grapple with this "atrophy of artistic taste"? How did they function
within and manipulate the Moscow art market?

It is important to remember that from about 1904 to about 1914—that is,
the Silver Age—Moscow did not have an intricate, sophisticated art market of

---

[2] For commentary on the "Exhibition of Art Works from Antiquity," see Moskvich, "Moskovskaia vystavka khudozhestvennykh proizvedenii stariny," in *Mir iskusstva* 6 (1901): 325. See
also D. Nikoforov: *Sokrovishcha v Moskve* (Moscow: Universitetskaia tipografiia, 1901).

[3] J. Bowlt, trans., *Benedikt Livshits: One and a Half-Eyed Archer* (Newtonville: Oriental Research Partners, 1976), 81; first published in Russian in 1933.

the kind that New York, Paris, and Milan have today. For example, there was no specialist auction house, and the first private commercial art gallery, the Le Mercier Gallery,[4] appeared there only in 1909. In other words, we are concerned here only with the beginning of an art market in the Madison Avenue sense, a promising development cut short by the October Revolution, never to be renewed except in the umbrageous world of private collecting, wheeling, and dealing that exists in Moscow today. Conservative, moderate, and radical artists practiced a wide range of artistic systems. Various clienteles had various tastes, and, while some Moscow merchants possessed an extremely refined understanding of art, many did not. Collecting, cataloging, and connoisseurship were occupations that grew apace in prerevolutionary Moscow, and the nouveaux riches acquired all manner of artifacts—from samovars to French Impressionists paintings, from icons to Japanese prints—but not for financial investment. Some collectors acquired works of art simply because ownership offered a traditional status symbol; others felt that the enormous walls of their Moscow *osobniaki* (mansions) needed pictorial relief and decoration. Still others maintained a serious and expert interest in their choice of subject, and they sought, restored, and cataloged their acquisitions with pride and joy. And a few collectors—such as Ostroukhov—were regarded as the ultimate scholarly authorities on particular areas of art history.

Moscow was not, and never has been, a major international art market, even though during the years from 1910 to 1925 it was one of the four or five axes of the international avant-garde (with Paris, Milan, Munich, and Berlin).[5] Like their illustrious predecessor, Catherine the Great, local collectors of antiquities, oriental art, Old Masters, and modern French painting bought works through galleries and auction houses in Berlin, Paris, Rome, London, and New York, but rarely in Moscow, unless, of course, their preference was for Russian icons or contemporary Russian painting.[6] One commercial Moscow

[4] Karl Avgustovich Lemerse (Le Mercier) had been an employee at the Avantso (Avanzo) art supply store in Moscow before opening a hat store and then a private gallery on Saltykovskii pereulok in Moscow. His gallery never really enjoyed social or commercial success and, in the early years, was dismissed as a feeble attempt to imitate Georges Petit and Durand-Ruel in Paris. The Le Mercier exhibitions were moderate in style and catholic in taste, although occasionally avant-garde artists were represented, for example, Ivan Puni at the "Exibition of Industrial Design" in 1915–1916. The kind of art favored by Le Mercier—paintings and Russian genre scenes by Aleksek Kharlamov and Fedot Sychkov—appealed to the petite bourgeoisie and had little relevance to the Moscow merchants. For some information on the Le Mercier Gallery, see I. Zilbershtein and V. Samkov, eds., *Valentin Serov v vospominaniiakh, dnevnikakh i perepiske sovremennikov* (Leningrad: Khudozhnik RSFSR, 1941), 1: 104; "Moskovskaia khronika" in *Apollon* 3 (1909–1910): 41.

[5] Perhaps the series of art and book auctions initiated in Moscow in 1987 will stimulate the formation of a Soviet "art market" in the Western sense. Of particular interest in this respect was the auction of contemporary Soviet artists organized by Sotheby's in Moscow on July 7, 1988.

[6] Indicative of this strong orientation toward Western centers for buying and selling art is the fact that Riabushinsky himself organized auctions of Russian collections in New York and other

gallery, Le Mercier, favored the decorative arts and eclectic shows, but it had only limited financial success because of this traditional bias toward the West. St. Petersburg did not fare much better, although the breakup of noble houses and the sale of their contents did contribute to a lively auction market there just before the Revolution, and there were art supply stores run by Ivan Avantso and Aleksandr Begrov. The one private art gallery in St. Petersburg, Nadezhda Dobychina's Art Bureau, founded in 1910, dealt only with contemporary Russian art (for example, Natan Altman, Lev Bakst, Marc Chagall, Boris Grigoriev, Kuzma Petrov-Vodkin) and gained a certain prestige thanks to the obdurate bargaining powers of its abrasive, no-nonense proprietress who "dealt with the artistic Olympi of both capitals as she would with her household menagerie" (fig. 4).[7]

Still, as we know from memoirs and telephone books of the period, Moscow had numerous *starieveshchiki* (junk dealers), flea markets, and old book dealers (who would often sell prints and paintings), and it was a regular pastime of the Moscow middle classes to visit the markets on Saturdays in search of knickknacks, engravings, and old porcelain. In other words, Moscow in 1904–1914 did not have an equivalent to our Madison Avenue or New Bond Street, but it already possessed the structure upon which such a market could have flourished. Moscow had two important public art museums—the Tretiakov Gallery and the Museum of Fine Arts, headed by the able Ivan Tsvetaev.[8] It had two major art schools—the Institute of Painting, Sculpture and Architecture and the Central Stroganov Institute of Technical Drawing, which also had its own museum—numerous private studios (for example, those of Fedor Rerberg and Konstantin Iuon), as well as reasonable art supply stores (a branch of Avantso's St. Petersburg store and the artist store on or near Kuznetsky Most), a good rental exhibition space, the Art Salon, on the Bolshaia Dmitrovka, and regular exhibitions featuring retrospectives, one-man shows, and group shows.[9] The Moscow construction boom of the early twentieth century also encouraged the direct involvement of artists in public spaces. For example, Sergei Maliutin produced the folkloric decorations for the Pertsov Apartment House, and Fedor Shekhtel made the swirling organic decorations

---

cities (i.e., not in Moscow). See, for example, the auction catalog *Primitives and Other Old Master Belonging to Nicolas Riabouchinsky from the Collection of Prince Golinicheff-Koutousoff* (New York: American Art Galleries, 1916).

[7] Bowlt, *Benedikt Livshits*, 116.

[8] For information on Ivan Tsvetaev and the opening of the Museum of Fine Arts in Moscow (now called the Pushkin Museum of Visual Arts), see *Muzei* 3 (1982). The whole issue is devoted to the Pushkin Museum.

[9] The Art Salon was also known as the Mikhailova Art Salon. It operated from 1912(?) through 1917 and witnessed a number of important shows of modern Russian art: for example, Natalia Goncharova's large one-woman show in 1913, Konstantin Kandaurov's panorama of contemporary trends called "Exhibition of Painting, 1915" in 1915, and the first and second "Exhibitions of Contemporary Decorative Art" in 1916 and 1917.

Fig. 4. Aleksandr Golovin, *Portrait of Nadezhda Dobychina* (1920). Oil on canvas, 96.5 x 98.2 cm. State Russian Museum, Leningrad.

for the Stepan Riabushinsky villa, which he also designed. Aleksandr Iakim-chenko made panneaux for the interiors of several villas, while Sapunov and Sudeikin designed the interiors for cabarets. In other words, the private and public art commissions for vestibules, walls, club lounges, and evening costumes generated by Moscow's thriving capitalist economy also accelerated the trend toward the semblance of a professional art market. Indeed, by around 1906, just as the ''World of Art'' held its last exhibition in St. Petersburg and just as Sergei Diaghilev, a prime mover of the new art, began to concentrate his activities on Paris, so a new generation of Moscow artists and patrons manifested itself, communicating ideas through social gatherings, the press, and exhibitions.

Aesthetically and psychologically this generation differed from their more refined colleagues in the North. The poet Mikhail Kuzmin recorded his impressions during a trip to Moscow at this time: ''the loud Moscow accent, the peculiar words, the manner of clicking the heels as they walked along, the Tatar cheekbones and eyes, the moustaches twirled upwards, the shocking neckties, colored waistcoats and jackets, a certain bravado and implacability in their opinions and judgements involuntarily I thought: new people have come forward.''[10] These "new people," the Modernist artists, literati, and their patrons, many of whom associated with the Symbolist reviews *Iskusstvo* and *Zolotoe runo*, owed much of their success to the "art market." In fact, Modernist painting in Moscow could scarcely have developed without its complex artistic mechanisms, especially the social and cultural "mixers" that brought together artists and collectors, sellers and buyers.

By the mid-1900s the Moscow art market was diverse and developing, but a particular point of emphasis as far as the Girshmans, the Morozovs, Ivan Troianovsky, and Nikolai Riabushinsky were concerned, was Moscow Symbolist painting, a primary ingredient of early Russian Modernism that prefigured what is now called the avant-garde. The painters and sculptors who supported the Symbolist aesthetic, some of whom were members of the Crimson Rose and Blue Rose groups (1904–1908) drew upon both European and domestic sources.[11] Thanks to their older colleagues, Viktor Borisov-Musatov and Mikhail Vrubel, artists such as Nikolai Feofilaktov, Pavel Kuznetsov, Aleksandr Matveev, Nikolai and Vasilii Milioti, Kuzma Petrov-Vodkin, Nikolai Sapunov, Martiros Sarian, Sergei Sudeikin, and Petr Utkin were aware of Gauguin and the Nabis, of Art Nouveau and Jugendstil. They were also close to the Russian Symbolist poets, especially Konstantin Balmont, Aleksandr Blok, Andrei Belyi, and Valery Briusov and, like them, appreciated the mystical philosophy of Vladimir Soloviev whose famous poem of 1892 summarized their worldview:

> Dear friend, don't you see
> That all that is seen by us
> is only a reflection, only shadows
> Of what the eye cannot see?[12]

The basic idea of Soloviev's poem—that the "real" reality is beyond the world of concrete appearances—appealed to both poets and painters of Russia's fin de siècle, and they endeavored to perceive and represent this higher harmony in their visionary poems and pictures. Kuznetsov, for example, felt that renewed attention to the primitive functions of the life cycle, especially pregnancy and childbirth, could remove the false outer shell of civilization and reconnect us with the cosmic essence. Utkin saw the ultimate truth to lie in astrological and meteorological changes, and Sapunov and Sudeikin inter-

---

[10] A. Belyi, *Mezhdu dvukh revoliutsii* (Leningrad: Izdatelstvo pisatelei, 1934), 244.

[11] For information on these groups, see J. Bowlt, "Russian Symbolism and the 'Blue Rose' Movement," *Slavonic and East European Review* (April 1973): 161–81.

[12] V. Soloviev, "Milyi drug, il'ty ne vidish' " (1892).

preted the carnival, the parade, and the theater in general as metaphors for the artificiality of everyday life. The kind of visual art that resulted was, like the concurrent poetry of Blok and Belyi, strange and enigmatic in its muted colors and abstracted imagery. Here fantasies of pale mothers and babies, shimmering fountains and pools, apocalyptic constellations, and theatrical masks seemed to question the very materiality of that materialist world constructed and supported by the Moscow merchants. Yet they were the individuals who acquired these visions, and their transactions constituted a major component of the Moscow art market: Riabushinsky and Troianovsky owned key Symbolist work by Kuznetsov; Genrietta Girshman, Ostroukhov, and Troianovsky owned paintings by N. Milioti; Morozov owned a major painting by Utkin; Riabushinsky also had works by Sapunov and Sarian; and other Moscow merchants such as Nikolai Karyshev and Evdokiia Loseva also acquired various pieces by the Blue Rose artists. The Girshmans entertained the Blue Rose artists in their home, Riabushinsky financed their one exhibition in 1907 and propagated their work in his magazine *Zolotoe runo*, Morozov and Shchukin invited them to inspect their private collections of European art, and everyone mingled at the Society of Free Aesthetics. How do we account for this curious compatability?

Obviously, both communities, the Symbolist painters and the Moscow merchants, were united by their mutual position as the artistic and social avant-garde of their time, rather like the radical Realists of the 1870s and 1880s vis-à-vis Tretiakov and Mamontov. Both parties possessed an entrepreneurial spirit that imparted a remarkable energy and optimism to their daily lives, and both, in that respect, assumed responsibility for establishing new and revolutionary structures in the society and culture of Russia. Last, but not least, some merchants—especially Nikolai Riabushinsky (fig. 5), his sister Evfimiia Nosova and Antonina Privalova—belonged to Moscow's gilded youth and partook of the bohemian privileges of all-night parties, tango dancing, and occult seances that the Symbolist poets and painters also enjoyed. In fact, the social encounters of artists and merchants at private homes and clubs played a vital role in the development of Moscow's art market, often leading to visits to studios, portrait commissions, and private subsidies, as well as the direct purchase of works.

Beginning in the late 1890s, the intellectual jour fixe became a key component of Moscow and St. Petersburg life. Many distinguished men and women of the time held regular meetings in their private homes—Konstantin Balmont's "Tuesdays," Briusov's "Wednesdays," Andrei Belyi's "Sundays," Viacheslav Ivanov's receptions at his "Tower" apartment, Diaghilev's Wednesday teas—many poetic, philosophical, dramatic, and occult issues were discussed and explored. Many intimate societies also pursued more specific interests, such as the Theosophical Circle, the Religious-Philosophical Society, the Spiritualist Circle (Briusov and the musician Vladimir Rebi-

Fig. 5. Photograph of Nikolai Riabushinsky (ca. 1912). Private collection.

kov played an enthusiastic part), the Way, and the House of Song. Moreover, these professional assemblies were matched by the many socialite salons that mushroomed in Moscow and St. Petersburg at the same time, offering entertainment as well as enlightenment.

By the mid-1900s several cultural salons and clubs established in Moscow were frequented by both art patrons and artists and writers. Chief among them were the Literary and Artistic Circle (the "Circle") and the Society of Free Aesthetics (the "Aesthetics"). These two clubs were the most important from the point of view of Moscow Modernism and the art market, although several similar societies, both formal and informal, existed simultaneously. In this respect, I should mention Vladimir Shmarovin's "Wednesdays," held regularly from 1886 through 1924, (fig. 6)[13] and Nikolai Teleshov's Wednesdays of the 1890s and 1900s.[14] Although the meetings were, in principle, open to

[13] On Vladimir Shmarovin and his "Wednesdays," see E. Kiseleva, *"Sredy" moskovskikh khudozhnikov* (Leningrad: Khudozhnik RSFSR, 1967).

[14] See N. Teleshov, *Zapiski pisatelia* (Moscow: Sovetskii pisatel, 1952), esp. chap. 3.

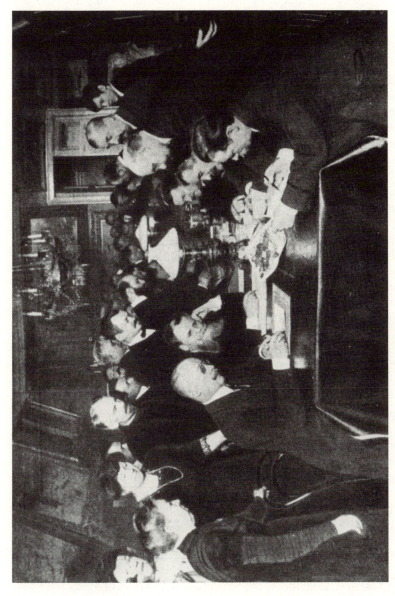

Fig. 6. Group photograph of artists at one of Vladimir Shmarovin's Wednesday Meetings, Moscow (ca. 1911). Reproduced in E. Kiseleva, *"Sredi" russkikh Khudozhnik* (Leningrad: Khudozhnik RSFSR, 1967), 17.

all artists and writers, a certain section of the intellectual community was favored: established artists and literati such as Levitan, Repin, Chekhov, and
Gorky. With the rise of a new generation of artists, the need was felt for a
more progressive, more tolerant cultural meeting place. This need was filled
by the foundation of the Circle and the Aesthetics. Both societies had direct
relevance to the Symbolist painters, especially the Aesthetics; they acted as
platforms for discussing artistic ideas, exhibiting pictures, and meeting representatives of the capitalist and intellectual hierarchies. However, the importance of these societies was not limited to their relevance to the Symbolist
artists alone, because both existed until the First World War (1916 and 1917,
respectively) and therefore witnessed and encouraged the rise of Neo-Primitiv-
ism and Cubo-Futurism.

The "Circle" was founded in 1899 by members of the former "Artistic
Circle" (*Artisticheskii kruzhok*) club, a meeting place primarily for actors and
musicians. The new Circle quickly became a focal point of Moscow's cultural
life, as its premises in the Vostrianovsky House of the Bolshaia Dmitrovka
began to draw representatives of all art media. Its library, restaurant, and bil-
liard hall were among its main attractions, but most popular were the Tuesday
discussions devoted to questions of art and literature. In the early 1900s these
"Tuesdays," now conducted by Balmont, Briusov, and V. Ivanov, took the
form of papers delivered by members followed by discussions between
speaker and audience. Many representatives of the Scorpion and Gryphon
publishing houses and of *Zolotoe runo* took part, and colleagues from St. Petersburg, such as Gippius and Merezhkovsky, were invited to attend. In this
way a wide arena was provided for communicating ideas between writers,
painters, and musicians. It is significant, therefore, that Balmont's *Three
Dawns* should have been produced at the Circle with decor by Nikolai Feofi-
lakov and Sapunov in 1906. The Tuesdays were not comfortable meetings of
a conservative intelligentsia, but were scenes of intense, often fierce, arguments between rival factions and anticipated the often violent disputes of the
leftists after 1908; indeed, the Circle sponsored some later Futurist meetings
in the Polytechnical and Historical Museums when such figures as David Bur-
liuk, Velimir Khlebnikov, and Vladimir Maiakovsky clashed—ideologically
and physically—with their audiences.

The Society of Free Aesthetics, especially relevant to the Moscow art market, was very active in its organizations of intellectual and artistic confronta-
tions. Of all the Moscow clubs, it was the most international and the most
sophisticated. Founded in 1906 on the Bolshaia Dmitrovka, the society arranged lectures, exhibitions, and dinner parties, and most of Moscow's artists
and patrons visited it. The comfortable, well-appointed club was conducive to
intimate discussion and contemplation: "You come in on to a staircase covered in blue-grey carpet, you turn into three or four rooms given over to us for
conferences; the same blue-grey walls; the carpets beneath your feet, the so-

fas, the armchairs and the little tables are of the same colors: blue-grey and blue-green; the light is dull.''[15] Under the auspices of Belyi and Briusov, the society did much to propagate Symbolism, although it broadened its interests considerably after 1909–1910 when mercantile members began to ''raise their voices.''[16] The intellectual membership of the society was actually dominated by painters and musicians, and writers were disproportionately few, mainly supporters of the magazine *Vesy* (Scales). Painters included all the Blue Rose artists, Goncharova, Larionov, Vasily Perepletchikov, Serov, Georgii Iakulov, and many others; musicians included Leonid Sabaneev and Aleksandr Skriabin; and foreign visitors included Matisse, Verhaeren, and Vincent d'Indy. As at other cultural clubs in Moscow and St. Petersburg, the society inspired a continuous cross-fertilization between the representatives of the various disciplines, resulting in many joint projects. Sudeikin, for example, collaborated with Bely on the idea of a puppet theater there with texts by Bely and designs by himself. In addition, carpets designed by Sudeikin were displayed in the rooms of the Society in 1907. In 1910 Briusov sanctioned a one-woman exhibition of Goncharova that caused a public scandal.[17] A Larionov exhibition was also held there in 1912.

The Society of Free Aesthetics lasted until 1917 when it closed, as Belyi recalled, because of an ''excess of lady millionaires'' among its members.[18] Of course, other meeting places in Moscow, such as the Polytechnic Museum, sponsored all kinds of public lectures, from Belyi's ''Art of the Future'' in 1907 and the Cubo-Futurist escapades of 1912–1913 to M. Lapirov-Skobl's discussion of interplanetary travel in 1924. There were also the bohemian cafés such as the Café Grecque on Tverskoi Boulevard that inaugurated Moscow's café culture—culminating in the brilliant, but ephemeral Café Pittoresque, which opened in January 1918.[19] All these institutions, but especially the Society of Free Aesthetics, can be regarded as symptoms of, if not stimuli to, the development of the Moscow art market to the wider appreciation of art, the establishment of particular artistic values, and the easier communication between vendor, collector, and supplier.

Recalling his experience of the Society of Free Aesthetics, Belyi wrote sardonically: ''Savva Mamontov, lots of them, suddenly caught on to us—it was almost pitiful. . . . Such couples (the Girshmans) appeared everywhere; the

[15] Belyi, *Mezhdu dvukt revoliutsii*, 244.

[16] A. Belyi, *Na rubezhe dvukh stoletii* (Moscow: Zemlia i fabrika, 1930), 219.

[17] See the references to Goncharova's 1910 exhibition in V. Briusov, *Dnevniki 1891–1910* (Moscow: Sabashnikovy, 1927), 142, 191, 192.

[18] Belyi, *Mezhdu dvukh revoliutsii*, 219.

[19] For Moscow's café culture, see V. Lobanov, *Kanuny* (Moscow: Sovetskii khudozhnik, 1968), esp. 80–92. For the Café Pittoresque, see S. Aladzhalov, *Georgii Yakulov* (Erevan: ATO, 1971), esp. chap. 5; A. Galushkina et al., *Agitatsionno-massovoe iskusstvo pervykh let Oktiabria* (Moscow: Iskusstvo, 1971), 100–101; V. Komardenkov, *Dni minuvshie* (Moscow: Sovetskii khudozhnik, 1973), 62–63.

husbands would give subisidies to societies trying to obtain something from us with the persistence of goats; the wives were langorous and, like Venuses, issued forth from a beautiful foam of muslin and diamond constellations.''[20] In spite of Belyi's ironic tone, the Girshmans, Ostroukhov, the Riabushinskys, Ivan Troianovsky, and, of course, Ivan Morozov and Sergei Shchukin, acted as positive forces in disseminating new artistic ideas, and purchasing works by the early Modernists from both public exhibitions and private showings. Troianovsky, in fact, "like a child, got carried away with every achievement of Larionov, Kuznetsov, Sudeikin.''[21] Additional support was provided by the regular soirées of Genrietta Girshman whose physical beauty inspired several portraits, for example by Serov in 1906, 1907 and 1911 and by Somov in 1911. Girshman was especially close to Sapunov and Sudeikin, whose pictures she collected, and to N. Milioti, who was rumored to have been her lover.

Of particular import to the general development of the Moscow art market and Russian Modernism were the names of the collectors Ivan Morozov and Sergei Shchukin, both members of the merchant community.[22] The most celebrated of the Morozovs in the sphere of art was Ivan, the owner of a complex of textile mills, whose collection of modern Western European paintings became internationally known (fig. 7). But in addition to his interest in French masters, Morozov purchased many works by young Russian painters, including Goncharova, Nikolai Krymov, Sarian, and Utkin; and Serov's portrait of him (1910) perhaps demonstrates the respect and sympathy that he enjoyed among the artists of his time. Starting his collection of French Impressionist and Post-Impressionist pictures only in 1903, Morozov soon owned one of the greatest collections of such art, rivaled only by that of Shchukin. His villa on Prechistenka, the interior of which had been reconstructed on the lines of an art gallery, boasted examples of Bonnard, Cézanne, Denis, Gauguin, Matisse, and Renoir. By 1917 the number of such pictures totaled 250. Morozov was in personal contact with many of these artists, and on his invitation Denis came to Moscow to paint panneaux for his villa. The music room, for example, Denis decorated with the story of Psyche. Morozov's collection of French paintings was cataloged by Sergei Makovsky in 1912 and published in *Apollon* (1912, no. 3–4).

Sergei Shchukin started his equally famous collection of modern Western European paintings about 1897 (fig. 8) and by the early 1900s he owned examples of all the principal Impressionists including Degas, Monet, and Renoir

[20] Belyi, *Mezhdu dvukh revoliutsii*, 224–25.

[21] Ibid., 225.

[22] For information on the collecting activities of Morozov and Shchukin, see B. Kean, *All the Empty Palaces: The Merchant Patrons of Modern Art in Pre-Revolutionary Russia* (London: Barrie and Jenkins, 1983). See also A. Fedorov-Davydov, *Russkoe iskusstov promyshlennogo kapitalizma* (Moscow: GAKhN, 1929), esp. chaps. 6, 7, 8.

Fig. 7. Pavel Pavlinov, *Portrait of Ivan Morozov* (1918). Reproduced in Lobanov, *Kanuny*, 146.

housed in his eighteenth-century villa on Znamensky pereulok. The most valuable part of his collection was a room devoted to Gauguin. In later years he included the Cubists such as Braque, Derain, Le Fauconnier, and Picasso, and artists of rather different trends, such as Liebermann and Redon. Like Morozov, Shchukin was in personal contact with Western artists, and at his invitation Matisse visited Moscow in October 1911, under the auspices of the Society of Free Aesthetics.[23] Shchukin's impressive collection overshadowed the more modest interests of his brother Petr, whose activities covered a more eclectic field, but his collections of Persian and Japanese art, Russian engravings and drawings and Russian icons and domestic utensils were particularly fine (fig. 9).[24] The catalog of Sergei Shchukin's Western masters was pub-

[23] For information on Matisse's visit, see Yu. Rusakov, "Matisse in Russia in the Autumn of 1911," *Burlington Magazine* (May 1975), 284–91.

[24] On Petr Shchukin and his collection, see P. Shchukin, comp., *Kratkoe opisanie Shchukin-*

Fig. 8. Dmitry Melnikov, *Portrait of Sergei Shchukin* (1915).
Present location unknown. Reproduced as the frontispiece to
B. Kean, *All the Empty Palaces* (London: Barrie and Jenkins,
1983).

lished in 1913, and the outline collection was recataloged upon its transfer to
the Pushkin Museum of Fine Arts in 1918 (then called the Museum of New
Western Painting).[25]

Through their collections, Morozov and Shchukin exerted an appreciable
influence on the formation of Modernist art in Russia, and Moscow artists such

skogo muzeia v Moskve (Moscow: Mamontov, 1895); see also Shchukin, *Vospominaniia P. I.
Shchukina (Moscow: Sinodalnaia tipografiia, 1911–12)*, five parts.

[25] See *Katalog Gosudarstvennogo muzeia novogo zapadnogo iskusstva* (Moscow: Gosudarstvennyi Muzei novogo zapadnogo iskusstva, 1928). Useful information is also contained in the
exhibition catalogs *Impressionist and Post-Impressionist Paintings from the USSR*, the National
Gallery, Washington, D.C., 1973; *Capolavori impressionisti e postimpressionisti dai musei so-
vietici* (Lugano: Thyssen-Bornemisza Collection, 1983).

Fig. 9. Photograph of one hall in Petr Shchukin's mansion in Moscow showing part of his collection (ca. 1895). Reproduced in P. Shchukin, *Kratkoe opisanie Shchukinskogo muzeia v Moskve* (Moscow: Mamontov, 1895), opp. p. 56.

as Goncharova and Larionov paraphrased a number of the Gauguin and Matisse canvases that they saw in these merchants' homes. But both men, rather aloof from Moscow's bohemia, led a conservative, patriarchal way of life. In this respect they differed markedly from Nikolai Riabushinsky—the prodigal son of the famous banking family and surely the most colorful of the Moscow patrons.[26]

Riabushinsky was a playboy and a dilettante, possessing neither the business acumen of his brothers Stepan (the banker) and Pavel (owner of *Utro Rossii*) nor the artistic refinement of Diaghilev whom, ostensibly, he chose to imitate. Nevertheless, Riabushinsky was fascinated by the new art and did much to propagate it. His luxurious review *Zolotoe runo*, what many called a

[26] On Nikolai Riabushinsky, see J. Bowlt, "Nikolai Ryabushinsky: Playboy of the Eastern World," *Apollo* (December, 1973), 486–93. On Riabushinsky and *Zolotoe Runo*, see W. Richardson, *"Zolotoe runo" and Russian Modernism* (Ann Arbor: Ardis, 1986). For contextual discussion, see P. Riabushinsky (signed Vladimir Riabushinsky), "Kupechestvo moskovskoe," *Den russkogo rebenka* (April 1951), 168–89.

"merchant's whim," produced a grand gesture; its Moscow panache and enthusiasm for Symbolism and Post-Impressionism did much to advance the cause of Moscow artists.[27] Riabushinsky also rendered a valuable service to modern art by financing and coorganizing four major exhibitions: the "Blue Rose" (1907), the international "Salon of the 'Golden Fleece' " (1908), and the two "Golden Fleece" exhibitions (1909–1910, the first of which was international).[28] Apart from collecting works by modern Russian and French artists, Riabushinsky painted profusely, contributed to exhibitions, wrote critical reviews, and even published a book of his own poetry (under the name of N. Shinsky).[29] To indulge his pleasures, Riabushinsky built himself a mansion in Petrovskii Park called the Black Swan; behind its neo-classical proportions the most outlandish events took place (fig. 10). There were cages for lions and tigers in the garden, at Christmas a huge fir tree would be erected and decorated with electric lights, and the interior boasted an impressive array of furnishings. To a large extent, his creative activity was questionable, merely a pretext for enjoying the license that an artist's life could afford. His maxim— "I love beauty, and I love a lot of women"—betrayed the kind of life he led.[30]

But whatever his personal faults, Riabushinsky was liberal with his financial resources. For example, in 1906 Riabushinsky commissioned a series of portraits of contemporary writers which resulted in Somov's remarkable heads of Blok and V. Ivanov. The same year he sent paints and brushes to Vrubel, then in Usoltsev's mental asylum, so that he could complete his portrait of Briusov in the same series. Also in 1906 Riabushinsky organized a curious competition with a cash prize for the most convincing depiction of the devil. Riabushinsky's prestige as a merchant Maecenas, while doubted and parodied in some quarters, did not go unrecognized by the tsar who received him in October 1906 and accepted the nine numbers of *Zolotoe runo* in handsome bindings "executed, according to rumors, by famous artists from a design by Riabushinsky himself."[31] Still, Riabushinsky was interested in not only promoting a magazine and art exhibitions but also enjoying the profits that the buying and selling of art could produce. This prompted him to consider building a Palace of the Arts in Moscow based on a shareholder scheme of five hundred shares at 1,000 rubles per share. The construction was to have been a permanent exhibition hall and museum of modern Russian art with auction

[27] Lobanov, *Kanuny*, 174.

[28] For commentary on the "Golden Fleece" exhibitions, see C. Gray, *The Great Experiment: Russian Art, 1863–1922* (London: Thames and Hudson, 1962), chap. 3; for exhibition lists (in French), see V. Marcadé, *Le Renouveau de l'art pictural russe 1863–1914* (Lausanne: L'Age d'Homme, 1971), 281–96.

[29] Riabushinsky published one book of his own poetry; N. Shinsky, *Stikhi* (Moscow: n.p., 1907).

[30] Quoted in S. Shcherbatov, *Khudozhnik v ushedshei Rossii* (New York: Chekhov, 1955), 41.

[31] As reported in "Iz zhizni," *Pereval* 1 (1906): 17.

Fig. 10. Photograph of one room in the Black Swan (ca. 1913). Works by Pavel Kuznetsov, leader of the Blue Rose group can be seen in the background. Private collection.

facilities; although Riabushinsky himself bought twenty-five shares, the project was never realized, due to his own financial collapse in 1909–1910. To counteract his losses, he auctioned some of his paintings in 1911 and 1916, and, in fact, much of his collection was destroyed by a fire in the Black Swan in 1914. Riabushinsky quickly restored his fortune and opened a Russian antique store on the Champs-Elysées, Paris. After the Revolution he was employed by the Soviets as a buyer and valuer for the new Commission Stores, but he soon emigrated to Paris, where he spent the remainder of his life as an antique dealer, traveling between Paris and Nice.

The patronal activities of Riabushinsky, Morozov, Shchukin, and the Girshmans played a central role in the development of Russian Modernism. The diversity and rapid proliferation of their collections in the late 1900s were symptomatic of the energy and versatility of the Moscow art market as a whole—qualities that also helped create another vital ingredient in that potpourri of artistic ferment, that is, periodicals and books devoted to modern art. Prominent among them were the magazines *Iskusstvo* and *Zolotoe runo*.

Iskusstvo was founded in 1905 by a cultured and wealthy Muscovite, Nikolai Tarovatyi, who, like Riabushinsky, had close personal ties with many artists. Tarovatyi's magazine filled the need for an artistic and doctrinal platform for the Symbolist poets and painters, and its articles and reproductions held a distinct bias toward Moscow. *Iskusstvo* treated only the initial stage of Modernism because it was forced to close after only the eighth issue in spite of strong financial support from Sergei Krechetov (Sergei Sokolov), director of the Gryphon publishing house. In 1906 its place was taken by *Zolotoe runo*, although on a much grander scale, and Tarovatyi was retained as art correspondent until his death in October of that year when the artist Vasilii Milioto (brother of Nikolai) succeeded him.

Iskusstvo provided the first opportunity for the new Moscow artists to submit graphic decorations to an art journal devoted wholly to their cause: examples of graphics by Anatolii Arapov, Feofilaktov, Sapunov, and other Symbolist artists as well as reproductions of paintings from current exhibitions appeared in most numbers. Although *Iskusstvo* was oriented strongly toward the Moscow Symbolists, it also paid attention to other Russian and Western movements. Tarovatyi himself appreciated the attainments of the St. Petersburg World of Art group and included Alexandre Benois, Mstislav Dobuzhinsky, Evgenii Lancéray, and Nikolai Rerikh as well as Moscow artists in his editorial staff. The wide diapason of articles indicated this artistic tolerance: Konstantin Siunnerberg contributed a lucid examination of Benois, Grabar, Fillip Maliavin, Somov, and Vrubel in an article entitled ''Five Artists''; Nikolai Vrangel wrote a long review of the ''Exhibition of Historic Portraits'' at the Tauride Palace; and Sergei Makovsky submitted a perceptive critique of Carrière's portraits. *Iskusstvo* even drew attention to the art of Mexico and Japan, a move that presaged the interest of the avant-garde artists such as Mikhail Larionov and Kazimir Malevich in primitive and Eastern cultures.

With the collapse of Tarovatyi's *Iskusstvo* in 1905, the urgent need for a well-organized, progressive art journal that would champion the ideas of the new art arose. This vacuum was filled in January 1906 when the first number of Riabushinsky's *Zolotoe runo*, one of the most exciting products of the Moscow art market, appeared. Undoubtedly, *Zolotoe runo* reflected the personal preferences of its owner, and its initial interest was in Symbolism, especially the art of the Blue Rose artists. But it did not ignore St. Petersburg. Indeed, the World of Art painter, Lancéray designed the magazine's cover for the 1906 and 1907 issues and augmented the Vrubel design for the subsequent numbers; moreover, during its first year of existence many St. Petersburg artists and critics contributed, including Benois, Siunnerberg, Filosofov, S. Makovsky, and Aleksandr Shervashidze. By 1908 *Zolotoe runo* had become an art journal rather than a literary review as a result of Riabushinsky's private desires— partly hostilities between him and Iurgis Baltrushaitis, Bely, Briusov, Gippius, and Merezhkovsky (all of whom resigned at the end of 1907) severed the literary connection, and partly the journal's close relationship with the "Blue Rose" and "Wreath" exhibitions in 1907–1908 molded the artistic interest.

Many important contributions appeared during the few numbers published, not least the successive presentations on Vrubel, Somov, Borisov-Musatov, and Bakst, a sequence that achieved a nice balance between the art of Moscow and that of St. Petersburg. Particular mention should also be made of two philosophical articles that related directly to the predicament of the Russian visual arts, that is, Benois's "Artistic Heresies" (1906, no. 2) and Imgardt's "Painting and Revolution" (1906, no. 5). The former opposed the contemporary fashion for extreme individualism in art, arguing that this would lead eventually to aesthetic chaos. Imgardt was more optimistic, implying that the next phase in art would be "visual music and phonic painting without themes"[32]—a gesture to the Symbolist search for artistic synthesism and a clear anticipation of abstract art.

Zolotoe runo ran out of funds in 1909 and was forced to close, although its last issues for that year did not appear until early 1910. By then the journal had served its purpose, for the apogee of Symbolism had passed. Its philosophy was replaced by the more abrasive gestures of the avant-garde. By and large, however, the Moscow merchants did not favor the extreme artistic manifestations of the avant-garde and expressed little interest in the abstract painting and sculpture, of say, Malevich and Vladimir Tatlin. Suprematist painting and "assemblages of material" were too radical even for that new and vigorous class,[33] and the exhibitions and societies that propagated these art forms after about 1910, for example, the Jack of Diamonds, were rarely patronized by the Girshmans, the Morozovs, the Riabushinskys, and the Shchukins.[34] In fact, the real avant-garde had no developed market, and if the public attended their exhibitions, it was out of curiosity and jocularity, not aesthetic delight. After all, how could one take seriously artists who painted their faces and wore wooden spoons in their buttonholes? In other words, the Moscow merchants were content to remain with the early Modernism that they had discovered in around 1905 and continued to buy works by Feofilaktov, Grabar, Kuznetsov, the Miliotis, Sarian, Serov, Somov, and Sudeikin until the Revolution. True, Shchukin acquired major Cubist paintings by Picasso, but to Malevich and Tatlin even these were hopelessly passé by 1915. How do we explain this sudden reticence on the part of Riabushinsky and his colleagues?

By 1912 the political and social mood of Moscow differed greatly from what it had been in 1905–1906, when the art of the Symbolist poets and painters had responded to a longing for peace in a society rocked by the first revolution and the tragedy of the Russo-Japanese War. On the eve of the First

[32] D. Imgardt, "Zhivopis i revoliutsiia," *Iskusstvo*, 5 (1905): 59.

[33] Tatlin referred to his first reliefs of 1914 as "assemblages of materials."

[34] On the Jack of Diamonds, see G. Pospelow, *Karo-Bube* (Dresden: VEB, 1985).

World War, the Moscow merchants seemed to awaken from this blissful state of retreat and realize that profound social transformation was inevitable and imminent in Russia. This growing unease and insecurity might explain their switch in artistic taste from the unusual in art to historicism and retrospectivism. The return to convention was manifest, for example, in the application of the neo-classical style to the new villas and dachas designed by Ivan Fomin and Shekhtel for the Moscow merchants. In turn, this was matched by their support of Acmeism, not Futurism, in literature and their acceptance of the more academic painting of Boris Grigoriev, Vasily Shukhaev, and Aleksandr Iakovlev. The new art magazines—*Apollon*, and *Stolitsa i usad'ba*—that replaced *Iskusstvo* and *Zolotoe runo* were now published in St. Petersburg, reflecting that city's sense of aesthetic measure, clarity, and proportion.

With the outbreak of war, this new conservatism among the Moscow merchants was consolidated, forcing an irreparable break between their artistic aspirations and the extreme developments of the avant-garde (for example, Malevich invented and exhibited his *Black Square* in 1915). By then the circle was fast closing. Surrounded by the misleading vividity of Kuznetsov's and Sarian's primitive landscapes, by the false logic of Matisse's and Picasso's still lives, by the irretrievable grandeur of Serov's portraits, and by the erotic knickknacks of Feofilaktov and Somov, the Girshmans, the Riabushinskys, the Morozovs, and the Shchukins encountered the October Revolution. The resultant closure of the stock exchange, the liquidation of assets, the nationalization of private collections, the ban on the exportation of art objects, and above all, the virtual disappearance of the merchant class led immediately to the collapse or at least transmutation of the Moscow art market.

PART FOUR

The Emergence of a Civil Society

Chapter 9

VOLUNTARY ASSOCIATIONS, CIVIC CULTURE, AND *OBSHCHESTVENNOST'* IN MOSCOW

Joseph Bradley

In early twentieth-century Russia the term *obshchestvennost'* signified the public sphere, a sense of public duty and civic spirit, increasingly in an urban context, and the groups possessing these values. In the Russian tradition, obshchestvennost' promoted activity for the public good rather than for private gain. Obshchestvennost' suggests the practical and purposive activity of the citizen rather than the state service of the government official or the visionary service of the revolutionary. Essential to developing a dynamic urban environment and Russian civic spirit at the end of the nineteenth century were the nation's growing number of voluntary associations. This chapter surveys the voluntary associations of Moscow, particularly those associations that promoted the public interest, remained somewhat aloof from the business of making a living, and pursued broadly philanthropic, educational, and cultural goals. I argue that had there been no associations, there would have been no obshchestvennost', as the term was understood by its proponents: voluntary organizations fostered sensibilities commonly thought of as "middle-class" in Western Europe and North America; and associational activity aided the development in Russia of a civil society independent of government.

The importance of voluntary associations has figured in several models of social theory and social history, and a brief look at a representative sample helps put the Russian case in proper perspective. "Americans of all ages and all dispositions constantly form associations," noted Tocqueville. The preeminent observer of voluntary associations in America provided a rationale for the historian: "Nothing in my opinion is more deserving of our attention than the intellectual and moral associations of Americans. Political and industrial associations of that country strike us forcibly; but the others elude our observation, or if we discover them, we understand them imperfectly because we have hardly ever seen anything of the kind. . . . In democratic countries

The writing of this paper was supported by a summer stipend from the National Endowment for the Humanities. The research was facilitated by the helpful staff of the Slavic Reference Library at the University of Illinois and by a faculty research grant from the University of Tulsa. I am grateful for the suggestions on earlier drafts offered by John Burnham, Paul Rahe, Barbara Reeves, Richard Silver, Richard Stites, Allan Wildman, and Callie Williamson.

the science of association is the mother of science.'' Indeed, Tocqueville claimed that along with institutions of local self-government, voluntary associations protected the citizens from both the central government and the excesses of the pursuit of private interest: ''If men are to remain civilized or to become civilized the art of association must develop or improve among them.'' Finally, Tocqueville posited a reciprocal relationship between civil and political associations: ''Civil associations pave the way for political ones, but on the other hand the art of political association singularly develops and improves this technique for civil purpose.''[1]

Specialized studies have demonstrated that associations and societies were essential ingredients to public life in Victorian Europe and America. Associations and the activities they sponsored were living examples of the economic power, creative spirit, paternalist good works, civic stewardship, and refinement of the middle classes. The libraries, lecture halls, workingmen's clubs, mechanics' institutes, temperance societies, exhibitions and museums, and the like, furthered education and self-improvement, provided rational amusements, dangled ladders of upward mobility from the social edifice, established community meeting grounds, aspired to mold respectable citizens, and offered national purpose and cohesion to a divided polity. At a time of urban social strife, the myriad of associations and organizations promoted a belief in shared values and the interaction of rich and poor in an attempt to blunt class antagonisms.[2] At the same time voluntary associations were important in shaping middle-class identities and in developing and reinforcing values, sensibilities, and cultural aspirations. In the United States, as Kathleen McCarthy argues, the notion of ''civic stewardship'' not only suggested commitment to an urban community and to the provision of essential social and cultural institutions, but the self-cultured patron of charities and the arts also became a new ''gentleman,'' identified in the public eye not with greed and brashness but with civic works and refinement.[3]

A century later Tocqueville's *Democracy* was recycled into postwar behaviorist social science and modernization theories that reaffirmed the individualistic ethic and ''democratic stability'' in the face of collectivist ideologies of

[1] Alexis de Tocqueville, *Democracy in America*, ed. Phillips Bradley (New York: Vintage, 1945), 2: 114, 118, 123.

[2] S. Elwitt, ''Social Reform and Social Order in Late Nineteenth-Century France: The Musée Sociale and Its Friends,'' *French Historical Studies* 11 (Spring 1980): 431–51; Alan J. Kidd and K. W. Roberts, eds., *City, Class and Culture: Studies of Social Policy and Cultural Production in Victorian Manchester* (Manchester: Manchester University Press, 1985); A. P. Donajgrodzki, ed., *Social Control in Nineteenth-Century Britain* (London: Croom Helm, 1977); H. E. Meller, *Leisure and the Changing City, 1870–1914* (London: Routledge and Kegan Paul, 1976); Peter Bailey, *Leisure and Class in Victorian England: Rational Recreation and the Contest for Control, 1830–1885* (London: Routledge and Kegan Paul, 1978).

[3] Kathleen D. McCarthy, *Noblesse Oblige: Charity and Cultural Philanthropy in Chicago, 1849–1929* (Chicago: University of Chicago Press, 1982), ix, 60–61.

the right and the left. Membership in associations was championed as individual and voluntary, rather than corporate and ascribed. Students of society traced such associational activity to the desire of the middle class to reach beyond the limits of traditional institutions such as family, church, and guild and to form social bonds with people of its own choosing. Moreover, according to a typical study, within the middle class, membership in associations was correlated with certain values and behavior such as individual self-confidence, cooperation, and trust. The high level of associational membership in the United States was further correlated with certain social factors such as a high level of female participation and high educational levels.[4] If modernization in the liberal tradition meant the ability to control one's own destiny, then associational activity was prima facie evidence of modernity.

Recently, social historians have constructed models for the formation of middle-class attitudes, sensibilities, and awareness in the nineteenth century. Stuart Blumin has identified formal and informal voluntary associations as one of five essential experiences in the process of middle-class formation in nineteenth-century America, contending that the emergence of reform organizations was directly connected to the crystallization of middle-class self-definition and awareness.[5] The experience of central Europe provides an even better comparative perspective for an analysis of the Russian case. Recently Geoffrey Eley and David Blackbourn have challenged the prevailing Marxist paradigm in nineteenth-century German historiography of a "failed" bourgeois revolution.[6] Despite its inability to dominate political society, the German bourgeoisie, Eley and Blackbourn maintain, was able to dominate civil society in the Hegelian sense by securing the market economy and capitalist relations, promoting private property rights and the rule of law, spearheading the movement of professionalization, and in general developing a public sphere separate and independent from the state. In particular, a network of voluntary associations was the "major agency through which the bourgeoisie set the tone in the material and cultural spheres of civil society." Moreover, associations

[4] These conclusions come from Gabriel Almond and Sidney Verba, *The Civic Culture* (Princeton: Princeton University Press, 1963), 211–15, 247–49. Other representative models include Reinhard Bendix, *Nation-Building and Citizenship* (New York: Wiley, 1964); Seymour Martin Lipset and Reinhard Bendix, *Social Mobility in Industrial Society* (Berkeley: University of California Press, 1959); and Lucian Pye and Sidney Verba, eds., *Political Culture and Political Development* (Princeton: Princeton University Press, 1965).

[5] Stuart Blumin, "The Hypothesis of Middle-Class Formation in Nineteenth-Century America: A Critique and Some Proposals," *American Historical Review* 90, no. 2 (1985): 299–338. Virtually the same argument has been made for England and France. See R. J. Morris, "Voluntary Societies and British Urban Elites, 1780–1850: An Analysis," *Historical Journal* 26 (1983): 95–118; and R. Holt, "Social History and Bourgeois Culture in Nineteenth-century France," *Comparative Studies in Society and History* 27 (1985): 713–26.

[6] Geoffrey Eley and David Blackbourn, *The Peculiarities of German History* (Oxford: Oxford University Press, 1984).

were essential in the process of class formation: "Associational life was one of the principal means by which various constituent groups of the bourgeoisie came together as a class." Finally, associational activity proceeded regardless of the political fortunes of the middle class. Indeed, the middle class was the most successful (and united) where its influence was the most quiet, natural, and anonymous; when it entered the political arena, the middle class became exposed, divided, and easily challenged by other groups.[7]

Not surprisingly, Russia does not occupy a prominent place in the social theory or social history of civil associations. In a comparison of associations of individuals under democratic and despotic governments, Tocqueville provides a sure guide to the fate of associations under autocracy:

> Despotism, which by its very nature is suspicious, sees in the separation among men the surest guarantee of its continuance and it usually makes every effort to keep them separate. . . . A despot easily forgives his subjects for not loving him, provided they do not love one another. He does not ask them to assist him in governing the state; it is enough that they do not aspire to govern themselves. . . . Equality places men side by side, unconnected by any common tie; despotism raises barriers to keep them asunder; the former predisposes them not to consider their fellow creatures, the latter makes general indifference a sort of public virtue.[8]

In a not altogether consistent theory of the relationship between political and civil society, Gramsci offered a succinct analysis of the Russian case: "In Russia the state was everything and civil society was primordial and gelatinous."[9]

Just how "primordial and gelatinous" was Russian civil society? The most important evidence comes from Russian voluntary associations. Tocqueville suggested a reciprocal relationship between civil and political associations and a correlation between voluntary organizations and limited government. Of course, for a long time these were virtually nonexistent in Russia. It was an extreme case of the continental pattern whereby officialdom rather than groups of private subjects took the initiative and whereby social needs were satisfied by traditional associations such as the family, the church, and the peasant

[7] Ibid., 148–19, 192–202, 259–60. The concept of "public sphere" (*Offentlichkeit*) comes from Habermas. See Peter Hohendahl, "Jürgen Habermas: 'The Public Sphere' (1964)," *New German Critique* 1, no. 3 (1974): 45–55, which includes Habermas's encyclopedic article, "The Public Sphere."

[8] Tocqueville, *Democracy in America*, 2: 109.

[9] Antonio Gramsci, *Selections from the Prison Notebooks*, ed. Quintin Hoare and Geoffrey Nowell Smith (New York: International Publishers, 1971), 238. Gramsci inherits the Hobbesian view, via Hegel and Marx, of a fractious, egotistical, destructive, anarchic civil society; this darker picture contrasts with the more positive view of civil society held by Locke, Rousseau, and Tocqueville. My evaluation of Gramsci's use of the adjective "primordial" becomes evident below. It may be worthwhile to note here that in its solid state a gelatin is hard and brittle, hence Gramsci's use of "gelatinous."

commune. Moreover, the Russian city never attained the corporate autonomy achieved over centuries by the European city. The city's inhabitants were grouped in hierarchical associations defined by tradition, law, and service to the state. In the eighteenth and early nineteenth centuries the purpose of the well-ordered urban economy and society was advancement of the wealth and power of the state and fulfillment of state needs. Despite the intention of Catherinian legislation to create a third estate and an urban community, the city came more under direct control of the state, and the electorate shunned involvement in municipal life. The city's limited public services were provided by the central bureaucracy, largely by the Ministry of Internal Affairs. As a result, the Russian city was little more than an administrative extension of the central government. Due to the artificiality of regulations governing employment and membership in the "town-estate," a government report in the early 1860s concluded that many towns were "distinguished from villages by purely formal, official differences."[10] Finally, it is commonplace in Russian history that the government repressed popular associations as sources of possible subversive activity and severely restricted the few associations permitted. To exist legally, an association required imperial approval, solicited through the Committee of Ministers.[11] Thus, the fears of a mistrustful government coupled with the numbing inactivity of an apathetic population for centuries swaddled organized public life.

Despite its size and economic importance, Moscow had few associations other than charitable societies before the era of the great reforms. Many organizations and societies, such as the English Club, the Society of Russian History and Antiquities, and the Literary Society were gentlemanly, clublike learned societies or groups, catering to the needs and interests of the nobility. Four of the city's societies were adjuncts of Moscow University. The Moscow

[10] Quoted in Daniel Brower, "Urbanization and Autocracy: Russian Urban Development in the First Half of the Nineteenth Century," *Russian Review* 42 (1983): 391. The standard works on the pre-Reform city are I. Ditiatin, *Ustroistvo i upravlenie gorodov Rossii* (Iaroslavl': G. V. Fal'k, 1877); P. G. Ryndziunskii, *Gorodskoe grazhdanstvo doreformennoi Rossii* (Moscow: Akademiia nauk, 1958); and J. Michael Hittle, *The Service City: State and Townsmen in Russia, 1610–1800* (Cambridge: Harvard University Press, 1979).

[11] Legislation concerning the establishment and supervision of societies went back to 1782. See A. D. Stepanskii, *Samoderzhavie i obshchestvennye organizatsii Rossi na rubezhe XIX–XXVV.* (Moscow: Moskovskii gosudarstvennyi istoriko-arkhivnyi institut, 1980). Useful introductions to Russian associations are "Obshchestva," in *Entsiklopedicheskii slovar'*, 82 vols. (St. Petersburg: Brokgaus i Efron, 1893–1902), 42: 607–28, and studies of the Soviet historian A. D. Stepanskii such as *Istoriia obshchestvennykh organizatsii dorevoliutsionnoi Rossi* (Moscow: Moskovskii gosudarstvennyi istoriko-arkhivnyi institut, 1979). Voluntary associations have not completely escaped the attention of Russian historians. See Jacob Walkin, *The Rise of Democracy in Pre-Revolutionary Russia: Political and Social Institutions under the Last Three Czars* (New York: Praeger, 1962), 121–52; and Marc Raeff, *Understanding Imperial Russia: State and Society in the Old Regime*, trans. Arthur Goldhammer (New York: Columbia University Press, 1984), esp. 129–45.

Agricultural Society, a learned society established in 1820, organized exhibits and conferences for peasants and in 1845 created the Moscow Literacy Society, which sponsored lectures and published books; however, this kind of public activity was rare at midcentury. Even important merchant organizations like the Moscow Stock Exchange Society did not exist until 1870.[12]

In midcentury, city guidebooks, unabashed boosters and image makers of the modern city, ignored Moscow's associations and "civic life." The 1868 guidebook, for example, informed the visitor that Moscow featured "heavenly cathedrals, royal palaces, aristocratic mansions, and innumerable shops and stores."[13] Yet within a generation, guidebooks began to notice something else about the city. Quite different are the images presented by the 1903 guidebook, for example. Its authors crowed: "Moscow has been transformed completely from a big village with an aristocratic air to a huge, crowded commercial and industrial city . . . adorned with museums, galleries, clinics, hospitals, charitable and educational institutions."[14] Moscow not only had been "transformed," but *completely* transformed. The "heavenly cathedrals, royal palaces, aristocratic mansions and innumerable shops and stores" that had impressed the author of the 1868 guidebook had given way to "museums, galleries, clinics, hospitals, charitable and educational institutions." The language and rhetoric of the compilers' preface reveals this transformation even better: this was a guidebook to meet *today's needs*; it was hoped that the book would be *useful*; the book strove to satisfy *practical goals*. The emphasis in the preface anticipates not only the greater detail but also the large type used in the later section on museums and galleries.

Voluntary associations and civic institutions had thus become a more important and more noticed feature of Moscow. In fact, by the end of the nineteenth century, in a nation not known for its joiners, private individuals were joining and organizing associations in unprecedented numbers, according to professional, occupational, philanthropic, and leisure interests. What associations were they joining? The 1912 City Directory listed more than six hun-

---

[12] *Moskva v 1872 g.* (Moscow, 1872), 54. On the absence of scientific and technical societies see N. N. Gritsenko et al., *Nauchno-tekhnicheskie obshchestva SSSR: Istoricheskii ocherk* (Moscow: Profizdat, 1968), 7.

[13] M. P. Zakharov, *Putevoditel' po Moskve*, 3d ed. (Moscow, 1868), 3.

[14] I. F. Gornostaev and Ia. M. Bugoslavski, *Putevoditel' po Moskve i ee okrestnostiam* (Moscow: Sytin, 1903), 36. The guidebook was prepared by the Standing Committee on Technical Education of the Moscow Section of the Russian Society of Engineers and published by Sytin; proceeds from its sale (a bound copy cost 1.25 rubles) went to support evening and Sunday classes for workers. For more on the changing images of the city, see Joseph Bradley, *Muzhik and Muscovite: Urbanization in Late-Imperial Russia* (Berkeley: University of California Press, 1985), ch. 2; Bradley, "Moscow: From Big Village to Metropolis," in *The City in Late-Imperial Russia*, ed. Michael F. Hamm, (Bloomington: Indiana University Press, 1986), 9–41; and Bradley, "The Writer and the City in Late-Imperial Russia," *Slavonic and East European Review* 64, no. 3 (1986): 319–38.

dred societies, organizations, clubs, and associations, covering a wide range of charitable, technical, literary, sporting, artistic, educational, cultural, and learned activities.[15]

Moscow's charitable organizations and mutual aid societies, such as the venerable Imperial Philanthropic Society and the Ladies Guardianship of the Poor, sponsored and maintained a broad range of institutions—hospitals, shelters and almshouses.[16] Moscow also boasted one of the most innovative and publicized charitable organizations in the country: the Municipal District Guardianships of the Poor.[17] Proponents claimed that by decentralizing poor relief and using volunteer case workers these guardianships would not only regenerate the poor but also transform the very concept of social service. Most mutual aid and consumers' societies were more recent in origin. Organized on the basis of trade or occupation, they reflected the increasing division of labor of the urban economy.[18] Benefit societies also existed for students and former students of various institutes and gymnasiums, as well as for Moscow's non-Russian minorities.

The increasing division of labor of the urban economy showed up also in the city's more than fifty vocational, technical, and medical societies. Many medical societies reflected a widespread concern with public health. Best known, particularly for its work in conjunction with the zemstvos, was the Pirogov Society of Russian Physicians, whose responsibilities included the Commission for the Diffusion of Knowledge about Hygiene.[19] The most

[15] *Vsia Moskva za 1912 g.* (Moscow: V. Chicherin, 1912). The city directory was divided into several sections, paginated separately. "Societies" can be found in the section of institutions, columns 808–947. Materials have also been taken from listings of "Clubs and Gatherings" and "Museums and Picture Galleries," cols. 1000–12. City directories were printed annually, beginning in 1894 in St. Petersburg and in 1897 in Moscow. The following discussion relies mainly on the 1912 City Directory; spot checks have been made for the years 1897, 1901, and 1907. For the sake of comparison, in 1897 St. Petersburg had approximately four hundred societies. No other city of the empire approached the two capitals in the number of associations. See also A. D. Stepanskii, *Obshchestvennye organizatsii v Rossii na rubezhe XIX-XX vv.* (Moscow: Moskovskii gosudorstvennyi istoriko-arkhivnyi institut, 1982); and A. D. Stepanskii, "Materialy legal'nykh obshchestvennykh organizatsii tsarskoi Rossii," *Arkheograficheskii ezhegodnik za 1978 g.* (Moscow: Nauka, 1979): 69–80. On the various laws pertaining to the establishment of assocations, reading rooms, public lectures, museums, and so on see K. G. Von-Plato, *Polozhenie o chastnykh obshchestvakh, uchrezhdaemykh s razresheniiami ministerstv, gubernatorov i gradonachal'nikov* (Riga, 1903); and K. Il'inskii, *Chastnye obshchestva i Sbornik Zakonov, rasporiazhenii pravitel'stva i reshenii Pravitel'stvuiushchego Senata* (Riga, 1913).

[16] Adele Lindenmeyr, "Public Poor Relief and Private Charity in Late Imperial Russia" (Ph.D. diss., Princeton University, 1980).

[17] For more discussion of the Guardianships, see Adele Lindenmeyr, "A Russian Experiment in Voluntarism: The Municipal Guardianships of the Poor, 1894–1914," *Jahrbücher für Geschichte Osteuropas* 30, no. 3 (1982): 429–51; and Bradley, *Muzhik and Muscovite*, 317–24.

[18] For an analysis of the urban labor force and occupational structure, see Bradley, *Muzhik and Moscovite*, 142–93, 359–70.

[19] Akademiia nauk SSSR, *Istoriia Moskvy*, 6 vols. (Moscow: Akademiia nauk, 1952–59), 5:

important technical societies were the Moscow Society of Architects, the Russian Mining Society, the Polytechnical Society, the Moscow Section of the Russian Society of Engineers, and the Society for the Dissemination of Technical Knowledge.[20]

In urban society an increasing division of leisure matched the division of labor and showed up in the city's sporting, artistic, educational, and cultural societies. Like other large European centers of the day, Moscow boasted several automobile, motorist, bicycle, and aviation clubs, as well as many other organizations promoting sports and hobbies. Also like large European cities, Moscow had several societies of spiritualists, mentalists, and theosophists.[21] Cultural and educational societies included the Moscow Literacy Society, the Moscow Free Library Society, the Moscow Society to Promote Educational Public Amusements, the Moscow Society to Organize Public Lectures, Libraries and Reading Rooms, the Moscow Society of Public Universities, and—that most Victorian of societies—the Temperance Society.[22] Finally, the most prominent of the learned societies were the Imperial Society of Natural Science, Anthropology and Ethnography, the Imperial Archeological Society,

---

429–38; Nancy Mandelker Frieden, *Russian Physicians in an Era of Reform and Revolution, 1856–1905* (Princeton: Princeton University Press, 1981), 179–99, 231–61. See also the papers by John F. Hutchinson, Julie V. Brown, and Samuel C. Romer in *Professions in Russia at the End of the Old Regime*, ed. Harley Balzer (Ithaca: Cornell University Press, forthcoming).

[20] On scientific and technical societies, see N. G. Filippov, *Nauchno-tekhnicheskie obshchestva Rossii, 1866–1917* (Moscow: Moskovskii gosudarstvenny istoriko-arkhivnyi institut, 1976) and N. N. Gritsenko et al., *Nauchnotekhnicheskie obshchestva SSSR*; Iu. A. Mezhenko, *Russkaia tekhnicheskaia periodika* (Moscow-Leningrad: Akademiia nauk, 1955) provides an excellent list of societies and bibliography of publications. On the Imperial Russian Society of Engineers (also known as the Russian Technical Society), see *Kratkii istoricheskii ocherk deiatel'nosti Imperatorskogo Russkogo Tekhnicheskogo Obshchestva s ego osnovaniia po 1 ianvaria 1893 g.* (Moscow, 1894); Harley D. Balzer, "Educating the Engineers: Economics, Politics, and Technical Training in Tsarist Russia" (Ph.D. diss., University of Pennsylvania, 1980); and Balzer, "Russian Technical Society," in *Modern Encyclopedia of Russian and Soviet History* 32: 176–80.

[21] A congress of spiritualists convened in 1906. See Veserossiiskii s"ezd spiritualistov, *Trudy* (Moscow, 1907).

[22] Sakharov, *Obzor deiatel'nosti Moskovskogo Komiteta gramotnosti* (Moscow, 1900). On the St. Petersburg Literacy Society, see D. D. Protopopov, *Istoriia Sankt-Peterburgskogo Komiteta gramotnosti, 1861–1895 gg.* (St. Petersburg, 1898). On associations of teachers themselves, see Christine Ruane Hinshaw, "The Soul of the School: The Professionalization of Urban Schoolteachers in St. Petersburg and Moscow, 1890–1907" (Ph.D. diss., University of California, Berkeley, 1986), esp. chap. 5; and Scott J. Seregny, *Russian Teachers and Peasant Revolution: The Politics of Education in 1905* (Bloomington: Indiana University Press, 1989). On temperance, see Marc L. Schulkin, "The Politics of Temperance: Nicholas II's Campaign against Alcohol Abuse" (Ph.D. diss., Harvard University, 1985); and George Edward Snow, "The Temperance Movement in Russia," *MERSH* 38: 226–34. For more on artistic associations, see Janet Kennedy, *The Mir Iskusstva Group and Russian Art, 1898–1912* (New York: Garland Publishers, 1977); John Bowlt, *The Silver Age* (Newtonville, Mass.: Oriental Research Publishers, 1979); Stuart Grover, "The World of Art Movement in Russia," *Russian Review* 32, no. 1 (1973): 28–42; and Robert Williams, *Artists in Revolution* (Bloomington: Indiana University Press, 1977).

the Moscow University Society of Amateur Naturalists, the Imperial Society of History and Antiquities, the Russian Literary Society, the Moscow Mathematics Society, the Moscow Society to Disseminate Scientific Knowledge, and the Moscow Agricultural Society.[23]

This brief survey is sufficient to indicate the number and variety of the city's organizations and associations at the beginning of the twentieth century. It is far from my contention that virtually overnight Russians had become compulsive joiners; yet this dramatic increase in the number of associations and in their visibility must be explained. Three causal factors—political, socioeconomic, and cultural—may be identified.

Like those of many plants that eventually robbed the old regime of nutrients, the seeds of civil association were sown by autocracy itself. By allowing nongovernmental institutions, such as the zemstvo, to play an active public role, the Great Reforms broke the monopoly of public life previously held by the autocrat and officialdom. For example, although approval from the central authorities of an association's charter still was required, beginning in 1862 the process of gaining such approval had devolved to several ministries.[24] The central government also granted Russian cities a measure of autonomy and permitted local political associations. In spite of limited franchise, apathetic electorate, and state supervisory functions, Moscow began to develop Russia's most active municipal government. Moscow was administered by civic-minded industrialists, entrepreneurs and professionals dedicated to expanding the city's public services.[25] During its first fifteen years the city council opened

[23] On the Agricultural Society, see Imperatorskoe Moskovskoe Obshchestvo sel'skogo khoziaistva, *Istoricheskaia zapiska o 30-ti letnei deiatel'nosti* (Moscow: A. A. Levinson, 1890). Many other societies published jubilee editions; for example, see *Istoricheskaia zapiska o deiatel'nosti Moskovskogo arkheologicheskogo obshchestva za 25 let* (Moscow: Sinodel'naia tip, 1890). On Russian science in the nineteenth century, see Alexander Vucinich, *Science in Russian Culture*, 2 vols. (Stanford: Stanford University Press, 1963, 1970). Two Soviet studies of learned societies in general are A. D. Stepanskii, "Nauchnye obshchestva pri vysshikh uchebnykh zavedeniiakh dorevoliutsionnoi Rossii," in *Gosudarstvennoe rukovodstvo vysshei shkoly v dorevoliutsionnoi Rossii i v SSSR* (Moscow: Moskovskii gosudarstvennyi istoriko-arkhivnyi institut, 1979), 210–39; and T. I. Vzdorpov, *Istoriia otkrytiia i izucheniia russkoi srednevekovoi zhivopisi XIX v.* (Moscow: Iskusstvo, 1986), 126–68. I am grateful to Christine Ruane for bringing this book to my attention.

[24] Stepanskii, *Samoderzharie i obshchestvennye organizatsii*, 6.

[25] James Bater, "Some Dimensions of Urbanization and the Response of Municipal Government: Moscow and St. Petersburg," *Russian History* 5, pt. 2 (1978): 46–63. Many of Moscow's mayors, such as Sergei M. Tret'iakov (in office, 1876–1882), Nikolai A. Alekseev (1885–1893), Konstantin Rukavishnikov (1893–1896), and Nikolai I. Guchkov (1905–1912), came from prominent merchant families. For more on the civic activity of the Moscow merchants, see P. Buryshkin, *Moskva kupecheskaia* (New York: Chekhov, 1954); Thomas C. Owen, *Capitalism and Politics in Russia: A Social History of the Moscow Merchants, 1855–1905* (Cambridge: Cambridge University Press, 1981); Alfred Rieber, *Merchants and Entrepreneurs in Imperial Russia* (Chapel Hill: University of North Carolina Press, 1982); and Jo Ann Ruckman, *The Moscow*

schools and hospitals, launched municipal public works projects, and involved itself in many areas of public health, housing, and urban transport.
As professionals and entrepreneurs became more and more interested in the
city around them, the city council began to play a more activist and reformist
role in urban affairs. Yet the "civic" significance of such municipal activism
went far beyond the additional street car route or sewage line. In the eyes
of a municipal social services commission, developing individual initiative
(*samodeiatel' nost'*) and public morality were goals of city government.[26] In
this way, Moscow became Russia's leading city in the movement for municipal autonomy and expansion of social services, and the City Council catalyzed
the cultivation of private initiative and civic vision.

A second important cause of the expansion of associational activity at the
end of the nineteenth century was the rapid process of urbanization and industrialization. The saga of Russian economic growth, railroad expansion, foreign investment, and generation of wealth in the 1880s and 1890s is familiar
to students of Russian history; by the eve of World War I, Russia had become
one of the major world producers of textiles, coal, iron, steel, and oil. Moscow was the fastest growing of Europe's metropolises, and smaller boom
towns sprang up virtually overnight. The diffusion of science and technology
and the specialization of the labor force meant an increasing need for technical
training, especially of the adult population. Literacy and public education
were spreading rapidly, and although the rural population may have used the
new literacy for their own utilitarian ends, there is evidence that among the
lower white-collar occupations and the skilled workers in the cities, horizons
were expanding rapidly.[27] For urban women of leisure, opportunities for education and independence materialized so suddenly that Russia was arguably
ahead of its time.[28] Predictably, expectations grew even faster. No matter how
active Moscow's municipal government, it was unable to keep up with the
increasing needs and demands of its residents; into this vacuum stepped the
city's public-oriented associations.

A third explanation for the growth in voluntary associations can be found in

---

Business Elite: A Social and Cultural Portrait of Two Generations, 1840–1905 (DeKalb: Northern
Illinois University Press, 1984).

[26] I develop this argument more in "Moscow: From Big Village to Metropolis." For more on
the city government, see Walter Hanchett, "Moscow in the Late Nineteenth Century: A Study in
Municipal Self-Government" (Ph.D. diss., University of Chicago, 1964); and Robert Thurston,
Liberal City, Conservative State: Russia's Urban Crisis, 1906–1914 (Oxford: Oxford University
Press, 1987).

[27] Ben Eklof, *Russian Peasant Schools: Officialdom, Village Culture, and Popular Pedagogy,
1861–1914* (Berkeley: University of California Press, 1986); and Jeffrey Brooks, *When Russia
Learned to Read: Literacy and Popular Literature, 1861–1917* (Princeton: Princeton University
Press, 1985).

[28] Richard Stites, *The Women's Liberation Movement in Russia: Feminism, Nihilism, and Bolshevism, 1860–1930* (Princeton: Princeton University Press, 1978).

the increased interest in Russian national culture and Russian public issues during the second half of the nineteenth century. Many manifestations of this interest are well known—populism, "small deeds" liberalism, the discovery of native and folk themes in art.[29] The lode of material regarding folk culture and the native land beckoned learned and philanthropic associations such as the Society of Natural Science, Anthropology and Ethnography and the Moscow Archaeological Society. The Moscow Slavic Conference and Ethnography Exhibition of 1867, sponsored by the former society, was a product of and further promoted this interest in native culture.[30] Likewise, one ingredient of the "singular popularity and fertile activity" of the Moscow Archaeological Society was its study of Russian archaeology and local monuments.[31]

Moments of national pride or shame galvanized the public to step in where autocracy was unable, or unwilling, to satisfy national needs. Thus, for example, the War with Turkey in 1877–1878 stimulated private, voluntary relief activity. Moreover, the unpopularity of the war in certain quarters prompted a wave of "unofficial" sorrow for the fallen soldier and generated Russia's first antiwar songs and paintings.[32] Later, government efforts to relieve the famine of 1891 were widely perceived to be inept; this brought on feelings of guilt among the educated classes, prompted more private voluntary relief efforts, and stimulated further associational activity.[33] Not all moments of national anguish were directed against the autocracy. When two decades of unrelenting radical pressure against the foundations of Russia's social and political order culminated in the assassination of Alexander II, the "Tsar-Liberator," on March 1, 1881, the destructiveness of the radical intelligentsia was attacked. In place of the "quarrelsome and contentious," to recall Locke, Russia needed the "industrious and rational," and the era of small deeds liberalism championed sober, practical, and constructive associational activity.

Few would argue that Russia needed practical, constructive activity. Did Moscow's voluntary associations fill the bill? An analysis of the membership,

[29] See Theofanis George Stavrou, ed., *Art and Culture in Nineteenth-Century Russia* (Bloomington: Indiana University Press, 1983), esp. essays by S. Frederick Starr, Elizabeth Kridl Valkenier, and Alison Hilton.

[30] Obshchestvo liubitelei estestvozaniia, antropologii i etnografii, *Vserossiiskaia etnograficheskaia vystavka i slavianskii s''ezd* (Moscow: Katkov, 1867). See also L. D. Alekseeva, "Moskovskii universitet i stanovlenie prepodavaniia etnografii v dorevoliutsionnoi Rossii," *Vestnik Moskovskogo universiteta*, ser. 8; *Istoriia* no. 6 (1983): 54–62.

[31] Vzdorpov, *Istoriia otkrytiia*, 139–40.

[32] Recall, for example, Vereshchagin's "Apotheosis of War." The warrior in Mussorgsky's "Polkovodets," the final song in the composer's cycle of "Songs and Dances of Death," is Death, who "surveys the ghastly field with pride" and proclaims "the Victory is mine! . . . Men shall forget what you fought for today." These statements about the futility of war and the "unofficial sorrow" they reflect must be contrasted with the "official," bombastic, and warlike sorrow for war dead that is a well-known feature of both tsarist and Soviet governments.

[33] Richard G. Robbins, Jr., *Famine in Russia, 1891–1892* (New York: Columbia University Press, 1975).

goals, internal and external conflicts, and political participation of Moscow's voluntary associations is beyond the scope of a short essay, and only a tentative answer can be offered here. Three important ongoing public activities may be singled out—publications, education, and sponsorship of museums and exhibitions. As David Blackbourn has argued regarding Germany, associational activity was most influential when it was quiet, natural, and anonymous.

The many bulletins, minutes of meetings, and transactions spread information about the parent society and contained news about similar societies in other cities. In this way, publications provided a national networking at a time when national organizations, unions, and even congresses were anathema to the autocracy. Many serials also contained scholarly and scientific articles that disseminated information regarding the field of interest of the parent society. These publications acted as the conveyor belts along which passed Russia's cultural intermediaries—teachers and physicians, for example—in their attempts to enlighten the common people. Most prolific in issuing publications were the Pirogov Society of Physicians and the Society of Natural Science, Anthropology, and Ethnography.[34] More popular publications included the Pirogov Society's booklets on public hygiene, the lectures and summaries of the Society of Public Universities, published by Sytin, the Readings for the Home and the Programs for Self-Education published by the Society for the Dissemination of Technical Knowledge, and many others.[35]

By offering classes, by systematically studying educational questions, or by organizing public lectures and opening libraries and reading rooms, several associations were directly involved in urban education. A few societies—the Polytechnical Society, the Russian Society of Engineers, and the Society for the Dissemination of Technical Knowledge—sponsored sections that studied and formulated educational policy.[36] Given the existence of both private schools and a public primary school system and given the needs of a growing

[34] A bibliography of the publications of the latter society is contained in *Izdaniia obshchestva: Bibliograficheskii ukazatel'*, 2 vols. (Moscow, 1894–1913), reprinted from the society's *Izvestiia*, vols. 89, 127. Among the publications of the Pirogov society were *Zhurnal, Trudy s''ezdov, Zemsko-meditsinskii sbornik, Obshchestvennyi vrach, Russkaia zemskaia meditsina, Zemskaia sanitarnaia statistika*. Other important serial publications included: Moskovskoe obshchestvo rasprostraneniia estestvennykh znanii, *Izvestiia*; Moskovskoe obshchestvo sel'sko-khoziaistva, *Trudy* (1877–1917); and Moskovskoe politekhnicheskoe obshchestvo, *Biulleteni* (1893–1914).

[35] On the public universities, see Iu. S. Vorob'eva, "Moskovskii gorodskoi narodnyi universitet im. A. L. Shaniavskogo," *Gosudarstvennoe rukovodstvo vysshei shkoloi v dorevoliutsionnoi Rossii i v SSSR* (Moscow: Moskovskii gosudarstvennyi istoriko-arkhivnyi institut, 1979), 170–89. On the readings for the home, see Obshchestvo rasprostraneniia tekhnicheskikh znanii, Komissiia po organizatsii domashnego chteniia, *Programmy dlia samoobrazovaniia* and *Programmy domashnego chteniia* (Moscow: I. D. Sytin, 1895–1900). V. Storozhev reviewed the activities in "Piatiletie moskovskoi komissii po organizatsii domashnego chteniia," *Obrazovanie*, no. 2 (February 1898): 36–54.

[36] The Society of Russian Engineers had a Commission for Technical Education. See its *Trudy*, 1874–1897.

and increasingly specialized urban economy, this involvement in education emphasized technical, vocational, and adult education.[37] Actual classes were offered by the Society for the Dissemination of Vocational Education, the Society to Study and Disseminate Accounting, and the Society of Retail Trade. In conjunction with the municipality, several societies ran general, vocational-technical, and business schools, many of which also organized adult education programs in the evening and on Sundays. For example, both the Russian Society of Engineers and the Society for the Dissemination of Technical Knowledge ran mechanics' schools and sponsored public lectures and free drafting classes. In 1893 the latter society initiated correspondence courses, modeled after British and American self-education programs.[38] Business schools, many of which opened in the 1890s and demonstrated the business community's commitment to education, also contributed to the rapid expansion of secondary education in Moscow. For example, in 1897 the banker Aleksei S. Vishniakov organized the Society for Commercial Education to give technical training to clerks already employed and to prepare young students for careers in business.[39]

Public lectures, reading rooms, and public libraries facilitated the efforts at general adult education. The first public lecture hall was opened in 1874 by the Commission to Organize Public Readings, itself founded by the Society to Disseminate Useful Books. According to the society's annual reports, at first the audience regarded the lecture hall as a place of entertainment where for two kopecks one could see magic lantern shows. By the 1890s, however, this attitude allegedly changed, and the "public began to regard the lecture halls as centers created for their continuing education and an enormous number of people began to flock to them."[40] In 1898 the Society to Organize Educational Public Amusements began to sponsor public lectures, along with slide shows, promenades, concerts, and plays.[41] Other societies opening reading rooms or organizing public lectures were the Society to Study and Disseminate Ac-

[37] Vocational, technical, and adult education have received little attention. See O. Kaidanova, *Ocherki po istorii narodnogo obrazovaniia v Rossii i v SSSR* (Berlin: Petropolis Verlag, 1939), and S. Elkina, *Ocherki po agitatsii, propagande i vneshkol'noi rabote v dorevoliutsionnoi Rossii* (Moscow: Gosizdat, 1930); these contain chapters on technical, vocational, and adult education. Prerevolutionary studies include V. P. Vakhterov, *Vneshkol'noe obrazovanie naroda* (Moscow: Sytin, 1896); and V. P. Vakhterov, *Vsenarodnoe shkol'noe i vneshkol'noe obrazovanie* (Moscow, 1917), E. O. Vakhterova, *Kak organizovat', otkryt', i vesti voskresenuiu shkolu (klassy) dlia vzroslykh v gorode i derevne* (Moscow, 1909); V. I. Charnolusskii, *Nastol'naia kniga po vneshkol'nomu obrazovaniiu* (St. Petersburg, 1913).

[38] *Istoriia Moskvy* 4: 662.

[39] Owen, *Capitalism and Politics*, 153.

[40] P. V. Krotkov, "Deiatel'nost' Komissii po ustroistvu v Moskve publichnykh narodnykh chtenii," *Izvestiia Moskovskoi gorodskoi dumy*, pt. 1 (July–August 1896): 22–27.

[41] "Obshchestvo sodeistviia k ustroistvu obshcheobrazovatel'nykh narodnykh razvlechenii," *Izvestiia Moskovskoi gorodskoi dumy*, pt. 1 (June 1898): 17–18.

counting, the Pirogov Society, the Society of Public Universities, the Society of Free Public Libraries, the Society for the Diffusion of Technical Knowledge, and the Temperance Society.[42] Similar to British and American university extension programs were the city's two public (or "people's") universities, the first run by the Society of Public Universities and the second, the Shaniavskii Public University, run by the City Council.[43] Their "public" goals were clearly stated: "The Public University is a free cultural institution with a single goal—the diffusion of science among all strata of the population. . . . The basic goal of the [Shaniavskii] University is to disseminate advanced scientific education and instill a love of science and knowledge among the people."[44] All programs of adult education aimed at nothing less than "the democratization of knowledge," "the levelling of social classes," and "the breaking of all barriers between people."[45]

Perhaps the most visible example of civic activity on the part of the city's associations was the creation of museums and exhibitions. Two organizations stand out in this type of civic activity—the Moscow Section of the Russian Society of Engineers and the Imperial Society of Natural Science, Anthropology and Ethnography. The former, in 1901, founded the Museum for Assistance to Labor. Modeled after the Paris Musée Sociale, the Museum for Assistance to Labor launched a two-pronged effort to practice what was called "social," as opposed to political, economy.[46] The museum collected data to help management improve the material conditions of workers; it also organized public lectures, classes, and exhibitions to help workers improve themselves. The museum became a focal point for progressively inclined professionals and the representatives of craft and clerical associations, but it also participated in the Zubatov experiment of "police socialism." In 1905 it sheltered the organizations and meetings of bakers and railway and municipal employees, organized the first All-Russian Conference of Representatives of Professional Unions, and even provided the hall for the first two meetings of what was to become the Moscow city soviet.[47]

Best known for its broad educational activities was the Museum of Science

---

[42] B. Raymond, "Libraries and Adult Education: The Russian Experience," *Journal of Library History* 16 (1981): 394–403; N. F. Sumtsov, "Organizatsiia obshchestvennykh razvlechenii," *Obrazovanie*, no. 1 (January 1898): 29–43.

[43] See *Pervyi Vserossiiskii s"ezd deiatelei obshchestv narodnykh universitetov i drugikh prosvetitel'nykh uchrezhdenii chastnoi initsiativy*, *Trudy* (St. Petersburg: Sever, 1908); and El'kina, *Ocherki*, 209–15.

[44] *Vsia Moskva za 1912 g.*, cols. 259–60.

[45] V. Storozhev, "Po povodu otcheta Moskovskoi Kommissii domashnego chteniia," *Obrazovanie* 3 (1897), 75.

[46] On the Paris Musée sociale, see S. Elwitt, "Social Reform and the Social Order," 431–51.

[47] Laura Engelstein, *Moscow 1905: Working-Class Organization and Political Conflict* (Stanford: Stanford University Press, 1982), 81, 100, 116, 156, 163. The museum published pamphlets on the trade union movement beginning in 1906.

and Industry, built on the basis of the Russian Exposition of Science and Industry in 1872. Organized jointly by the Society of Natural Science, Anthropology and Ethnography and the City Council, the museum was an example of cooperation between associations and the city government. Beginning in 1878 the Museum sponsored public lectures, discussions, and Sunday tours pitched at the worker.[48] By the turn of the century, the museum resembled an open university; indeed the Society of Public Universities sponsored classes on law, economics, literature, natural sciences, and medicine all held at the museum.[49] At first attended largely by the intelligentsia and lower white-collar workers, these classes attracted more and more blue-collar workers.[50] By providing meeting halls and auditorium space free of charge to numerous other societies, the museum became a civic center, contributing substantially to both adult education and civic life.

The Museum of Science and Industry was only one of many museums through which Moscow's educated classes tried to spread learning and culture to the general public by means of permanent exhibitions. Among the many special exhibitions which were also held in Moscow were expositions of Ethnography (1867), Anthropology (1879), Geography (1892), Archaeology (1890), Agriculture (1864), Electricity (1892), Art, Architecture and Construction (1904), and Photography (1902).[51] But perhaps best known for their lavishness were the Exposition of Science and Industry in 1872 and the All-Russian Exposition of Industry and the Arts ten years later.[52]

Grand expositions in Russia, like those all over Europe and America during the second half of the nineteenth century, were major events that displayed the latest developments in science, industry, and the arts and showed off native industry and crafts to foreign visitors.[53] The 1882 Exhibition of Industry and the Arts in Moscow was no exception.[54] Its official Report recognized that everywhere industry—in the broadest sense, that is, the productive capacities

---

[48] "Voskresnye ob"iasneniia kollektsii" were published in fourteen installments in the society's *Izvestiia* beginning in 1878.

[49] N. N. Pozdniakov, "Politekhnicheskii muzei i ego nauchno-prosvetitel'noi deiatel'nosti 1872–1917 gg.. Rabota peredovykh russkikh uchenykh v Politekhnicheskom muzee," *Istoriia muzeinogo dela v SSSR* (Moscow: Gosudarstvennoe Izd-vo kul'turno-prosvetitel'noi literatury, 1957), 129–58.

[50] *Istoriia Moskvy* 4: 636; 5: 469–70.

[51] Many special purpose exhibitions are listed in Mezhenko, *Russkaia tekhnicheskaia periodika*.

[52] On the 1872 Exposition Obshchestvo liubitelei estestvoznaniia, antropologii i etnografii, see *Obshchee obozrenie Moskovskoi politekhnicheskoi vystavki* (Moscow: Moskovskii universitet, 1872); and Marietta Shaginian's historical novel, *Pervaia Vserosskiiskaia* (Moscow: Molodaia gvardiia, 1965).

[53] Guy Stanton Ford, "International Exhibitions," *Encyclopedia of the Social Sciences* (New York: Macmillan, 1933), 6: 23–27.

[54] The following discussion is based on *Otchet o Vserossiiskoi khudozhestvenno-promyshlennoi vystavke 1882 g. v Moskve* 6 vols. (St. Petersburg: V. Bezobrazov, 1884).

of a nation—had become the major determinant of a nation's power and prestige. A nation could display its power and prestige by displaying its industrial,
scientific, and cultural achievements. Fittingly, the phrase "industrial celebra-
tion" was used repeatedly as a synonym for the exhibition. By discovering
that Russian industry was capable of producing articles of taste and refinement, foreigners would recognize that Russia was truly an educated, well-
ordered (*blagoustroennaia*) European nation.

Impressing Europeans, of course, has been a venerable tradition in Russia,
but Europeans were not the most important people to impress. One intended
benefit of the exposition was bolstering Russian self-esteem regarding its own
industry, long assumed by Russians themselves to be inferior. To prosper in
the modern age, the report argued, industry needed the spirit of risk, self-
confidence, enterprise, forward movement, competition, and public discussion (*glasnost'*). But the recent wave of terror and government repression,
coupled with the alleged propensity of Russia's upper classes to "self-accu-
sation and negativism," had paralyzed society and, with it, economic life.
Russia was plagued by "negative attitudes" and "groundless pessimism."
Hence the most important "moral consequence" of the exhibition was restor-
ing faith in the nation's strength.

In this type of civic activity the resemblance between Moscow and Victorian cities in Europe and America is striking. Students of what has been called
the "museum movement" agree that the Victorians placed much emphasis on
the utility of museums for education, self-improvement, cultural enrichment,
rational leisure, social unity, civic pride, and national purpose.[55] Moreover,
through such philanthropies and activities for the public good, business interests and professionals of Europe and America presented a claim to social leadership and to stewardship over the worker.[56]

Moscow's voluntary associations contributed significantly to the formation of
sensibilities, commonly thought of as middle-class in Western Europe and
North America and to the development of Russian obshchestvennost'. By providing forums for Russia's burgeoning professional groups and by emphasizing the values of merit and technical competence, the city's associations promoted professionalization, so important to the formation of middle-class
identity in Victorian Europe and America. Indeed, given Russia's archaic estate structure and the increasing discontent of liberal professionals over their
lack of rights and perquisites and the impediments to national organization, as

---

[55] See, for example, Kenneth Hudson, *A Social History of Museums: What the Visitors Thought*
(London: Macmillan, 1975), 46; David Burg, *Chicago's White City of 1893* (Lexington: University Press of Kentucky, 1976); and D. K. Van Keuren, "Museums and Ideology: Augustus Pitt-
Rivers, Anthropology Museums and Social Change in Later Victorian Britain," *Victorian Studies*
28 (1984): 171–89.

[56] McCarthy, *Noblesse Oblige*.

Gregory Freeze has recently reminded us, it is hard to imagine professionalization without local voluntary associations.[57] In addition, through philanthropies the city's entrepreneurs and professionals claimed stewardship over the worker and thereby developed an important ingredient of Western middleclass identity: belief in individual self-improvement for the aspiring accomplished by means of adult education and rational use of leisure. Like the instruments of education and literacy, organizations and activities aimed at the worker aspired to "enlarge the mind," "make better citizens," and improve taste. Voluntary associations reinforced values commonly associated with the middle classes and commonly regarded as deficient in autocratic Russia: opportunity, individual initiative, autonomy, self-reliance, self-improvement, a spirit of enterprise, industriousness, rationality, the ability to control one's destiny, and a belief in science and progress.

Voluntary associations arguably played an even greater role in developing Russian obshchestvennost'. Associations provided meeting grounds and conveyors between the new entrepreneurial, professional, and cultural elites and between the new elites and the state. For example, according to a Soviet historian, the public meetings and the *"nesoslovnyi kharakter"* (nonestate nature) of the Moscow Archaeological Society allowed "village priests, *meshchane*, peasants, and women to sit alongside the customary aristocrats and even members of the imperial family."[58] The myriad of societies and associations that sprang up in the last two generations before the Revolution offered an opportunity to correct the alleged spasms of public life, to introduce elements of equilibrium and steadiness, to provide outlets for the "industrious and rational," and to achieve national unity and reconciliation. More important, associations cultivated a capacity for individual initiative channeled toward certain spheres of practical activity—education, civic culture, rational leisure, the public good—that avoided both the selfish and rapacious pursuit of gain rejected by Russian Orthodoxy and traditional Russian culture and the nihilism of the radical intelligentsia rejected by Russian liberals. Associations were marriages of self-interest with the public interest, of individualism with the common good, and (so striking a feature of the Russian art world at the time) of European imports with old Russian culture. Thus, associational activity promoted that sense of public duty and civic spirit that had been missing from Russian national life.

Associational life was not without its contradictions, which became more visible in the 1905 Revolution. Although discussion of associations' participation in national politics lies outside the scope of this paper, one contradiction may be readily noted. Many associations promised a breakdown of the barriers

[57] Gregory Freeze, "The Soslovie (Estate) Paradigm and Russian Social History," *American Historical Review* 91, no. 1 (1986): 28–29.

[58] Vzdorpov, *Istoriia otkrytiia*, 140.

of tradition, the estate system, and state service, yet they also promoted new identities and groupings based on craft, profession, culture, and choice. Inevitably, as conflicts arose within organizations, as among the teachers in 1905, and between organizations and the government, new barriers divided no less than old.[59] Herein lies an important flaw in *obshchestvennost'* and in Russia's nascent civil society, which was hardly as "primordial" as Gramsci believed. In its attempts to limit the central power, to create new and autonomous centers of power, and to train the populace in political skills, it became an increasingly articulate competitor to autocracy and officialdom in an effort to reconstitute political society. Yet, civil society remained "gelatinous" and brittle; obshchestvennost' created new fault lines and fissures. To extend Gramsci's argument, not only was civil society unwilling or unable to defend the state, but it was also unable to defend itself.

Nevertheless, voluntary associations did not create the conditions in which they existed. I allow Tocqueville the last word. How to protect the individual from arbitrary rule in both aristocratic and democratic countries concerned the Frenchman. Aristocratic countries abounded, he argued, in wealthy and influential individuals who could not easily be suppressed. Democractic countries, lacking such individuals naturally, could create them artificially: "I think that private citizens, by combining together, may constitute bodies of great wealth, influence, and strength, corresponding to the persons of an aristocracy. . . . An association for political, commercial, or manufacturing purposes, or even for those of science and literature, is a powerful and enlightened member of the community, which cannot be disposed of at pleasure or oppressed without remonstrance and which, by defending it own rights against the encroachments of the government, saves the common liberties of the country."[60] As associations *saved* the common liberties in a democratic country, they aspired to *create* them in an autocratic country.

[59] See the essays by Ruane and Eklof and by Balzer in this volume, and Jonathan Sanders, "The Union of Unions: Political, Economic, Civil and Human Rights Organizations in the 1905 Russian Revolutionary" (Ph.D. diss., Columbia University, 1985). I discuss national congresses, an extremely visible and political form of associational activity in "Reform from Below: Association, Assembly, and the Autocracy, 1906–1914," a paper presented for the Kennan Institute Conference, "Reform in Russian and Soviet History: Its Meaning and Function," May 5–7, 1990. On the evolution of civil society in the post-1905 period, see Manfred Hagen, *Die Entfaltung politischer Offentlichkeit in Russland, 1906–1914* (Wiesbaden: F. Steiner, 1982).

[60] *Democracy in America*, 2: 342.

Chapter 10

IDEOLOGY, IDENTITY, AND THE EMERGENCE OF A MIDDLE CLASS

William G. Wagner

Despite important differences between and among them, prerevolutionary Russian liberals and, until recently, Western historians of Russia generally have shared a common paradigm for interpreting Russia's past. At the basis of each group's explanation of Russian history lies an idealized account of Western European, especially English, history according to which the emergence of a middle class ultimately gave rise to liberalism, parliamentary government, and political democracy. Russian liberals and Western historians alike thus portray post-Petrine Russia as either broadly conforming to this allegedly normal pattern of development or deviating from it. But in either case their principal concern has been to explain the fate of political democracy—either its limited success or its stunted development—in Russia. Moreover, central to these explanations has been the relative strength of a middle class whose degree of development is measured by the extent to which its members professed democratic values. Hence, in the view of prerevolutionary Russian liberals and many Western historians, the spread of education, the introduction of limited representative institutions, and economic growth prior to the First World War were producing an informed, civic-minded public—*obshchestvo*—capable of acting independently in political affairs and thereby overcoming the unbalanced relationship that had existed historically between the autocratic state and Russian society. Although divided between liberals and socialists, this civic-minded public was united in its opposition to the allegedly arbitrary authority of the tsarist regime, which in turn represented an anachronistic impediment to progress. In contrast, other Western historians have emphasized the continued strength of the state relative to society and, especially, the absence of a middle class capable of forcing the autocracy to share its power. Thus, regardless of their disagreement over the prospects for political democracy in Russia, adherents of both views depict the tsarist state as alienated from society and unified in its resistance to liberalizing reform.

Although yielding many useful insights, this approach to Russian history can obscure as much as it reveals about Russia's recent past. In particular, by emphasizing the conflict between the state and society, it tends to exaggerate both the degree of unity within the tsarist state and the extent of the state's

isolation from educated society. Moreover, by identifying the middle class—
or obshchestvo—with democratic values, whether liberal or socialist, it can
understate the extent of ideological diversity within educated society and obscure the effect of this diversity on social and political stability in the final
years of the tsarist regime. These problems derive in part from the tendencies
both to assume that a homogeneous set of values and beliefs, that is, a specific
consciousness or ideology, is natural for a given sociological group and to
interpret the absence or limited expression of these attitudes as evidence of
this group's weak or even deformed development. If this assumption is abandoned, however, and the possibility—and even likelihood—of fundamental
ideological diversity within a sociologically defined class is accepted, then the
history of Late Imperial Russia appears differently.

From this perspective both the state bureaucracy and the privileged and educated elements of society appear to have been divided along similar ideological lines. Members of both groups responded to the educational, social, and
economic changes taking place in post-Emancipation Russia by formulating
various competing ideologies that redefined their self-identity, social role, and
the criteria for determining social status in ways that also explained these
changes.[1] In addition, ideological allies within state officialdom and educated
society were frequently divided by occupational, institutional, gender, or other
rivalries. These ideological and other conflicts produced fragmentation as
much as cohesion within the bureaucracy and Russian obshchestvo on the eve
of the First World War, thereby complicating both the efforts of the government to deal with the problems confronting it and the subsequent search by
Western historians for a Russian middle class. This conflict and fragmentation
can be seen clearly in the attempts to reform divorce law made by the government and the Orthodox Church in the early twentieth century.

Throughout the imperial period, Russian marriage law both reflected and
sought to reinforce the patriarchal values and hierarchical relations that underlay the autocratic regime, traditional Russian society, and the Orthodox
Church. Drawing heavily on church teachings, the law proclaimed the husband to be head of the family and granted him extensive authority over his
wife, including the power to control her place of residence, employment, and
access to higher education. A wife in turn was obligated to live with her husband and obey him completely. Reinforcing the husband's authority, the law
considered marital strife a personal affair and consequently left the efforts of
a husband to discipline his wife outside its purview. Thus, Russian law in
effect completely subordinated a wife to the power of her husband and left her
no means of legal redress apart from a criminal action for severe injury.[2]

---

[1] My definition of ideology owes much to the ideas of Clifford Geertz; see particularly his essay
"Ideology as a Cultural System," in *The Interpretation of Cultures* (New York, 1973), 193–233.

[2] *Svod zakonov Rossiiskoi Imperii* (St. Petersburg, 1857), 10:1, arts. 100–108, 2202, and 1–
118 generally on marriage.

This religious and patriarchal conception of marriage made divorce difficult to obtain, particularly for members of the Orthodox Church. Each faith recognized officially by the state defined and administered its own rules for divorce, and those established by the Orthodox Church were among the most stringent. The church permitted divorce only for prolonged disappearance, criminal exile to Siberia, sexual incapacity arising before marriage, or adultery, which required proof by several eyewitnesses. Spouses guilty of adultery, abandonment, or sexual incapacity, moreover, were permanently prohibited from remarrying.[3] Nor did marital separation provide a feasible alternative to divorce. Because separation was formally prohibited except for members of the Catholic faith, informal agreements to separate were unenforceable and left women especially in a vulnerable position. A woman living apart from her husband had no right to his support, and the husband in turn could impede his wife's ability to support herself by controlling her passport or refusing her permission to enter employment. Their children, too, could be declared illegitimate, subjecting them to harsh legal disabilities as well as severe social stigmas.[4] Dissolving a marriage thus proved extremely difficult under Russian law. Indeed, as church leaders stated repeatedly, the purpose of the law was to discourage divorce as a violation of the holy sacrament of marriage.[5]

By all accounts, the principles underlying imperial law accurately reflected the relations and attitudes that prevailed in marriages within all social groups in Russia during the early nineteenth century. Social life tended to be organized around patrilineal family networks and local communities in which parental arrangement of marriages to benefit the family, unequal relations based on age and gender, and subordination of the individual to the group predominated. Prior to midcentury, moreover, juridical and theological writing as well as tsarist educational policy also firmly supported the principles of patriarchal authority and inequality embedded in the law.[6] Although resulting partly from tsarist censorship, this support also derived from conviction. Not hesitant to criticize other aspects of Russian law, the noted professor of civil law at Kazan University, Dmitry Meier, in his influential treatise first published posthu-

---

[3] Ibid., arts. 45–60, and 11:1, *Ustav dukhovnykh del innostrannykh ispovedenii.*

[4] Ibid., 10:1, arts. 119–63, 1119.

[5] *Tsentral'nyi gosudarstvennyi istoricheskii arkhiv* (Leningrad), hereafter *TsGIA*, f. 1405, op. 542, d. 663, ll. 117–23; f. 796, op. 445, d. 417, ll. 1–13, pp. 4–21; f. 797, op. 91–1898, d. 53, ll. 77–78.

[6] For example, see A. I. Kranikhfel'd, *Nachertanie rossiiskago grazhdanskago prava v istoricheskom ego razvitii* (St. Petersburg, 1843), 10–14, 19, 28–40, 51–55; K. A. Nevolin, *Polnoe sobranie sochinenii K. A. Nevolina* (St. Petersburg, 1857, 1858), 3: 45–87, 92–151, 246–63, 303–90; Arkhimandrit Fotii, "Vzaimnyia khristianskiia otnoshcniia suprugov," *Strannik* 8(1861): pt. 2, 63–69; B. Engel, *Mothers and Daughters. Women of the Intelligentsia in Nineteenth-Century Russia* (Cambridge, 1983), 23–27; G. Freeze, *The Parish Clergy in Nineteenth-Century Russia. Crisis, Reform, and Counter-Reform* (Princeton, 1983), 133–39, 178–79; and N. Riasanovsky, *Nicholas I and Official Nationality in Russia, 1825–1855* (Berkeley, 1959), 91–96.

mously in 1858 described marriage as a social institution governed primarily by religious and moral laws. He therefore accepted both ecclesiastical jurisdiction and the relationship of authority and obedience between husband and wife, which underlay substantive law, as corresponding to the nature and purpose of marriage.[7]

By the 1860s, however, a number of developments had begun to undermine the social as well as the ideological foundations of the law. By emphasizing individuality, personal judgment, and merit over uncritical acceptance of tradition and ascribed status within a collective group, these developments led especially educated Russians to question the existing basis of social relations and status and to reconceptualize the nature of marriage accordingly. Perhaps foremost among these developments was the spread of specialized higher education, which contributed to occupational as well as bureaucratic professionalization by emphasizing the allegedly rational solution of problems by those with technical expertise. The social composition of the elite created by this process cut across existing sociolegal categories as people from outside the nobility gained access to higher education, noblemen deprived of their serfs by the Emancipation of 1861 abandoned their estates and sought alternative sources of income, and women were admitted to some professions. The growth of industry and commerce as well as the extension and increased functional specialization of the state administration expanded both the opportunities for employment and the influence of members of this educated and professional elite. As a result of these developments, members of this elite began to perceive social relations in terms of occupation, personal merit, and educational background rather than family and social estate.

This shift in self-perception also gained impetus from several cultural and intellectual trends during the nineteenth century. In their training and occupational practice, members of the professional elite were exposed to specialized Western European literature that emphasized the rights, health, or development of the individual. In the first half of the century, literary and philosophical romanticism likewise focused attention on the individual's emotions, feelings, and personality, while many theories of political economy dominant in the latter part of the century stressed the necessity of releasing the individual's energies for economic development.

These developments provoked a controversy within the educated elite over the nature of marriage. By the late nineteenth century, considerable pressure was accumulating for reform of divorce law. But far more was at stake in this controversy than simply alleviating the problems said to be caused by outdated and restrictive legal rules. Reform of the law unavoidably involved redefining fundamental social relationships, the nature of authority, and the relationship between the state and the Orthodox Church. Advocates of reform believed that

---

[7] D. I. Meier, *Russkoe grazhdanskoe pravo*, 2d ed. (St. Petersburg, 1862), 499–562.

it would help provide the foundation for a society based on legality, civil equality, and, frequently, greater public participation in political life; conservatives opposed reform as a threat to social and political order. This ideological and political conflict within educated society and state officialdom became intertwined with institutional rivalries within the government, which themselves often reflected the competing interests of different professional groups. Members of the emerging professional elite in turn used legal reform as a means to promote their own occupational interests, particularly at the expense of the church. At the same time, the Orthodox Church itself became torn by reform proposals that in part reflected more fundamental conflicts over its structure, governance, and doctrines.

Reflecting this diversity of objectives, efforts to reform the law during this period arose chiefly from two separate sources. On the one hand, a series of commissions formed in the Ministry of Justice proposed to relax divorce laws substantially in order to protect wives who were mistreated by their husbands and to eliminate the widespread fraud that existed in divorce cases. Although directed toward practical ends, these proposals also challenged traditional conceptions of authority by emphasizing individual rights, elevated the secular over the religious aspects of marriage, and greatly extended the influence of the Ministry of Justice, the civil courts, and the jurists who dominated these institutions.[8] At the same time, a parallel series of committees established by the Holy Synod, the main governing body of the Orthodox Church, became deeply divided over whether to allow divorce more frequently while endeavoring to defend the religious nature of marriage and the church's jurisdiction over it.[9] Both efforts eventually merged in an interdepartmental commission formed in 1916 under the auspices of the Holy Synod to resolve the disputes blocking reform of the law. This commission, however, proved unable to overcome the ideological, occupational, and institutional conflicts that divided its members.[10]

The juristic case for reform was summarized in the draft civil code prepared by a special Editorial Commission that had been formed by the Minister of Justice in 1882. Indeed, the commission's proposals, published between 1899 and 1902, underlay all subsequent projects advanced by the ministry. Consisting entirely of jurists, the commission reflected the composition of the legal profession as a whole. Although hereditary nobles predominated, several members had belonged originally to other social estates. Because few nobles

[8] *Grazhdanskoe ulozhenie. Kniga vtoraia. Semeistvennoe pravo* 2 vols. (St. Petersburg, 1902), and *TsGIA*, f. 797, op. 91–1898, d. 53; op. 92–1901, d. 81a/81b; op. 92–1906, d. 68; op. 92–1914, d. 185; op. 96, d. 271; 1405, op. 542, d. 666–68, 670–72.

[9] *TsGIA*, f. 796, op. 445, d. 417, 420–21; f. 797, op. 96, d. 219. See also S. P. Grigorovskii, *O razvode. Prichiny i posledstviia razvoda i brakorazvodnoe sudoproizvodstvo. Istoriko-iuridicheskie ocherki* (St. Petersburg, 1911).

[10] *TsGIA*, f. 796, op. 445, d. 417.

on the commission owned land, most members of the commission relied primarily on the exercise of their professional expertise for their livelihood as well as for their status and self-esteem. They also shared specialized legal training in institutes of higher education, long careers in various fields within the legal profession, and a belief in the importance of law in regulating social and civil relationships.[11] Not surprisingly, therefore, their proposals reflected the dominant views within juridical writing on marriage law by the late nineteenth century.

Members of the commission used comparative historical methodology and sociological theory to formulate an evolutionary explanation of marriage that emphasized both the universality of the process and the progressive development of individuality, equality, legality, and knowledge. This explanation in turn deflected conservative criticism of the commission's proposals by demonstrating their historical legitimacy as well as their social utility and justness. According to this scheme, sociolegal development consisted of two parallel processes in which the conjugal family (*sem'ia*) gradually displaced the patrilineal kin-group (*rod*) and the autonomous individual gradually emerged from subordination to patriarchal authority. The two processes were considered closely interrelated, with the conjugal family, restructured on allegedly moral principles, creating the environment that enabled the individual's fullest development. Although members of the commission, like jurists generally, disagreed over the causes of this transition from clan to family, they all agreed that it transformed both the family's structure and its distribution of authority. In their view, the blood ties and patriarchal authority that bound the patrilineal clan together weakened as state law, religious precepts, reason, and economic development overcame the primitive conditions, instinctual nature, and physiological needs of early human society. This process gradually provided the individual with a separate social identity as well as the economic and legal ability to survive apart from the clan. As the individual gained autonomy, the commission argued, marriage came to be based more on the spouses' voluntary choice and their emotional affinity than on parental arrangement and calculated interests of the clan. Having freely chosen their wives, husbands no longer considered them chattel and outsiders to their clan but spiritual and moral partners. As affection between spouses gained primacy over kinship, the commission claimed, patriarchal authority gave way to a relationship based on mutual rights and moral obligations.[12]

Comparing Russian with Western European sociolegal development, the

---

[11] *Grazhdanskoe ulozhenie. Pribavlenie k proektu grazhdanskago ulozheniia.* (St. Petersburg, 1906), 57–61; and *TsGIA*, f. 1364, op. 15, d. 347, 400, 464, 471, 572, 588, 602, 670, 673, 722, 724, 767, 793, 848, 932, 1015. See also A. I. Lykoshin, "Pamiati A. A. Knirima (K istorii sostavleniia proekta grazhdanskago ulozheniia)," *Zhurnal ministerstva iustitsii* 10 (1905): 1–28.

[12] In addition to the references cited in note 8, see *Grazhdanskoe ulozhenie. Kniga chetvertaia. Nasledstvennoe pravo* (St. Petersburg, 1903), esp. the introduction.

commission concluded that Russia had reached the stage in this evolutionary process where the function of the family was to enable the fullest possible development of each member and to foster civic-spirited, patriotic, and productive citizens. This function could only be fulfilled, the commission contended, when family relations corresponded in practice to the equality of rights, mutuality of obligations, and affection that should exist naturally between family members. By supporting unlimited authority, demanding unquestioning obedience, and preserving inequality among family members, however, existing law distorted these relations and thereby prevented attainment of the family's social objectives. The commission claimed, for example, that granting the husband unlimited authority over his wife only encouraged his mistreatment of her. Likewise, it argued that compelling spouses to live together when the affective relations between them had broken down merely led to mutual hostility, degeneracy, and violence, all of which threatened the spiritual as well as physical well-being of both the spouses and their children.[13]

To avoid these harmful results, the commission proposed to limit the authority of the husband and to enhance the rights and legal security of his wife, in part by expanding the grounds for divorce, allowing marital separation, and shifting jurisdiction over both types of cases to the civil courts. In the view of the commission, allowing dissolution of a marriage or separation of the spouses when cohabitation proved unbearable for one or both partners would help ensure equality between spouses as well as provide relief for wives abused by their husbands. To justify secular jurisdiction in these cases, the commission claimed that jurists were better trained than priests to discover and weigh the facts in divorce actions. Perhaps more significant, the commission also attempted to distinguish rigidly between the external form and the internal relations of a marriage. Although recognizing the right of the church to determine the ceremony and rules governing entry into marriage, it argued that the relations between spouses once a marriage had been concluded should be regulated by the state in the public interest.[14]

While expressing a similar world view, the parallel demands for reform made by nonjurists reflected the particular perspective and interests of each group. At meetings of medical societies as well as in the committees established by the Holy Synod after 1906, physicians and psychologists favoring reform of the law stressed that marriage was a physiological and spiritual relationship that satisfied important human needs, especially that of procreation.

---

[13] *Grazhdanskoe ulozhenie. Semeistvennoe pravo*, 278–79, 296–98, 490–92, 516, and arts. (with commentary) 3, 108–40, 148–52, 163, 172–73, 176–77, 179, 197–99, 202, 253–54, 257, 284–302, 311–36; and *TsGIA*, f. 797, op. 91–1898, d. 53, ll. 29–70.

[14] *Grazhdanskoe ulozhenie. Semeistvennoe pravo*, iv–v, 42–52, 272–74, 278–80, 287–90, 296–98, 309–26, 331–32, 336–37, 341 and arts. (with commentary) 1–9, 12, 15–56, 59–88, 96–105, 112, 141–77, 179, 181, 186–96, 202, 216–24, 229, 233, 260.

Marriages therefore should be dissolved, they argued, whenever the physiological function of marriage could no longer be served or the mental union
between spouses became impossible. Compelling spouses to remain together
under these circumstances merely led to degeneracy, spread harmful diseases,
and endangered the physical and psychological health of other family members, thereby undermining the well-being of society. Reformist physicians
thus advocated including a number of mental and physiological maladies, to
be verified by medical experts in each case, among the grounds for divorce.[15]
Similarly, while often criticizing the inadequacy of proposals to reform the
law made by government committees, liberal and radical journalists invariably
supported them as a means of fostering progressive values and relationships
that they hoped would undermine the patriarchal foundations of the tsarist order.[16] The feminist movement, dominated by women drawn from Russia's
privileged and educated elites, likewise strongly favored relaxation of divorce
law as one way to break down the legal and cultural barriers that perpetuated
the inequality of women, impeded their access to education, and barred them
from many professional careers as well as social activities.[17]

While the reforms of the law demanded by jurists, physicians, journalists,
and feminists generally could be reconciled, those advocated by ecclesiastical
reformers could not. To be sure, important similarities existed. The theologians and ecclesiastical scholars who favored reform employed the same comparative-historical methodology and sociological theories as jurists to support
their argument that the church canons governing divorce did not constitute
immutable rules but embodied general principles whose external form varied
over time to suit changing historical conditions. The practical meaning of
these canons therefore had to be redefined in each historical situation to ensure

[15] For example, see *Obshchestvo russkikh vrachei v pamiat' N. I. Pirogova. Dnevnik shestogo
s"ezda russkikh vrachei* (Kiev, 1896), 12: 1; and supplement, 66–69; ibid., *Dnevnik sed'mogo
s"ezda* (Kazan, 1899), 3: 21–25, 13: 281–87; ibid., *Desiatyi s"ezd* (St. Petersburg, 1907);
L. Bertenson, *Fizicheskie povody k prekrashcheniiu brachnago soiuza. Nesposobnost' k brach-
nomu sozhitiiu. Bolezni. Durnoe ili zhestokoe obrashchenie* (Petrograd, 1917); "Zhurnal zasedaniia grazhdanskago otdeleniia Iuridicheskago Obshchestva 24 fevralia 1896," *Zhurnal iuridicheskago obshchestva pri Imp. S.-Peterburgskom Universitete* 10 (1896): supplement, 8–22;
TsGIA, f. 797, op. 91–1898, d. 53, ll. 34–70 (pp. 33–37); and f. 1405, op. 542, d. 671, ll. 2–34
(pp. 21–45), 106–97 (pp. 163–65), 256.

[16] For example, see *Russkie vedomosti* 299 (1898): 2, and 3 (1899): 2; "Popravki semeinago
prava," *Nedelia* 5 (1898): 145–49; *Vestnik evropy* 2 (1900): 812–18, and 4, 801–3; *Russkaia
mysl'* 2 (1898): 186–88, 12 (1902): 428–30, and 1 (1903): 38–40; and I. V. Gessen, "Razdel'noe
zhitel'stvo suprugov," *Pravo* 49 (1911): 2755–67, and 50, 2842–51.

[17] For example, see *Trudy pervago vserossiiskago zhenskago s"ezda pri russkom zhenskom
[Vzaimno-blagotvoritel'nom] obshchestve v S.-Peterburge 10–16 dekabria 1908 goda* (St. Petersburg, 1909), 11, 60–62, 344–48, 359–67, 374–86, 494–95, 512–19, 549–57, 589, 742, 754–
60, 768, 825; "Zasedanie komissii Ushinskago," *Pravo* 16 (1905): 1324–29, and M. Ia. Perga-
ment, "K predpologaemoi reforme brakorazvodnago protsessa," *Soiuz zhenshchin* 5–6 (1908):
15–18.

that the essential purposes of a Christian marriage be achieved. Like other advocates of reform, ecclesiastical reformers concluded that contemporary conditions necessitated expansion of the grounds for divorce. Compelling spouses to remain together once the spiritual bond between them had dissolved, they asserted, merely led to degenerate behavior that undermined rather than fulfilled the goals of a Christian marriage. But for ecclesiastical reformers, reform of the law also represented a means to reinvigorate the church spiritually and thereby increase its influence over society. They therefore opposed any proposal to shift jurisdiction over divorce cases to the civil courts because it would exclude the church from an important area of social life.[18]

Despite this conflict, however, the similarities between juristic, medical, ecclesiastical, and other advocates of reform demonstrate that elements of a common identity were emerging within a significant part of Russian obshchestvo by the early twentieth century. The campaign to reform divorce law—and civil law generally—both reflected and partly created the values, images, and aspirations defining this identity. Indeed, the image of marriage expressed by proponents of reform legitimized their ideals, values, and hopes more than it reflected the reality experienced by most Russians, especially the peasantry and lower urban strata, during this period.

By emphasizing freedom of choice and equality in marriage, it suggested that formal legal estates should be replaced by civil equality for all subjects. In criticizing patriarchal authority as subject to frequent abuse, it implied that social and political authority generally should be limited by civil and perhaps political rights enjoyed by all. The historical view of marriage as progressing toward equality and freedom for the individual likewise explained the changes occurring in Late Imperial Russia in a way that provided the educated and professional elite with considerable status, influence, and self-esteem. Through their understanding of this evolutionary process and their technical expertise, members of this elite could contribute to the development of Russia, in part by adjusting the law to their perception of contemporary social needs. Opposition to reform could be dismissed as the self-interested yet doomed attempt by outdated social groups to maintain their privileges. Thus demands to reform the law in accordance with this progressive image of marriage represented in part an attempt by advocates of reform to transform society to reflect their own social, professional, and sometimes even political values and interests.

Given these implications, the proposals made by the Editorial Commission and other advocates of reform not surprisingly provoked intense opposition

---

[18] In addition to the references to *TsGIA* in notes 8 and 9, see *Zhurnaly i protokoly Predsobornago Prisutstviia* (St. Petersburg, 1906–1907), 2:15–16 (4th sect.), 245, 320–23, and 4:97–138 (3rd sect., zhur. no. 24), 1–88 (comb. mtg., 3rd, 6th, and 7th sects., zhur. 1–4).

from conservatives, both within and outside the government. Yet opponents of reform did not simply represent the members of outdated classes clinging desperately to anachronistic privileges. In fact, they often shared the same social background, education, and careers as their progressive adversaries. Sergei Lukianov, for example, who helped block reform of the law while ober procurator of the Holy Synod between 1909 and 1911, was a respected pathologist and former professor of medicine. Konstantin Pobedonostsev, ober procurator from 1880 to 1905, was a noted jurist whose father had been a professor at Moscow University. Indeed, Pobedonostsev presented perhaps the most articulate defense of existing law in his influential treatise on Russian civil law first published between 1868 and 1880 and republished several times thereafter.[19] As an adviser to Alexander III and Nicholas II, Pobedonostsev also strongly influenced state as well as church policy toward divorce and on several occasions managed to block reforms proposed by the Ministry of Justice.[20]

In opposing reform, Pobedonostsev used the same comparative-historical approach as his adversaries and similar sociological theories to show that the relationships of authority and obedience supported by the law existed naturally in marriage and were necessary to preserve order within both family and society. According to him, the discipline and respect for authority fostered in the patriarchal family grew into social discipline and respect for state authority, which helped maintain social stability and political order. Reforms of the law that weakened this authority, especially by allowing wives to challenge or leave their husbands, would therefore undermine public order by subverting the family.[21]

For similar reasons Pobedonostsev defended the religious basis of marriage and consequently opposed all efforts to shift jurisdiction over divorce cases to the civil courts. The infusion of Christian ideals, he argued, had not only transformed marriage from a physiological and instinctual into a moral and spiritual relationship, but it had also strengthened marriage by making it an indissoluble sacrament patterned on the relationship between Christ and the church. This doctrine of indissolubility as well as the principle of submission to authority contained in Orthodox teaching reinforced the role of marriage in inculcating individual and social discipline, not least by discouraging irresponsible decisions over marriage and compelling spouses to remain with one another regardless of each other's faults.

Like other conservative jurists who opposed reform, Pobedonostsev also argued that existing law represented the cumulative outcome of Russia's historical development and thus embodied unique national and Orthodox

[19] K. P. Pobedonostsev, *Kurs grazhdanskago prava*, 4th ed., 3 vols. (St. Petersburg, 1896).

[20] *TsGIA*, f. 797, op. 91–1898, d. 53, ll. 1, 71–79, 92–97, 100–112, 114–24.

[21] Pobedonostsev, *Kurs* 2: 1–18, 44, 56–58, 79–84, 93–96, 110–13, 116–26, 166–68, 172, 176, 182–87.

traditions. To disrupt these traditions through reform based largely on foreign models would destabilize the social and political order and deflect Russia from its natural course of development. In contrast to progressive reformers, Pobedonostsev therefore interpreted the development of the law as a sign of vitality rather than disintegration. This long development proved, he asserted, that basic legal principles had survived for centuries, adapting successfully to constantly changing social and economic conditions. Rejecting demands to reform divorce law as an attempt to introduce inappropriate Western European institutions like civil marriage into Russia, he ascribed these demands to the irresponsible infatuation of intellectuals with abstract and alien ideas, especially the doctrines of socialism and unfettered individualism.

The doctrine of individualism in particular, declared Pobedonostsev, "strives insistently toward the complete destruction of any authority in all spheres of human life and, rejecting it in *religion*, in the *state*, and in *society*, just as decisively banishes it from the *family*."[22] The reforms of divorce law proposed by progressives would contribute to this erosion of authority, he feared, by undermining the traditional power of the husband and disrupting the cooperative relationship that had developed historically between the Orthodox Church and the tsarist state. Weakened by reform, neither family nor church would be able to constrain the egotistical impulses of individuals, who consequently would sacrifice state and collective interests to their selfish desires and personal whims.[23]

Conservative theologians and clergy, especially the bishops dominating the Holy Synod, voiced similar fears. Like Pobedonostsev, they viewed people as weak and egotistical, needing firm control. But in addition to a threat to public order, they saw in the proposals of the Ministry of Justice, of jurists generally, and even of the committees formed by the Synod, challenges to episcopal authority as well as to religious faith and Orthodox doctrine. Although the projects drafted by jurists entailed secularization of the power to define and administer marriage law, the proposals formulated by ecclesiastical reformers implied a change in both the nature of church doctrine and the power to interpret it.

Ecclesiastical conservatives consequently responded to demands for legal reform by reasserting the traditional interpretation of Orthodox doctrine. This doctrine, they declared, established absolute rules that were universally applicable regardless of historical circumstances. From this perspective, marriage was considered an inviolable sacrament that should be dissolved only for the single reason accepted by Christ—adultery. Divorce for other reasons was considered sinful, a temptation to the faithful to evade their Christian respon-

[22] Ibid., 96, emphasis in original.
[23] Ibid., 20, 26–28, 32–33, 36–38, 41–55, 58, 61, 69–72, 79–78, 93–101, 105–6, 110–11, 114–26, 177–78, 191–94, 210.

sibilities and yield to their weaknesses. Ecclesiastical conservatives thus concluded that reform of divorce law would only accelerate the deterioration of Christian morality that they believed was already taking place in Russian society under the influence of secularizing intellectuals. Exclaimed Metropolitan Vladimir of Moscow when rejecting the proposals drafted by a Synodal committee in 1908, ''Need we speak of how dangerous it would be to set off on the path of such concession especially in our time, when the materialistic world view has declared relentless war on Christianity, when we are threatened by the most dreadful revolution—the rising up of the spirit of this world against the spirit of God's [world]?''[24] Such sentiments left little room for compromise.

Arguments against reform advanced by conservative journalists and physicians essentially echoed those made by Pobedonostsev and clerics like Metropolitan Vladimir.[25] Embedded in all these arguments was a view of marriage that expressed values, attitudes toward the individual and authority, and a vision of historical development that were antithetical to those held by proponents of reform. Whereas progressive reformers defined marriage as a matrix of mutual rights and obligations that arose from affective relationships and fostered the individuality of both spouses, conservatives portrayed it as an institution based on patriarchal power, obedience to authority, and unequal status that protected society against the individual. Conservatives believed these latter relations were necessary for preserving order in the family and stability in society, but reformers argued that by unduly constraining the individual they intensified discontent and therefore destabilized society. The historical explanation of marriage offered by conservatives likewise suggested that order and stability derived from both continuity in the form of constancy rather than change and authority by a paternalistic elite. This elite could include the educated and professionals, who saw themselves as defending national traditions and order against the self-interested and socially destabilizing pretensions of their reformist opponents. Thus, for conservatives, too, marriage law represented an instrument for shaping the relations, attitudes, and values of society in accordance with their own beliefs and interests.

By the early twentieth century, then, two conflicting views of marriage had emerged within educated Russian society as well as within state officialdom

---

[24] *TsGIA*, f. 796, op. 445, d. 417, ll. 1–13, p. 18. For the views of ecclesiastical conservatives in general, see the references cited in note 18.

[25] For example, see N. Znamenskii, ''Malen'kiia zametki po povodu tolkov o razvode,'' *Moskovskiia vedomosti* 70 (1900): 2, and 71, 2; I. Kashkarov, ''Polurazvod i razvod,'' *Ibid.*, 61 (1900), 2, and 62, 2; N. N., ''Brak, otdel'noe zhitel'stvo i razvod,'' *Grazhdanin* 26 (1901): 7–9; Provintsial, ''Zametki otnositel'no proekta o razdel'nom zhitel'stve suprugov,'' *Ibid.*, 8 (1900), 8–9; the references to meetings of the Pirogov Society cited in note 15; and the views of Luk'ianov, *TsGIA*, f. 1405, op. 542, d. 671, ll. 106–97 (pp. 131–34).

and the Orthodox Church. Each view stemmed from a different ideological vision of Russia's future, and each offered an important role to the educated and professional elite. This association of marriage with ideological belief complicated and politicized any attempt to change divorce law because every proposal was perceived in terms of its implications for social organization, political authority, and church-state relations. The result was a legislative impasse. Conservatives within the government, often allied with their counterparts in the Duma and the State Council, used their institutional power to block measures proposed by reformist officials, who were supported, in turn, by liberal elements within educated society. Indeed, of the many projects for reform drafted during this period, only one concerning marital separation was ever enacted into law, in 1914. After the left and the right in the Duma and the State Council split over the measure, this bill passed only because the moderate conservatives controlling both legislative chambers were persuaded that it would provide relief for mistreated wives without transforming or disrupting fundamental social relationships. Their support in turn rested partly on the Holy Synod's acceptance of the bill. The Synod dropped its opposition to the proposal only after being assured by the Ministry of Justice that the new law would not empower the civil courts to grant a formal separation but only enable them to regulate the relations between spouses who had separated in fact.[26]

This conflict over reform of divorce law in the early twentieth century reveals sources of both unity and disunity within the educated and professional elite that emerged in Late Imperial Russia. Clearly, both proponents and opponents of reform valued specialized expertise and used it to resolve disputes over social and political issues. Both likewise believed that civil law shaped as well as reflected social relations and values and therefore sought to use the law to fashion society in accordance with their own attitudes, beliefs, and interests. This ability to use specialized education, willingness to engage in public debate over sociopolitical issues, and paternalistic desire to shape social development in correspondence with ideological beliefs bound the educated and professional elite together and set it apart from the rest of Russian society. To this extent, the picture painted by prerevolutionary Russian liberals and Western historians seems accurate. During the nineteenth century the tsarist

---

[26] *TsGIA*, f. 797, op. 91–1898, d. 53, ll. 125–9, 137–224, op. 96, d. 219, ll. 1–4, op. 92–1906, d. 68, l. 33, *Gosudarstvennaia Duma. Stenografcheskii otchet. 1911 g. Tretii sozyv, sessiia chetvertaia* (St. Petersburg, 1911), 2: 1652–62; ibid., *1914 g. Chetvertyi sozyv, vtoraia sessiia* (St. Petersburg, 1914), 2: 362–427, *Gosudarstvennaia Duma. Prilozheniia k stenografcheskim otchetam. Chetvertyi sozyv, vtoraia sessiia [1913–1914 gg.].* (St. Petersburg, 1914), 2, no. 134; *Gosudarstvennyi Sovet. Stenografcheskii otchet. Vos'maia sessiia [1912–1913]* (St. Petersburg, 1913), 1114–1215; *Gosudarstvennyi Sovet. Sessiia VIII, Kommisiia* (St. Petersburg, 1913), no. 2; Grigorovskii, *O razvode*, 330–41; and Gessen, "Razdel'noe zhitel'stvo suprugov."

educational system had helped to create a civic-minded society capable of participating in political life. But Russian obshchestvo was more diverse and spoke with more voices than generally admitted. The educated and professional elite was often divided by competing occupational, institutional, and other interests. More significant, higher education and specialized expertise proved compatible with various irreconcilable ideological perspectives that could either support or challenge the autocratic regime. The conflict resulting from this ideological diversity reflected the fragmentation of the educated and professional elite that prevented it from developing a common identity capable of providing political cohesion.

Tsarist officials were split along similar lines. By complicating an already complex legislative process, this division within state officialdom reduced the ability of the government to deal effectively with the crises confronting it. The likelihood of deadlock over legislation seemed to grow the more directly a proposal affected the reality or symbolic representation of power and authority.

These legislative struggles and impasses embittered both proponents and opponents of reform toward the bureaucracy. While progressives blamed the bureaucracy for the inadequacy or lack of reform, conservatives accused it of undermining the existing sociopolitical order by carrying reform too far.[27] Despite this hostility toward the bureaucracy, educated society was not as isolated from it as either Russian liberals or Western historians have claimed. Apart from socialism, the same ideological divisions split both state officialdom and the educated and professional elite. Members of both groups struggled to adapt their self-perceptions and world views to the conditions of early twentieth-century Russia.

Given this ideological division, the assumption that the existence of a larger middle class in Late Imperial Russia would have introduced political democracy and thereby avoided revolution seems problematic. Although development of an educated elite did create liberal groups that advocated the introduction of civil rights and political democracy, other members of the same elite continued to support the principles underlying the autocratic regime. Still others embraced radical socialist or mystical religious doctrines. The resulting ideological and political conflicts helped destabilize the tsarist regime by eroding faith in the values that sustained it, by irreconcilably dividing the elites on which it relied and by impeding its ability to deal effectively with the problems it confronted. Thus, contrary to the view commonly offered in Western historiography, it would seem that a major source of instability in Russia on the eve of the First World War was not the absence but the presence of a nascent

[27] For example, compare the reaction of the liberal and conservative press to the reform of inheritance law enacted in 1912: *Russkie vedomosti* 38 (1912): 1; *Rech'* 41 (1912): 2, and 42 (1912): 2; and "Dnevnik," *Grazhdanin* 8 (1912): 12–13.

middle class, a middle class that was as ideologically and politically divided as were the middle classes elsewhere in Europe during this period.[28] This diversity suggests both the complexity of the sociological phenomenon of the middle class, in prerevolutionary Russia and elsewhere, and the danger of identifying it with a particular ideology or political system.

[28] For example, see P. Gay, *The Bourgeois Experience. Education of the Senses* (New York, 1984), 17–68; D. Blackbourn and G. Eley, *The Peculiarities of German History: Bourgeois Society and Politics in Nineteenth-Century Germany* (New York, 1984); and W. Reddy, *Money and Liberty in Modern Europe: A Critique of Historical Understanding* (Cambridge, 1987), 1–33.

Chapter 11

THE ZEMSTVO AND THE DEVELOPMENT OF A
RUSSIAN MIDDLE CLASS

Charles E. Timberlake

THE ORGANS of rural self-government in Russia, the *zemstva*, promoted the growth of a new socioeconomic stratum that did not fit into the existing estate, or *soslovie*, system of tsarist society. In and of themselves, zemstvo institutions constituted the first communications network that conveyed new concepts and values (among them "middle-class" ideas) from the cities to the villages. In this discussion I focus on the centrality of a communications system to the dissemination of ideas to rural areas and the importance of the zemstva in creating these networks.

By hiring tens of thousands of specialists with higher or "middle" educational degrees and dispersing them among the provincial capitals and district towns of European Russia, where before the Great Reforms the number of such jobs had been infinitesimal, the zemstva were giving birth to and nurturing a socioeconomic stratum of professionals (with salaried occupations) and their assistants that in Western European societies scholars include in the "middle class." Because there were zemstvo administrative offices (where most specialists, excluding teachers and nurses, worked) in 350 provincial capitals and district towns, the zemstva were instrumental in creating a Russian version of a middle class.

The zemstva also promoted a notion of middle class in a different concept of "service." The nature of zemstvo service so contrasted with tsarist civil service—virtually the only employment opportunity for specialists prior to the Great Reforms—that it produced a new consciousness or self-perception among its deputies and hired specialists. Working in the villages, "in the midst of the *narod*," these people came to see themselves as agents from an "all-estate" (all-soslovie) body rendering service to the broad public of the empire. They contrasted their service to the narod with the service performed by tsarist bureaucrats whom the zemstvo activists considered alienated from the population by an elaborate set of titles, niches, and ranks and by their primary location in the capital city of St. Petersburg. They considered the tsarist civil service system to be tied to the pre-Emancipation idea of *soslovnost'* by which state service was considered the preserve of the noble soslovie.

By 1900, most educated Russians had also become cognizant of the differ-

ences between the web of zemstvo agencies and the services they provided
and the autocracy's network of agencies and the civil servants who staffed
them. In 1900 the vice-governor Kondoidi of Samara labeled the autocracy
and its servitors the "first element," elected deputies who met annually in
zemstvo assemblies formed the "second element," and the zemstvo army of
some seventy thousand hired specialists composed the "third element."[1]

Some zemstvo deputies from the nobility and the urban professionals saw
in the future a Russian society transformed by integrating the *sosloviia* that
existed in pre-Emancipation Russia into a modern society (*obshchestvo*) of
citizens differentiated not by soslovie status but by occupation. The concept
of such a transformed society they called *obshchestvennost'*, and they contrasted it to soslovnost' by which they meant the desire to retain a segmented,
unintegrated society that preserved traditional disparities in privilege and obligation.

This essay is divided into two parts. The first part discusses the zemstva
collectively, explaining their common characteristics and common tasks, establishing the geopolitical boundaries within which zemstvo institutions existed, presenting total numbers of provincial and district zemstvo assemblies,
and explaining the way in which the typical zemstvo structured its executive
board (*uprava*). The second part of the essay analyzes the zemstvo institutions
in one province, Tver, as a case study of expanding zemstvo work and corresponding growth in zemstvo personnel.

The Zemstvo Statute of 1864 explained the tasks of the zemstva as "caring
for local economic needs and wants." In specifically illustrating appropriate
activities within this rather hazy arena, the statute mentioned construction and
maintenance of local roads and administrative buildings; promotion of public
education and public health; maintenance of hospitals and prisons; collection
of food reserves for time of famine; measures for protecting livestock from
various diseases; promotion of local trade and industry; assistance to postal
operations; management of charitable institutions and relief work; prevention
of fires and administration of fire insurance; supervision of certain properties
previously under the control of governmental agencies; and arrangements for
conducting local elections to the zemstvo assemblies. The zemstva had the
rights to address petitions to the government through the provincial governor
and to submit legal questions to the Judicial Senate.[2] Even if one stopped with
this list, one could already see the need for veterinarians, doctors, teachers,
and an office staff to perform all these tasks.

Still other clauses seemed intent to leave a broader range of activities open
to the zemstva. The clause that gave them the right to "care for local economic

---

[1] L. D. Briukhatov, "Znachenie 'tret'iago elementa' v zhizni zemstva," *Iubileinyi zemskii
sbornik, 1864–1914*, ed. B. B. Veselovskii and Z. G. Frenkel (St. Petersburg, 1914), 186.

[2] *Polnoe sobranie zakonov Rossiikoi imperii* 39 (1864): pt. 1, 2.

needs and wants,'' for instance, provided those zemstvo members who wanted the broadest possible sphere for zemstvo activity with an ''elastic clause'' (much as the U.S. Constitution's clause allows Congress to ''provide for the general welfare'') to justify virtually any project that the tsarist government did not veto. Because of the magnitude and diversity of these duties, the authors of the zemstvo statute empowered the zemstva to employ a staff of specialists (*vol' nonaemnye sluga*).

The Zemstvo Statute of 1864 provided for the creation of district and provincial zemstvo institutions in 33 provinces of European Russia. By 1875 they had been organized in 35 provinces, but on March 20, 1882, the government reorganized the Don Cossack Region, ending separate zemstvo institutions in the region. From 1882 until 1911, 34 provinces, containing 359 districts, had zemstva (except one district in Bessarabia, making a total of 358 district zemstva). During this period with 34 provincial zemstva, plus 358 district zemstva, a total of 392 zemstva existed as employers of specialists. In 1911 zemstvo institutions were created in the western provinces of Kiev, Volynia, Podolia, Vilna, Minsk, and Mogilev, and the following year they were created in Astrakhan, Orenburg, and Stavropol provinces. From 1912 to 1917 zemstvo institutions existed in 43 provinces of European Russia and in 440 or the 441 districts within those provinces, for a total of 483 zemstva as employers of specialists.[3]

As zemstva increased their activities and their budgets, they expanded their executive boards. The structure of a typical zemstvo board evolved from a rather simple body into an elaborate bureaucracy in some provinces. Initially, the typical board was composed of an elected ''chairman,'' who received a salary, and elected ''members''—two to three at the district level, three to four at the provincial level—without salary. By statute, each could elect up to six ''members,'' but they rarely had this many.[4] In provinces where zemstva were most active, they soon divided their assigned tasks into categories, creating bureaus, commissions, councils, and departments within the zemstvo board to manage tasks grouped into a category. They then hired a manager of each agency, and then assistants for those managers, secretaries, bookkeepers, and other office personnel. Thus, the bureaucracy grew both horizontally through the addition of new agencies and vertically through hiring more personnel within each agency. Common examples of such subagencies are statistical department, department of public education, bureau of zemstvo fire insurance, bureau of health.[5]

---

[3] See Charles Timberlake, ''The Leningrad Collection of Zemstvo Publications,'' *Slavic Review* 26 (1967): 474–78.

[4] See Kermit McKenzie, ''Zemstvo Organization and Role in the Administrative Structure,'' in *The Zemstvo in Russia: An Experiment in Local Self-Government* (Cambridge, 1982), 52–56.

[5] For a detailed illustration, see the data on the Tver provincial zemstvo board in the second part of this chapter.

As the zemstva added agencies to the institutional skeleton created in the Zemstvo Statute of 1864, their network expanded farther across the countryside and reached deeper into the Russian village, especially as the zemstva created both elementary school and public health systems. This institutional infrastructure attracted the attention of an emerging group of university-educated sons of nobles who spurned service in the tsarist bureaucracy in favor of working among the peasantry and of professional practitioners who had settled in the provincial capitals because they wished to use the network of zemstvo institutions as a mechanism for transforming the village in the image of more developed industrial nations of Western Europe.

Other urban groups were also attracted to the zemstva as a possible mechanism for gathering and distributing information. Before the existence of the new institutions, such groups as the Free Economic Society that assumed the task of improving agriculture and the rural economy had no means beyond the tsarist communications system to distribute their literature to the villages or gather information about the status of agriculture. They were constantly disappointed that so few governors and governors-general bothered to distribute and collect the questionnaires that the society sent from St. Petersburg.

Without an effective means of communication and in an essentially oral culture, an urban group could not share its knowledge and therefore could not help improve the rural economy. It could only peer into the darkness of the village and respond to the occasional spark that appeared in the form of a letter from a peasant or priest requesting literature on some instrument or practice. In response, the society could only mail into the otherwise impenetrable village copies of its journal or diagrams and explanations of new devices and improved practices and wonder whether its efforts had produced any effect.[6]

By 1880, the zemstva had built extensive elementary school systems in the villages, and they hired teachers, usually trained in secondary or higher schools located in a major city, to move to the village to teach in a zemstvo school. To varying degrees, teachers brought new ideas to the villages. Various groups sought to use the network to infuse still more radical ideas into the village. Still others, such as the Literacy Committee of the Free Economic Society, merely sought to help the zemstva work more efficiently at spreading literacy. The society viewed this work as a prerequisite for the rapid dissemination of ideas in a country composed largely of isolated villages. Thus, an essential way in which the zemstva helped in the growth of a middle class was to build institutions that constituted a communications network to bring ideas of change to the countryside.

These institutions promoted new social consciousness by allowing profes-

---

[6] Joan Pratt, ''The Russian Free Economic Society, 1765–1915'' (Ph.D. diss., University of Missouri-Columbia, 1983). See 36–44 for the Free Economic Society's frustrating survey efforts utilizing the bureaucracy from 1765 to 1804, and 207–10 for the vastly improved survey conducted through the zemstva in the 1870s.

sionals and members of the nobility to focus their energies on the provinces. As elected members of the city duma or the zemstva, they could remain in the province and work more closely with the local people and institutions they wished to change. These educated noblemen and specialists sought consciously to use the zemstva and city dumas to produce social change in Russia's provincial capitals, district (*uezd*) towns, and particularly in the villages. To that end, they established institutions that formed the fiber of what we commonly call middle-class society in Western Europe—savings banks, a health care system of hospitals and clinics, elementary and secondary schools, postal networks, including postal roads. The socioeconomic complexity and institutional multiplicity characteristic of an urban industrial culture contrasted sharply with the relatively simple socioeconomic relationships and institutional structure of Russian district towns and villages when there were no social classes before the Great Reforms.

The judicial institutions created in 1864 were to some degree agencies of the zemstva in that the zemstva elected the county's justices of the peace, paid their salaries, and built and maintained their jails. These institutions also served as conduits for Western secular values: the justices of the peace, serving as judges and legal teachers in the Russian village, demonstrated, not always perfectly, the principles of rule by law and equality of all groups before the law and administered justice by using peasant juries in place of the pre-Emancipation system of separate courts for the separate sosloviia. All these concepts were extracted from middle-class urban, industrial society of Western Europe and written into the Russian legal reform of November 20, 1864. Obviously such transplants did not take root overnight in new soil; nonetheless, the necessary impetus was in place.

By the end of the century the zemstva provided employment opportunities for tens of thousands of specialists, another way in which the zemstva helped develop a Russian variant of a middle class. Before the zemstva appeared in the 1860s, a Russian with professional training had little choice about his employer. He or she looked almost exclusively to an agency of the tsarist government in the national capitals or, less likely, in a provincial capital. Because the tsarist government controlled virtually all the educational institutions that trained specialists, it could determine which specializations would be emphasized. By controlling admissions, it could determine the numbers and gender of the specialists to be trained. Thus, the government determined, consciously or unconsciously, the size of the pool of professional specialists available in Russian society.[7] The government's major concern in creating universities and special educational institutions was to assure itself a supply of reliable, well-

---

[7] I have developed this argument at some length in Charles Timberlake, ''Higher Learning, the State, and the Professions in Russia,'' in *The Transformation of Higher Learning, 1860–1930*, ed. Konrad H. Jarausch, Historisch-Sozialwissenschäftliche Forschungen, vol. 13 (Stuttgart, 1982; Chicago, 1983), 321–44.

trained civil servants.[8] With the emergence of the institutions of the Great Reforms, and the zemstva in particular, the tsarist government had a competitor for the pool of specialists. Conversely, specialists had a choice of employers. As zemstva built schools, hospitals, and other institutions, they employed teachers, doctors, statisticians, and agronomists. By 1900 a "zemstvo service," known popularly after 1900 as the third element, staffed zemstvo agencies and institutions.

While this new market expanded job opportunities for specialists, it also provided a new environment in which to work. Leaving the city to work in the Russian village altered consciousness. For many people, in zemstvo work as well as in the literary circles of Moscow and St. Petersburg, zemstvo service enjoyed much more approval than "state service." The distinction between the two was a part of the evolution of the consciousness of a society, obshchestvo, beginning to function independently of the central government. Thus, the zemstva not only swelled the numbers of the Russian middle class by offering new employment alternatives but also contributed to a separate identity among these employees by creating a new provincial surrounding for their work.

As a major employer of specialists, the zemstva created a second civil service corps (the third element) that competed with the tsarist government for scarce trained talent. The personnel needs of the zemstvo, coupled with new demands from other quarters of Russian society—city dumas, the independent courts, a developing commercial-industrial sector—produced upward pressure on the government to create new special schools, to open the universities to larger numbers of students, and to add new departments and programs of study to the university curriculum. The zemstva supported expanded enrollments in intermediate- and higher-level educational institutions by establishing a significant number of scholarships to enable students to come to the major cities from the provinces. By attaching the condition that upon completion of the course of studies each scholarship recipient repay the zemstvo by a minimum number of years of remunerated service in a zemstvo institution, the zemstva played a major role in socializing provincial youths to urban values that they, in turn, brought back to the village during their years of required service.[9]

The combined needs of zemstva, state, and private enterprise for trained specialists during the period of rapid industrialization after 1885 expanded and diversified the numbers and types of special educational institutions. Unwill-

---

[8] See James C. McClelland, *Autocrats and Academics: Education, Culture and Society in Tsarist Russia* (Chicago, 1979); Richard Wortman, *The Development of a Russian Legal Consciousness* (Princeton, 1976); and Walter Pintner, "The Russian Higher Civil Service on the Eve of the 'Great Reforms,' " *Journal of Social History* 8 (1975): 55–68.

[9] See Charles Timberlake, "Tver Zemstvo's Technical School in Rzhev: A Case Study in the Dissemination of Secular and Revolutionary Ideas," in *Religious and Secular Ideas in Late Tsarist Russia*, ed. Charles Timberlake (forthcoming from University of Washington Press).

ing to alter the curriculum of its universities to meet the nation's new needs, the tsarist government expanded, instead, the system of special educational institutions erected and maintained by its various ministries. These were devoted primarily to the new technologies, such as civil engineering, surveying, electrical engineering, "commercial sciences," and even aviation.[10] And the government allowed, with its usual concerns for proper bureaucratic supervision, much broader latitude for private persons and institutions to create special schools, especially for the education of women.[11] In the field of teacher training, the zemstva themselves began founding educational institutions such as teachers' seminaries and teachers' institutes. Although these were not "higher" educational institutions, they trained large numbers of elementary teachers who found employment—indeed, were required to teach for a specified period—in the zemstvo schools.[12]

This expanded market for specialists, in turn, stimulated the central government, the zemstva themselves, and private persons and groups to open more schools at all levels to train specialists for zemstvo service. The creation of schools, of course, increased the need for teachers, an area of critical shortage in post-Reform Russia. The infrastructure that the zemstva helped create perpetuated training and employment of specialists and thereby the growth of a "middle" group.

In addition to developing an assortment of skilled specialists and professionals, the zemstva also spread these specialists throughout the 34 (and later 43) provinces of European Russia, rather than clustering them in the two national capitals as the tsarist government did its civil servants. Each provincial zemstvo maintained at least one office for its board in the provincial capital, which generally had the zemstvo hospital, library, teachers' seminary, zemstvo bank, progymnasium for girls, orphanage, and various bureaus. The professional staff of those facilities added a significant middle-class component of specialists to the population of the provincial capitals.

In the 358 district towns (county seats), the zemstvo maintained a board office and, depending upon the wealth of the area and the combination of personalities elected to the zemstvo assembly, repeated in miniature the construction of service facilities and hiring of staff that the provincial zemstvo provided in the provincial capital. Virtually every district zemstvo board had a library; many built hospitals and progymnasiums for girls. Zemstvo special-

---

[10] See the chapters by Patrick Alston and James McClelland in *Transformation of Higher Learning*, ed. Jarausch. See also Timberlake, "Tver Zemstvo's Technical School," 335, for the Moscow Agricultural Society's futile efforts to establish agronomy as a special program of studies in the universities.

[11] See the section on "Zhenskoe obrazovanie" in D. Margolin, *Spravochnik po vysshemu obrazovaniiu*, 3-oe izdanie (Petrograd, 1915).

[12] N. A. Korf, "Nashi uchitel'skiia seminarii," *Vestnik Evropy* 4 (1883): 786–851; B. B. Veselovskii, *Istoriia zemstva za sorok let*, 4 vols. (St. Petersburg, 1909–1911), 4: 6–8; hereafter *Istoriia zemstva*. Allen Sinel, "Educating the Russian Peasantry: The Elementary School Reforms of Count Dmitrii Tolstoi," *Slavic Review* 28, no. 1 (1968): 49–70.

ists, such as veterinarians and agronomists, served the entire district from an office located in the district town. Collectively the 34 provincial zemstva and the 358 district zemstva formed 392 separate entities, each with its own staff. Because in each province one city served both as district seat and provincial capital—for example, the cities of Tver and Moscow were the district seat and the provincial capital—the total number of cities and towns to which the zemstvo contributed a middle-class population was 358.[13]

While district zemstvo employees formed a component of an emerging middle class in the district towns, other district zemstvo specialists lived and worked permanently in the villages. Performing zemstvo services in the villages on a permanent basis were often one to three elementary school teachers and a paramedic maintaining a clinic (fel'dsherskii punkt). Many of these employees had studied on zemstvo stipends in the provincial capital or in a city in another province.[14] Other zemstvo specialists, such as agronomists, veterinarians, statisticians, and fire insurance agents, visited while peforming their duties.

Statistics reveal the extent of zemstvo employment of specialists. In fiscal year 1909–1910, among the zemstva's more than 70,000 specialists were, for instance, the following numbers of specialists in three selected categories: 39,651 teachers in 25,047 schools (or 110.4 teachers and 69.8 schools per district, on average); 3,022 doctors (or 8.5 per district); and 975 veterinarians (or 2.7 per district). The average number of teachers in a district has some close relationship to reality, for schools were located in the villages. The averages for doctors and veterinarians are purely arithmetical. The current quality of our data base on Imperial Russia does not allow us to determine the numbers actually living and working in each district.[15]

The zemstvo institutions of Tver province employed specialists in an increasingly broad range of specializations and increased significantly the number of specialists within each category from 1866, the first year of their existence, to 1881, with particularly large increases in staff occurring in the last three years of the 1870s. In 1866, they employed only 17 people, classified in five categories (see Table 11.1).[16]

---

[13] Charles Timberlake and James Malloy, "Introduction," in B. B. Veselovskii, *Istoriia zemstva* (reprint; Cambridge, Eng.: Oriental Research Partners, 1973), v–vii.

[14] Samuel Ramer, "The Zemstvo and Public Health," in *The Zemstvo in Russia*, 294–98.

[15] The estimation of 70,000 zemstvo employees is in Veselovskii, *Istoriia zemstva*, 3: 465. The totals for individual specializations were compiled from data in ibid., 4: 229–34. Although the government census of 1897 showed 104,808 zemstvo employees, I have chosen to use Veselovskii's figures as more reflective of full-time, salaried employees because they qualified for participation in the zemstva's pension fund. The means for determining primary employment for the purposes of the census are less clear. If occasional laborers are included among zemstvo employees, the number is certainly greater than 70,000. See Hugh Seton-Watson, *The Russian Empire, 1801–1917* (Oxford, 1967), 536, for a summary of the census figures.

[16] *Sbornik materialov dlia istorii Tverskogo gubernskago zemstva 1866–1881 gg.* 10 vols. (Tver, 1883), 1: 284–85.

TABLE 11.1

Tver Zemstvo Employees, 1866

Office staff, provincial board	2
Office staff, district boards	10
Doctors & veterinarians	2
Fel'dshers (nurses)	1
Teachers (male—1; female—1)	2
Total	17

By 1881, the zemstvo institutions of Tver province employed 669 people in nine classifications. The following year, the provincial zemstvo's committee on retirement insurance compiled a list of zemstvo employees eligible for benefits.[17] That list shows 773 persons employed in 18 separate job categories. From 1866 to 1882, the number of employees rose from 17 to 773, an average annual increase of more than 44 new employees.

During that same period the zemstvo added thirteen new categories (indicated with an asterisk in Table 11.2). The title and number of persons employed under each category reveal the zemstva's major commitment to education and health care. If we combine all positions related to health care—doctors and veterinarians, hospital supervisors, wardens of insane asylum, pharmacists, feldshers, and managers of the orphanage—the total number of health care specialists is 218, or 28 percent of total zemstvo employees. The 419 teachers comprised 54 percent of the zemstvo staff. Thus, providers of health care and teachers accounted for 637 of the total 773 positions, or 82 percent of all zemstvo employees. Although the statistics for 1882 do not distinguish between male and female, the data for 1881 did. In 1881 of 669 employees 163 were women: teachers, 156 (of 383); feldshers, 5 (of 113); doctors or veterinarians, 2 (of 39). Almost half (308) of the zemstvo employees had been hired between 1879 and 1881.[18]

The data in Table 11.2 allow us to see the range of specialists employed by the zemstva. Furthermore, by showing the distribution of specialists among the districts, these figures show the geographic distribution of middle-class specialists in this province of mixed industrial-agricultural economy.

The distribution of employees throughout the districts was fairly even. If we assume that the 70 employees of the provincial board lived in the city of Tver and if we add a reasonable number of the 64 specialists employed by the Tver district zemstvo, assuming that they, too, lived in the city of Tver, we see that the zemstvo contributed approximately 100 permanent positions of employment to that city. (This calculation is based on the assumption that

---

[17] Ibid., 280–81.
[18] Ibid., 284–85.

TABLE 11.2
Tver Zemstvo Employees, December 1882

Title	Province	Districts	Total
Doctors and veterinarians	4	34	38
Secretaries*	1	12	13
Bookeepers*	1	12	13
Office manager, insurance dept.*	1	0	1
Head of statistical dept.*	1	0	1
His assistant*	1	0	1
Heads of desks (deputies of secretaries & bookeepers)*	10	25	35
Clerks (& registering clerks)*	18	32	50
Technicians:* senior	1	0	1
junior	3	0	3
Supervisor of printing plant*	1	0	1
Typesetters & printers*	5	0	5
Zemstvo insurance agents*	12	0	12
Supervisors of zemstvo hospitals*	1	11	12
Warden of insane asylum*	1	0	1
Provincial pharmacist and district hospital pharmacists* (incl. one feldsher)	1	12	13
Feldshers	6	147	153
Manager of the orphanage*	1	1	1
Teachers	1	418	419
Totals	70	703	773

* New category.

approximately 30 of the 38 teachers employed by Tver district zemstvo would have lived and taught in other towns or villages in the district.) The remaining 639 employees were dispersed rather evenly among the other eleven districts, ranging from the lowest number at 44 to the highest number of 66, with the exception of Bezhetsk, which was well above the norm with 98 employees, 65 of whom were teachers.

As Table 11.3 shows, by 1891 the number of zemstvo specialists in Tver province who were included in the retirement fund, had risen to 941.[19] Part of that increase was that chairmen and members of the zemstvo boards were added to the retirement fund, for an increase of 40. The remaining 901 represented an addition of 168 employees in the eight years since the end of 1882. Table 11.3 shows that the zemstvo retirement system had begun to make more formal distinctions than before among its specialists. By 1891, it had orga-

[19] *Materialy dlia istorii Tverskogo gubernskago zemstva 1886–1908 gg.*, 10 vols. (Tver, 1909), 6: 102–3; hereafter *Materialy*.

TABLE 11.3
Tver Zemstvo Employees, 1891

	Job Title	Province	Districts	Total
I	1. Board chairmen	1	12	13
	2. Provincial board members	3	—	3
	3. Senior doctors (provincial hospital and Burashevo colony) (1,000 rubles pension)	2	—	2
				18
II	1. District board members	—	24	24
	2. Secretaries	1	12	13
	3. Bookkeepers	1	12	13
	4. Manager of statistical department	1	—	1
	5. Manager of insurance office	1	—	1
	6. Senior technician	1	—	1
	7. Zemstvo insurance agents	13	—	13
	8. Zemstvo doctors and veterinarians	6	44	50
	9. Principal of Maksimovich school[a]	1	—	1
	10. Head teacher, Maksimovich school[a]	1	—	1
	11. Teachers, Maksimovich school[a]	3	—	3
	12. Provincial board cashier	1	—	1
	13. Assistant to manager of the statistical department	1	—	1
	14. Manager of the economic department, Burashevo colony (600 rubles pension)	1	—	1
				124
III	1. Desk heads, assistant secretaries, assistant bookkeepers	8	26	34
	2. Assistants to senior technician	2	—	2
	3. Supervisor of printing plant	1	—	1
	4. Female warden of the orphanage	1	—	1
	5. Provincial pharmacist and pharmacists in district hospitals	1	12	13
	6. Supervisor, provincial hospital	1	—	1
	7. Teachers,[b] Maksimovich school[a]	7	—	7
	8. Clerks in provincial hospital and Burashevo colony	2	—	2
	9. Assistant insurance agents	4	—	4
	10. Librarian (400 rubles pension)	1	—	1
				66
IV	1. Clerks and receiving clerks	15	32	47
	2. Typesetters and printers	5	—	5

TABLE 11.3 (*cont.*)

Job Title	Province	Districts	Total
3. Medical and veterinary feldshers, feldshers, and midwives	15	144	159
4. Supervisors of district hospitals	—	—	11
5. Teachers and their assistants	1	494	495
6. Counters, statistical department	3	—	3
7. Manager of the school fund	1	—	1
8. Burashevo pharmacist's assistant	1	—	1
9. Burashevo laundress	1	—	1
10. Burashevo housekeeper	1	—	1
11. Supervisor, Novotorshok orphanage (200 rubles pension)	1	—	1 / 725
V 1. Clerk in Burashevo colony	1	—	1
2. Supervisors in the provincial hospital and Burashevo colony	5	—	5
3. Provincial hospital laundress	1	—	1
4. Housekeeper, Maksimovich school[a] (120 rubles pension)	1	—	1 / 8
Totals	177	824	941

[a] A teachers' school for girls.

[b] Of the seven teachers, four are women and three are men.

nized all its full-time employees into five groups and set a uniform retirement benefit for specialists within each category. The range in annual pension was quite substantial; specialists in group I received a pension nearly nine times the amount allocated to specialists in group V. The gradations for annual pensions were: group I, 1,000 rubles; group II, 600; group III, 300; group IV, 200; and group V, 120. The 18-person elite within zemstvo service in Tver province were the chairman and 3 elected members of the provincial board, the chairmen of the 12 district zemstvo boards (a total of 16 bureaucrats), and the 2 senior doctors, one of whom was Dr. M. P. Litvinov who for many years headed the zemstvo's famous, innovative colony for the mentally ill near the village of Burashevo. (Ironically, in the Soviet era it has been one of the most notorious psychoprisons for dissenters.)[20] The major categories of employees in health care and education—teachers and feldshers—were in group IV, next to the bottom.

By 1910, for which we have partial figures, full-time employees in the Tver zemstvo totaled more than 2,000. Raw numbers that B. B. Veselovsky compiled in an appendix to the last volume of his mammoth history of the zemstva yield a firm figure of 2,004 employees in only three specializations: doctors

[20] Harvey Firestone, *Soviet Psychoprisons* (New York, 1979).

(101), veterinarians (11), and teachers (1,892). Missing from these numbers are the specialties classified in groups II and III on the 1891 retirement fund rolls, a total of 190 people in 1891. Also excluded are all specializations in group III other than teachers, an additional 230 persons, for a total of 420 persons not included in Veselovsky's compilation. Assuming continued average increases in personnel in this eleven-year period, the number of 420 would have increased also to raise the total number of persons employed by the zemstva of Tver province in 1910 to approximately 2,750 to 3,000. Given Veselovsky's calculation of approximately 70,000 total zemstvo employees in the 34 provinces with zemstva in 1900, the average number of employees per province would be approximately 2,100, a figure close to our estimation. Because Tver was one of the more active zemstva in Russia and because it had just instituted universal elementary education in the province in 1910, therefore undertaking a major increase in number of elementary teachers, we would expect them to be at least slightly above average in number of employees.

As the number of employees increased, the provincial zemstvo board also developed a significantly more complex structure. In 1908 the zemstvo board had ten departments staffed by 46 persons with 37 job titles to manage the provincial zemstvo's many activities. In addition to the elected positions of chairman and three members, agencies with hired staff for them were as follows: secretariat (5 job titles, 8 employees), library (2 titles, 2 employees), bookkeeping (6 titles, 9 employees), statistical department (4 titles, 2 employees), road department (8 titles, 15 employees), highway department (2 titles, 4 employees), educational reference department (3 titles, 2 employees), sanitation department (4 titles, 1 employee), economic department (2 titles, 0 employees), watchmen (1 title, 3 employees).[21]

This case study shows that the zemstvo institutions of Tver province were a major employer of a broad range of specialists. Although they had little need for people with law degrees—the most popular degree at Russian universities from 1860 to 1917 and the best road into the tsarist civil service—and needed historians and philologists only as teachers in middle-level schools, the zemstva actively recruited specialists with the other two degrees offered at Russian universities: medicine and the natural sciences. Still greater was the need for specialists trained in the middle and higher special educational institutions: feldsher schools, teacher-training schools, commercial schools, the polytechnic institutes.

The experience of the zemstva in Tver province shows that this new market expanded rapidly. The 3,000 positions in 1910 represented an average annual increase of approximately 65 new positions for the 46-year period from 1866 to 1910. Applying this same average to all Russia's zemstva, the 70,000 positions existing in 1900 (a period of 34 years) represented an annual average

---

[21] *Materialy* 6: 292–93.

increase of 2,647 specialists to the zemstva's collective work force. Considering that in 1880 total enrollment in the seven universities in the empire, excluding Warsaw University, was 7,230 students, scattered among all the classes, many of whom were in the five-year course in medicine, we see that the zemstva were annually adding to their collective work force more people than the universities were graduating.[22] Although most zemstvo employees (teachers and feldshers) did not require university degrees, others, such as doctors, did. Together with the tsarist government and the emerging group of factory owners, the zemstva substantially contributed as employer to the growth of a middle class in Russia.

The role of the zemstva as employer and creator of a set of modern urban institutions applied on the provincial and district as well as on the national level. In the case of Tver, the ratio between employees of the district zemstva and the provincial zemstvo was approximately 10:1. Thus, approximately 90 percent of all zemstvo employees were probably living and working in towns and villages. In the district towns and provincial capitals zemstvo employees formed a significant cluster.

It is difficult to determine by these methods the degree to which these middle-class specialists came to reside in the villages and bore a middle-class consciousness into the village. Other areas of zemstvo activity still require the appropriate analysis. For instance, in Tver, the zemstva created and supported an extensive network of producers' cooperatives, such as the cheese-producing cooperative that achieved national recognition under the leadership of Mr. Vereshchagin, and it gave considerable support to the handicraft (*kustar'*) industries. But did participation in these ventures play any role in converting a peasant's soslovie identity into a broader consciousness of obshchestvennost'? In the 1870s, the peasantry seems to have considered Tver zemstvo's role in founding and funding cooperatives as merely the work of outsiders from a government agency providing grants to aid the peasantry in its traditional seasonal handicrafts industries.[23] Detailed studies examining longer periods of time are necessary before drawing conclusions about the impact of zemstvo work on the peasantry's perceptions of itself or the zemstva. The data presented in the case study of Tver are adequate, nonetheless, to demonstrate the existence of a Russian version of an emerging middle class, divided into categories indicating approximations of relative status, distributed geographically throughout the provincial capitals and towns of European Russia by 1910.

Did the zemstvo personnel exhibit a consciousness that distinguished them from reforming landlords who acted out their sense of noblesse oblige? Cer-

[22] *Statistika rossiiskoi imperii*, Vyp. 3 (St. Petersburg, 1890), 1.

[23] Pamela Sears McKinsey, ''Kustar' Metalworking: The Tver' County Nailmakers and the Zemstvo Cooperative Movement,'' *Canadian Slavonic Papers* 24, no. 4 (1985): 365–84.

tainly, one sees a sense of obligation to serve the narod in virtually every group one analyzes in late tsarist Russia: revolutionaries, zemstvo activists, tsarist bureaucrats, even industrialists. But did zemstvo deputies (the second element) and zemstvo-hired specialists perceive themselves as acting out of a sense of their noble soslovie origins? Certainly the nobility dominated provincial zemstvo assemblies.[24] Although no categorical answer can be given to this question for either group of zemstvo adherents, one can find numerous instances in which zemstvo deputies referred to themselves as members of "society," obshchestvo, and they contrasted their work in the zemstva to government service, *gosudarstvennaia sluzhba*. In 1894, the government offered certain categories of zemstvo employees (doctors, paramedics, technicians, among others) the chance to become members of the civil service system. At its annual session that year, the provincial zemstvo assembly voted that "to make [these categories] into civil servants (*chinovniki*) would be pointless and contradictory to the spirit of all the zemstvo's work which has always attracted a service staff not because of superficial distinctions." The provincial board argued that because the only practical benefit of membership in tsarist civil service was the right to participate in the government pension fund, employees of the Tver zemstvo had nothing to gain, for the retirement plan of the Tver zemstvo was equally beneficial.[25]

Zemstvo deputies saw themselves as being outside government and inside society, but not part of narod; thus, they constituted a middle group. Although a nobleman might also perceive himself as separate from the government, liberal zemstvo deputies in Russia had objectives distinct from the nobleman's patriarchal interest in the welfare of his servants. The noble's obligation was based on the assumption that society would remain static in the soslovie system. In the case of the zemstvo staff and hired professionals, service was aimed at producing social change that would lead Russia along the path of Western European development.

The sense of noblesse oblige assumes a system of social orders tied to a rural, agrarian society. In that context, the nobility's obligation, to society in general was primarily an obligation to the enserfed masses. In the zemstva, legislators were not homogeneous. Although definitely dominated by the nobility, the zemstvo assemblies, in the most rural areas of European Russia, had a sizable contingent of vocal urban professionals: doctors, bankers, statisticians, merchants, and university professors. As time passed, representatives of peasant groups played a larger role, particularly in the district zemstva.

Little study has been devoted to the social origins of the third-element spe-

[24] N. M. Pirumova, *Zemskoe liberal'noe dvizhenie* (Moskva, 1977).
[25] *Materialy* 6: 291.

cialists.[26] In the case of Tver the members of the elite (group I in the retirement plan) tended to be descendants of noble families, but lower-ranking employees were not. Certainly the teachers and feldshers the most numerous group of employees, were not primarily descended from the nobility. But even if we allowed that third-element specialists, too, were not primarily of noble origin, we would still be observing the embourgeoisement of the gentry. For example, the senior doctor of Tver provincial hospital, Mikhail Petrunkevich perceived himself much more as a doctor and zemstvo leader than as a member of the nobility.[27] Likewise, his brother, the famous zemstvo activist Ivan Petrunkevich, entitled his memoirs *Notes of a Public Figure* (Zapiski obshchestvennogo deiatelia).

It is also true that traditional social orders—represented by terms like "nobility" "clergy," and "peasantry"—had become so amorphous by 1900 that to attach such a label to a doctor, lawyer, engineer, or university professor would communicate very little. Although government graphed specialists onto the soslovie and civil service system, a scholar communicates much more effectively by using the language of classes than the language of sosloviia.[28] As a consequence of easy access to universities, sons of nobles were transforming themselves into liberal professionals in a rapidly urbanizing and industrializing society. Although they might have been born and raised on estates in rural Russia, sons of nobles left the country for the universities, then took positions in urban areas. Of those who returned to manage the family estate, many converted their holding into a factory-in-the-field (*ekonomiia*) type of commercial agriculture. (This type of noble was far more likely than one who merely rented his land on shares to become active in the second element of the zemstvo.)

Although the zemstva's role in creating a middle class through transforming segments of the nobility and peasantry and providing them with nontraditional occupations was only one cause for the emergence of a middle class in Late Imperial Russia, theirs was a major role, especially in the province, beyond the bounds of the two capitals.

[26] The most detailed study of this group is N. M. Pirumova, *Zemskaia intelligentsiia i ee rol' v obshchestvennoi bor'be do nachala XX v.* (Moskva, 1986).

[27] See Charles Timberlake, "Petrunkevich, Mikhail Il'ich," in *The Modern Encyclopedia of Russian and Soviet History* 28 (1982): 50–53.

[28] Seymour Becker illustrates this point quite convincingly in his book, *Nobility and Privilege in Late Imperial Russia* (DeKalb, 1985). See also Charles Timberlake, "The Middle Classes in Late Tsarist Russia," in *Social Orders and Social Classes in Europe since 1500: A Study in Social Stratification*, ed. Michael Bush (Longman House, 1990), for an analysis of the evolution of the language of the professions and the government's efforts to meld the newly borrowed Western terms with existing terms in the Table of Ranks.

PART FIVE

The Professionalization of the Intelligentsia

Chapter 12

THE PROBLEM OF PROFESSIONS IN IMPERIAL RUSSIA

Harley Balzer

RUSSIAN LIBERALISM suffered not only from the small size of the educated public but also from its fragmentation, isolation, and political immaturity. The experience of Russian professionals certainly demonstrates the weakness of the emerging middle class. Caught between the peasant masses and a government that resisted professional autonomy, Russian professionals discovered that available Western models offered scant guidance in dealing with the social, political, and cultural challenge posed by Russia's unique mix of state activism and social underdevelopment. In England and the United States, professionals constituted a, and some argue the, crucial element of the middle class.[1] On the Continent, and especially in Russia, the social and political geography was different.

In *Russian Physicians in an Era of Reform and Revolution*, Nancy Frieden, has emphasized that Russian professionals experienced a Janus-faced relationship with the state. State intervention and encouragement constituted an indispensable precondition of economic and social developments; however, the state simultaneously blocked attempts at autonomous professional organization. To be sure, an ambivalent relationship to the state also existed in Western countries, where professional groups relied on state power to enforce their monopoly position.[2] In Russia this ambivalence was more extreme and forced a constant interplay of professional and political demands. At the same time, political demands raised the issue of forming coalitions with other groups. Although the Liberation Movement (*Soiuz osvobozhdeniia*) pointed the way toward such coalitions, they tended to fragment after 1905.

Rather than evolving from independent corporate groups on a guild model, Russian professions, but not their professional organizations, were fostered by the Russian state. The state monopolized the institutions of higher education,

---

[1] Harold Perkin, *The Rise of Professional Society: England Since 1880* (London: Routledge, 1989); Perkin, *The Origins of Modern English Society, 1780–1880* (London: Routledge and Kegan Paul, 1969); and Burton J. Bledstein, *The Culture of Professionalism: The Middle Class and the Development of Higher Education in America* (New York: W. W. Norton, 1976).

[2] Nancy Mandelker Frieden, *Russian Physicians in an Era of Reform and Revolution, 1856–1905* (Princeton: Princeton University Press, 1981), 14; Magali Sarfatti Larson, *The Rise of Professionalism: A Sociological Analysis* (Berkeley: University of California Press, 1977); Thomas L. Haskell, ed. *The Authority of Experts* (Bloomington: Indiana University Press, 1984).

using them to train personnel when it required medical, technical, pedagogical, legal, and other specialized skills. Yet many Russian professionals came
to perceive their interests and the proper performance of their professional
activity as requiring freedom from state tutelage. If there were no indigenous
models of social organization, there were plenty from abroad, and Russian
professionals sought to emulate their European counterparts' corporate status,
independence, and prestige.[3]

Russia's professionals sought to reduce state interference in their activities,
while still requiring state power to achieve their professional programs. The
state had a similar agenda: to use the professionals for specific purposes, while
allowing only that degree of autonomy and independence absolutely essential
to the performance of specific services.

The reciprocal nature of this ambivalence is important. Most top Russian
government officials had little sympathy for either the professionals or their
program. The two groups came from different milieux and, with a few exceptions, did not mix easily. Professional specialists usually received their education at universities or specialized institutes, while most top government officials attended the nobility's elite schools or military academies. As recent
studies by Daniel Orlovsky and Richard Robbins have shown, this "culture
gap" was eroding as specialists with a profile similar to the professional experts increasingly occupied positions in the staffs of many ministries.[4] Even
the Ministry of Internal Affairs, which did not share this "expertization,"
experienced some movement toward professional standards on the part of its
most arbitrary wielders of power—the provincial governors.

While in many respects conforming to a continental pattern of professional
development, Russia was also unique, mainly in the sharpness of discontinu-
ities and contradictions. If the ancien régime persisted on the rest of the Continent, how much more was it still a factor in Russia?[5] "Uneven" is not really
strong enough to describe fully the simultaneous existence of advanced industrial islands in a sea of peasant economic activity—perhaps "ragged" better
conveys the image.[6]

---

[3] The development of Russian professional groups and the literature on the topic are discussed
in Harley Balzer, ed., *Professions in Russia at the End of the Old Regime* (Ithaca: Cornell University Press, forthcoming).

[4] Daniel T. Orlovsky, "Professionalism in the Ministerial Bureaucracy on the Eve of the Feb-
ruary Revolution of 1917," and Richard G. Robbins, Jr., "The Limits of Professionalization:
Russian Governors at the Beginning of the Twentieth Century," in Balzer, ed., *Professions*; also
Robbins, *The Tsar's Viceroys: Russian Provincial Governors in the Last Years of the Empire*
(Ithaca: Cornell University Press, 1987).

[5] Arno J. Mayer, *The Persistence of the Old Regime* (New York: Pantheon, 1981); Eugen Weber, *Peasants into Frenchmen* (Stanford: Stanford University Press, 1976).

[6] The seminal work on this topic is Alexander Gerschenkron, *Economic Backwardness in Historical Perspective* (Cambridge: Belknap Press of Harvard University Press, 1966), particularly
the title essay. For a more recent formulation, see Daniel R. Brower, "Urban Revolution in the

At the turn of the century Russia was an underdeveloped nation, and Russian professions and professionals manifest patterns familiar to students of underdeveloped societies in the twentieth century.[7] One important common feature of "development" is the existence of a small elite, isolated from the bulk of the population and seeking to assist and educate those masses using social and political ideologies that are regarded with suspicion by the government. Another is the paradox that most educated specialists are employees of the very state they seek to challenge.[8]

Although Russian professionals were a relatively small group, they were highly concentrated. One corollary of a small, highly concentrated professional stratum was its closeness. At least in the case of urban professionals, everyone knew everyone else. A few schools in Moscow and St. Petersburg educated the overwhelming majority of specialists in any field. Most engineers, for example, came from St. Petersburg technical institutes; most lawyers and more than one-third of all physicians were graduates of Moscow University.[9] This "professional geography" requires more attention to flesh out the important relationships and provide detail on the various circles (*kruzhki*) and interrelationships. Recent research has demonstrated the importance of the *kruzhok* and its offspring, the scientific school, for political and scientific development.[10]

Late Russian Empire," in Michael F. Hamm, ed., *The City in Late Imperial Russia* (Bloomington: Indiana University Press, 1986), 319–53, 325–26; also David S. Landes, *The Unbound Prometheus: Technological Change and Industrial Development in Western Europe from 1750 to the Present* (Cambridge: Cambridge University Press, 1969).

[7] For one of the most recent formulations, see Teodor Shanin, *Russia As A 'Developing Society'* (New Haven: Yale University Press, 1985), and Shanin, *Russia, 1905–07: Revolution as a Monument of Truth* (New Haven: Yale University Press, 1986). Concerned with peasants, Shanin does not devote much attention to the question of professions or the middle class. His "snapshot" of social classes totally ignores the professional groups; see *Russia As A 'Developing Society'*, 119. Although he does appreciate the radical character of the Union of Unions, he devotes no time to elucidating its composition; see *Russia, 1905–07*, 74–75.

[8] The literature on elites in underdeveloped or "modernizing" societies is vast. For good discussions, see David E. Apter, *The Politics of Modernization* (Chicago: University of Chicago Press, 1965); and Lucian W. Pye, *Politics, Personality and Nation Building: Burma's Search for Identity* (New Haven: Yale University Press, 1964).

[9] Charles Timberlake does a good job of illustrating these connections in "Higher Learning, the State and the Professions in Russia," in *The Transformation of Higher Learning, 1860–1930*, Konrad H. Jarausch, ed. (Chicago: University of Chicago Press, 1983), 321–44; see also A. E. Ivanov, "Geografiia vysshei shkoly Rossii v kontse XIX-nachale XX vv.," in *Istochnikovedcheskie i istoriograficheskie aspekty russkoi kul'tury* (Moscow: Academy of Sciences SSSR Institute of History, 1984), 160–86.

[10] Mark Adams, "The Founding of Population Genetics: Contributions of the Chetverikov School, 1924–1934," *Journal of the History of Biology* 1, no. 1 (1968): 23–39, and Adams, "Science, Ideology and Structure: The Kol'tsov Institute, 1900–1970," in *The Social Context of Soviet Science*, ed. Linda L. Lubrano and Susan Gross Solomon (Boulder, Colo.: Westview Press, 1980), 173–204; Kendall Bailes, *Science and Russian Culture in an Age of Revolution: V. I.*

Beyond the cities and their close-knit circles, Russian professionals frequently experienced cultural isolation. The growing professional stratum was caught between a seemingly hostile government and the even more hostile "dark masses." Nancy Frieden has shown the experience of physicians in the countryside, and Ben Eklof and Scott Seregny have graphically portrayed the situation of village teachers who sought to play the role of "culture bearers" to the peasants.[11] Such isolation was especially frustrating when professional journals constantly reported on the activities of professional "brethren" in Europe.

A sense of isolation and affinities based on education and knowledge make professionals closely resemble the intelligentsia, and the two groups overlap considerably. But they are not identical. One could be an *intelligent* without being a professional, much less a member of a profession; not all professionals meet everyone's definition of an intelligent. Membership in the intelligentsia derived (and still derives) from a combination of self-ascription and group acceptance. Family tradition plays an important role; any intelligent can describe his or her *vospitanie*—literally "upbringing," but really implying moral education and inculcation of values. Members of the intelligentsia most often refer to a specific family member or surrogate relative who was their *vospitatel'*, and they distinguish between where they received their formal education and where they received their vospitanie.[12] The issue is increasingly divisive in contemporary Soviet society, with some analysts finding the need to codify the popular reference to the real (*nastoiashii*) *intelligent*.[13]

One factor differentiating professionals from the intelligentsia is professionals' identification with an international community of specialists. The intelligentsia, by contrast, despite its international intellectual, personal, and even organizational connections, is not comprehensible outside the context of a special Russian ethos.[14] Based on their vospitanie, social conscience, and fre-

---

Vernadsky and His Scientific School, 1863–1945 (Bloomington: Indiana University Press, 1990), chap. 5; and Harley D. Balzer, "Educating Enginieers: Economic Politics and Technical Training in Tsarist Russia" (Ph.D. diss., University of Pennsylvania, 1980), chap. 2.

[11] Frieden, *Russian Physicians*; Ben Eklof, *Russian Peasant Schools: Officialdom, Village Culture, and Popular Pedagogy, 1861–1914* (Berkeley: University of California Press, 1986); and Scott J. Seregny, *Russian Teachers and Peasant Revolution: The Politics of Education in 1905* (Bloomington: Indiana University Press, 1989).

[12] This conclusion was initially based on observation of the present-day Soviet intelligentsia. I have subsequently found ample documentation in the numerous autobiographies of members of the prerevolutionary intelligentsia collected by Vengerov, preserved in the archives of Pushkinskii Dom, Fond 377. I am grateful to Alan Kimball for bringing this material to my attention.

[13] "Podvizhniki: O traditsiiakh otechestvennoi intelligentsii," *Pravda*, March 10, 1987, 3.

[14] Russia was hardly the only country with an intelligentsia, although I can recall lengthy arguments in graduate school and around Soviet friends' tables over whether America has a "real" intelligentsia or "merely" intellectuals. In Russia, the intelligentsia has often been associated with opposition political activity, but this creates difficulty with figures like M. N. Katkov. On the intelligentsia, see Philip Pomper, *The Russian Revolutionary Intelligentsia* (Arlington

quently their political concerns, most Russian professionals were also *intelligenty*, and if the conflicting roles strike us as contradictory, individuals at the time apparently managed the dual identities without undue difficulty.

The "professional program," adumbrated by most Russian professionals and heavily influenced by European models, also combined at least two closely related elements that received unique emphasis in the Russian experience: first, an acceptance of the legitimacy of the state's role, even as professionals sought to emancipate themselves from state tutelage; second, a powerful strain of social conscience coursing through the entire Russian intelligentsia. The Janus-faced relationship with the state has caused many historians, the present writer included, to focus on conflicts between professionals and the tsarist government. These battles, however, should not obscure the evidence that many Russian professionals tolerated and even welcomed a degree of government involvement well beyond the state-professional collaboration seen in Germany. What is striking is not so much the structure of the state role as its legitimacy—a legitimacy that stemmed from the political culture, from the simple need for protection from the sometimes hostile masses, and most of all from the need for assistance in carrying out medical, educational, and other social programs.

In seeking to implement their social programs, Russian professionals evinced a messianic tone reflecting their roots in the Russian intelligentsia. The intelligentsia culture included a strong sense of social responsibility, far more demanding than simple noblesse oblige. Members of the intelligentsia felt not merely a responsibility but a compelling duty—to their peers, to their country, and to the *narod*—to fulfill the mission of educating, uplifting, and modernizing the Russian masses. In their search for allies in pursuit of these goals, professionals repeatedly found that the state was both the greatest obstacle and the most promising source of assistance. Only the state had the resources to carry out the desired transformation and the raw power needed to mobilize a reluctant population.

Although the intelligentsia culture, opposition to autocracy, and assertions of independence dominated the Russian professional program in the years preceding the 1905 Revolution, alternative models were available for Russian professionals interested in fostering Russia's development. In an autocracy, the possibility of utilizing the immense power of the autocrat to further a specific program was enormously tempting. Russian reformers throughout the nineteenth century sought to achieve their goals by maneuvering into a position where they could speak in the name of the Tsar, and members of the professions were not immune to the attractions of this path. Alliance with

Heights, Ill.: AHM Publishing Co., 1970); Richard Pipes, ed., *The Russian Intelligentsia* (New York: Columbia University Press, 1961); and V. R. Leikina Svirskaia, *Intelligentsiia v Rossii vo vtoroi polovine XIX veka* (Moscow: Mysl', 1971), and Svirskaia, *Russkaia intelligentsiia v 1900–1917 godakh* (Moscow: Mysl', 1981).

autocratic power was always a plausible alternative professional program. Ivan Vyshnegradsky was one of the first professionals to appreciate this opportunity, and it was carried to its greatest extent by Sergei Witte.[15] In the period after 1905 it became an even more attractive option.[16]

The basic organizational form of modern professions is the autonomous professional association. Beginning in the period of Great Reforms, growing numbers of Russian professionals voiced a desire to establish such professional organizations. In a context where formal organization was proscribed, they sought alternative mechanisms to foster group identity. Scientific societies, school alumni associations, mutual assistance societies, and professional congresses assumed heightened importance in the absence of "real" professional institutions.[17] The scientific societies created at educational institutions could never stray too far from their charters because the institutions themselves were closely monitored and coordination among them was haphazard. But individuals could engage in informal group activity, and many did.[18]

Professional congresses (s"ezdy), the most important forum for the development of professional groups, were also a major cause of conflict with the government. Permitted to convene on a district and province basis beginning in the 1860s, teachers held an All-Russian Congress in 1872. Lawyers sought to use their congresses as the basis for expressing professional aspirations, first in the Moscow Legal Society and subsequently in its St. Petersburg counterpart. Physicians perfected the technique and carried it further than any other prerevolutionary professions.[19]

Groups that succeeded in convening congresses often provided an umbrella under which other nascent professions could meet and organize. Zemstvo stat-

[15] Balzer, "Educating Engineers," 166–70, 368–69, 401–6.

[16] See John Hutchinson's discussion of G. E. Rein, "Politics and Medical Professionalization After 1905," in Balzer, ed., *Professions*. This model is typical in other developing or modernizing societies, for example Ataturk in Turkey. See Apter, *The Politics of Modernization*.

[17] A. V. Ushakov pays particular attention to the mutual assistance societies as early forms of organizational activity in *Revoliutsionnoe dvizhenie demokraticheskoi intelligentsii v Rossii, 1895–1904* (Moscow: Mysl', 1976), 43–46; A. D. Stepanskii provides important detail on the role of scientific societies; see A. D. Stepanskii, "Nauchnye obshchestva i s"ezdy Rossii na rubezhe XIX–XX v.i literatura voprosa," *Istochnikovedcheskie i istoriograficheskie aspekty Russkoi kultury* and Stepanskii, "Nauchnye obshchestva pri vysshikh uchebnykh zavedeniiakh dorevolutsionnoi Rossii," *Gosudarstvennoe rukovodstvo vysshei shkoloi v dorevolutsionnoi Rossii i v SSSR* (Moscow, 1979).

[18] Bailes, *Science and Russian Culture*. Stepanskii points out that when a 1907 law finally legitimized student scientific circles the existence of political parties rendered them less significant to the political process.

[19] F. G. Panachin, *Uchitel'stvo i revoliutsionnoe dvizhenie v rossii (XIX–nachalo XX v.).* (Moscow: Pedagogika, 1986), 85ff. Brian Levin-Stankevich, "The Transfer of Legal Technology and Culture: Law Professionals in Autocratic Russia," in Balzer, ed., *Professions*; Frieden, *Russian Physicians*; and N. M. Priumova, *Zemskaia intelligentsiia i ee rol'v obshchestvennoi bor'be* (Moscow: Nauka, 1986).

isticians held a congress in 1887, but subsequent meetings were prohibited. They managed, nevertheless, to gather in subsections of the Ninth Congress of Naturalists and Physicians (1894), the Moscow Juridical Society (1898), and the Free Economic Society (1900). The 1901 Eleventh Congress of Naturalists and Physicians was "essentially a congress of statisticians."[20] Further research into the activity of other groups would undoubtedly reveal similar patterns.

The tensions between organization-oriented professionals and a resistant government escalated in a cyclical fashion: The government forbade formation of a professional organization; the group received permission to convene a congress instead; the congress petitioned for creation of a professional organization; the government responded by forbidding future congresses. A variation on the theme was the effort by some professional groups to host an international congress in their specialty. Combining a thirst for international scientific recognition with an end run around prohibitions on professional gatherings, these proposals were almost invariably judged inopportune or ahead of their time by the government.[21] As a result increasing numbers of professionals considered their professional programs impossible to fulfill without a solution of the political issue.

Physicians were the first Russian professionals to succeed in gaining state acceptance of their professional activity. Scientific expertise and practical value put doctors in a position to engage in an unprecedented level of professional organization. Their success largely stemmed from sheer necessity. The leaders of Russia's organs of local government were never permitted to collaborate, but their physician-employees had to work in concert if epidemics were to be held in check, much less prevented. The necessity for communication among public health practitioners spurred development of professional journals and eventually a professional association of Russian physicians. The Pirogov Society evolved a "professional idea" based on scientific expertise, sacrifice, and public service.[22]

The crisis of famine and disease in 1891–1893 required major involvement by specialists in Russian society, particularly physicians, and accelerated the development of professional demands.[23] Despite government assurances that adjusting railroad tariffs would rectify the food situation, those who witnessed the hunger and misery were compelled to act. They came away from the

[20] Pirumova, *Zemskaia intelligentsiia*, 138–39.

[21] TsGIA, F. 733, op. 160, d. 215.

[22] Frieden, *Russian Physicians*, 106–8; Pirumova, *Zemskaia intelligentsiia*; and Pirumova, *Zemskoe liberal'noe dvizhenie: Sotsial'nye korni i evoliutsiia do nachala XX veka* (Moscow: Nauka, 1977).

[23] On the famine of 1891–1892, see Richard G. Robbins, Jr., *Famine in Russia, 1891–1892* (New York: Columbia University Press, 1975), esp. chaps. 9, 10. On the response by physicians, see Frieden, *Russian Physicians*, chap. 6.

experience with a heightened belief in the efficacy of their initiatives and with their appetites whetted for greater involvement in social activity. Many Russian professionals believed their service to society and state would be acknowledged, and the important contributions that could be made by autonomous professionals would overcome the government's wariness about independent groups. Government failure to alter its policies in recognition of the groups' efforts induced many of Russia's would-be professionals to join forces with the growing "liberation movement."

Leadership during the early 1890s was in the hands of *aktivisty* among the professionals. Virtually every profession contained a faction arguing that their professional program was essential to Russia's salvation. It was commonly assumed that this program could be achieved only as part of a major political transformation that would limit the autocracy while it freed society—and the professions in particular—to improve the life of their country. The proponents of this professional program were not necessarily a majority in most professional groups; for example, around 1905 the Pirogov Society included perhaps one-quarter of Russian physicians. Often these self-appointed leaders or activists became spokesmen by virtue of their energetic role and the apathy of others. A similar phenomenon was at work in the leadership of the zemstvos.[24]

Events in Russian political and economic life encouraged the professional activists, and their activity in turn helped foster the growing Liberation Movement. For many, the struggle for professional organization and autonomy was inseparable from the larger movement for political change. In some professional groups, political and economic motivations were intricately intertwined. Among engineers, a massive expansion of educational opportunities in the late 1890s followed by economic recession after 1900 generated a serious unemployment problem. In this situation, young engineers turned to professional associations and mutual aid societies for personal assistance, and their individual needs merged with the growing activism of these groups in the broader political realm.[25]

While engineers may have experienced unemployment more acutely than other professionals—a function of their close relationship to economic conditions and the enormous increase in their number during the previous decade—other groups also responded to changing economic conditions, most notably

[24] The process is described by Roberta Manning, "The Zemstvo and Politics, 1864–1914," in *The Zemstvo in Russia*, Terence Emmons and Wayne S. Vucinich, ed. (Cambridge: Cambridge University Press, 1982), 133–76. See also Hutchinson, in *Professions*, Balzer, ed.; Stepanskii, "Nauchnye obshchestva pri vysshikh," 229–30; Eklof, *Russian Peasant Schools*, 243–47; Ronald Hayashida, "The Unionization of Russian Teachers, 1905–1908: An Interest Group Under the Autocracy," *Slavic and European Education Review*, no. 2 (1981): 1–16; and Jonathan Sanders, "The Union of Unions: Economic, Political and Human Rights Organizations in the 1905 Russian Revolution" (Ph.D. diss., Columbia University, 1985).

[25] The fullest discussion of economic factors in development of the engineering profession is in Harley Balzer, "The Engineering Profession in Tsarist Russia," in *Professions*, Balzer, ed.

physicians and teachers. Among physicians, competition for the coveted salaried (state) positions increased in the final decade of the nineteenth century, pushing a greater portion of the medical profession into generally less lucrative private practice. After 1900, these pressures were accentuated by inflation: the appearance of even larger numbers of new graduates, and increased government measures to punish politically active individuals.[26] Teachers, too, experienced increasing competition and straitened economic circumstances, and in the villages they were pressured to play a political role interpreting events for the peasantry.[27]

The 1905 Revolution was a crucial watershed for professional organizations and the entire Russian middle class. For nine brief months in 1905, from Bloody Sunday to the issuing of the October Manifesto, it appeared that the forces unifying Russian educated society were unstoppable, that the combined front against autocracy could not be denied, and that the leadership of radical professionals would emerge victorious over that of professional radicals.[28]

The major institutional representatives of professional groups in 1905 were the Liberation Movement (*Soiuz osvobozhdeniia*) and its offshoot, the Union of Unions. Professional groups that found their organizational efforts frustrated were encouraged to consider unions the most effective means for articulating both their professional demands and the broader political goals of the Liberation Movement. Beginning with the Writers Union in the mid-1890s, a growing number of professions established union organizations under the umbrella of the developing Liberation Movement.

The experience of 1905 politicized large segments of the Russian population, and not just the obvious cases, such as physicians who treated the victims of Bloody Sunday. Political awareness and activity fundamentally increased among numerous groups in Russian society. The Union of Liberation consciously sought to use existing professional organizations while also fostering new groups as instruments of political activity. In addition to further politicizing the professional context, their efforts spurred the process of professionalization among groups that had only dimly perceived such interests before Bloody Sunday. Union fostering had an impact among not only the groups targeted by the Union of Liberation but also other professions that emulated or spun off from the first unions. Political and professional agendas became thoroughly intertwined.

[26] Frieden, *Russian Physicians*, 217, 220.

[27] Eklof, *Russian Peasant Schools*, 246; Scott Seregny, "Professional Activism and Association Among Russian Teachers, 1864–1905," in *Professions*, Balzer, ed., and Seregny, *Russian Teachers and Peasant Revolution*, 86–98.

[28] The treatment of 1905 draws heavily on the contributions to Balzer's *Professions*. For general background, see Sanders, "The Union of Unions"; Abraham Ascher, *The Revolution of 1905: Russia in Disarray* (Stanford: Stanford University Press, 1988); and Shmuel Galai, *The Liberation Movement in Russia, 1900–1905* (Cambridge: Cambridge University Press, 1973).

The interweaving of professional activity and the Liberation Movement was evident from the start. The Union of Liberation held its founding congress in St. Petersburg, January 2–5, 1904. It coincided with the physicians' Eleventh Pirogov Congress and the Third Congress on Technical and Professional Education. The authorities were so concerned with the two large professional meetings—they closed the Technical Education Congress January 6—that they essentially lost the Union of Liberation in the tumult. Under the guise of commemorating the emancipation, the Union of Liberation undertook to organize banquets explicitly for political agitation.

In the months before Bloody Sunday, there was no reason to expect a violent outburst. Opposition activity focused on the banquet campaign and mobilizing public opinion, but reform from above was the dominant hope of the professional middle class. Moderate political reforms were preferable to radical change, and by no means was political transformation to be accompanied by social revolution. During this period professional unions and meetings of professional organizations served as a mechanism to mobilize and politicize groups that could not otherwise assemble legally.

January 9 changed the situation drastically. Activists, such as L. I. Lutugen and other leaders of the Union of Engineers, set about organizing unions in St. Petersburg. In March and April 1905 four unions held founding congresses in St. Petersburg at the behest of the Liberation Movement: writers, lawyers, professors, and engineers and technicians. Although not identical, all four groups basically followed what would become the Kadet line. The Writers Union played perhaps the most visible role, but engineers and technicians frequently took the most radical stance. Lawyers also played leading roles in the Liberation Movement, viewing it as a step to leadership of the entire nation. The Academic Union was consistently the most timid of the Union of Unions groups. Professors always felt a dual responsibility to keep the universities open and continue education, while also providing moral leadership to the Liberation Movement.

In Moscow, by contrast, the union movement was dominated by zemstvo employees: medical personnel, veterinarians, agronomists and statisticians, and primary school teachers. As zemstvo employees, they were less hampered by the bureaucracy than their counterparts in the St. Petersburg professions, and their emphasis on economic issues and social status reflected this difference. Many unions, including pharmacists, veterinarians, bookkeepers, office workers, and the critically important railroad workers, arose independent of the nurturing activities of the Liberation Movement. These groups developed their own identity and organization in struggles over economic benefits and working conditions, and in some instances they learned that political struggle was the only guarantee of hard-won benefits.[29]

---

[29] Sanders, "The Union of Unions"; also Sanders, *"Drugs and Revolution."* On Moscow

For a time, shared goals obscured significant differences among and within professional groups and even between members of the same profession in different cities. Leadership was in the hands of the previously existing professional leadership and those controlling the major professional journals. As leader of the Union of Unions, Pavel Miliukov sought to unite professionals and zemstvo personnel into what could become a constitutional-democratic party, hoping that growth of the union would compensate for the lack of "critical mass" in any single profession. But he could not forestall increasing radicalism.[30] The political current in the spring and summer of 1905 moved consistently leftward. Professionals reacted strongly to politically motivated dismissals. When unions pledged to support any individual who was dismissed, they put the entire organization in the hands of its most radical members.

With peasants still passive and most bourgeoisie neutral, workers and members of the professional intelligentsia were in the forefront of the battle against autocracy. Yet radicalization was not universal. Autocracy had its supporters, as did the simple ideology of "law and order." Far from all the professionals supported the radical aktivisty even at the height of revolutionary fervor. As the revolutionary wave subsided, political and other divisions within professional groups became increasingly decisive.

The October Manifesto split the Union of Unions, as it did the entire liberal movement. Now there were legitimate political parties as an alternative to the unions' opposition activity, and many believed that legal professional associations would inevitably follow. With a first step taken in the political evolution, many liberals and professionals sought a "third side" to the barricades, hoping to find a middle path between autocratic repression and revolutionary violence.[31]

The general strike cost the Union of Unions much support. When the St. Petersburg Soviet was arrested on December 3, only engineers, pharmacists, and clerks were willing to support another strike. The first group to withdraw formally was the Academic Union. Professors dropped out in January 1906 to consolidate their professional gains and ensure the integrity of nonpolitical educational institutions. Thereafter the union movement gradually dissolved,

groups, see Laura Engelstein, *Moscow, 1905: Working-Class Organization and Political Conflict* (Stanford: Stanford University Press, 1982), 115, 120; Ushakov, *Revoliutsionnoe dvizhenie*; and Pirumova, *Zemskaia intelligentsiia*.

[30] Miliukov failed so dismally in reconciling zemtsy and professionals at the Third Union of Unions Congress in Finland on July 1, 1905, that he denied having been there; in fact, he chaired the session. Paul Miliukov, *Political Memoirs, 1905–1917*, ed. Arthur P. Mendel (Ann Arbor: University of Michigan Press, 1967), 34; cf. Sanders, "The Union of Unions." See also Ascher, *The Revolution of 1905*, 143.

[31] The "third side of the barricades" is explored by V. V. Shelokhaev, *Kadety-glavnaia partiia liberal'noi bruzhuazii v bor'be s revoliutsiei, 1905–1907 gg.* (Moscow: Nauka, 1983).

though the proliferation of unions and other formal organizations for a time obscured the extent of the fragmentation.[32]

The history of the professions in 1905 is somewhat distorted by the role of the Union of Unions. The Union was less an expression of professional maturity than a highly convenient tactic. Because congresses and professional meetings were the only public gatherings sanctioned by the government, they took on a political role, essentially replacing political assemblies. The unions fit a national mood of flexibility and solidarity, providing legal and ostensibly nonpolitical fronts for antigovernment activity. After the autumn of 1904 these groups became increasingly political, and additional groups were added to the ranks of unionized occupations and professions. Some, like teachers, had a long professional history. Others, like railway workers and pharmacists, developed their own identity and organization in struggles over economic goals and working conditions. The October Manifesto accentuated divisions between older intelligentsia unions (writers, lawyers, academics, but *not* engineers) and the newer, less established professional groups like the pharmacists.

Important cleavages existed within professional groups as well. Virtually all professional unions faced a divisive question about including technicians, assistants, and other secondary level employees. Engineers accepted technicians as partners in their Union of Engineers and Technicians, but many engineers were never happy with this gesture. Physicians had to resolve the divisions between private and zemstvo doctors and also cope with demands for recognition from feldshers and other paraprofessionals.[33] Professional unions were ambivalent about including these auxiliary employees. Their numbers increased the groups' strength, but their economic demands and more radical political stance, along with the existence of intraprofessional issues, made the alliance uneasy. They generally were accepted as long as they deferred to leadership by the "real" professionals.

Members of the semiprofessions were themselves pulled in two directions. They wished to emulate the style and tenor of the real intellectuals, but they were also attracted by the economic promises of Socialist Revolutionary and Social Democrat programs. Members of these groups were frustrated when they performed the same duties as credentialed specialists but did not receive commensurate pay or recognition.

The experience of Russia's first popular revolution demonstrated both the potential and the limits of professional activism. Within a remarkably short period of time, existing groups increased in size and expanded their range of

[32] Samuel D. Kassow, "The University Professoriate in Tsarist Russia," in *Professions*, Balzer ed.; and Kassow, *Students, Professors, and the State in Tsarist Russia* (Berkeley: University of California Press, 1989); Sanders, "The Union of Unions."

[33] The problem of paraprofessionals is discussed by Balzer, Ramer, and Seregny in Balzer's *Professions*; for the issue in other settings, see Amitai Etzioni, ed., *The Semi-Professions and Their Organization* (New York: Free Press, 1969).

activity, while many professions that had not previously sought to form independent groups strove to organize. Yet the questions these groups confronted in determining their character—whom to include, what demands should receive priority, where to stand on political issues as opposed to economic and professional concerns—revealed lines of division precluding the formation of large, cohesive organizations that might have exerted a decisive influence on the political outcome.

The 1905 Revolution was a high watermark for Russian professional unions.[34] Despite the achievements of the Union of Unions, virtually no one in 1912–1914 or during the First World War suggested that it should be resurrected. In 1905, the professional and union movement provided a convenient screen for political activity, while simultaneously helping to advance the particular professional programs of individual groups. Mixing professional and political concerns, to some extent dictated by government opposition to public activity, also enhanced the flexibility of the opposition movement and encouraged its solidarity. Yet, while providing legitimate cover, the Liberation Movement masked profound political differences among professionals and between them and other elements of the educated class.

After October 1905, the evolution of political parties brought the differences into sharper relief, while the political importance of professional groups as front organizations diminished. The barriers to unity posed by class, party, and the structure of work became apparent. At the same time the government, having been burned by the role of professional groups in 1905, refused to sanction broad professional associations and sought to punish the professional activists. Fragmentation was accentuated by the situation within most professions, where a striving for personal as opposed to collective goals dominated, and the leadership of liberationists was challenged by individuals favoring a more conciliatory relationship with the government.

Heightened political awareness and activity during the 1905 Revolution did not lead to greater unity within Russia's professional groups. In most professions the period after 1905 was characterized by fragmentation and disarray, as the obstacles to unity became more evident. Cleavages within professions—particularly noticeable among engineers, physicians, and teachers—were present in varying degrees within all groups. To some extent subdividing professional groups is a normal process, reflecting increasing functional differentiation as emerging specialties assert their unique occupational niche. But the extent of professional subdivision in Russia in these years is striking.[35]

[34] The term professional union is used here in a Western sense, not in the Soviet usage *profsoiuz*, which refers to workers' unions as well as trade unions in a broader sense.

[35] Edwin Layton has described this process brilliantly for the American engineering profession in *The Revolt of the Engineers: Social Responsibility and the American Engineering Profession* (Baltimore: John Hopkins University Press, 1971), 40–42. For similar differentiation among Russian engineers, see Balzer, "Educating Engineers," 417–20; and "The Engineering Profession"

By 1907, leadership in many professional groups was slipping from the hands of the highly politicized adherents of the Liberation Movement. New leaders reflected increasing diversity and the proliferation of specialized associations in many fields. In addition, for large numbers of lawyers, physicians, engineers, and others, the general European economic upswing made this a time to make one's fortune, a period when careerism dominated. Even a committed Bolshevik like Leonid Krasin used these years to rise to a prominent position with the Siemens Corporation.[36]

In some instances, new leaders represented a markedly different professional agenda. Every profession included individuals who were relatively conservative—men like Rein in the medical profession. They now became more assertive, voicing their belief that the professional program could best be attained through cooperation with autocratic power. In this context we can understand why the most hated tsarist ministers of education were those from the university professorate. The conservative trend among students was apparent as well. Surveys of the *studenchestvo*, the group from which future professionals were drawn, show both a marked decline of identification with left-wing political groups in these years and an increased willingness to be identified with the political right.[37]

In analyzing this right shift in the leadership of professional groups after 1905, the role of government repression should not be discounted. By 1906 administrative reprisals forced the Union of Unions to turn attention to economic assistance for unemployed members—especially teachers, but also physicians and then others as well. Massive dismissals, as in the case of teachers, had a devastating effect on the activists while dissuading others from following in their footsteps. Zemstvo boards and private employers took advantage of the opportunity to rid themselves of "troublemakers," particularly among such groups as engineers and pharmacists.[38]

It would be valuable to investigate in detail the purge of professionals in these years to see if any relationship existed between various groups' functional roles and the extent of dismissals. The tsarist government frankly admitted that it could not fire all the questionable or undesirable specialists teaching in its higher educational institutions because there were not adequate cadres to replace them.[39]

---

in *Professions*, Balzer, ed. The number of engineering societies, for example, grew from nine to at least twenty one in the decade after 1905.

[36] Lyubov Krassina, *Leonid Krasin: His Life and Work* (London: Skettington & Sons, 1929), p. 40.

[37] See Kassow and Hutchinson in Balzer's *Professions in Russia*. The authors of the brochure *K kharakteristike sovremennogo studenchestva* (Petersburg, 1910) were shocked to find anti-Semitism among the students they surveyed, and they contrasted this to the "moral stance" of the earlier generation of students.

[38] Seregny, "Professional Activism," in *Professions*, Balzer, ed.; Sanders, "The Union of Unions."

[39] TsGIA, f. 25, op. 5, d. 3, ll. 67.

The fate of professional groups paralleled, to a degree, that of workers' unions, which also saw membership of individual unions decline while new, more specialized organizations developed.[40] While workers renewed their strike activity in 1912–1914, most Russian professionals remained aloof. They continued to pursue individual professional programs and to appeal to the government for recognition and autonomy. If the war forced the government to accept some of these demands, the regime successfully turned back initiatives to create additional national professional organizations. When the tsarist regime fell in February 1917 the change was welcomed by most professional groups, but they could claim little credit for the overthrow.[41]

The growing diversity within Russian professions in the period from 1907 to 1914 and their inclination to refrain from opposition activity raises a serious question regarding the "revolutionary situation" from 1912 to 1914. The strike movement that developed in the two years before the outbreak of World War I was large and sometimes effective, but the movement was not the same broad-based struggle against autocracy seen in 1905. The professional intelligentsia did not join with the workers, making the prewar movement much less significant as a threat to the regime.[42]

Recent scholarship on the social history of the prewar period permits us to go even further in evaluating the extent of social fragmentation in tsarist Russia. Virtually all groups of the professional intelligentsia were deeply divided. Even the Imperial Army experienced a split between different images of professional development.[43] Other researchers have documented the weakness of the merchant-entrepreneur groups and the gulf between these groups and the professional middle class;[44] the fragmentation and isolation of the gentry and their continuing dependence on the state;[45] and the tensions between second

[40] Victoria E. Bonnell, *Roots of Rebellion: Workers' Politics and Organizations in St. Petersburg and Moscow, 1900–1914* (Berkeley: University of California Press, 1983), 202–9.

[41] Tsuyoshi Hasegawa, *The February Revolution: Petrograd 1917* (Seattle: University of Washington Press, 1981); Marc Ferro, *The Russian Revolution of February 1917*, trans. John Lamb Richards; (Englewood Cliffs, N.J.: Prentice-Hall, 1972); Diane Koenker, *Moscow Workers and the 1917 Revolution* (Princeton: Princeton University Press, 1981); and Donald J. Raleigh, *Revolution on the Volga: 1917 in Saratov* (Ithaca: Cornell University Press, 1986), 110–11.

[42] This theme is developed in Kendall Bailes's "Conclusion" to Balzer's *Professions*. The most complete statement of the "revolutionary situation" is by Leopold Haimson, "The Problem of Social Stability in Urban Russia, 1905–1917," *Slavic Review* 23, no. 4 (1964): 619–42, and 24, 1 (1965): 1–22. The best analysis of the strike movement in these years is in Bonnell, *Roots of Rebellion*.

[43] William C. Fuller, Jr., *Civil-Military Conflict in Imperial Russia, 1881–1914* (Princeton: Princeton University Press, 1985), chap. 1.

[44] Alfred J. Rieber, *Merchants and Entrepreneurs in Imperial Russia* (Chapel Hill: University of North Carolina Press, 1982).

[45] Leopold Haimson, "Introduction: The Russian Landed Nobility and the System of the Third of June," in *The Politics of Rural Russia, 1905–1914*, Leopold Haimson, ed. (Bloomington: Indiana University Press, 1979); Roberta Manning, "Zemstvo and Revolution: the Onset of Gentry Reaction, 1905–1907," in *The Politics*, ed. Haimson; Manning, "The Zemstvo and Politics";

and third elements in the zemstvos, particularly over professional issues such as administrative control and budgets.[46]

In retrospect, it is evident that the political education of Russian professionals—and of Russian obshchestvennost' in general—remained incomplete. The solution to the "professional problems" would have been a development corresponding to that of other industrial societies: continued growth of functionally specialized professional groups according to occupation; and legitimation of broader, more inclusive membership societies encompassing a much larger number of the specialists and middle-level personnel in particular occupational groups. While this development was indeed underway, the state refused to accept the legitimacy of the larger, more politically active organizations. Here the immaturity of both government and obshchestvennost' was most apparent. The professionals and other groups had not learned how to articulate their demands, and the government had not learned how to listen to them, perceiving every move for autonomy as a threat to the autocracy. The failure of the middle to hold thus stemmed from two related causes: the number of professionals and other members of the middle class was not large enough to dominate electoral politics, much less the politics of the streets; absent numerical weight, Russia's nascent third force could hold power only if it exhibited political skills and maturity that Russia's tsarist rulers had prevented it from developing. After six decades of Stalinism, we are witnessing a process of professional organization reasserting itself in the Soviet Union, now with a much larger number of professionals. Once again the legitimacy of the professional program is a barometer of social and political maturity.

and Manning, *The Crisis of the Old Order in Russia: Gentry and Government* (Princeton: Princeton University Press, 1982); and Robert Edelman, *Gentry Politics on the Eve of the Russian Revolution: The Nationalist Party, 1907–1917* (New Brunswick: Rutgers University Press, 1980).

[46] See Manning's works cited in note 45; and Terence Emmons, *The Formation of Political Parties and the First National Elections in Russia* (Cambridge: Harvard University Press, 1983).

Chapter 13

CULTURAL PIONEERS AND PROFESSIONALS:
THE TEACHER IN SOCIETY

CHRISTINE RUANE AND BEN EKLOF

FEW INDIVIDUALS would consider schoolteachers the quintessential professionals. Low pay, low status, and the predominance of women in the field have kept the teaching profession from becoming a career option to which many middle-class children aspire. In the eyes of society, teachers are "contaminated" from working with children. In the words of one scholar, their work is only "semiprofessional" because "their training is shorter, their status is less legitimated, their right to privileged communication less established, there is less of a specialized body of knowledge, and they have less autonomy from supervision or societal control than 'the' professions."[1]

However, despite their relegation to the lower ranks of the professional hierarchy, teachers have long wanted to raise their professional standing. Throughout Europe in the nineteenth and twentieth centuries, teachers formed organizations demanding greater autonomy, better training programs, and more self-regulation—typical demands of any occupation seeking to raise its professional status. Russian schoolteachers were no different from their European counterparts. They, too, formed a professional movement during the late nineteenth century and demanded greater respect, social status, and autonomy for the important work they performed.

What makes the Russian case so striking and important for scholars is the conjunction of these professional demands with political demands for restructuring Russian society. Moreover, these same individuals were calling for the creation of a kind of civil consciousness, which they called *obshchestvennost'*, to replace the old *soslovie* mentality. Russian professionals wanted their own special place in society where they could live and work free of government interference and free to make their own independent contribution to Russian life. They wished to belong to neither the nobility nor the bureaucracy; instead, they wanted to create a new sphere of activity outside the government. As the government became more intransigent, Russian teachers began to fight for their beliefs through professional and political activism.

This chapter examines the goals of the teachers' professional movement as a way of understanding the development of a civil consciousness. Teachers

---

[1] Amitai Etzioni, *The Semi-Professions and Their Organization* (New York, 1969), vi.

served as "cultural pioneers" entrusted with the task of promoting this new civil consciousness—a belief in science, progress, individual advancement—and with spreading knowledge, the key to the new society. Moreover, Russian teachers make an excellent case study because the history of their professional development demonstrates the tensions inherent in the professional and political movements as well as in the development of obshchestvennost' in Russia.

Yet the most salient feature of the Russian teaching profession as it developed over the course of the nineteenth century was its heterogeneity. The school system itself extended downward from the prestigious classical gymnasiums and lycees to the two-year literacy schools, supervised by the Holy Synod. The personnel who operated the schools were just as diverse as the schools.

At the top of the teaching profession were the male secondary schoolteachers, who in 1880 were mostly married sons of the nobility, bureaucrats, and the clergy. Boasting a university education, these men entered the teaching profession as members of the government civil service with all the privileges and ranks such service entailed. Many were authors of various works in their area of specialization or in the field of pedagogy. As a way of improving their standing in the civil service as well as gaining greater financial renumeration, many secondary schoolteachers served on various government committees.[2]

Perhaps the greatest change occurring in the teaching profession in Russia during the nineteenth century was the feminization of that profession, which began in earnest after 1871. As early as 1882 the St. Petersburg Commission on Education instituted a policy of hiring only women to teach in the new municipal primary schools; other cities and zemstvos soon followed suit. The St. Petersburg school officials believed that teaching was women's "natural" profession, and it helped prepare women for marriage by encouraging their nurturing instincts. It took women longer to gain access to teaching jobs in the secondary schools, but in 1911 women were finally allowed to teach in any secondary school of their choice.[3]

The women who taught in the primary and secondary schools shared many traits. The majority were daughters of the nobility, clergy, and *meshchanstvo*. They were graduates of the women's gymnasiums, institutes, and higher courses. Most women teachers were young and unmarried, and the majority taught fewer than ten years before leaving the profession.[4] For most women, teaching served as a way of earning a living before marriage. Teaching for

[2] Christine Ruane Hinshaw, "The Soul of the School: The Professionalization of Urban Schoolteachers in St. Petersburg and Moscow, 1890–1907" (Ph.D. diss., University of California, Berkeley, 1986), 58–72; V. R. Leikina-Svirskaia, *Intelligentsiia v Rossii* (Moscow, 1971), 154.

[3] F. G. Panachin, *Pedagogicheskoe obrazovanie v Rossii: istoriko- pedagogicheskie ocherki* (Moscow, 1979), 49.

[4] Hinshaw, "The Soul of the School," 58–72.

them was not a career, but rather a way-station until their "real" work as wives and mothers began.

In contrast to urban teachers, Russian rural teachers were a sundry group, but as time passed a growing percentage came from humbler origins. Between 1880 and 1911 the proportion of teachers of peasant origins rose from 30 percent to 49 percent, while the proportion from the clergy declined from 38 percent to 22 percent and, from the nobility, from 11 percent to 7 percent. Together with *meshchane*, peasants by 1911 made up an absolute majority of teachers; but among women, no single social group accounted for more than one-third of the total.[5] Similarly, rural teachers received their training in a variety of schools, including clerical seminaries (20 percent), specialized educational institutions (19 percent), and gymnasiums and progymnasiums (33 percent); the balance were from either secondary schools providing no pedagogical instruction or elementary schools that granted teaching certificates.[6] They were a young lot. In 1911, roughly seven out of ten were under thirty years of age. By contrast with women teachers, 50 percent of male zemstvo teachers and 40 percent of male church schoolteachers were married and more likely to put down roots in the village. If marriage and hearth improved the teachers' rapport with the peasants, then the feminization of the profession meant that a vital link was missing.

Given this information about the profile of Russian schoolteachers, no unified social portrait can be drawn. Sharp discordances among schoolteachers were based on gender, class, location, and level. Thus, the teaching profession, to gain a group identity, had to draw together individuals from the already existing estates and merge them into an entirely new group—a professional middle class with a new set of values and attitudes toward work and society.

If social cohesiveness was not a unifying force for teachers, one other factor was: namely, teachers' experiences both in and out of the classroom. When teachers were finally given the opportunity to meet and discuss the problems of the Russian educational system, they discovered that their common experiences united them in a way that offset the other social, political, and cultural divisions. As teachers began to meet in various pedagogical and mutual aid societies, they found a common sense of grievance against what they considered arbitrary government control of the classroom and undue interference in teachers' private lives; they decried inadequate school facilities and overcrowding that occurred at all levels of the school system; they also expressed indignation at the lack of respect accorded teachers by the rest of society. This common work experience and sense of shared grievances served as a founda-

[5] Ministerstvo narodnogo prosveshcheniia, *Odnodnevnaia perepis' nachal'nykh shkol Rossiisskoi imperii proizvedennaia 18 ianvaria 1911*, 16 vols. (St. Petersburg, 1916), 16: 95; Leikina-Svirskaia, *Intelligentsiia*, 163.

[6] *Odnodnevnaia perepis'* 16: 86, 56, sec. 3.

tion for developing a professional ethos among teachers, emphasizing self-worth, individual advancement, and autonomy. As the teachers' professional movement began to gain momentum in Russia in the late 1890s and particularly after 1900, several common themes emerged in the writings and speeches of the professional activists: the poor material status of teachers, the absence of legal recourse against abuse by educational authorities, and a widespread lack of respect for the important work teachers performed. Teachers' professional organizations paid particular attention to the plight of the rural teacher, most victimized by the Russian educational system.

Perhaps because of the low esteem of the craft, few countries have paid their primary schoolteachers well. Russia was no exception; in the 1860s the annual wage of the teacher fluctuated from 12 to 150 rubles. Beginning in the 1890s provincial zemstvos began offering salary supplements to the districts to bring wages up to 360 rubles. The government initiated a pension plan in 1900, and the 1908 School Bill stipulated that all districts receiving government aid for school expansion had to pay a minimum salary of 360 rubles, with periodic supplements of 50 rubles. By 1911 the average salary of teachers in all rural primary schools was 343 rubles for men and 340 for women.[7] Even among secondary schoolteachers, the best paid of all urban teachers, there was much dissatisfaction, although urban teachers tended to complain more of financial insecurity than actual want—a major distinction between primary and secondary schoolteachers.

How adequate was this income for teachers' needs? Abundant direct testimony documents that teachers, particularly in the countryside, faced extreme hardship, sacrifice, and deprivation. A study of teachers in the Moscow district in 1900 showed that only 15 percent were free of debt.[8] The same budget studies showed that married teachers with two children spent 74 percent of their annual income (372 rubles) on food; those with three children spent 86 percent. Poverty drove teachers to give private lessons on the side, teach crafts, conduct private readings, work as insurance agents, even hire out as farm laborers (*batraki*), shepherds, or housepainters.[9] Such teachers, it might be noted, had over fifty hours weekly of contact time with students. In extreme cases, teachers left the profession to become clerks in the state-run liquor stores, police constables, tax officials, even pest exterminators.

The difficulty rural teachers had in receiving even this pittance graphically

---

[7] *Odnodnevnaia perepis'* 16: 95. For provincial programs, see V. I. Farmakovskii, "Nachal'-naia shkola Ministerstva narodnogo prosveshcheniia," *Russkaia shkola* 10, no. 10 (1899): 168–87. For a detailed discussion, see Ben Eklof, *Russian Peasant Schools: Officialdom, Village Culture, and Popular Pedagogy, 1861–1914* (Berkeley, 1986), 215–20.

[8] V. V. Akimov, "Zemskaia deiatel'nost' po narodnomu obrazovaniiu v Moskovskoi gubernii," *Zhurnal Ministerstva narodnogo prosveshcheniia*, n.s., 8, sec. 3 (1907): 15–17.

[9] Salomatin, *Kak zhivet i rabotaet narodnyi uchitel'*, 2 vols. (St. Petersburg, 1910), 188–90; V. Charnoluskii, *Zemstvo i narodnoe obrazovanie*, 2 vols. (St. Petersburg, 1910), 2: 272–97.

illustrates their low social status. The way they had virtually to beg for their pay shows just how compromised they were by their location between two cultures. Teachers seldom could count on prompt payment from the village commune, and wages frequently arrived several months late, particularly during the lean spring season. Scarcity did not always cause the delay; when a teacher was not in good standing with local peasant officials, they could pull the purse strings to harass or humiliate the teacher. One vicious peasant clerk and his drunken friends regularly entertained themselves by forcing the local teacher to dance for his salary.[10]

The fact that rural teachers had to grub for their salaries before the local zemstvo speaks eloquently of their low standing before the nobility running these institutions. Even more important, such treatment had to tarnish the image of teachers in the eyes of the villagers: although not "one of us," they were also not people of any standing in the outside world. Or why were doors slammed in their faces, why were they treated as inferiors? The teacher was sometimes called a "cultural pioneer," but this description had its limits. Instead, rank-and-file teachers, though genuinely committed to the cause of spreading enlightenment, were also acutely sensitive of their status as semi-professionals; they believed their salaries only further reduced them in the eyes of the people. Although pursuing a noble profession—even a mission—they endured treatment by both population and officialdom that did not befit that mission. This hurt pride was evident when teachers were denied servants by the local community and were "even forced to carry their own firewood and water." As one teacher noted, "I consider these tasks incompatible with the lofty title of teacher."[11] It is most curious that a mixture of Populism, a belief that basic education was the key to progress and therefore a calling, and dire poverty led to extreme status anxiety among Russia's teachers.

The legal status of teachers often made their lives miserable and once again showed how little teachers were respected by either the people or the authorities. As one teacher noted, everyone seemed aware of teachers' obligations, while no one recognized their rights. Vulnerability began with legislation concerning hiring, confirmation, and dismissal, for all sides recognized that teacher selection was undoubtedly the single most important means of exerting effective control over schooling, as teachers were caught between progressive educators and conservative officials. Control extended far beyond the confines of the school day, reaching deeply into the teachers' personal life. The government was extremely apprehensive about political contamination of the village community by radical teachers. Because it could not supervise daily classroom routines, the government tended to overreact to claims that teachers

[10] V. Evteev, ed., *Trudy pervogo vserossiiskogo s''ezda predstavitelei obshchestv vpomoshchestvovaniia litsam uchitel'skogo zvaniia*, 2 vols. (Moscow, 1907), 1: 473.

[11] Ibid., 1: 477.

were spreading sedition or corrupting the youth. In turn, anyone familiar with the ways of the political system could threaten the teacher with political suspicion in order to extort, blackmail, terrorize, even force sexual favors from the teacher.

In some instances the inspector appropriated the right to intervene in every aspect of the teachers' personal life. An egregious example of such interference was the infamous instructions given teachers by Inspector Iablochkov of Tula in the 1890s, calling for strict morality, consultation with officials before marriage, and complete submission to authority. Iablochkov also called long hair "disgusting" on men and forbade women to wear their hair in buns, cautioned against "brightly colored jackets" or tobacco ("animals get by without it").[12] Inspectors sometimes confiscated teachers' internal passports to control their movement.

Among the authorities who exercised some control over the teacher's life, particular mention should be made of the local priest who, according to the 1874 Education Statute, was responsible for the moral and religious tone of the school. According to the former teacher Salomatin, conflict between teacher and priest was endemic and usually ignited by pupils performing poorly at their religion lessons or on religious tests.[13] He recorded instances when teachers ran into trouble for refusing to teach religion classes for the priest (for which the latter was paid). The priest sometimes took offense if the teacher or pupils failed to attend church regularly, to help out with the services, or to sing with the choir. Teachers were sometimes dismissed after being denounced by the local priest for attending a gathering at which there was vodka and dancing. Thus, Salomatin claimed that teacher and priest lived together "like cat and dog." Of course, not all inspectors or priests were officious or overbearing; many were in fact dedicated to popular enlightenment. Still, the potential for abuse was there. That it occurred is attested by Anikin, who wrote, "just read the pedagogical chronicle in the education periodicals, and your hair will stand on end."[14]

Women teachers proved particularly vulnerable to harassment by local school officials. In 1912 the local school board in Chistopolsk required prospective women teachers to submit not only a certificate of political reliability but also medical proof of their virginity.[15] Perhaps the most infamous of all

[12] Cited in P. F. Kapterev, *Novye dvizheniia v oblasti narodnogo obrazovaniia i srednei shkoly* (Moscow, 1913), 29.

[13] Alexander Tarnovskii, *Ob ob''iazannostiakh uchitelia nachal'nogo narodnogo uchilishcha* (Moscow, 1896), 104–5, 107, 176–81; Ia. K., "Pravovoe polozhenie narodnogo uchitelia," *Russkaia shkola* 19, no. 5–6 (1908): 140.

[14] Salomatin, *Kak zhivet*, 176–81. Another figure who sometimes made life miserable for the teacher was the local school trustee. For a discussion, see Eklof, *Russian Peasant Schools*, chap. 5, and Hinshaw, "The Soul of the School," chap. 4.

[15] Tarnovskii, *Ob ob''iazannostiakh*, 3, 35, 37.

these various interventions into women teachers' private lives occurred not in some remote corner of the Russian countryside but in St. Petersburg itself. In 1897 the St. Petersburg Commission on Education changed the hiring requirements for personnel in the municipal primary schools. Teacher candidates now had to be between the ages of eighteen and thirty, unmarried or widowed without children. These new rules did not permit the commission to fire married teachers who were already teaching in the schools, but these teachers now had to apply to the commission for permission to remain in their rent-free apartments. The intended effect of these new rules was clear: the commission wanted to hire young, single women unencumbered by husbands or children. Despite a number of articles that appeared in the press condemning these new rules as "draconian," the St. Petersburg City Duma approved them in October 1897.[16] These rules became the chief source of friction between the teachers and the Commission on Education, but they were not repealed until 1913. Many provincial inspectors throughout Russia pursued a similar policy—either refusing to hire or firing women who married.

Another complaint among teachers was their spiritual and intellectual isolation. In this area urban teachers were much more fortunate than their rural counterparts. Urban teachers had access to books, periodicals, and other sources of intellectual stimulation; however, the urban teachers complained bitterly that they had little time to devote to such intellectual and cultural pursuits because they were overworked and exhausted by their daily labors. Once again they complained that even when they did have some free time, they did not have the financial resources to spend on such activities.

All teachers agreed, however, that rural teachers suffered the most from their intellectual isolation. Convincing evidence of the rural teachers' low intellectual horizons and lack of interest in the outside world can be found in the many studies of teachers' reading habits carried out near the turn of the century. Teachers were potential conduits of modern culture, but if they read little, they were not likely to bring much that was new to the village. V. V. Petrov's study of Moscow province in the 1890s showed that 60 percent had fewer than fifty books in their possession. Despite an extensive library network in that province, only 17 percent to 30 percent of teachers used it. From 1894 to 1898 only eighty teachers, out of roughly eight hundred, used the special pedagogical libraries housed in district zemstvo executive board offices.[17]

---

[16] "Poriadok opredeleniia na uchitel'skie dolzhnosti v nachal'nykh uchilishchakh goroda S.-Peterburga," *Izvestiia S.-Peterburgskoi dumy* 19 (1897): 129–32; and A. Strannoliubskii, "Nesostoiatel'nost' S.-Peterburgskoi Gorodskoi Dumy v dele narodnogo obrazovaniia," *Obrazovanie* 10 (1897): 151. For a further discussion of the marriage issue, see Christine Ruane, "The Vestal Virgins of St. Petersburg: Schoolteachers and the 1897 Marriage Ban," *Russian Review* (forthcoming).

[17] Blinov, "Narodnyi uchitel'," in *Vseobshchee obrazovanie v Rossii*, ed. D. Shakhovskoi et

Thus, teachers felt an acute sense of status anxiety. They were mocked and bullied by the upper and middle echelons of society for their lack of cultural refinement and material status; the peasants distrusted them as outsiders or *prishlye*. Rural teachers, in particular, were caught between two worlds, two cultures. As one teacher commented: "One could say that he [the teacher] has departed one shore without reaching the other."[18]

But not all teachers gave up in despair or sank to the level of the country-side. Beginning as early as the 1860s a small group of Russian educators and teachers dedicated themselves to improving the status of Russian teachers through the development of professional organizations. These pedagogical and mutual aid societies began first in the big cities of the empire but slowly spread to the countryside, looking for ways to help teachers both materially and intellectually. As teachers began to meet and discuss mutual problems, many concluded that the problems of the schools or the profession could not be solved until some fundamental change occurred in the Russian political and social structure. Until Russian citizens gained respect and autonomy from their government—values intrinsic to the development of obshchestven-nost'—there could be no meaningful change in Russia. For teachers, the real enemy was the heavy hand of the Ministry of Education, which interfered so frequently in their lives, denied them legal protection, and kept them in pov-erty. Encouraged by the growing strength of the underground radical move-ment and the other professional movements, teachers, particularly after 1900, began to make stronger demands for both educational and political change. A significant number of teachers also sought redress *through* the Ministry of Ed-ucation, by inclusion in the Table of Ranks as employees of the state, entitling them to the corresponding benefits and status. It is a yet unresolved issue how many teachers turned to the state and how many to the opposition.[19]

When Russia finally exploded in revolution in January 1905, the teachers' professional movement—not necessarily all teachers—eagerly joined in the Liberation Movement with its own list of demands for the government. Fol-lowing the killing in Kursk of several gymnasium students by Russian police on February 12, 1905, members of the Moscow Pedagogical Society pub-lished a manifesto "Notes of the Moscow Secondary Schoolteachers." The article began with the by-now widespread phrase, "It is impossible to live this way any longer" (*Tak dol'she zhit' nel'zia*) and called for an end to the bu-reaucratic and police regime in the schools as well as the convention of a

---

al. (Moscow, 1902), 72; V. V. Petrov, *Voprosy narodnogo obrazovaniia v Moskovskoi gubernii* (Moscow, 1897–1907), 2: 36–37; N. I. Bratchikov, "Uchebnovospitatel'naia chast' v nachal'noi shkole," *Russkaia shkola* 20, no. 2 (1909): 127.

[18] Evteev, *Trudy*, 1: 266.

[19] On this, see especially Scott J. Seregny, *Russian Teachers and Peasant Revolution: The Politics of Education in 1905* (Bloomington, 1989).

national assembly of elected representatives.[20] Following this highly publicized statement by Moscow teachers, thousands more began to join whatever
local teachers' organization they could find. And now, after years of dream-
ing, for the first time professional activists began to plan openly for the creation of an all-Russian teachers' union to represent teachers' interests to the
Ministry of Education and provide teachers with a tool for achieving some
professional and political goals.

The first national meeting of the new All Russian Union of Teachers and
Education Activists (VSU) took place in June 1905. For some the meeting was
a truly joyful occasion as these teacher activists finally saw the culmination of
all their years of hard work. However, as debate began over the nature of the
new union, the mood of ebullience quickly dissolved in rancorous debate.
Ironically, the delegates now completely agreed on the educational reforms
necessary to advance their professional interests. At the very first meeting the
teacher delegates unanimously approved the professional goals for the union:
(1) creation of a unified ladder system of education; (2) introduction of free,
universal education; (3) elimination of the religious element in the school; (4)
freedom to instruct as teachers saw fit and in the language of the local population; (5) right of any individual or organization to establish an educational
institution; and (6) local control of education.[21] These goals clearly expressed
the aim of the teachers, which was to establish an autonomous teaching profession. In achieving this independence from the bureaucratic authorities,
teachers hoped not only to win a secularized, democratic, decentralized school
system providing universal access at all levels but also, in so doing, to gain
the respect they so deeply craved from the rest of Russian society.

Problems arose, however, when the delegates began to discuss political
goals. There were essentially three points of view on the place of politics in
the new teachers' union. The most conservative of the teachers believed that
the VSU had no business interfering in Russian political life; that should be
left to the tsar and his advisers. Another group of delegates felt that teachers
should concern themselves with politics, but that these pressing political issues must remain separate from the union's professional activities. The third
group believed most emphatically that the All-Russian Teachers' Union could
not hope to achieve any of its professional goals unless it adopted political
ones as well.

The debate over the union's platform worked itself out in a curious fashion.
Two positions were put forward. Supported by the rural delegates, the union
leadership submitted a platform incorporating both political and professional
points and supporting many goals of the Socialist Revolutionary party (SR),

[20] "Zapiski prepodavatelei moskovskikh srednikh uchebnykh zavedenii," *Pravo* 6 (Feb. 13,
1905): 424–25.
[21] TsGAOR, f. 6862, op. 1, d. 46, ll. 17–18.

although the platform clearly stated that the union would not become affiliated with any one political party. On the other side, a coalition of urban teachers, led by the Social Democrats, proposed a strictly professional platform for the union; this proposal also included demands for an eight-hour day, an end to the war, and a declaration of teacher solidarity with the working class, demands associated with the Social Democratic party in 1905.[22] The leader of the Social Democratic faction, N. A. Rozhkov, even threatened to leave the union if the strictly professional platform was not adopted. Despite this threat, the delegates voted 109 to 40 to adopt the SR-influenced professional-political platform. The Social Democrats, joined by other urban teachers in a dramatic display, walked out of the meeting.[23]

The results of this schism in the All-Russian Teachers' Union were far-reaching, for it marked an end to the short-lived unity of the teaching profession that activists had worked so hard to achieve. Although the All-Russian Teachers' Union advocated a moderate political program tailored to appeal to all progressive political parties, it nevertheless came to represent the interests of rural teachers and became associated with the Socialist Revolutionary party, to which most politically active rural teachers belonged. As one rural teacher succinctly put it, "the rural teacher must act as an SR, otherwise the peasants will not heed him."[24] This attitude seems to suggest that rural teachers in 1905 did not act according to any developing notion of professional identity, but rather that teachers' views of this new civil consciousness were meant to bridge these social antagonisms. Instead, they chose to identify themselves with the peasantry and its political organizations. Indeed, many teachers became the elected representatives for the peasants in the First and Second Dumas. According to Seregny, "teachers' support for the Peasant Union perhaps best reflected the fact that after October [1905], if not before, teachers viewed the rural masses as their salvation."[25]

Among urban teachers, there is no such clear-cut identification of teachers with one particular social category. Instead, urban teachers' political views covered the entire Russian political spectrum. In an interesting replay of the June debate in the All-Russian Teachers' Union, the Moscow City Teachers' Union took up the question of political involvement in the fall of 1905. This time those favoring political neutrality for the union won.[26] Despite the at-

[22] The Social Democrats led the fight against the political and professional platform because they believed that such a platform would unite the teachers with the liberal bourgeoisie rather than the proletariat. See L. K. Erman, *Intelligentsiia v pervoi russkoi revoliutsii* (Moscow, 1966), 91–92.

[23] TsGAOR, f. 6862, op. 1, d. 46, ll. 18–24 and d. 57, ll. 20–21.

[24] Scott Seregny, "Professional and Political Activism: The Russian Teachers' Movement, 1864–1908" (Ph.D. diss., University of Michigan, 1982), 614.

[25] Ibid., 810. However, see also Eklof, *Russian Peasant Schools*, 243–47.

[26] TsGAOR, f. 6862, op. 1, d. 84, ll. 224–225.

tempts of some teachers to impose a specific political program on the Moscow Teachers' Union, the majority realized that no one political program could satisfy all the teachers. Having lost control of the national Teachers' Union, the Moscow teachers did not want to risk losing their local professional union to any one political party.

After the June 1907 coup, teachers lost all the gains that they had made up to that point. Thousands of teachers were arrested in the repression following the Revolution of 1905, and many others were harmed in the peasant violence that erupted in late 1905 and 1906. Teachers' unions were banned, and membership in all the professional organizations dropped precipitously. By 1908, it looked to many as though the teachers' movement had been crushed.

In the months following the end of the 1905 Revolution, many teachers were left to wonder just what had happened to the unity of their professional movement, which had been destroyed not by government arrests and repression, but from within by the teachers themselves. What had gone wrong? Why had their professional movement descended so abruptly into rancorous debates and political division? For the historian, the reasons for the failure of the teachers' movement do much to highlight the enormous social and political tensions Russia was experiencing in the early years of the twentieth century.

The chief reason for the movement's disintegration in 1905 was the perhaps unavoidable superimposition of larger political goals upon the professional movement. This, in turn, demonstrated the strengths and limitations of the development of obshchestvennost' in Russia. Professional and political movements did well in the pre-1905 period because the goals they espoused—autonomy, self-worth, respect for the individual in society and service—had a broad appeal in a country frantically trying to catch up with the West. Workers, peasants, nobles, and professionals all felt aggrieved by the autocracy, although, as Roberta Manning and others have demonstrated, the nobility clung to notions of hierarchy and privilege and opposed not the autocracy but its policies. Once the Revolution of 1905 came and these very same groups began to live according to these new values, the Liberation Movement dissolved into antagonistic factions with no common vision for Russia's future.

Despite their claims of solidarity, teachers perhaps more than any other aspiring professional group, were highly segmented, both vertically and horizontally. Secondary school teachers looked down upon teachers in primary schools. Most urban teachers did not feel that they shared much with their rural cousins. Once primary school teachers came together to form a union, they realized that the views of urban and rural teachers on Russian society were different, even contradictory. Urban teachers were, after all, from the educated elite. When these urban teachers were confronted by their rural counterparts in the highly charged atmosphere of 1905, the issues dividing them became more important than their mutual interest in improving Russian education and creating an autonomous profession. Years later as one teacher activist described the situation: "Professional interests were forgotten; they thought about them [only] in so far as they were connected with political work."[27] In short a concern to maintain boundaries and hierarchy among teachers overwhelmed the struggle for professional autonomy vis-à-vis the state. Ideology, as we have shown, played a major role, but Klaus Frolich has shown that the SR party appealed to rural teachers because it was most democratic internally and not only recruited but also promoted within its ranks large numbers of the lower intelligentsia.

Moreover, it is not clear that the political views of the leadership of the teachers' movement accurately reflected the position of rank-and-file teachers. But for many teachers in their schools acute dissatisfaction with the low status of the teaching profession was accompanied by the hope that the government would improve the teachers' lot. Social mobility was undeniably the major goal of large numbers of teachers of humble origins, as demonstrated by the turnover of personnel, the search for government rank and a government uniform (in the secondary schools), and by persistent petitions for free tuition and free boarding facilities at school for their children. Many teachers actually welcomed the government drive, begun with the 1908 School Bill, to remove rural schools from zemstvo control and incorporate them directly into the Ministry of Education hierarchy, thereby making teachers official employees of the state. The zemstvo had long treated the teachers as hirelings; perhaps, they thought, the government would at least put uniforms on them and give them ranks. One need only turn to the many fictional teachers depicted in the works of Anton Chekhov to confirm this pervasive status anxiety, isolation, and striving for acceptance—whether by obshchestvo or vlast'.

However, the development of a professional ethos and obshchestvennost' among schoolteachers was further complicated by the urban/rural divide among them. If one associates the rise of the professions with industrialization and urbanization, then professionalization becomes an urban phenomenon, at least initially. But Russian schoolteachers lived and worked in the cities *and* the countryside. As we have seen, rural teachers prior to and during the 1905 Revolution were caught between two cultural worlds, while urban teachers felt themselves part of urban life and culture. This suggests that among urban teachers it is possible to find the beginnings of a civil consciousness at the turn of the century, but among rural teachers this same development remained stillborn. At the same time, after 1908, educational expansion by zemstvos and the government led to improved salaries and benefits and an enhanced role in the effort to modernize Russia. Preliminary research on the activities of urban teachers in the post-1907 period indicates that urban teachers continued to press for professional recognition until World War I. This suggests that urban

---

[27] N. Popova, "Moskovskaia oblastnaia organizatsiia Vserossiiskogo Uchitel'skogo Soiuza," *Narodnyi uchitel'*, no. 11 (November 1925): 47.

teachers continued to view themselves as part of a developing profession in the prewar period. At the same time, however, rural teachers continued to feel themselves isolated from Russian educated society, yet not part of the village community either. Thus, the development of obshchestvennost' may have remained a strictly urban phenomenon with few roots in the countryside.

Another factor that helps explain both the failure of the teachers' professional movement and the full development of obshchestvennost' in Russia is the place of women teachers in the profession. As we have seen, for many women their commitment to teaching was temporary. This attitude had a profound impact on the professionalization of women teachers because it meant that men did not accept women teachers as equals: male teachers did not believe women were as committed to the betterment of the profession because they had no long-term career plans. Moreover, even those women teachers who asserted their rights as professionals found little support among their male colleagues. The many regulations against women teachers, especially married ones, demonstrated that Russian society did not approve of such professional women. Indeed, many felt that women should not be independent and autonomous individuals. When St. Petersburg teachers tried to repeal the prohibition against married women teachers in 1905, they received support not from teachers' organizations but from woman's groups, a sure sign that this issue was a ''woman's'' issue and not one that concerned the teaching profession as a whole. The message was clear: women's particular needs and concerns were of interest only when they coincided with the interests of the men teachers. How, then, could the teachers' professional movement hope to succeed when close to half the members of the profession did not feel welcome within the profession? And, more important, how could obshchestvennost', with its emphasis on independence and autonomy, develop if women were not included?

Thus, the teachers' professional movement failed. Teachers had a clear-cut program of educational reforms that would improve their working lives, but they also recognized that these reforms depended upon a profound political and social transformation of Russia. One urban teacher summarized the feelings of many in the profession in 1907: ''Obviously, it is necessary to wait for a new public (*obshchestvennyi*) awakening, which will again shake up the teachers' union, will unite the large circle of teachers, and will clear the path for professional, union work.''[28] The real problem, however, was that teachers did not agree on what the new Russia should be—whether social justice or political reforms should be given priority. There was no one vision of a modern Russia that all teachers shared. Until such a common vision could be found, neither teachers' professional aspirations nor a civil consciousness could be achieved.

[28] P., ''Iz zhizni korporatsii moskovskikh gorodskikh uchitelei,'' *Uchitel'* 5 (March 31, 1907): 29.

PART SIX

The Creation of a Public Culture
Beneath the Elites

"GOING TO THE INTELLIGENTSIA": THE CHURCH AND ITS URBAN MISSION IN POST-REFORM RUSSIA

GREGORY L. FREEZE

AS THE PACE of industrialization and urbanization quickened in post-Reform Russia, these processes of social change inevitably generated a host of new problems and issues, for not only state and society but also the Russian Orthodox Church. To be sure, from the 1860s the Church had tended to regard the modern city as a cultural antipode to traditional Orthodoxy and to hypostasize the Church's identification with the village and its way of life. It is hardly surprising that many clergymen distrusted, even despised, the intelligentsia, not only the radical wing that abjured revealed religion in favor of materialistic ideologies but also the more staid, moderate segments of *obshchestvo* (educated society). Predictably, the Church also felt unsure of its hold on the city's lower strata, especially the workers who manned the new factories that were springing up all across the urban landscape. This antiurbanism, though muted and not systematically articulated, was not limited to reactionary bishops; even liberal priests expressed anxiety about the secular city and tended to idealize the ignorant but pious villagers as the bastion of Orthodoxy.[1] Unlike the corrupted townspeople, the "people"—ordinarily equated with the gray masses in the village—seemed to preserve their traditional piety. This rural orientation predisposed the Church to focus on the problems of the rural parishes and clergy and, by default, to neglect the needs of its urban mission.[2]

This essay forms part of a larger project, "Church and Society in Imperial Russia, 1750–1914," which at various stages has been supported by the International Research and Exchanges Board, the Fulbright Faculty Research Program, and the Alexander von Humboldt-Stiftung. A special thanks is due to the staff of the Central State Historical Archive in Leningrad and the Slavic Library of Helsinki University.

[1] For examples of the latter, see "Letopis' tserkovnoi i obshchestvennoi zhizni v Rossii," *Tserkovnyi vestnik*, no. 17 (1906): 553 (hereafter *TsVk*). "Tserkov' i rabochii vopros," *TsVk*, no. 40 (1906): 1285–89.

[2] The ecclesiastical press, whether central or diocesan, gave little attention to the Church's urban mission—a tendency reflected by the preponderance of such village-oriented church journals as *Rukovodstvo dlia sel'skikh pastyrei*. For this one-sidedness, see the critical comments in "Neskol'ko slov o gorodskom dukhovenstve," *Smolenskie eparkhial'nye vedomosti* (1908), no. 19. This tendency was already apparent by the 1850s; see, for example, the complaint in the memoir by I. S. Belliustin that, while concern had been voiced about the miserable condition of

To be sure, the Church did not altogether ignore the spiritual needs of the city, and, especially from the 1890s amidst the resurgence and restructuring of the Liberation Movement (*osvoboditel'noe dvizhenie*), it made a new effort to reach various segments of urban society.[3] For all its earnestness, however, this urban mission ultimately failed to "urbanize" Orthodoxy, to carve out a salient niche for the Church in the teeming cities of the empire. This essay examines one dimension of that urban ministry, namely, the attempt to reach "upward" to the educated, propertied strata that claimed to embody *obshchestvennost'* or articulate civil society. In part, the Church's diffident, unproductive response derived from the very frailty of obshchestvennost', which was simply too inchoate to elicit much clerical attention, let alone trigger a radical shift in ecclesiastical thought and policy.[4] But the obstacles to an urban mission were manifold. Given the Church's genuine interest, however, the problem is to elucidate why it had such difficulty in adapting Orthodoxy to the city and its educated, middling strata. This essay seeks to consider why the Church took a new interest in the city, how it perceived and responded to the secular, self-conscious obshchestvennost' of the city, and why this urban mission gradually slipped downward on the Church's agenda.

To answer these questions, this essay draws upon three main sources—the archive of the Holy Synod, various official publications of the Church, and the ecclesiastical press. The Synodal archive not only provides data on the official policy of the Church but also contains voluminous quantities of diocesan reports on ecclesiastical activity at the grassroots.[5] Useful insights are also to be gleaned from Synodal publications, especially those of the various preconciliar commissions.[6] But of paramount importance is the ecclesiastical

---

the rural clergy, the plight of urban clergy had been virtually ignored. See Belliustin, *Description of the Clergy in Rural Russia*, ed. and trans. G. L. Freeze (Ithaca, 1985).

[3] For the reform era, see the discussion and references in Julia Owalt, *Kirchliche Gemeinde und Bauernbefreiung: soziales Reformdenken in der orthodoxen Gemeindegeistlichkeit Rußlands in der Ära Alexanders II* (Göttingen, 1975).

[4] This author, at least, is skeptical of attempts to exaggerate the coherence or comprehensiveness of a "middle-class" ideology and consciousness, even at the end of the ancien régime. Traditional historiography has slighted the urban strata, yet their coherence and cohesiveness should not be exaggerated; that is all the more the case given the dearth of research on stratification, mobility, subcultures, and, in particular, the dynamics of group formation and aggregation. At the very time that such phantasmagoric collectivities as obshchestvennost' wafted through city boulevards, countervailing forces of geographic, occupational, and ethnic divisions produced an irresistible tendency toward disaggregation and differentiation. For some preliminary comments, see the introduction to G. L. Freeze, *From Supplication to Revolution: A Documentary Social History of Imperial Russia, 1760–1906* (New York, 1988).

[5] The synodal archive is located in Tsentral'nyi gosudarstvennyi istoricheskii arkhiv SSSR, f. 796; hereafter TsGIA SSSR.

[6] Particularly important are *Otzyvy eparkhial'nykh arkhiereev po voprosu o tserkovnoi reforme*, 3 vols. (St. Petersburg, 1906); *Zhurnaly i protokoly zasedanii Vysochaishe uchrezhdennogo pred-*

press—the "thick journals" of the ecclesiastical academies that examined the Church's role on a higher level,[7] the diocesan press (particularly for those dioceses with major urban centers),[8] and the new, socially oriented periodicals that directly addressed the issue of the Church's secular mission.[9] Together these sources provide multiple perspectives on the Church's encounter with urban Russia—a subject virtually ignored in the existing scholarship.[10]

Curiously enough, until the mid-nineteenth century the Church appeared highly satisfied with urban piety and its own status in the city. Indeed, it was strongly entrenched in cities, with a high density of churches and clerics that conferred an impressive social preponderance and enabled the Church to pursue its mission with zeal and effect. The Church also found it possible to accommodate the commercial values of an urban economy; thus it approved of hard work, accepted the legitimacy of fair profits and property, and even as-

---

sobornogo prisutstviia, 5 vols. (St. Petersburg, 1906–1909); and the materials in *Predsobornoe soveshchanie*, 5 vols. (St. Petersburg, 1912–1916).

[7] This essay draws upon *Khristianskoe chtenie* (St. Petersburg, 1821–1917); *Bogoslovskii vestnik* (Sergiev Posad, 1892–1918); *Trudy Kievskoi dukhovnoi akademii* (Kiev, 1860–1917); and *Pravoslavnyi sobesednik* (Kazan', 1855–1917).

[8] The diocesan press, which emerged in the 1860s as *eparkhial'nye vedomosti* (sometimes bearing a different nomenclature, such as *Izvestiia po . . . eparkhii*), is of stupendous magnitude. This chapter draws upon the diocesan press in the two capitals (*Izvestiia po S.-Peterburgskoi eparkhii* and *Moskovskie tserkovnye vedomosti*) as well as a few other dioceses—Vladimir, Kazan', Khar'kov, Smolensk, and Tver: *Vladimirskie eparkhial'nye vedomosti* (Vladimir, 1865–1918); *Izvestiia po Kazanskoi eparkhii* (Kazan', 1867–1918); *Vera i razum* (Khar'kov, 1884–1917); *Smolenskie eparkhial'nye vedomosti* (Smolensk, 1865–1918); *Tverskie eparkhial'nye vedomosti* (Tver', 1877–1918).

[9] Of greatest importance is the weekly published under the auspices of the St. Petersburg Ecclesiastical Academy, *Tserkovnyi vestnik* (St. Petersburg, 1874–1917), which was deeply concerned about the Church's role and position in society; through its editorials, reports, and correspondence it provides valuable material on the Church's inner mission to the city. Of considerable importance too are the socially oriented journals, which sometimes incorporated the phrase "Church-societal" in their title; of particular value was a periodical published in Kazan during the latter phases of the 1905 Revolution, *Tserkovno-obshchestvennaia zhizn'* (Kazan', 1906–1907), and a St. Petersburg paper founded in 1912, *Tserkovno-obshchestvennyi vestnik* (St. Petersburg, 1912–1914).

[10] Useful material can be gleaned from John S. Curtiss, *Church and State in Russia: The Last Years of the Empire, 1900–1917* (New York, 1940); Gerhard Simon, "The Russian Orthodox Church and the Social Question in Russia before 1917" (Paper presented to the Conference on the Millenium on Christianization in Russia in Uusi Valam, Finland, September 1988); and especially J.M.H. Geekie, "The Church and Politics in Russia, 1905–1917: A Study of the Political Behavior of the Russian Orthodox Clergy in the Reign of Nicholas II" (Ph.D. diss., University of East Anglia, 1976). However, Curtiss made only perfunctory use of archival materials and the latter none at all. The Soviet historian P. N. Zyrianov (*Pravoslavnaia tserkov' v bor'be s revoliutsiei 1905–1907 gg.* [Moscow, 1984]) did consult archival materials, but he examined only the files indicating counterrevolutionary activity by clergy and ignored others, especially those with countervailing evidence.

serted their providential nature, with the proviso that private wealth be used to further divine purpose, especially through dispensing charity.[11] Moreover, the Church was generally satisfied with the moral-religious condition of townsmen and even regarded the religiosity of the city as superior to that of the village. Indeed, although the urban inhabitants also gave grounds for concern, the most important difficulty was not unbelief but Old Belief, manifested in the untoward influence of Old Believer merchants. Nevertheless, when bishops began filing regular annual reports in the mid-nineteenth century, they showed virtually no concern about religious indifference among the city's educated elites or popular classes.[12] Statistics on religious observance (that is, the annual data on confession and communion),[13] the higher literacy rate,[14] the greater availability of catechism instruction,[15] the superior education of

[11] In typical statements from the mid-eighteenth century, the Orthodox Church taught that wealth was not inherently evil, only that it must be acquired honestly and used to further the Lord's ends—not for wasteful consumption. For example, the children's catechism of Metropolitan Platon (Levshin), delivered this admonition: "In the words of the Apostles, the wealthy should not be arrogant, rely upon their riches, excessively seek wealth, and regard every means of self-enrichment as permissible and indulge in luxury; they should not be miserly, but generous toward the poor and indigent; they should use their wealth for the Lord's honor and for general welfare and to support themselves in a decent manner." See "Kratkii katikhizis dlia obucheniia malykh detei pravoslavnomu khristianskomu zakonu" in Platon (Levshin), *Sochineniia*, 6 vols. (Moscow, 1780), 183. For similar statements in sermons, seminary textbooks on moral theology, and ecclesiastical literature for popular edification, see *Nastavlenie o sobstvennykh viaskogo khristianina dolzhnostiakh* (St. Petersburg, 1788), f. 1, verso; Gavriil (Titlinov) and Platon (Levshin), *Sobranie raznykh pouchenii na vse voskresnye i prazdnichnye dni*, 3 vols. (St. Petersburg, 1776), 1: 76–77; Ioann Kochetov, *Nachertanie khristianskikh obiazannostei po ucheniiu greko-rossiiskoi tserkvi* (St. Petersburg, 1838), 81–83, 145–47; Filaret (Drozdov) *Slova i rechi*, 3 vols. (Moscow, 1848–1861), 3: 388 (1858 sermon); P. Soliarskii, *Nravstvennoe pravoslavnoe bogoslovie* (St. Petersburg, 1869), 262–65; Gavriil (Zheltikov), *Nravstvennoe bogoslovie primenitel'no k programme seminarskogo kursa* (Tver', 1883), 661–79.

[12] See, for example, the collection of reports from 1855 in TsGIA SSSR, f. 796, op. 137, g. 1856, d. 2398.

[13] Compiled from the 1770s and throughout the nineteenth century (and now available in the annual files of the synodal archive in TsGIA SSSR, f. 796), the annual statistics on confession and communion did not give grounds for fear of dechristianization in the city; indeed, if authorities had cause for alarm, it pertained mainly to the rural population, which, for various practical reasons (distance from the parish church, travel to attend fairs, or employment away from the community) tended to show a higher rate of absenteeism and omission.

[14] Higher literacy in the city was frequently cited in episcopal reports, with the notation that it correlated directly with higher levels of religious knowledge and consciousness. Both because the literate had traversed religious texts and because they were better prepared to comprehend and retain catechistic instruction, the bishops laid great value on primary education for the faithful, the peasantry not excepted. Indeed, for this very reason the Church made vigorous (if ineffective) efforts, even before the Great Reforms, to encourage priests to open parish schools.

[15] Although since the mid-eighteenth century the Church had sought to require catechization, by the 1850s such instruction was still limited to parishes in towns and a few isolated rural parishes. The failure to catechize in the village was partly attributable to the parish clergy (who lacked the requisite training and time), but the main problem was the parishioners—not only their illiteracy, but also their sporadic attendance, which rendered systematic teaching impossible.

urban priests,[16] and the generous donations for church construction[17]—all were adduced as evidence of religious health in the city. Although illegitimacy rates, routinely regarded as one sign of moral-religious condition in nineteenth-century Europe, were noticeably higher in the city, they were low by comparison with contemporary European standards and aroused little concern among clerics in pre-Reform Russia.[18]

The religious condition of the village was sharply different. Not that the Church found peasants wanting in piety; on the contrary, bishops and priests consistently acknowledged the peasants' profound fear of God and veneration of the Church. But rural believers, it was emphasized, had scant comprehension of their faith and remained ignorant of rudimentary prayers, the Ten Commandments, and the creed. The Church had, to be sure, made vigorous efforts to raise the religious consciousness of its rural flock, but with scant success. In the face of massive illiteracy, indifference or even opposition of serfowning squires,[19] and geographic dispersion, the rural priest found it nearly impossible to instruct his flock in the rudiments of the faith.[20]

After midcentury, however, the Church grew increasingly disenchanted with the city. In part, that attitude derived from dechristianization among the lower classes, especially the factory workers who gradually lost their faith in

[16] Service records demonstrate statistically what was already a commonplace in ecclesiastical life: urban parishes were assigned ordinarily to candidates with higher educational qualifications—either a diploma from a theological academy or at least high marks in the seminary. Given the travails of priesthood in the village, combined with its enervating physical toil and sheer material privation, urban parishes were choice appointments reserved to ordinands with the best education. For an incisive critique of this practice, see the case of I. S. Belliustin described in G. L. Freeze, "Revolt from Below," in *Russian Orthodoxy under the Old Regime*, ed. Theofanis Stavrou and Robert Nichols (Minneapolis, 1978), 90–124.

[17] The Church, not without cause, regarded expenditures and contributions for parish churches (construction, renovation, and decorative enrichment) to be a measure of popular piety; on that account, the city gave no cause for concern. Apart from the annual episcopal *otchety*, see the summary overview in each year's official report of the chief procurator (*Izvlecheniia iz vsepoddanneishego otcheta po vedomstvu pravoslavnogo ispovedaniia* published under various titles from 1836 until 1914).

[18] Data from various dioceses in the 1820s show extremely low rates of illegitimacy (2 to 5 percent); see TsGIA SSSR, f. 796, op. 104, g. 1823, d. 1367. Scattered reports for cities suggest slightly higher proportions, but nothing to compare with the skyrocketing statistics in the contemporary West. More remarkable than the statistics is the Church's silence on this whole question, which was attributable not to indifference or lack of authority, but to the small magnitude of the problem; only in the post-Reform era, when rates rose sharply (especially in the cities), did the Church register alarm. For the problem of later data on illegitimacy, see David L. Ransel, "Problems in Measuring Illegitimacy in Prerevolutionary Russia," *Journal of Social History* 16 (1982): 111–27.

[19] See G. L. Freeze, "The Orthodox Church and Serfdom in Prereform Russia," *Slavic Review* 48 (Fall 1989): 361–87.

[20] See Gregory L. Freeze, "The Rechristianization of Russia: The Church and Popular Religion, 1750–1850" (forthcoming in *Studia Slavica Finlandensia* [Yearbook of the Neuvostoliittoinstituutti, Helsinki], Tomus 7 (1990).

village Orthodoxy, the *bytovoe pravoslavie* that was functionally meaningful to the rhythms of rural life but bore little relevance to the needs of urban existence.[21] Initially, however, the bishops were far more concerned about educated society, not just the radical intelligentsia that espoused materialist and atheistic philosophies but also the more moderate segments of educated society that seemed so vulnerable to religious indifference and Western culture.[22] It would be false, however, to identify anti-Western sentiments with the Church; apart from countervailing tendencies,[23] critical attitudes toward the West were commonplace in post-Reform society, as vibrant in the radical left as among archconservatives, among *narodniki* as well as *pochvenniki*. More important in explaining the Church's alienation from liberal obshchestvo was the latter's assault—through the press, *zemstvo*, and state organs—upon ecclesiastical prerogatives, especially the clergy's role in public education, their exemption from taxation and other duties, their opposition to easier divorce and separation, and their demand for state repression of dissenters and apostates.[24] In short, it is hardly surprising that the clergy felt increasingly alienated from educated urban elites and inclined to focus their energies and hopes on the proverbial piety of the Russian peasant.

In the late nineteenth century, however, the Church began to reevaluate this negative attitude toward the city and its inhabitants. To be sure, the bias against the city persisted, especially among clergy in dioceses with low levels of urbanization. But some segments of the Church, especially liberal priests in the two capitals and the faculty of ecclesiastical schools, emphasized the importance and feasibility of the inner mission to the city. While much of their interest focused on the working class and such social problems as poverty and alcoholism, they also called on the Church to reassess its relationship to educated, propertied strata. How, though, did the Church conceive of these educated, propertied strata in the city? Where did it place this category within its larger conception of the social order in Late Imperial Russia?

In essence, the clergy continued to use the traditional categories—common people (narod) juxtaposed to educated society (obshchestvo or intelligentsiia).[25] The latter, defined principally by culture, could not be directly corre-

[21] For the concept of *bytovoe pravoslavie*, see G. A. Nosova, "Bytovoe pravoslavie (na materialakh Vladimirskoi oblasti)" (Kand. diss., Institut etnografii, Moscow, 1969).

[22] For a typical statement, see Ioann Petropavlovskii, *Obshchedostupnye stat'i v zashchitu khristianskoi very protiv neveriia* (Moscow, 1881).

[23] Indeed, the Church evinced a continuing interest in ecumenical ideas; see G. V. Florovsky, "Orthodox Ecumenism in the Nineteenth Century," *St. Vladimir's Quarterly* 14 (1956): 2–53, and L. A. Boerneke, "The Dawn of the Ecumenical Age: Anglican, Old Catholic and Orthodox Reunion Negotiations of the 1870s" (Ph.D. diss., University of Minnesota, 1977).

[24] For a preliminary overview of these problems, see Igor Smolitsch, *Geschichte der russischen Kirche*, ed. G. L. Freeze, vol. 2, (forthcoming in *Forschungen zur Osteuropäischen Geschichte*, Bd. 45).

[25] For typical examples, see "S novym godom," *TsVk*, no. 1 (1904): 2–4; "Letopis' tserkovnoi

lated to anything so geographically or socially specific as the urban middle class; after all, significant parts of the professions and semiprofessions—such as the teachers in elementary schools—lived and worked in the countryside, not the city. Although this simplistic, archaic social analysis might be partly attributed to the Church's more general failure to elaborate a positive social ideal,[26] in fact the Church was simply employing ideas of educated society, which based its own identity upon cultural, not social or economic, categories.[27] Nevertheless, in the late nineteenth century the Church did renew its interest in a mission to the intelligentsia that consciously shared a secular urban culture and described itself variously as obshchestvo, intelligentsiia, and obshchestvennost'.[28]

There were several reasons for the clergy's new willingness to reconsider its negative view of the educated and propertied elements in society. One was the development of a "this-worldly" theology, which rejected earlier tendencies to remain apart from secular issues and to focus exclusively on the celestial goals. This new current of theology, which had emerged in the 1860s and gained ground ever since,[29] argued that the Church, like Christ, must come into the world and infuse His principles and precepts into secular society and relations. Thus Vladimir Solov'ev wrote in the late nineteenth century that the Church is of *this* world and must exert its influence accordingly: "The Church must gradually make [state and society] similar to itself by introducing the

---

i obshchestvennoi zhizni," *TsVk*, no. 11 (1905): 344; *Zhurnaly i protokoly* 1: 37–38; V. Z. Zavitnevich, "Chto sleduet ponimat' pod tak nazyvaemym razryvom russkogo intelligentnogo obshchestva s narodom?" *Trudy Kievskoi dukhovnoi akademii*, no. 7 (1907): 351–94 (hereafter *TKDA*) S. N. Bulgakov, *Dva grad*, 2 vols. (Moscow, 1911), 2: 131.

More broadly, as the case of ecclesiastical social thought suggests, analysis of Russian civic consciousness should not lose sight of the narod; whether as counterpoise to urban culture and society, or as the embodiment of elemental violence, the narod—no less than the state—figured directly in the formulation of urban identities and strategies for social and political change. In a word, Bürgertum is comprehensible only in contradistinction to Bauerntum.

[26] For acerbic comments about the Church's want of a social ideal, see G. S. Petrov, *Tserkov' i obshchestvo* (St. Petersburg, 1906), p. 27.

[27] Stratification based on culture rather than economic criteria was hardly unique to Russia; compare the rise of the Bildungsbürgertum in nineteenth-century Germany, with a parallel development in self-descriptive terminology. See especially the essays in Werner Conze and Jürgen Kocka, *Bildungssystem und Professionalisierung in internationalen Vergleichen* ("Industrielle Welt," Bd. 38) (Stuttgart, 1985).

[28] Clerical writers used the terms *obrazovannoe obshchestvo* and *intelligentsiia* almost interchangeably; the latter was far broader than the narrower notion of "revolutionary" intelligentsia and approximates more closely the older term *obshchestvo*, which roughly corresponded to the German *Bildungsbürgertum*.

[29] For a discussion of the first prominent exponent, see G. L. Freeze, "Die Laisierung des Archimandriten Feodor (Bucharev) und ihre kirchenpolitischen Hintergründe. Theologie und Politik in Rußland der Mitte des 19. Jahrhunderts," *Kirche im Osten* 28 (1985): 26–52. For a typical post-Reform statement, see A. Gromachevskii, *Prakticheskie zadachi deiatel'nosti sel'skogo pravoslavnogo sviashchennika*, 2d ed. (St. Petersburg, 1890), pp. 5–6.

principles of love and accord into all dimensions of human life."[30] After the turn of the century, such comments—relatively rare a few decades earlier—became ubiquitous in the clerical press. Typical was the statement that "Christ was not only divine, but also human," and hence "it is necessary to realize the universal truth here on earth, so far as that is possible for man."[31] While this new engagement tended to focus on the lower strata and their needs, it also embraced an effort to build new ties to educated society—through personal contacts, publications, lectures, and public discussions. All that marked a salient departure from the adversarial relationship that had developed during the Great Reforms and post-Reform decades.

The appeal of the new theology rested, at least in part, on recognizing a decline in the Church's appeal and influence among the faithful, especially in the city. Amidst growing evidence that the Church was losing its battle against both religious indifference and religious deviation, where the Old Belief and especially the new sectarian movements were cause of mounting concern in the Church, some clergy drew the conclusion that only a more socially engaged Church could retain or regain the loyalty of the faithful. They argued—with desperate urgency as Revolution swept across the Russian Empire in 1905—that the Church must address the laity's worldly needs to remain relevant, not only to mediate and moderate social conflict but also to sustain the trust and love of its flock.[32] Like their fellow clergy in Western and Central Europe, liberal clergy in Russia warned that the Church must become more involved in temporal issues or risk losing its influence over the people. Under the circumstances, it is clear why an activist social theology became so attractive by the turn of the century, as the Liberation Movement gained momentum and made the impassiveness of the Church appear unconscionable. In some clerical circles, at least, it was plainly imperative that the Church must either join forces with the intelligentsia or risk ceasing to be a force at all.

But the clergy's interest in educated obshchestvo also derived from the realization that the latter had also begun to reconsider its earlier attitudes toward religion and the Church. Neo-Kantian idealism, even Tolstoianism, as well as the new currents in art and literature all provided compelling evidence that the intelligentsia had begun to free itself from antireligious, materialistic philosophies and to take a new interest in spiritual questions.[33] This reorientation led

[30] Quoted in V. Myshtsyn, *Po tserkovno-obshchestvennyn voprosam*, 2 vols. (Moscow, 1905–1906), 2: 30.

[31] "Nashi zadachi," *Khristianin*, no. 1 (1907): 14.

[32] For typical statements, see Ieromonakh Mikhail, "Pochemu nam ne veriat?" *TsVk*, no. 5 (1905): 138–41; "Iz zapisnoi knizhki sviashchennika," cited in Myshtsyn, *Tverskovno-obshchestvennye voprosy*, 1: 21–22; Soiuz revnitelei tserkovnogo obnovleniia, "[Zapistka] ob otnoshenii tserkvi i sviashchenstva k sovremennoi obshchestvenno-politischeskoi zhizni," *Tserkovno-obshchestvennaia zhizn'*, no. 14 (1906): 507.

[33] See the discussion and bibliography in Christopher Read, *Religion, Revolution and the Russian Intelligentsia 1900–1912* (London, 1979).

directly to attempts at colloquy and rapprochement between Church and intelligentsia—the most famous case of which was the Religious-Philosophical Society in St. Petersburg. At sessions convened in 1902–1903 and attended by both clerics and the lay intelligentsia, the two parties deliberated such delicate questions as the mutability of Orthodox canon, the significance of marriage, and the need for religious tolerance. Although the intelligentsia's participation has been exhaustively and repeatedly studied, it is no less important to appreciate the clergy's interest and participation in the venture.[34] And it was no accident that the first topic on the agenda was "the intelligentsia and the Church." Although the anxious chief procurator of the Synod, K. P. Pobedonostsev, grew restless and finally ended these encounters, the publication of their minutes, even in censored form, demonstrated a possible union of Orthodoxy and intelligentsia.[35]

Indeed, it was argued that only through the collaboration of Church and intelligentsia could both parties achieve their respective goals—the spiritual and material uplifting of the people. Liberal clergy, though still critical of the intelligentsia's materialistic philosophy, nevertheless praised the latter for its desire to help the downtrodden and liberate the nation from the oppressive bureaucracy.[36] Even so prominent and venerable an organ as the journal of the Moscow Academy wrote that, compared to the inaction of the clergy, the intelligentsia proved more Christian than the Church.[37] Furthermore, some clerics pointed out that the Church and intelligentsia had a common foe—the bureaucratic state, which not only sustained an unjust social order but also had a highly deleterious effect on the Church and its mission.[38] Moreover, some clergy argued that the Church and intelligentsia needed each other and represented complementary forces in society. Liberal clergy, in particular, stressed that the Church, which had seemed so indifferent to secular questions and lacked a coherent social gospel, could learn from the social teachings of the intelligentsia. At the same time, the intelligentsia needed the Church: hitherto the intelligentsia had failed abysmally in pursuit of its vainglorious mission— and not least because it had been unable to understand and appreciate the religious concerns of the people.[39]

---

[34] That lay focus also pervades the meticulous analysis offered in Jutta Scherrer, *Die Petersburger Religiös-Philosophischen Vereinigungen* ("Forschungen zur Osteuropäischen Geschichte," Bd. 19) (Berlin, 1973); see also P. Scheibert, "Die Petersburger religiös-philosophischen Zusammenkünfte von 1902 und 1903," *Jahrbücher für Geschichte Osteuropas* 12 (1964): 513–60.

[35] The published minutes of the meetings are available in *Zapiski Peterburgskikh religiozno-filosofskikh sobranii (1902–1903 gg.)* (St. Petersburg, 1906).

[36] See, for instance, "Tserkov' i rabochii vopros," *TsVk*, no. 40 (1906): 1287.

[37] Myshtsyn, "Iz tserkovnoi pechati," *Bogoslovskii vestnik*, no. 11 (1905): 575.

[38] Myshtsyn, *Po tserkovno-obshchestvennym voprosam*, 1: 64.

[39] See, for instance, "Doklad V. A. Ternavtseva, 'Russkaia tserkov' pred velikoi zadachei,'" in *Zapiski*, 5–23, and Igumen'ia Ekaterina, "Monastyr' i khristianskii asketizm," *TsVk*, no. 42

Significantly, not only liberal but also conservative segments in the Church manifested a growing interest in ties to the laity. For conservatives, however, the primary goal was neither to combat dechristianization nor to foster social change but to emancipate the Church from the deleterious consequences of state tutelage. Hence the Church, like virtually every other segment of late Imperial Russia, had its own "liberationist" goals. It would be misleading, however, to assume that this connoted nothing more than a desire to sunder the fetters of the secular state. On the contrary, that "destatification" was a precondition for the more important and urgent goal of revitalizing the Church through the restoration of conciliarism (*sobornost'*).[40] Although the primary objective was to achieve ecclesiastical autonomy, conciliarism—especially among liberal clergy—came to include recognition that the laity should be given greater responsibility and authority in the Church, especially at the parish level, but in some degree at higher levels (as in diocesan assemblies and national church councils). Indeed, if the Church sundered its political and economic dependence upon the secular state, it would have to base itself ever more firmly upon the support and engagement of the laity.[41] In a word, conciliarist ideas predisposed the clergy to look more closely at society, including the educated segments that could be expected to play a prominent and positive role in national, diocesan, and parish councils.

But for the most part the Church was interested in neither the intelligentsia nor obshchestvo in and for itself. To be sure, significant and influential segments of the clergy evinced genuine interest in developing its ties to educated society, but the goal was to forge ties with a useful collaborator to help lead the people and resist the state. Indeed, the clergy—liberal as well as conservative—generally tended to assume a supraclass position, to argue that the Church (as the church of *all* the people) must remain above particular social classes or political parties. That supraclass posture was not only consistent with Church tradition and conciliarist principles, but it also reflected the su-

---

(1904): 1323. A variant of this argument is found in the priest M. Senatskii's *Dukhovenstvo i intelligentsiia v dele religiozno-nravstvennogo i umstvennogo razvitiia naroda* (Nizhnii-Novgorod, 1903), which argues that the intelligentsia's moral deficiencies made clerical participation in the emancipation movement all the more necessary.

[40] The disenchantment with the state, which mounted steadily since the Great Reforms, came to a peak in the early years of the century and led to the determined demand for reform in 1905. Such sentiments, rooted in frustration over the failure to solve the Church's problems and disgruntlement over state policies, especially in religious toleration, impelled even conservative bishops to demand a "free church" and, correspondingly, to seek closer fusion of Church and society. See the discussion and references in G. L. Freeze, *Parish Clergy in Nineteenth-Century Russia; Crisis, Reform, Counter-Reform* (Princeton, 1983); and Freeze, "Tserkov', religiia i politicheskaia kul'tura na zakate starogo rezhima'' (Paper presented to the International Colloquium on the Working Class and the Development of the Revolutionary Situation in Early Twentieth-Century Russia, June 1990, Leningrad).

[41] For the social implications of church reform movements, see the explicit comments in "Letopis' tserkovnoi i obshchestvennoi zhizni v Rossii," *TsVk*, no. 32 (1905): 1013.

praclass propositions deeply embedded in Russian political culture, be it the ideology of Tsarism or the intelligentsia.

Specifically in this sense the Church also responded to obshchestvennost'— the emerging social identity of the educated, propertied middle strata in the city. This self-descriptive term was by no means a new phenomenon in Russian society; ever since the mid-nineteenth century various terms had circulated to describe a collectivity based more on education and values than property: obshchestvo (since the 1840s), intelligentsiia (since the 1860s), and ultimately obshchestvennost' (by the early twentieth century).[42] This new obshchestvennost' stood in juxtaposition to state authority (*vlast'*), and, though not reducible simply to a middle "urban class," it did refer primarily to the educated, propertied strata in the city.[43] Although the volume of clerical writing on the subject and specific use of the term was limited, obshchestvennost' did find its way into the ecclesiastical lexicon.

The result, however, was not a recognition of the new corporate identity, but an attempt to appropriate it for ecclesiastical purposes in the form of a "Christian obshchestvennost'." It is hardly surprising that, amidst the tumult of revolution and the Church's own ambitions for a greater social role, some clerical writers emulated the language current in lay society as they endeavored to bring the Church closer to the contemporary world. The important point, however, is that they did not merely praise secular obshchestvennost' or urge clerical support for it, but sought to superimpose the Church's own role and aspirations.

Significantly enough, the new language of obshchestvennost' held at least three different meanings for clerical writers. First, in a meaning plainly derivative of the general usage as secular "public opinion," obshchestvennost' represented a counterplea for a public opinion based on Orthodox Christian principles with the expectation that it would exert a healthy influence on the contemporary world. Indeed, as one observer pointed out, all other groups were hastily organizing to express and defend their interests, and hence it was incumbent upon the Church to do likewise.[44] How to achieve this was unclear: whether through the Christianization of an existing obshchestvennost' or through the creation of a Christian public opinion under the hegemony of the Church.[45] A second, related usage of obshchestvennost' connoted something

---

[42] For the rise of *obshchestvo* in the 1840s, see Anthony Netting, "Russian Liberalism: The Years of Promise, 1842–1855" (Ph.D. diss., Columbia University, 1967); on the intelligentsiia, see Otto W. Müller, *Intelligentsia: Untersuchungen zur Geschichte eines politischen Schlagwortes* (Frankfurt, 1971).

[43] For a pioneering study of obshchestvennost' in the interrevolutionary years, see Manfred Hagen, *Die Entfaltung politischer Öffentlichkeit in Rußland 1906–1914* (Wiesbaden, 1982).

[44] S. Troitsky, "Tserkovnyi sobor i miriane," *TsVk*, no. 46 (1905): 1446.

[45] As one writer argued, no attempt to improve social relations could succeed unless the necessary prerequisite—uplifting of individual morality—had been achieved; and for that a Christian public opinion must play a vital role ("Obzor vnutrennei tserkovno-obshchestvennoi zhizni Ros-

like "sociability," where public opinion was reified to express the union of
Church and society. Such usage bore distinct overtones of a still more popular
term in clerical parlance—*sobornost'*—and aimed at greater Christian solidarity, for the sake of achieving both social justice and the spiritual well-being of
individual believers.[46] A third and rather uncommon usage of obshchestvennost' referred to the restructuring of the secular world after Christian precepts;
in this case "Christian obshchestvennost' " meant Christian socioeconomic
relations. This definition lay close to the new theology of temporal engagement and summons to reconstruct society on the basis of Christian principles.[47] The ambiguous, shifting connotation of the word, as well as its rarity,
above all suggests the difficulties and limits inherent in the Church's effort to
define its new urban ministry.

Nevertheless, the Revolution of 1905–1907 raised aspirations for some kind
of Christian obshchestvennost' to an unprecedented level. Although an institution as large as the Church, manned by a complex hierarchy of clerical servitors, was bound to show extreme variations in behavior and attitude, substantial segments of the parish clergy clearly did become involved in the
Liberation Movement, usually by silent assent, sometimes by active engagement. Apart from clerical radicals like Grigorii Petrov and Archimandrite Mikhail,[48] entire assemblies of clergy in some districts and dioceses adopted resolutions explicitly supporting the Liberation Movement and demanding that
the Church—like state and society—be rebuilt along radically new lines.[49]
And even after the revolution subsided, the clergy nevertheless continued to
seek ties to the intelligentsia, most notably in the establishment of new religious-philosophical societies in St. Petersburg, Kiev, and Moscow.

Yet these efforts came to naught: by the outbreak of World War I, it was
clear that the Church had failed to establish an effective urban mission and

---

sii," *Pravoslavnyi sobesednik*, no. 2 [1905]: 341). See also "Mneniia i otzyvy," *TsVk*, no. 44
(1906): 1420–22, and the programmatic statement of a religious periodical in Kiev, duly titled
Narod (The People) (reprinted in *TsVk*, no. 16 [1906]: 502–3).

[46] For example, see "Nashi zadachi," *Khristianin*, no. 1 (1907): 12; A. Saragda, "O tserkovnoi obshchestvennosti," *TsVk*, no. 13 (1913): 398–400.

[47] Thus the liberal Union of Church Renewal supported all efforts toward "the creation of a
Christian *obshchestvennost'* by establishing among Christians more perfect forms of fraternal
relations with respect to both social and material matters." See "Soiuz tserkovnogo obnovleniia
v Peterburge," *Tserkovno-obshchestvennaia zhizn'*, no. 5 (1906): 186. Similar was the demand
by the liberal clerical paper in Kiev, *Narod*, that "the Christian truth penetrate not only private
life but also the domain of social relations"; see "Mneniia i otzyvy," *TsVk*, no. 16 (1906): 502.

[48] For examples of their views, see Archimandrite Mikhail (Semenov), *Khristos v vek mashin*
(St. Petersburg, 1907); G. S. Petrov, *Dumy i vpechatleniia* (St. Petersburg, 1907).

[49] For example, see the explicit support of the liberation movement voiced by the clerical assemblies in Vladimir (Gosudarstvennyi arkhiv Vladimirskoi oblasti, f. 556, op. 1, d. 4423, ll. 1–
98), Viatka (TsGIA SSSR, f. 796, op. 187, g. 1906, d. 6677, ll. 19–25), Ialta (ibid., d. 6571),
and Tambov (TsGIA SSSR, f. 797, op. 76, otd. 3, st. 5, d. 10).

forge new ties to urban society. It did not totally abandon the effort; the clerical press still carried appeals to create the Christian obshchestvennost'.[50] But such appeals had little concrete effect, and most observers candidly conceded the disappointing results of the Church's mission to the intelligentsia. As one clergyman wrote at the end of 1910, "the lack of cohesiveness in our Church community" had had unwholesome effects on the Church and had undermined the long-overdue cause of internal Church reform. Thus, apart from the notorious division between the white and black clergy, the Church suffered no less from a lack of sobornost' embracing laity as well as clergy: "The main, overwhelming majority of laymen (both from the common people and the intelligentsia) are not in the least interested in the life of the Church. For them, Church membership has simply become a certain kind of juridical condition, religion a matter of internal personal experience; and they do not even think about collaborative creation in matters of Church and religion or about the application to society (*obobshchestvlenie*) of the Church's ideals."[51] Nor, as some candidly admitted, had the Church registered any significant success in its mission to the intelligentsia.[52] As World War I drew near, leading Church journals offered an exceedingly dismal picture of the results from Church efforts to establish Christian obshchestvennost'.[53]

Why then did the Church fail to establish Christian obshchestvennost'— whether as a new liaison to lay public opinion or as the formation of a distinct and separate ecclesiastical-lay community? Indeed, given the enormous volume of ecclesiastical publications, why was the question of Church-intelligentsia and especially "obshchestvennost' " (secular or Christian) given relatively little attention?[54]

Certainly one important factor was repression from above: rigorous censorship, disciplining of liberal clergy, and the general atmosphere of repression after 1907 combined to still hopes and expectations of reform and revitalization. After the "clerical liberation movement" reached its peak in 1906, Church authorities gradually tightened control over diocesan clergy and quashed their bold demands for liberation, whether in the Church or in society at large. At the same time, the bishops took steps to punish, silence, and in some cases defrock liberal and outspoken clergy, including such key figures

[50] "Nashi zadachi," *Khristianin*, no. 1 (1907): 12.

[51] "Na poroge novogo goda," *TsVk*, no. 1 (1911): 1–4.

[52] "Mneniia i otzyvy," *TsVK*, no. 22 (1910): 664–66.

[53] "K voprosu o prikhode," *TsVk*, no. 14 (1913): 417–18; "Tserkov' i obshchestvo," ibid., no. 26 (1914): 780.

[54] The number of articles devoted specifically to the question of urban society, obshchestvennost' and the Church's mission there is exceedingly small, even in such socially oriented periodicals as *Tserkovno-obshchestvennyi vestnik* and *Tserkovnyi vestnik*, both of which were published in St. Petersburg.

as Georgii Petrov and Archimandrite Mikhail.[55] Pressure also emanated from secular sources: not only official state authorites, zealous in repressing clerical activists, but also private groups like the Union of Russian People were extraordinarily active in identifying liberal clergy and demanding their removal.[56] Finally, following an inconsistent and uncertain policy in 1905 and early 1906, from late summer 1906 the Synod demanded that the clergy play a "constructive" role in exposing revolutionary parties and supporting those "legal" parties (from the Octobrists rightward) that stood for order.[57] Unquestionably this conservative political role, especially as oppositionist sentiment mounted in educated society after 1912, did little to kindle good relations between the Church and obshchestvo.[58] Nor did the Church even manage to sustain its tie with more moderate, even conservative elements, as its conflict with the Octobrists in the Third and Fourth Dumas demonstrated.[59]

It would be misleading, however, to attribute the Church's failings solely to the repressive activities of reactionary bishops and bureaucrats. Censorship notwithstanding, ecclesiastical periodicals still had considerable latitude and in fact continued to publish some articles on the urban mission and Christian obshchestvennost'. Yet they chose not to do so. Nor did the various religious-philosophical societies enjoy a groundswell of support and mature into broader, effective fusion of Church and intelligentsia. In a word, although repression from above surely played a role, other more important, more durable factors acted to impede efforts by the Church to win influence in educated society.

One important barrier was the enduring isolation of the clergy as a closed estate. Despite various attempts since the 1860s to dismantle the rigid hereditary lines, the clergy was still overwhelmingly composed of the clergy's own

[55] The Synodal files abound with such cases, all of which had to be reviewed and approved by the Holy Synod; for the case of Petrov, see TsGIA SSSR, f. 796, op. 187, g. 1906, d. 6668. See also V. V. Brusianin, *Sud'ba pervykh deputatov* (St. Petersburg, 1906).

[56] The Synod hewed a cautious line, declining to issue blanket injunctions that such banners be placed in parish churches and instead directing each bishop to decide the question himself; see its resolutions from 1907 to 1908 in TsGIA SSSR, f. 796, op. 187, g. 1906, d. 775. For cases where prelates opposed the Union, see the report from Saratov in TsGIA SSSR, f. 796, op. 189, g. 1908, d. 8393.

[57] For the Synod's new policy, expressed in a circular from its presiding prelate (Metropolitan Antonii) on August 31, 1906, see TsGIA SSSR, f. 796, op. 187, g. 1906, d. 775, ll. 11–12.

[58] For the Church's role in the elections to the Fourth Duma, see the file in TsGIA SSSR, f. 796, op. 194, g. 1912, d. 1207. See also F. Jockwig, "Kirche und Staatsduma: Zur politischen Aktivität der Russisch-Orthodoxen Kirche am Vorabend der Revolution," in *Wegzeichen: Festgabe zum 60. Geburtstag von Prof. Dr. H. M. Biedermann* ("Das östliche Christentum," NF, vol. 25) (Würzburg, 1971), pp. 446–50, and Vladimir Rozhkov, *Tserkovnye voprosy v Gosudarstvennoi dume* (Rome, 1975).

[59] See especially Rozhkov, *Tserkovnye voprosy*, for a detailed analysis and bibliography on the Duma debates.

sons.[60] In social psychology, this fact doubtless encouraged the clergy—even its more liberal segments—to give considerable attention to their own estate's needs, at the risk of neglecting or even contradicting the larger interests of society.[61] Furthermore, with a separate juridical status as a special service population of the Church, the clergy had limited opportunities and rights to establish ties with the laity or, for that matter, with members of their own estate.[62] A further obstacle was social background: the clergy in urban parishes often came from a rural milieu. The urban parishes, because of their superior income and cultural advantages, were regarded as prized appointments and given as rewards to top-ranking seminarians, regardless of their geographic origin. Indeed, to judge from service records of the 1890s, sons of urban priests, given their easier access to secular schools and the gymnasium, tended to leave the clerical estate in disproportionately high numbers; by contrast, their country cousins had to rely upon the ecclesiastical schools that aimed to channel its graduates into church service.[63] Although the clergy generally found it difficult to establish ties with the laity, this was especially true for priests from rural backgrounds.

A second important barrier was the disorganization of urban parishes, which were often described as the weakest link in the entire ecclesiastical organization. Part of the problem was demographic: the urban parish ordinarily had a relatively large number of parishioners, making it virtually impossible for the priest to minister to the needs of or even perform nominal rituals for the massive flocks under his charge.[64] Nor was the city parish even territorially or socially fixed; because the Russian Church had no system of formal registration for membership (that is, to attach members to a particular parish), townspeople could drift from parish to parish—or attend none at all.[65] Some

---

[60] For example, see the comments in "Mneniia i otzyvy," *TsVk*, no. 3 (1905): 73–75, and Gregory L. Freeze, "Between Estate and Profession: Russian Clergy of the Ancien Régime in Comparative Perspective" in *Social Structures and Stratification in Modern Europe*, ed. Michael Bush (forthcoming).

[61] Even the "socially conscious" resolutions by clerical assemblies in 1905–1906 dealt almost exclusively with demands of the parish clergy—for greater power in Church administration, salaries, improvements in ecclesiastical schools, and the like. For a typical example, see the resolutions of parish clergy in Smolensk in early 1906 in "Zapiska deputatov eparkhial'nogo s''ezda dukhovenstva v fevrale 1906 g.," *Smolenskie eparkhial'nye vedomosti*, no. 5 (1906): 223–24.

[62] This disunity, all the more palpable amidst the hectic organizational developments elsewhere in contemporary society, impelled the clergy to repeat demands for a "Union of Russian Clergy." See, for example, the resolutions of the Smolensk clergy; (TsGIA SSSR, f. 796, op. 186, d. 657, 1. 163, and "Otkliki dukhovenstva," *TsVk*, no. 10 (1905): 318.

[63] For some interesting comments on the clergy in Moscow, see the valuable memoir by N. P. Rozanov in Otdel rukopisei Gosudarstvennoi Biblioteki im. V. I. Lenina, f. 250 (N. P. Rozanov), k. 2, d. 1.

[64] See "Letopis' tserkovnoi i obshchestvennoi zhizni," *TsVk*, no. 16 (1906): 516.

[65] "Izvestiia i zametki," *TsVk*, no. 5 (1911): 135; "Pastva S. Peterburgskoi eparkhii v 1910

priests complained too that their parishes were enormously complex in social terms; whereas the rural priest dealt with a more or less homogeneous population of peasants, the city priest ministered to parishioners from a bewildering variety of social statuses.[66] In a word, the urban parish was so territorially amorphous, so socially heterogeneous, and so numerically overpopulated that even the most conscientious priest had difficulty establishing strong bonds to his flock.[67]

A third set of obstacles to the rapprochement between Church and educated urban society was ideology and values. Apart from the clergy's predictable antipathy to such intellectual fashions as Nietzscheanism and sensualism, it also looked askance at the intelligentsia's unorthodox interests in religious matters. Even the publication of *Vekhi* evoked a cautious response,[68] while movements like "God seeking" offered only undeniable proof of the distance that remained between the intelligentsia and clergy.[69] Nor could Orthodox writers feel comfortable endorsing all elements of civil consciousness, especially the exaltation of individualism; rather, the clergy, as indeed most elements in prerevolutionary society,[70] was more inclined to emphasize collective values and responsibilities.

Perhaps even more important was the special identity and self-conception of the clergy as a supraclass force, beyond any party and any class. That attitude had deep roots in the traditional political culture, mirroring the state's own supraclass identity, but it also drew upon the "other-worldly" theology of pre-Reform Russia and continued to exercise a strong influence on Orthodox thought. It is hardly surprising that conservative Church authorities inclined toward this view, especially during the revolutionary upheavals of 1905–1907, and reminded the clergy that their service "stands higher and above any parties."[71] Significantly, this same notion also pervaded the think-

---

g.," *Izvestiia po S.-Peterburgskoi eparkhii*, no. 3 (1912): 4; L. S. "Ob otnosheniiakh studentov uchebnykh zavedenii k religii i pravoslavnoi very," *TsVk*, no. 5 (1911): 135.

[66] G. "Pervye shagi gorodskogo pastyria," *TsVk*, no. 3 (1905): 68–71; M. Kalynev, "O postanovke missionerskogo dela v gorodskikh prikhodakh," *Zhurnaly i protokoly*, 2: 359; "Golos sel'skogo sviashchennika v vidu vyborov v Gosudarstvennuiu Dumu," *TsVk*, no. 10 (1906): 297.

[67] By 1913 clergy testified that they knew their flock but slightly; "Sviashchennik i sovremennoe obshchestvo," *TsVk*, no. 39 (1913): 1202–3.

[68] For positive assessments of *Vekhi* as evidence of the crisis in the intelligentsia, see K. A. Smirnov, "*Vekhi* o russkoi intelligentsii," *Vera i razum*, no. 24, (1909): 709–23; more critical readings are to be found in I. A. "*Vekhi*," *Khristianin*, no. 8 (1909): 685–87; T. Lokut', "Ideinyi krizis intelligentsii," *Khristianin*, no. 1 (1912): 65–70.

[69] "Bogoiskatel'stvo vne tserkvi," *TsVk*, no. 58 (1908): 1169–71; "Mneniia i otzyvy," *TsVk* no. 19 (1908): 568–70; "Ot redaktsii," *Tserkovno-obshchestvennyi vestnik*, no. 1 (1912): 1–3.

[70] Significantly enough, the predominant term and ordering principle was obshchestvennost', stressing the collective element vis-à-vis the state, rather than a more individualist-directed *grazhdanstvennost'*. Thus the predominant notion in the Russian prerevolution was not *citoyen*, but *société*.

[71] Metropolitan Antonii to Bishop Vladimir of Kishinev (January 21, 1906) in TsGIA SSSR, f. 796, op. 187, g. 1906, d. 775, 1. 3.

ing of liberal clergy. The diocesan assembly in Vladimir declared in 1905: "The clergy must not remain aside but rather should have sympathy for the liberation movement (in the spirit of the Manifesto of 17 October), without, however, adhering to any political party [and] only approving what is good and condemning what is bad, from a Christian point of view."[72] Indeed, as the very conception of a Christian obshchestvennost' implied, the Church's goal was not simply to fuse the Church with educated society but to create some larger multiclass community or public opinion. Hence attention was focused almost exclusively on the creation of inclusive social organizations, both at the national level (as a sobor) and at the local level (as a parish).[73] Characteristically, when the Church debated the question of lay participation in the sobor, it prescribed only territorial—not social—representation.[74] As earlier, the Church still avoided attempts to make its mission more socially specific (beyond the crude distinction between urban and rural) or to refine its conception of the social order. Hence the Church could neither commit itself to the narrower vested interests of urban middle classes, which indeed became more distinctly pronounced in the wake of the revolution, nor abandon its instinctive commitment to the interests of the lower social strata.

Finally, it seems that the Church's neglect of educated society derived in part too from its preoccupation with a perceived religious crisis in the village. Whereas the Church was still confident of the peasantry's basic piety on the eve of 1905, this self-assurance was utterly devastated in the wake of the revolution. The decline of religious sentiment in the village became a source of acute concern in the Church, and the ecclesiastical press wrote candidly that popular piety had been greatly weakened by the cumulative effect of the market, factory, newspapers, and revolution.[75] Indicative of the concern was the

---

[72] "Ekstrennyi s"ezd," *Kliaz'ma* no. 14 (1906).

[73] For example, see "Korrespondentsiia iz Saratova," *TsVk*, no. 41 (1905): 1297–99. This social inclusiveness informed, similarly, the provisional parish statute of 1917: "The purpose of the parish is for Orthodox Christians at each place of residence to unite into one church commune [*tserkovnaia obshchina*] at a parish church, and through the medium of the parish staff have communal unity in prayers, sacraments and Christian teaching, with mutual assistance to each other in achieving salvation through a good life, Christian enlightenment and charity." *Vremennoe polozhenie o pravoslavnom prikhode* (Petrograd, 1917), 3–4.

[74] "Mnenii i otzyvy," *TsVk*, no. 10 (1906): 298; *Zhurnaly i protokoly*, 1: 37–38, 2: 670 (program).

[75] Prot. D. T., "ot chego sovremennogo dukhovenstva utratilo vliianie na narod," *Izvestiia po S.-Peterburgskoi eparkhii*, nos. 13–14 (1914): 29–30; "Novogodnye dumy," *TsVk*, no. 1 (1914): 1–4; V. Beliaev, "Religioznyi krizis," *TsVk*, no. 10 (1914): 289–92; "Iz inoeparkhial'noi zhizni," *Izvestiia po S.-Peterburgskoi eparkhii*, no. 20 (1909): 22–23; "Pastva S.-Peterburgskoi eparkhii v 1910 godu," *Izvestiia po S.-Peterburgskoi eparkhii*, no. 3 (1912): a4–5, no. 4 (1912): 3–8; Prot. I. Vostorgov, "Bludnoe vremia," *Moskovskie tserkovnye vedomosti*," no. 5 (1911): pril., 1–4; Prot. I. Butkevich, "Slovo v den' Novogo Goda," *Vera i razum*, no. 1 (1909): 1–9; "Nashi prikhodskie nuzhdy," *Prikhodskie chteniia* [appendix to *Tserkovnye vedomosti*]; "Episkop o religiozno-nravstvennom sostoianii nashego prikhoda," *Tserkovno-obshchestvennyi vestnik*, no. 10 (1913): 8–10.

Church's response to the general discussion of "hooliganism" in 1912–1913, which most bishops recognized as a widespread problem (in villages no less than cities) and which they attributed to a general decline in religiosity.[76] Even the official reports of the Church, which drew upon diocesan accounts, offered dismal assessments.[77] At the same time, those segments of the population that still possessed religious sensibility were drawn in massive numbers to the Old Belief and the various sects that proliferated in the last decades of the old regime. Faced by an apparent erosion of its rural base, the Church elected to concentrate its resources and power on the village that seemed the last bastion of Orthodoxy amidst a tidal wave of dechristianization and dissent in the final years of the old regime.[78]

In conclusion, the Church perceived and responded to the emergence of middle-class Russia—if by that we mean the liberal obshchestvo in post-Reform Russia. It is important to emphasize that the Church's response sprang from various motives—a desire to implement the new theology, concern about irreligious tendencies in the city, and fear that the Church would be entirely forgotten amidst the Liberation Movement. But in the end the effort failed to have much effect. Ultimately, the church was too committed to its supraclass values and mission, especially when obshchestvo itself seemed more committed to its own internal needs than the larger needs of the nation as a whole. Although the Church did not altogether lose interest in the city and obshchestvennost', it nevertheless put its priorities elsewhere—above all, in the village. As the ecclesiastical press and leading clergymen conceded, the Orthodox Church plainly failed to establish an effective urban ministry that would have enabled it to help shape consciousness and organizational ties of middle-class urban society.

[76] See diocesan responses in TsGIA SSSR, f. 796, op. 195, g. 1912, d. 3223.

[77] See, for instance, the analysis of the chief procurator's 1912 report by A. Papkov, "Trevozhnoe sostoianie nashei tserkvi (strashnaia kniga)," *Tserkovno-obshchestvennyi vestnik*, no. 10 (1914): 5–7.

[78] It is significant that the Church organized recurring conferences on the inner mission, but these focused solely on the struggle against the Old Belief, sects, and non-Orthodox confessions—not on the Church's mission in the city, whether among workers, petty townspeople, or the educated and propertied strata.

Chapter 15

V. M. DOROSHEVICH: THE NEWSPAPER JOURNALIST AND THE DEVELOPMENT OF PUBLIC OPINION IN CIVIL SOCIETY

LOUISE MCREYNOLDS

THE COMMERCIAL daily newspaper materialized in post-Reform Russia as "the dominant discourse of the nascent middle class."[1] In other words, it created a public space where those most concerned with social and economic progress could bring information together with ideas. On the one hand, the commercial revolution underway required technologically advanced media for circulating the economic information that fueled it. More important, the readers and advertisers who formed the crucial nexus of the group responsible for economic change needed new modes for expressing their social and political values as they battled rigid traditional structures to establish their claims as a legitimate power base.[2] The proliferation of commercially based mass-circulation newspapers satisfied both demands, providing an internal dynamic to intellectual as well as socioeconomic change.

Using the daily newspaper as a source for studying these changes proves especially insightful because, although as a medium of communications the Russian variant owed much of its structure to the preceding Western models, the contents of Russia's newspapers challenged many aspects of the West's claims to cultural imperialism. Frustration with their own patriarchal political system did not lead to an embrace of Western ideas and institutions, as those growing into a civil society looked to their own national achievements for an identity that would be neither imitative nor derivative. The daily paper, the

A version of this essay was presented at the annual AAASS convention in Boston in November, 1987. I thank Donald J. Raleigh and Nicholas V. Riasanovsky for comments on that earlier draft. The International Research and Exchanges Board (IREX) and the Fulbright-Hays Committee provided funding to conduct my research.

[1] Richard Terdiman, *Discourse/Counter-Discourse* (Ithaca: Cornell University Press, 1985), 119. Here Terdiman refers generally to the nineteenth-century commercial press.

[2] Two recent studies deal with the development of a corporate or class identity among tsarist Russia's merchants and entrepreneurs; although both mention the merchant press, neither study examines in depth the role of newspaper journalism in this process. Alfred J. Rieber, *Merchants and Entrepreneurs in Imperial Russia* (Chapel Hill: University of North Carolina Press, 1982); and Jo Ann Ruckman, *The Moscow Business Elite: A Social and Cultural Portrait of Two Generations, 1840–1905* (DeKalb: Northern Illinois University Press, 1984).

mass medium through which they could communicate as a group with shared interests, played a key role in articulating those interests.

A novel medium of communications, the daily newspaper required a new kind of journalist to mediate between events and readers, and the potential for influence was great. A new language was needed, as were personalities whose expressed views would be shared by the thousands of readers necessary to keep the paper prosperous. Vlas Mikhailovich Doroshevich became the most popular of these mediators because his language made him widely accessible and his opinions struck responsive chords among readers looking for guidance at the end of Russia's old regime. Described by a contemporary as "a child of the newspaper . . . but more talented, more candid, stronger than the rest," Doroshevich played an active role in every major journalistic development from 1881 through 1917.

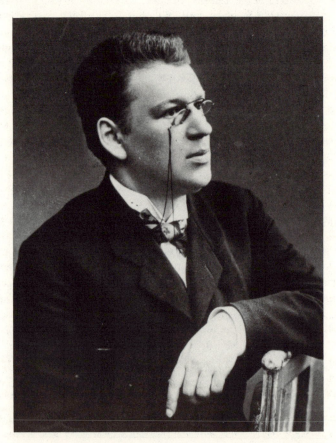

Fig. 11. Photograph of V. M. Doroshevich, "King of the Feuilletonists" (ca. 1900).

Contradictory sources make it difficult to reconstruct Doroshevich's childhood accurately, but we know that he was born in 1864 with *ersatz* printer's ink in his blood. His father, an unsuccessful writer, died young, leaving his mother, Alexandra Sokolova, with three small children. Disinherited by her wealthy provincial gentry family for marrying beneath herself, the well-educated Sokolova turned to journalism to earn a living. Whether because of poverty, professional ambition, or pressure to flee abroad for dabbling in left-wing politics in the 1860s, Sokolova abandoned her son in infancy, leaving him with only a note asking that he be named for Blaise Pascal. The wayfaring mother returned after ten years and successfully took her boy's adoptive father, a Muscovite landowner named Doroshevich, to court to reclaim him. Young Vlas never forgave her for this, and later, when the two found themselves working for the same newspapers, their relations were frosty to the point of making colleagues uncomfortable.[3] Regardless of the personal relations between the two, through his mother the boy was exposed to all aspects of newspaper journalism.

A hooligan before the term was coined, the boy chafed under the strictures of traditional Russian life. He scorned the tsarist educational system, which he described as "heartless, soulless" and "a chancellory for turning out young bureaucrats."[4] Readers could readily identify with his nonelitist upbringing, delighting in his mocking nostalgia for Moscow's Gymnasium No. 1, the only school from which he supposedly had not been expelled.[5] One of his most popular literary creations was "Ivanov Pavel," a dim-witted peasant schoolboy only slightly less stupid than his surroundings.

Doroshevich's background, personality, and desire to become a writer led him in 1881, at age seventeen, quite logically to Moscow's most recent entrant into the world of journalism, N. I. Pastukhov. A semiliterate bar owner, Pastukhov had decided to take the advice of the reporters who gathered at his watering hole and was opening his own newspaper, *Moskovskii listok* (The Moscow Flyer). Instead of competing directly with the heavily politicized Moscow press—M. N. Katkov's *Moskovskie vedomosti* (The Moscow News) and its "liberal opposition" *Russkie vedomosti* (The Russian News)—Pastukhov aimed to attract an untapped audience with a new kind of daily by appealing directly to their tastes for entertainment and the desire to read about their own lives. As the political press braced itself to fend off the reaction following Tsar Alexander II's assassination, readers responded enthusiastically to Pastukhov's inexpensive blend of hard news, peppered with gossip about the personal lives of the Moscow merchantry. Sensitive to his readers'

---

[3] The biographical information is from S. V. Bukchin, *Sud'ba fel'etonista* (Minsk: Nauka i tekhnika, 1975); B. G., "A. I. Sokolova. Nekrolog," *Istoricheskii vestnik* 135, no. 3 (1914): 954–59; and Vladimir Pokrovskii, *Moskva*, no. 12 (1965): 203.

[4] Bukchin, *Sud'ba fel'etonista*, 15.

[5] V. M. Doroshevich, "Iz literatury i zhizni," *Vestnik znaniia*, no. 6 (1904): 230–32.

unsatiated appetites for entertainment, Pastukhov added serialized romances and dramas, illustrated with woodcuts, driving circulation up to thirty thousand within the first year.[6]

The 1880s, generally slighted in the historiography as little more than a decade of repression, stand out as the decade when commercially based, mass-circulation newspapers began to establish themselves as public institutions. They challenged the authority of the "prestige press," the so-called "thick" journals, edited and published by Russia's elite *intelligentsia*.[7] This intelligentsia held a unique position in Imperial Russia. Commonly accepted as a discrete social category, they looked on themselves as "the embodied 'intelligence,' 'understanding,' or 'self-consciousness' of the nation."[8] Supreme idealists, they had difficulty coming to terms with the Russian reality of an obscurantist autocracy and ignorant peasantry, a quandary that severely alienated them from both tsar and people. Nor could they find comfort in the growth of a literate middling stratum developing independently of their control. Deeply distrustful of newspapers, these intellectuals took refuge in the editorial offices of the thick journals, where they directed their discourse to an audience much like themselves.[9]

Reporters, however, measured their influence by the quantity rather than the intellectual quality of their readers. Because they also held readers' confidences, newspaper journalists must be considered intellectuals, but they stood apart from the elite group because they did not believe that intelligence had been entrusted to them for safekeeping. Widely read and wildly popular, Doroshevich was the prototype for this new type of intellectual figure. Newspaper publishers like Pastukhov and others who made their marks in the 1880s—for example, A. S. Suvorin of *Novoe vremia* (The New Times) and S. M. Propper of *Birzhevye vedomosti* (The Stock Market News)—sought readers by offering a product fundamentally different from thick journals. The newspaper's economic basis mandated that it either attract readers by the tens of thousands or bow out to the competition. Disdainful of this market mentality in publishing, the intelligentsia refused to write for the popular press, leaving it to newcomers such as the young Doroshevich to shape its development as a medium of communications.

[6] On *Moskovskii listok*, see Kn. B. A. Shchetinin, "Legendarnyi izdatel'," *Istoricheskii vestnik* 25 (1911): 1030–43; and Jeffrey Brooks, *When Russia Learned to Read* (Princeton: Princeton University Press, 1985), 118–25.

[7] I borrow here from Ithiel de Sola Pool's characterization of politicized media directed toward elite audiences. Described in his *The Prestige Press: A Comparative Study of Political Symbols* (Cambridge: MIT Press, 1970), 33.

[8] Martin Malia, "What Is the Intelligentsia?" in *The Russian Intelligentsia*, ed. Richard Pipes, (New York: Columbia University Press, 1961), 3.

[9] Malia describes these journals as "vehicles for almost all creative culture under the old regime" and "the *intelligentsia*'s sole means for making the ideal impinge upon the real." Ibid., 14.

Although journal writers and newspaper reporters probably did not use different sides of their brains for thinking, as one observer argued, they clearly interpreted their roles as communicators differently.[10] The very nature of the newspaper, shouting facts today that could change by tomorrow, was inimical to Russia's muses. Alexander Herzen scorned reporters as "grasshoppers, devouring events before they have time to ripen," but Doroshevich found his worth in the immediate relevance of newspapers.[11] At ease with the limitations inherent in his vocation, he wrote that "the talented [newspaper journalist] must remember that his art—like the art of an actor—is creative for only a moment, and then dies with him."[12]

The two were not so far apart as Herzen might imagine. At issue was style, not substance. Doroshevich cast Herzen in the role of political mentor; the former recalled how reading the latter's *From the Other Shore* as a schoolboy had shaped many of his attitudes toward society and politics.[13] This example makes flesh the connection between the established and the new intelligentsia, emphasizing at the same time the significance of their disparate media. Heirs to the same Russian revolutionary intellectual tradition, they found different means of expressing it to different audiences. Doroshevich communicated many of Herzen's frustrations with the established order to the nonintelligentsia readers whom the exiled writer disdained.

Beginning his career at *Moskovskii listok* proved invaluable to Doroshevich, for he learned early how to cultivate mass appeal. He worked in all departments for Pastukhov, including helping his publisher set up a special edition of the paper to cover the annual Nizhnii Novgorod trade fair. But his feuilletons, often satirical, written under the pen name "The Jolly Muscovite," earned him renown as "The King of Feuilletonists." Although his early writing career also took him to several popular magazines, such as *Budil'nik* (The Alarm Clock) and *Razvlechenie* (Entertainment), he quickly recognized the greater influence possible through the daily paper. Entertaining readers was not enough for him; he began contributing hard news stories and editorials to *Moskovskii listok*. Here he introduced the anti-Westernism that remained a cardinal feature of his outlook throughout his career.[14] His readers at *Moskovskii listok* included a goodly number from the "less cultured merchants, business men, shopkeepers and serving people" or those suffering from both an economic disadvantage and an inferiority complex vis-à-vis the West; they therefore welcomed his sentiments.[15]

[10] "Obo vsem," *Russkoe bogatstvo*, no. 2 (1887): 174–84.

[11] Quoted in M. Gal-in, "Sredi khronikerov," *Russkaia mvsl'*, no. 5 (1913): 19.

[12] Bukchin, *Sud'ba fel'etonista*, 251.

[13] V. M. Doroshevich, *Sobranie sochinenii*, vol. 4 (Moscow: Tovarishchestvo I. D. Sytina, 1905), 1–6.

[14] Doroshevich's early career is detailed in Bukchin, *Sud'ba fel'etonista*, 17–38.

[15] Brooks, *When Russia Learned to Read*, 128.

Doroshevich's professional opportunities were limited at Pastukhov's paper, though, by the combination of his publisher's politics and his own journalistic ambitions. Industrialization brought increased wealth and opportunities, and the groups comprising the middle stratum grew increasingly pluralistic, a fact reflected in the increasing variety of newspapers. Anti-Semitic and generally conservative, Pastukhov contented himself with one segment of Moscow's readership, and he did not try to expand circulation beyond the profitable forty thousand.[16] Breaking with Pastukhov, Doroshevich's route to national recognition took the same detour as many of his colleagues, through the smaller but widely respected *Odesskii listok* (The Odessa Flyer). Odessa had become a haven for journalists from the two capitals "hiding out" from censors until controversies cooled down; thus, many of Russia's best journalists spent a part of their careers in this port city. Writing for *Odesskii listok* raised his standing among colleagues and gave Doroshevich a following among the better educated and more politically progressive readers than those who would have picked up Pastukhov's daily. His appearance did not go unheralded; Odessa residents Kornei Chukovsky and Leon Trotsky remembered their childhood enthusiasm for his columns in the 1890s.[17] Doroshevich's popularity at the two different kinds of newspapers confirmed his ability to attract followers from all intellectual strata.

At *Odesskii listok* Doroshevich not only broadened his audience, but, more important, he also extended his horizons when he began to travel as a foreign correspondent, visiting Western Europe, the United States, and the Far East in the 1890s. His most significant trip for the Odessa daily, though, was not abroad, but to the Russian penal colony on the remote outpost of Sakhalin Island in 1896. In response to the outcry raised by Anton Chekhov's graphic report on the island prison in the "thick" journal *Russkaia mysl'* (Russian Thought) in 1894, Doroshevich brought prison life to newspaper readers. His sensational depictions thrust him into the national spotlight.[18]

These vignettes from Sakhalin, laced with the sex, violence, and human suffering of life in the penal colony, had something for every imagination. He reacquainted readers with Sofia Bliuvshtein, the infamous "Golden Hand," a pickpocket, seductress, and suspected murderess whose escapades had captured front pages in the 1880s.[19] Although he put off many intellectuals with

[16] Between 1882 and 1917, circulation for *Moskovskii listok* rose from 30,000 to a peak of 45,000 in 1910. To compare this with other Russian dailies, see Louise McReynolds, "News and Society: *Russkoe slovo* and the Development of a Mass-Circulation Press in Late Imperial Russia" (Ph.D. diss., University of Chicago, 1984), 220–26.

[17] Leon Trotsky, *My Life* (New York: Pathfinder, 1970), 65; and Bukchin, *Sud' ba fel' etonista*, 45–46. It should be noted, however, that Chukovskii later considered Doroshevich's writing style a literary embarrassment.

[18] The Sakhalin stories appeared in a variety of newspapers, and in 1903 I. D. Sytin collected and published them with ample photographs. This two-volume collection went through at least one more edition in 1907.

[19] V. M. Doroshevich, *Sakhalin* (Moscow: Tov. Sytina, 1907), 8–10.

his penchant for vulgar detail, the topic was too important to be ignored.[20] As with Herzen, the primary objection was to style, but it was precisely the way he described this inherently political subject in deliberately lurid prose that brought in the middle-and lowbrow audience he sought to cultivate. Lev Tolstoi's admiration for these stories notwithstanding, Doroshevich met his goal of appealing to a broad rather than elite readership.[21]

Doroshevich's search for a somewhat base common denominator left him an outcast among the intelligentsia. *Sovremennyi mir* (The Contemporary World) editor Sergei Melgunov thought him "the basest of men."[22] For years the symbolist poet Aleksandr Blok refused to sell his poetry to the newspaper this "untalented scoundrel" edited because he abhorred the idea of being associated with Doroshevich.[23] Even Maksim Gorky, who leaned toward the melodramatic and enjoyed a substantial following from the lower and middle strata, worried that his own writing resembled Doroshevich's emotional style.[24]

Neither Doroshevich's popularity nor influence can be properly understood without considering his use of language. This reflected the "new journalism" that had developed in Russia and the West in the 1880s, with a strong bias toward middling groups as they wrestled with elites for a befitting place in the social order.[25] Doroshevich activated the passive, drawing readers into the drama of life as it unfolded around them. For example, he often wrote feuilletons in the form of conversations where he stood outside as an observer, replicating dialogues. This writing convention underscored the daily newspaper's authority in reconstructing reality; turning readers into eavesdroppers enhanced Doroshevich's "claims to professional competence and verisimilitude."[26] Poking fun at two groups with one feuilleton, Doroshevich let the merchantry comment on the decadent movement in the arts. Doroshevich "listened" as two merchants' daughters struck up a fast friendship on a train. One confessed to be married to a poet calling himself "Oskar Wildovich," and the disenchanted discussants resolved that decadents were good-for-nothings, currying favor with the middle class for their money.[27] A literary voyeur of the highest caliber, he left didacticism to those who moralized from the pages of the thick journals. He had no need for editorial comment; for example, he

[20] Bukchin, *Sud'ba fel'etonista*, 82–117, discusses the impact of these stories on public opinion.

[21] "Tolstoi o literature i iskusstve," *Literaturnoe nasledstvo*, nos. 37–38 (1939): 542.

[22] S. Mel'gunov, *0 sovremennvkh literaturnvkh nravakh* (Petrograd: Tipografiia Vil'de, 1916), 29.

[23] Aleksandr Blok, *Sobranie sochinenii* (Moscow: Izdatel'stvo Gos. Khud. Lit., 1963), 148.

[24] Bukchin, *Sud'ba fel'etonista*, 238.

[25] Michael Schudson discusses some historiography of the relationship of class to the language of journalism in his *Discovering the News* (New York: Basic Books, 1978), esp. chap. 3.

[26] Ibid.

[27] V. M. Doroshevich, "Dekadenty," *Rasskazy i ocherki* (Moscow: Sovremennik, 1986), 13031.

reported selections verbatim from a trial of twenty peasants accused of murdering an Odessa banker in his home. When one defendant pulled off her sweater to show the court the wounds from the police investigation, Doroshvich ended his account with the judge's admonition: "Defendant, try to conduct yourself properly."[28]

Once Doroshevich had established himself nationally with the Sakhalin stories, he was not long for Odessa. He moved to St. Petersburg where, together with A. V. Amfiteatrov, another celebrated journalist with whom he had "served time" in Odessa, and populist writer G. P. Sazonov, he began to publish *Rossiia* (Russia), a short-lived daily whose celebrated closing would ensure its place in history. Heavily subsidized by two progressive industrialists, Savva Morozov and M. O. Albert, *Rossiia* was intended to offer Petersburgers an alternative to Suvorin's powerful, conservative *Novoe vremia*.[29] The intensity of their rivalry inspired Doroshevich's most often reproduced feuilleton, "The Aged Executioner." Following this pointed attack on Suvorin's influential literary critic V. P. Burenin for the latter's sharp critique on the young poet Sergei Nadson shortly before Nadson's untimely death, Doroshevich earned the grudging respect of some of his critics.[30]

As at *Moskovskii listok,* Doroshevich worked in every department. Covering the local courts became one of his most frequent assignments, a beat he especially enjoyed because he regretted the generally low quality of crime reporting in the Russian press.[31] Deeply influenced by his experiences on Sakhalin, he interpreted crime as a manifestation of society's deeper problems. In accordance with the reformist sensibilities of many from the middle class, he presented the accused as victims of their circumstances instead of portraying society threatened by criminals, the image found in *Novoe vremia*. Doroshevich never shunned graphic detail or refrained from pulling at heartstrings in pursuit of readers. In his coverage of the trial of a woman who had suffocated her baby, for example, he provided a biography of the impoverished and abused mother to explain why she had hoped to give her infant salvation through death.[32] Later in his career, he demonstrated the heretofore unprecedented power of the press when he mounted an editorial campaign that successfully freed two brothers wrongly convicted of murder.[33]

Rossiia, on the verge of becoming a major force in St. Petersburg after its

[28] V. M. Doroshevich, "Pytki," *Russkoe slovo* (hereafter Rs), nos. 102 and 104, May 4, 6, 1907.

[29] A. N. Bokhanov, *Burzhuaznaia pressa Rossii i krupnyi kapital* (Moscow: Nauka, 1984), 72.

[30] "Staryi palach" is reprinted in Doroshevich's *Rasskazy i ocherki* (Moscow: Moskovskii rabochii, 1966), 234–40. Burenin responded in kind by linking his literary adversary to the legendary outlaw Vanka Kain. *Dnevnik A. S. Suvorina* (Moscow-Petrograd: Izd. L. D. Frenkel', 1923), 256.

[31] Bukchin, *Sud' ba fel' etonista*, 131.

[32] "Detoubiistvo," republished in *Rasskazy*, 311–19.

[33] Vladimir Pokrovskii, "Vlas Doroshevich," *Moskva*, no. 12 (1965): 203.

first two years, was closed in January 1902 for a flagrant breach of the censorship. Amfiteatrov wrote a none-too-subtle exposé of social misconduct among the ruling Romanov family. Lest any readers be unable to identify his caricatures, he called them the "Obmanov" family, an obvious pun that means "swindlers." Adding insult, he named the characters Nick and Alex after the most recent tsars.[34] The public was surprised that the article was published, not that the government closed the paper. Suvorin speculated that Amfiteatrov had written it to attract attention out of jealousy for Doroshevich's popularity.[35] Whatever his motives, Amfiteatrov put the "King of Feuilletonists" out of a job. Doroshevich at last agreed to work for the publisher who had been courting him for years, I. D. Sytin.

The two were well matched as editor and publisher. An entrepreneur who had begun as an apprentice to a provincial merchant, trading furs and branching into publications, Sytin began by tapping into the market for the newly literate after the Great Reforms and rose to become tsarist Russia's foremost book publisher. Sytin had purchased the rights to the Sakhalin stories, and since 1898 Doroshevich had been an occasional contributor to Sytin's nondescript Moscow daily, *Russkoe slovo* (The Russian Word).[36] Thereafter Doroshevich published exclusively with Sytin until he left *Russkoe slovo* in the summer of 1917 primarily because of political differences with the other editors.

The terms of Doroshevich's contract attested to Sytin's faith that he would bring a mass audience that included readers from all social strata with him. Doroshevich had "general supervision" of the paper, the power to make final decisions, and the obligation to contribute feuilletons for the Sunday paper and at least fifty-two other articles on contemporary issues during the course of the year. Sytin could not interfere with Doroshevich's management, and no one could edit his copy. Sytin did, however, require an insurance policy: Doroshevich was obligated to work within the confines of the censorship or the contract was void. Doroshevich received an annual salary of 40,000 rubles, plus an estimated 20 percent of the newspaper's profits.[37] Within three years, circulation had quadrupled to 117,000; by 1917 its circulation of one million made *Russkoe slovo* one of the world's largest newspapers.[38] As Doroshevich noted, *Russkoe slovo* was a genuinely "public" institution because its readers

---

[34] "Old Gentleman" [one of Amfiteatrov's pen names], "Gospoda Obmanovy," *Rossiia*, no. 976, Jan. 14, 1902.

[35] Quoted in Bukchin, *Sud' ba fel' etonista*, 159.

[36] Sytin wrote the two had been "friends since youth," but their paths did not appear to cross regularly before 1902. Sytin's autobiographical article in Rs, no. 41, Feb. 19, 1917.

[37] The terms of his contract were derived from several sources: Bukchin, *Sud' ba fel' etonista*, 166; A. N. Bokhanov, "Russkie gazety i krupnyi kapital," *Voprosy istorii*, no. 3 (1977): 119; and, I. A. Volkov, *Dvadtsat' let po gazetnomu moriu* (Ivanova-Voznesensk, 1925), 70–71.

[38] McReynolds, "News and Society," 226.

came from all social backgrounds.[39] A desire for information and opinions about the many changes and opportunities unfolding around them united these readers through their newspaper.

Doroshevich achieved national celebrity status, further indication of the esteem with which reporters were held in the public's imagination. One reader reportedly sued Sytin (unsuccessfully) because Doroshevich's column did not appear daily.[40] Feuilletonists at provincial newspapers compared themselves to him and invented personal associations with him as indications of their own importance; editors of other papers referred to their most prominent journalists as "our Doroshevich."[41] Many readers of another Moscow daily, in response to a survey on what they wanted to read more, included Doroshevich among the most popular and respected contemporary authors when they included him with Gorky and Tolstoi as contributors they wanted to their newspaper.[42]

Relishing his wealth and notoriety, Doroshevich developed a flashy personal style. He once wrote, "I want people to read me, not about me," and left scant clues to his personality.[43] A portly man and clean shaven, he was caricatured by his widow's peak, broad nose and mouth, and his pince-nez. Driving the same ostentatious make of automobile as Nicholas II, he was easy to spot in the streets of Moscow.[44] He wrote several feuilletons from the gaming tables in Monte Carlo. A gourmand, he did not have a reputation as a heavy drinker that many of his colleagues enjoyed.[45] Doroshevich loved the theater, had himself tried acting briefly, and struck up professional friendships with such luminaries as Konstantin Stanislavsky and Fedor Shaliapin.[46] His marriages, both of which failed, were to glamorous actresses much younger than himself. The first marriage produced his only child, Natalia, who became a popular feuilletonist for the nascent Soviet press.

His flamboyant manner created an image that, at first glance, contradicted the stridently antimaterialist barbs he tossed at the West. In fact, Doroshevich did not reject the high life in general, but rather the notion that wealth for its own sake was an acceptable social value. He defended his readers against a West that was encroaching culturally as well as economically. As the nation began to industrialize, the presence of Westerners in Russian commerce became more conspicuous, especially because Western Europeans controlled

[39] *Polveka dlia knigi* (Moscow: Tovarishchestvo I. D. Sytina, 1916), 420. On the readership of Russkoe slovo, see also McReynolds, "News and Society," 64–67.

[40] E. G. Golomb and E. M. Fingerit, *Rasprostranenie pechati v dorevoliutsionnoi Rossii i v Sovetskom soiuze* (Moscow: Sviaz', 1967), 15.

[41] M. Turinskii, "Gazety v provintsii," *Istoricheskii vestnik* 128, no. 4 (1912): 163; and Volkov, *Dvadtsat' let po gazetnomu moriu*, 16–17.

[42] *Utro rossii*, no. 321, Dec. 10, 1910.

[43] Bukchin, *Sud'ba fel'etonista*, 111.

[44] Bokhanov, "Russkie gazety," 119.

[45] V. A. Giliarovskii, *Moskva gazetnaia* (Moscow: Moskovskii rabochii, 1960), 219.

[46] Pokrovskii, "Vlas Doroshevich," 207, 209.

many major Russian industries and manufactories. Doroshevich objected vehemently to what he considered this exploitation of Russia by outsiders. Moreover, his antipathy toward the West was not an end in itself; he wrote much that suggested he believed Russia's Eastern roots grew deeper than its Western, calling on readers to forge an individualistic rather than imitative sense of themselves.

One of Doroshevich's first important works on Russia's position at the geographical and political crossroads, *The China Question* (Kitaiskii vopros), coauthored by Amfiteatrov, appeared in 1901. Acrimoniously anticolonial, the stories shared the theme that Russia should seek political alliances in the East rather than the West. In one tale, "The *Muzhik* Ivan and the Old Dragon," for example, these two neighbors (obviously symbolizing Russia and China) enjoy such harmonious relations that, in a reminder of the recently constructed Trans-Siberian Railway, the dragon allows the landlocked Ivan to lay water pipes across his land. They see their tranquility shattered, though, when Ivan joins the Liberal Movement then fashionable in St. Petersburg, cozying up to Dzhon Dzhemsovich Bull, a repugnant English factory owner living in the Russian capital but merciless toward his native workers. Bull and his cronies try literally to beat their civilization into the hapless dragon. The story ends with the conflict unresolved, as peasant and dragon commiserate on why they can no longer live together in peace.[47]

The late nineteenth century was a time of eastward expansion of the Russian empire, and envy of Western profiteers in the Far East undoubtedly colored Doroshevich's perspectives. He did not, however, refer to China or other Eastern countries as rightfully situated in a Russian "sphere of influence." On the contrary, he specifically opposed Russian imperialism. His primary concern was that Western culture, in the guise of the imperialist Bull, was absorbing the Russian national identity.

The relationship of Russia to the West had generated intense conflicts among educated Russians for generations, and Doroshevich brought the famous debates between Westernizers and Slavophiles of the pre-Reform era to a new audience in the pages of the popular press. The debate in the mass-circulation dailies was less philosophical than when it had been argued in the thick journals because the experiences of the two groups of readers with Western culture differed so greatly. Newspaper readers were more likely to know about Europe and America from reporters such as Doroshevich instead of from traveling or studying abroad as the intelligentsia had. The basic issue, though, had remained the same across the generations: was Russia a backward nation, inferior to the West, or were Russians endowed with an inherent cultural superiority?

[47] A. V. Amfiteatrov and V. M. Doroshevich, *Kitaiskii vopros* (Moscow: Tov. Sytina, 1901), 3–28.

Doroshevich promoted feelings of national self-confidence. In the early twentieth century, most of the Russian intelligentsia would have agreed with Westernizer Peter Struve that, "before Western European culture the Russian man feels himself in the position of a schoolboy and an ignoramus; even when he hates something foreign and antipathetic to him, he cannot avoid valuing it and feeling ashamed before it."[48] Doroshevich dismissed Westernizers such as Struve and comforted those readers who were insecure about their Russian-ness by reminding them of the inferiority of Western culture.[49] From his trav-els as a foreign correspondent, he could tell readers how Russia was viewed abroad. He queried Spaniards, for example, on an issue of great interest to Russians: whom did they prefer, Tolstoi or Dostoevsky?[50] Russian national integrity was at stake and instead of feeling insecure, Doroshevich exhibited a cocky arrogance about his heritage.

Doroshevich often parodied European manners and values, giving his read-ers the opportunity to feel as smug as he did. "Burzhui" translated as an object of contempt, not a synonym for Russia's middle class. Doroshevich described a new game in "bourgeois Paris," for example, where "winners" arrive home without being mugged along the way.[51] Contemptuous of Amer-ica, he saw "the dollar is everything."[52] Those Russians and the natives of colonized countries who aped Westerners likewise fell victim to Doroshe-vich's pen.[53] Social hypocrites populated his West: He discussed a drunken Austrian rambling on about Russia's chronic problems with alcohol and told of a Spaniard who took him to a bullfight and there began to berate Russians for their "barbarism."[54] Not even on her deathbed could Doroshevich find sympathy for Queen Victoria, his symbol of "bourgeois Britian."[55] To under-score British duplicity, he pointed out that he personally enjoyed many close friendships among the Japanese, whereas the British refused them entrance to their private clubs and referred to them in racial slurs.[56]

Doroshevich's aversion for the West had political implications when it car-ried over into his attitude toward the liberal political movement in Russia, that is, to those parties that would be presumed most attractive to the middle class as it might equate to the Western social grouping. He had firmly supported the strikers in the 1905 Revolution, excited that "the country is at last deciding

[48] Quoted from Jeffrey Brooks, "*Vekhi* and the *Vekhi* Dispute," *Survev* 19, no. 1 (1973): 32.

[49] Doroshevich satirized Struve and his Westernizing colleagues in a feuilleton, "P. B. Struve," Rs, no. 156, July 8, 1907.

[50] "Rossiia v Espanii," Rs, no. 83, March 26, 1902.

[51] "Igry," Rs, no. 214, Sept. 19, 1907.

[52] Bukchin, *Sud'ba fel'etonista*, 67.

[53] "Dzhentlmeny," Rs, nos. 350, 353, 356, Dec. 17, 20, 23, 1898; and "Anglichane i ia-pontsy," in his *Vostok i voina* (Moscow: Tov. Sytina, 1905), 117–31.

[54] From Bukchin, *Sud'ba fel'etonista*, 20–30.

[55] Ibid., 143.

[56] Ibid., 66–67.

its own fate,'' and became malevolent toward those liberals who compromised with the tsarist government in order to put down the Moscow uprising so bloodily.[57] In "The Whirlwind" (*Vikhr'*) he satirized those groups whom he associated with the Russian burzhui, who supported convocation of the State Duma, Russia's ineffectual quasi-legislative body because it would protect their social positions and property.[58] When the Western-oriented Kadet party tried to buy into *Russkoe slovo* in 1906, Doroshevich threatened to resign.[59] He mocked Russian politics in general, explaining "I have no political convictions. It is my duty to teach them to others."[60] In a comic blend of cynicism and acumen, Doroshevich predicted that in fifty years the same tsarist ministers would still be distributing the same inconsequential news releases to his grandson that they were handing him.[61]

The last satirical feuilleton he wrote for *Russkoe slovo*, published in December 1916, decried the rampant profiteering from the acute shortages of consumer goods brought about by World War I. The title character of "The Genius," a stockbroker imprisoned for usury, nonetheless exuded confidence that his services would be needed by the Western-style government he anticipated would emerge in Russia after the war.[62] This also reflected one aspect of Doroshevich's changing attitude toward the war: Initially he placed responsibility solely on German militarism, but by 1916 he was blaming the government in Petrograd as he voiced personal doubts about continuing the slaughter.[63]

When the autocracy collapsed in February 1917, most editorial policy makers at the mass-circulation dailies quickly moved behind the provisional government. Doroshevich sought a compromise between socialist parties and government, and the combination of his failing health and growing political differences between himself and others at *Russkoe slovo* precipitated his resignation in May.[64] He intended to continue writing feuilletons, but his opinions contradicted those of others on the editorial board. In June he moved south to the warmth of Sevastopol.[65]

Between May and October, Doroshevich produced a pamphlet of eight feuilletons that illustrated the confusion with which he faced the revolutionary upheaval. His greatest fear was of civil war, and he floundered for a means to

---

[57] Ibid., 177.

[58] Sytin later published in pamphlet form "Vikhr'," a collection of feuilletons that appeared first in 1906 in Rs.

[59] Bokhanov, "Russkie gazety," 119.

[60] Pokrovskii, "Vlas Doroshevich," 201.

[61] Feuilleton in Rs, no. 19, Jan. 24, 1914.

[62] "Genii," Rs, no. 286, Dec. 17, 1916.

[63] See his only work translated into English, *The Way of the Cross*, intro. by Stephen Graham (New York: Putnam, 1916).

[64] Bukchin, *Sud'ba fel'etonista*, 211.

[65] Ibid., 212; and feuilleton in Rs, no. 119, May 28, 1917.

avoid this. He appealed to the socialists to recognize that compromise would be necessary to save the country, even suggesting that Lenin would come around to Zinoviev's moderate position.[66] However loathesome he had considered the autocracy in 1905, it had survived and therefore spared him and the many who shared his amorphous politics from assuming the responsibility of government.

Ultimately, however, Doroshevich welcomed the October Revolution as an alleged moral victory of peace over money. He praised the cease-fire inaugurated by the Bolsheviks because it represented the superiority of Russian war aims vis-à-vis the West. Never a member of any political party, he joined those Russians for whom the October Revolution held the promise of unlimited potential because the government had at last been turned over to the Russian people. This move to the left was consonant with his sense of nationalism. "The Russian revolution never dreamed about being a revolution only in Russia," he argued. "It always dreamed about being revolution in the whole world. Don't tell us 'doctor, heal thyself' because we've already set an example for you."[67]

Having rejected Russia's Westernizers, Doroshevich proved willing to listen to Lenin when the latter could show signs of genuine support. During the Civil War, when the White Army held the Crimea, he refused to support these forces, proclaiming grandly that he "did not want to spoil [his] epitaph."[68] He gave public lectures on how Russia could benefit from the experiences of the French Revolution and worked briefly with his daughter as correspondent for the fledgling Soviet news agency, ROSTA.[69]

The last year of Doroshevich's life was tragically marred by illness and rejection. He returned to Petrograd in 1920 with great expectations of a literary career in the new socialist order. Extremely ill, he languished in a clinic, with time for only one more feuilleton. In his final statement, a nonsatirical damnation of the Romanovs, he vented his spleen against the past and heartened that Russians at last appeared in control of their future.[70] He died a few hours before his fifty-eighth birthday, February 22, 1922, and was buried quietly in the Volkov cemetery, next to General Trepov's would-be assassin and someone with whom he shared much both intellectually and politically, Vera Zasulich.[71]

The "King of Feuilletonists" was a new type of celebrity for twentieth-century Russians; he mirrored the social and economic changes that had made

---

[66] *Pri osobom mnenii* (Kishinev: n. p., 1917), 33.

[67] Ibid., 103–4.

[68] Pokrovskii, "Vlas Doroshevich," 201.

[69] N. V. Doroshevich, "Korol fel'etonistov v poslednye gody zhizni," *Prostor*, no. 4 (1971): 93, 97.

[70] This feuilleton, "Nikolai II," was published posthumously in *Ekran*, no. 26 (1922): 7–9.

[71] He had praised her revolutionary contributions in June 1917, in *Pri osobom mnenii*, 34–35.

his audience equally distinct as a new social group. One of Doroshevich's biographers observed that he was "a child of his times" and would not have developed as he had in any other epoch.[72] Very much a "child of the newspaper," no other medium would have allowed him to reach millions of readers with his opinions on social and political problems. Equally important to Doroshevich's evolution was the intellectual climate in which he grew up. The late nineteenth century witnessed great strides in education in Russia, and the growing middle and lower levels of literate society began to question political and intellectual tradition. Doroshevich became a prominent figure by responding to their doubts. Considerably less estranged from the public at-large than the intellectuals who shied away from his unreserved approach, he gave readers a point of reference in their changing world.

The point cannot be stretched to say that Doroshevich told his readers what to think, but it is undeniable that he was telling them what to think about.[73] Arguing throughout his career that the greed and self-interest of Western politics and culture made them unworthy subjects for imitation, he counselled readers to look for uniquely Russian solutions to their problems. True to himself, when he lost his fancy car and exorbitant salary, he supported those who had taken them in the name of the greater national good he had long believed in. If not all his fans embraced the Bolsheviks as openly as he did after 1917, the consistency of both Doroshevich's thought and popularity complicate the accepted interpretation that the liberal movement failed in Russia because of the limited strength of the middle class.[74] Those readers who believed, as Doroshevich had, that the West was bankrupt would not hold enough store in liberalism to fight for it.

[72] Pokrovskii, "Vlas Doroshevich," 202.

[73] Here I am paraphrasing Bernard C. Cohen, quoted in Maxwell E. McCombs and Donald L. Shaw, "The Agenda-Setting Function of the Mass Media," in *Reader in Public Opinion and Mass Communications*, ed. Morris Janowitz and Paul M. Hirsch, 3d ed. (New York: Free Press, 1981), 128.

[74] I am building here on an argument put forth by Michael Karpovich, "Two Types of Russian Liberalism," in *Continuity and Change in Russian and Soviet Thought*, ed. Ernest J. Simmons (Cambridge: Harvard University Press, 1955), 129–43.

Chapter 16

THE LOWER MIDDLE STRATA IN REVOLUTIONARY RUSSIA

Daniel Orlovsky

In the Soviet Union today, reformers and public opinion in general are trying to come to terms with the shape of Soviet society.[1] It is by now clear that the traditional categories of worker and peasant can account for neither the complexities of the current society nor its twentieth-century historical antecedents. Unfortunately, this recognition must work against the fact that most social history of twentieth-century Russia and the Soviet Union is written in terms of workers and peasants.[2] This is true even if we add the crude categories of intelligentsia or "employee," the other mainstays of Soviet statistical compilations. The point is that Soviet and Late Imperial Russian society were always finely textured evolving entities that embraced many different layers, groupings, and occupations. It would be difficult to understand the twentieth-century transformation of Russian society, or even the possibility of a civil society, let alone classes, without a clear sense of the layering in what was after all a remarkably dynamic and fluid social setting. This essay provides a general picture of what I term the "lower middle strata" in revolutionary Russia, from roughly 1900 through the revolutions of 1917 and the establishment of Soviet power. The essay aims to fill in yet another of those "blank pages" in Russian and Soviet history to which Gorbachev refers by bringing to light the contours of remarkably diverse and powerful groups of white-collar workers,

---

[1] See V. M. Selunskaia, *Sotsial'naia struktura sovetskogo obshchestva: istoriia i sovremennost'* (Moscow, 1987) and the work of T. Zaslavskaia. Both promote the idea of a layered society of many occupations and strata. In the West the most forceful statement of this view is Moshe Lewin, *The Gorbachev Phenomenon: A Historical Interpretation* (Berkeley, 1988).

[2] For Late Imperial Russia, the picture is better thanks to the recent works on the social estates (sosloviia), nobility, merchants (including the bourgeoisie), clergy, women, the military, and the professions. See especially work by Manning, Hamburg, and Becker; Owen, Rieber, Ruckman, and West; Freeze, Fuller, Bushnell, and the collection of essays on the professions edited by Harley Balzer and Kendall Bailes. See also A. Ben Eklof, *Russian Peasant Schools: Officialdom, Village Culture, and Popular Pedagogy, 1861–1914* (Berkeley, 1986), Scott Seregny, *Russian Teachers and Peasant Revolution: The Politics of Education in 1905* (Bloomington, 1989); and Christine Ruane Hinshaw's Ph.D. dissertation (Berkeley, 1987) and her essay in this volume.

employees, technical, managerial, and professional personnel who proved the essential leavening in revolutionary state building.

In revolutionary Russia, the history of the lower middle strata, by which I mean those social layers located between the property-owning or higher-status professional "middle class," on the one hand, and blue-collar factory or peasant agrarian labor, on the other, which are organized by occupations other than direct physical labor in the production process, reveals important similarities to the history of their counterparts in the industrialized European countries and the United States before World War I. In Europe, white-collar occupations grew along with capitalism in new industrial and commercial enterprises.[3] The new occupations differentiated themselves from the older petite bourgeoisie of craftsmen, small shop owners, and accumulators of property. At first, in Germany and France, for example, certain white-collar workers viewed themselves as the beneficiaries of capitalism and thus saw their occupations, distinct from the blue-collar occupations, as vehicles for social mobility. The downswings of capitalist development, however, led to economic hardship and insecurity and the creation of white-collar interest groups and unions that saw the possibility of alliances on the left with the factory proletariat. When the socialist parties failed to adjust their doctrines or organizations to embrace these lower middle strata, white-collar organizations easily attached themselves to right-wing movements that promised to curb the excesses of capitalist development, restore the "old values," and promote a "healthy" nationalism.[4] European white-collar workers appeared to have no class identity of their own. They wavered between left and right, though their deeply rooted sense of themselves as different from blue-collar workers and their somewhat higher social status in relation to factory workers made for an easy transfer of allegiance to the nationalist right.

Russia also produced significant and growing numbers of white-collar employees, technical personnel, professionals, and quasi-professionals by the end of the nineteenth century. According to the 1897 census, 10.6 percent of the empire's population (13,386,392 of a total 125,640,021) belonged to the legal category of the *meshchanstvo*, a low-status urban group that provided many recruits to the occupations accessible to the lower middle strata. This estate represented the second largest population category after the peasantry, which counted an enormous 77.1 percent of the Russian population or

---

[3] See, for example, Jürgen Kocka, ed., *Angestellte im europaischen Vergleich: Die Herausbildung angestellter Mittelschichten seit dem spaten 19. Jahrhundert* (Gottingen, 1981), and Kocka, *White-collar Workers in America: A Social-Political History in International Perspective* (London, 1980).

[4] See the superb study of Philip Nord, *Paris Shopkeepers and the Politics of Resentment* (Princeton, 1986), and Hans Speier, *Angestellte vor dem Nationalsozialismus* (Gottingen, 1977).

96,896,648 people.[5] Some major occupation categories that fall within the lower middle strata are listed in the census in Table 16.1.[6]

The census also notes 103,760 independent household heads employed in public (zemstvo and town duma) and estate institutions, 12,174 engaged in private legal activities (including lawyers, notaries, and their office employees), 129,607 teachers and others employed in education, 25,141 representatives of the academic, artistic, and literary worlds, 78,992 medical professionals and employees, 54,096 administrators of private commercial and industrial firms, and 6,762 employees of private railroad and shipping companies.[7]

The layering of Russian urban society was even more pronounced on the eve of World War I. See Tables 16.2 and 16.3 for statistics for St. Petersburg (1910) and Moscow (1912).[8]

TABLE 16.1
Population by occupation, 1897 Census

Occupation	Number
Administrative and judicial	42,034
Officials	6,612
Office employees (administrative and judicial)	44,481
Watchmen/guards	21,162
Diplomats	380
Officers—police/gendarmes	10,425
Policemen, firemen	94,150
Administrators (total)	223,314

[5] Of course, the 1897 census still used the empire's problematic estate (*soslovie*) categories for its aggregate figures. The data are broken down by occupation, however, permitting a good overview of lower-middle-strata formation. See *Obshchii svod po imperii rezul'tatov razrabotki dannykh pervoi vseobshchei perepisi naseleniia proizvedennoi 28 ianvaria 1897 goda*, 2 vols. (St. Petersburg, 1905), 1: 1–3. On the estate system, see Gregory L. Freeze, "The Soslovie (Estate) Paradigm and Russian Social History," *American Historical Review* 91, no. 1 (1986): 11–36. On the slippery concept of the meshchanstvo see Manfred Hildermeier, "Was war das Mescanstvo?" in *Forschungen zur osteuropaischen Geschichte*, Band 36 (Berlin, 1985), 15–53. The use of the term "lower middle strata" here includes those occupations often placed under the following rubrics: intelligentsia, *meshchanstvo*, employees (*sluzhashchie*), state bureaucrats or rankholders (*chinovniki*), the Third Element, and so forth.

[6] The census also provides figures for dependent family members, which are in all cases quite significant.

[7] *Obshchii svod po imperii*, 256–64.

[8] For St. Petersburg, see A. G. Rashin, *Naselenie Rossii za 100 let (1811–1913 gg.): Statisticheskie ocherki* (Moscow, 1956), 325. Rashin's figures, which represent a crude attempt to build up the size of the working class at the expense of white-collar employees, come from *Petrograd po perepisi 15 dekabria 1910 g.naseleniia*, chast' 2, vyp. 1: *Raspredelenie naseleniia po gruppam zaniatii* (Petrograd, 1915).

For Moscow, see Rashin, *Naselenie Rossii*, 333. For a superb discussion of similar data drawn

TABLE 16.2
Petersburg population by occupation, 1910

Occupation	Number	Percentage
Employers of labor	44,300	3.7
One-person enterprise	76,000	6.5
Employees, industrial	40,700	3.4
Workers	504,000	42.5
Servants	189,000	15.9
Employees, nonindustrial	66,000	5.5
Rentiers	39,000	3.3
Caretakers of private or state institutions	55,800	4.7
Military	47,500	4.0
Temporarily unemployed	38,500	3.2
Total population	1,186,700	

TABLE 16.3
Moscow population by occupation, 1912

Occupation	Number	Percentage
Employees of labor	44,200	4.2
Employers using only family members	6,800	0.6
One-person enterprise	59,100	5.6
Family members in artisan production	15,700	1.5
White-collar employees		
In industry and commerce	92,300	8.8
Factory workers	165,900	15.6
Other industrial workers	126,800	12.1
Workers, transport, apartment houses, and commerce	111,300	10.6
Service—home	99,100	9.4
Apprentices—commercial and artisan	41,600	4.0
Police employees	32,400	3.1
Other employees and free professions	57,700	5.5
Other workers in institutions	23,100	2.2
Rentiers	19,200	1.8
Pensioners	43,800	4.2
Living in communal dormitories	55,400	5.3
Other, unemployed, no indication	57,600 [??]	5.5
Total population	1,051,300	

These figures indicate that, in addition to growing numbers of blue-collar factory workers, the capital cities contained numerous white-collar, professional, and "proto-professional" groups. The proto-professionals included sales clerks (*prikazchiki*), cashiers, bookkeepers, pharmacy employees, post, telegraph, and railroad employees, factory and enterprise clerks, middle-level managers, municipal, zemstvo, and other public-sector employees, paramedical personnel, teachers, statisticians, low-ranking technicians, agronomists, and the like. Much depends on who is counted as a worker, and on this subject there is no consensus, even among Soviet historians. Some include the numerous sales clerks, post, telegraph, and railroad employees among the workers, and others prefer to separate them from the working class as a source of petit-bourgeois contamination.[9] The point is that despite all sorts of evidence to the contrary, the mainstream of Soviet historiography—and, indeed, Western historiography, as well, though for somewhat different reasons—has attempted to downplay or ignore the role of nonworkers and peasants, the hated petite bourgeoisie in the revolutionary process of early twentieth-century Russia.[10]

Whatever the ideological motivation for the historians' repression of the lower middle strata, the Russian context in which these groups emerged had its own peculiarities. In Russia, a relatively new and highly concentrated capitalist sector coexisted with a much larger agrarian sector and peasant population.[11] In both sectors, however, the state and bureaucratic institutions still played an inordinately large role. One could argue that even before the October Revolution and the advent of "socialism," the state institutions and structures functioned as a surrogate market able to collect its own material and human capital. And this accumulation went on even as state and market institutions exhibited a high degree of mutual influence. These factors—in addition to the strong influence of indigenous anti-industrial populism and the relative weakness of the propertied and entrepreneurial middling social groups—all served to push Russia's growing lower middle strata to the left on the eve of the 1905 revolution. In the case of the lower-status white-collar occupations and proto-professionals, low wages, poor living and working conditions, pa-

---

from a slightly earlier period (1902) and a pioneering effort at mapping out Moscow's urban occupational layering, see Joseph P. Bradley, Jr., *Muzhik and Muscovite* (Berkeley, 1985).

[9] See the differing approaches to the problem of working-class borders in the following recent Soviet studies: Z. Z. Kruze, *Uslovie truda i byta rabochego klassa Rossii v 1900–1914 godakh* (Leningrad, 1981); Iu. I. Kir'ianov, *Perekhod k massovoi politicheskoi bor'be: Rabochii klass nakanune pervoi Rossiiskoi revoliutsii* (Moscow, 1987); and N. A. Ivanova, *Struktura rabochego klassa Rossii, 1910–1914* (Moscow, 1987).

[10] One major exception to this is the remarkable collective study of V. P. Buldakov, A. E. Ivanov, N. A. Ivanova, and V. V. Shelokhaev, *Bor'ba za massy v trekh revoliutsiiakh v Rossii: Proletariat i srednie gorodskie sloi* (Moscow, 1981).

[11] In addition to the classic works of Alekhsander Gershenkron on the subject, see the more recent study by Peter Gatrell, *The Tsarist Economy, 1850–1917* (London, 1986), 98–191.

triarchal relations in the work place, and lack of legal rights were the immediate causes of unrest among the lower middle strata in the revolutions of both
1905 and 1917. Economic hardship, the search for status and a political and
administrative role in the revolutionary process of state building, and a similar
quest for more status and authority in relation to those above them in workplace hierarchies and to propertied Russians in general motivated the lower
middle strata to strive for what they termed "democratization."[12]

My concept of the lower middle strata includes all the occupations and social groups that occupied space between the world of factory and agrarian
labor, on the one hand, and the entrepreneurial owners of capital and other
forms of property, on the other. It also signifies those who believed in the
process of democratization or the sharing of political and social power with
those who stood higher in workplace and larger social hierarchies. It is clear
that many higher-status professionals, administrators, and managers (doctors,
lawyers, engineers, bureaucrats, professors) should not be included in such a
category. Some of these individuals identified fully with propertied Russia
or even with the Old Regime political establishment. Many worked loyally
for the state in various administrative and professional capacities within
the framework of the ministerial bureaucracy—for example, lawyers in the
Ministry of Justice or the Senate, engineers in the Ministry of Communication, financial experts or economists in the Ministries of Trade and Industry and Finance, doctors in the Ministry of Internal Affairs or the military.
Others moved into opposition, first as members of the Union of Liberation and
later as mainstays of the liberal parties, especially the Kadets. In these roles,
many opposed the ambitions and organizations of their professional and white-
collar subordinates. Still, higher-status occupations and professions should be
included within the lower middle strata because the varied ideologies and political allegiances—liberal, conservative, technocratic, the project of free professions—did not preclude numerous representatives of these same occupations from joining or even leading the democratic movement in 1905–1907
and 1917 with their lower-status counterparts. Here one must be clear, however, to distinguish between the higher-status groups (lawyers, engineers, and
technical personnel, for example) and white-collar office clerks, shop personnel, and the like. For analytic purposes, the various layers or strata must be
disaggregated. The social and ideological uniqueness and the politics of the
various groups must be respected even while we recognize the social and political power of the whole.

In 1917, the social revolution of the lower middle strata involved a double
movement. First, there was the struggle within professional and institutional
settings as members of the lower middle strata took power from their white-

---

[12] I take up this idea at length in Orlovsky, *Russia's Democratic Revolution: The Provisional
Government of 1917 and the Origins of the Soviet State* (Berkeley, forthcoming).

collar superiors within those institutions. This was the case, for example, in
the zemstvos and town dumas where this process of democratization occurred
in the executive boards even before the provisional government's officially
sanctioned elections.[13] It also took place in the setting of many trade unions
and professional organizations. The second move was cumulative, represented
by the collective weight of numerous lower-middle-strata functionaries creating their own world of considerable political and social power by creating and
staffing an entire infrastructure—zemstvos, soviets, cooperatives, war industries committees, land and food supply committees, trade unions, professional
organizations and congresses, and the like—that was absolutely at the center
of revolutionary state building. The provisional government failed to take full
advantage of this infrastructure in its state-building agenda. The example of
the white-collar trade unions illustrates the volatility and dynamism within the
lower middle strata as well as that sector's aspirations to a major role in the
new revolutionary state. The post-October Bolshevik regime, far more attuned
to lower-middle-strata infrastructure and its aspirations, was largely successful
in harnessing the skills and energy of the white-collar plebians to the ''proletarian'' revolution. Actually, it appears that many white-collar workers and
other occupational groups willingly identified with the proletarian cause both
before and after October. Whether this attraction to the left, to alliances with
workers and peasants as opposed to the bourgeoisie, resulted in the lower middle strata influencing the nature of the socialist and populist movements themselves is a question that must remain at the heart of our understanding of the
revolutionary process and its outcomes.

During the late nineteenth century, white-collar workers in Europe and
America were important elements in a growing middle class or middle classes
that strove for political and cultural hegemony. Stuart Blumin has written eloquently of the growth of middling layers of society and a ''middle-class consciousness'' in nineteenth-century America.[14] According to Blumin, this middle class was not the consciousness-bearing bourgeoisie of Marxist theory; it
did not have to express itself in either an aggressive, self-conscious ideology
or any neat fashion in the political arena. Blumin focuses instead on class
awareness derived from ''convergences'' of personal, social, and workplace
experience. Types of work, patterns of authority and consumption, residential
location, family organizations and strategies, formal and informal voluntary
associations—all allow Blumin to posit the existence of disparate social
groups rooted in the burgeoning white-collar occupations that are united as a
middle class. The experience of the layers of Russian white-collar employees
and professionals may be viewed from a similar perspective, though the out-

---

[13] See Orlovsky, *Russia's Democratic Revolution*.

[14] Stuart M. Blumin, ''The Hypothesis of Middle-Class Formation in Nineteenth-Century
America: A Critique and Some Proposals,'' *American Historical Review* 90, 2 (1985), 299–338.

come was quite different. In the United States, the disparate groups united under a common cultural umbrella of shared sensibilities and mythologies; in Russia there was always more fragmentation. The property-owning bourgeoisie could not overcome its regional, ethnic, and ideological differences and unite into a *class* for itself. A broader middle class, as conceptualized by Blumin for the American case, was also a chimera due to the status conflicts within occupations and professions and the lower middle strata's identification with the left.

Recently, Marxist theoreticians and historians have confronted the issue of the petite bourgeoisie while discussing the obvious importance of technical and white-collar labor in twentieth-century capitalist and socialist economies and the emergence of either a new proletariat or a new bourgeoisie that might include white-collar labor.[15] Erik Olin Wright has put forth the notion of "contradictory class locations" that permits him to place different groups of white-collar workers and technical intelligentsia in either camp, depending on their role in the production process.[16] Clearly the lower middle strata may help form a middle-class hegemony, or it may attach itself to blue-collar workers under a proletarian or some other label. This implies an important point of interpretation in the historiography of the Russian Revolution and early Soviet period that depends so heavily on a model of proletarian hegemony. Though proletarian hegemony certainly existed as a means of legitimation and as an ideal, in the Russian case, it did not preclude white-collar gains or even a creative role for white-collar groups within the new proletarian state and society.

White-Collar Employees and Their Trade Unions in 1917

During 1917, both the higher status professional groups and the poorer white-collar workers were extremely active in politics and the process of state building. The story of the white-collar trade unions or mixed white- and blue-collar unions in 1917 reveals much about social differentiation, mobility, and the powerful movement of the marginalized white-collar employees against their superiors. It also tells us much about the creation of the Soviet state and its social and institutional foundations.

The materials on the white-collar trade union movement in 1917 reveal the following picture.[17] The trade union movement of the lower middle strata de-

[15] See especially the works of Nikos Poulantzas, *Classes in Contemporary Capitalism* (London, 1975), 193–97; Erik Olin Wright, *Class, Crisis and the State* (London, 1978), and the excellent discussion in Chris Smith, *Technical Workers: Class, Labour, and Trade Unionism* (London, 1987).

[16] See Wright, *Class, Crisis and the State*, and his recent modification of his theory in "What Is Middle about the Middle Class," in *Analytical Marxism*, ed. John Roemer (Cambridge, 1986), 114–40.

[17] My analysis is based upon the records of the congresses of such unions as the commercial

veloped during the 1905–1907 revolution as a response to poverty, poor working conditions, patriarchal authority structures, and lack of legal rights and
protection in relations with employers and the state.[18] It is important to distinguish between the union movement of the higher-status professions—the doctors, lawyers, engineers, professors and the like—and its counterpart among
the lower middle strata—the salesclerks, white-collar employees, low-ranking
railroad employees, land surveyors, office personnel in the state, public, and
private sectors, primary school teachers, paramedics, and other lower-ranking, miserably paid, and unprotected functionaries of the emerging capitalist
economy and the hybrid institutions of the traditional state. To some extent
these groups cooperated in the Union of Unions of 1905, though Jonathan
Sanders has shown that even then, the higher-status professions, many of
which supplied personnel to the Kadet party, were effectively opposed by the
radicalism of the lower-middle-strata unions that had joined the Union of
Unions.[19]

The main characteristics of the 1917 movement can be illustrated by the
cases of two prominent white-collar occupational groups, the post and telegraph workers and the commercial and industrial employees. The pattern is
one of intensive union formation beginning immediately with the February
Revolution, but along very decentralized lines defined by occupation, region,
locality, and even factory. Central union organs and congresses were held and
national bodies created, but often with little or no control over constituent
organizations. There was an early and pronounced move on the part of union
leaders and the rank-and-file to identify their cause as part of the class struggle, part of the general proletarian movement. Here we find that some union
leaders preferred to espouse class harmony and negotiation with enterprise
owners, but as 1917 wore on they were often pushed into more radical positions by rank-and-file pressures. The union members were for "democratization," by which they meant an all-out attack on the workplace hierarchy. They

---

and industrial employees, credit institution employees, the press of various unions, and union
histories.

[18] See, for example, A. M. Gudvan, *Ocherki po istorii dvizheniia sluzhashchikh v Rossii: do
revoliutsii 1905 goda*, Part 1 (Moscow, 1925) and *Normirovka truda torgovo-promyshlennykh
sluzhashchikh* (Petrograd, 1917); D. V. Antoshkin, *Ocherk dvizheniia sluzhashchikh v Rossii (so
vtoroi poloviny XIX veka)* (Moscow, 1921), and *Professional'noe dvizhenie sluzhashchikh 1917–
1924 gg.* (Moscow, 1927); Maks Gordon, *Iz istorii professional'nogo dvizheniia sluzhashchikh v
Peterburge: pervyi etap (1904–1909 gg.)* (Leningrad, 1925). See also three recent Soviet studies
of white-collar employee unions and their radical activities during the 1905 Revolution: P. S.
Liubarov, "Vystupleniia torgovykh rabochikh i sluzhashchikh v Rossii v 1905 godu," *Voprosy
istorii* 8 (1977): 20–35; N. A. Ivanova and V. V. Shelokhaev, "Vserossiiskaia pochtovo-tele-
graficheskaia zabastovka v noiabre 1905 godu," *Voprosy istorii* 10 (1976): 51–66; and Ivanova
and Shelokhaev, "Torgovye sluzhashchie v revoliutsii 1905–1907 gg.," *Istoricheskie zapiski* 101
(1978): 161–216.

[19] See Sanders, "The Union of Unions" and his recent article "Lessons from the Periphery-
Saratov, January 1905," in *Slavic Review* 40, no. 2 (Summer 1987): 229–44.

despised management personnel and at all times attempted to assert their own claims to either autonomy or a hand in management. Blue-collar unions at first supported the provisional government as the harbinger and protector of the democratic revolution, but by the summer of 1917 this changed completely. The movement became increasingly hostile to and distrustful of the government. The unions viewed the provisional regime as excessively bureaucratic and unresponsive, a distant and unsympathetic nonprovider and breaker of promises. As the union movement lost faith in government intentions and even in its legislation, it saw more and more need for centralization and strong organization to protect the lower middle strata in an unpredictable and threatening situation. The union movement thus evinced a willingness to strike to gain economic benefits and relief from its members' steadily worsening position. The strike movement ebbed and flowed according to the attitudes of employers and the general political situation.

A survey of the activities of two of the more prominent white-collar occupational groups and their unions in 1917 sheds light on the important role of the lower middle strata in the class struggle within revolutionary Russia.

Postal and Telegraph Workers in 1917

Postal and telegraph workers were especially active in 1917.[20] As was the case with the other white-collar unions of this period (e.g., railroad workers, paramedical personnel, teachers) a radical rank-and-file that was fragmented in its organizations according to occupational lines was led by a more conservative, though by no means antirevolutionary, union leadership drawn from managerial layers and rank-holders who supported the provisional government.

The post and telegraph movement began with the organizational form so common to the revolution: the formation of committees in the workplace and localities, with their de facto assumption of administrative functions and membership drawn from lower-ranking personnel. The first All-Russian Post and Telegraph Congress opened on May 14 in Moscow, with delegates from fourteen postal regions.[21] The delegates included 126 postal rank holders and only 51 lower employees (mailcarriers and the like). The Socialist-Revolutionary party (S-R) dominated the 56 delegates, but in fact party allegiances were largely unformed apart from the existence of a "socialist bloc."

The congress leaders hoped it would unify the movement, shape the local organizations into common forms, and formulate union positions on the crucial issues of wage scales, cost of living supplements, and tables of organization (*shtaty*). They also by definition had to consider relations with the Ministry of Post and Telegraph and the provisional government because they, like

---

[20] For the 1917 Union movement, the most thorough study is K. Bazilevich, *Professional'noe dvizhenie rabotnikov sviazi (1917–1918)* (Moscow, 1927).

[21] Ibid., 74.

many railroad and water transport employees, were employed by the central state bureaucracy. Although the congress had considerable authority before it opened, its delegates had great difficulty in defining policies consonant with the interests of the wide range of employees of the post and telegraph apparatus.

A first congress priority was to redefine relations with the ministry.[22] Speakers drew a portrait of the future ministry apparatus that included elected managers and chiefs and the transfer of administrative authority to elected collectives. This was one facet of democratization in the postal service.[23]

The congress faced pressure from provincial organizations for higher wages and quick expansion of the tables of organization, a welcome form of social welfare during the revolution and civil war, but weeks began to pass without the articulation of clear programs and strategies.[24] Several regional organizations in Petrograd and the south began to complain and demand greater activity and competence from the congress.[25] Critics complained that the delegates were poorly prepared for the issues and undisciplined. By the beginning of June, the provincial delegates had grown tired of endless speeches and began to speak of returning home.[26] After thirty-nine days, the congress finally elected a union central committee and completed its work.

In final declaration of democratic principles and intent, the congress abolished all hierarchies, ranks, and orders with their attached privileges and all occupational distinctions (legal and moral) between "higher and lower employees." All employees were to have equal rights if they fulfilled their duties by virtue of their personal qualities and special education or training. It is important to keep firmly in mind this grass-roots push for level or equal treatment within the hierarchies. It was not an attitude shared by the white-collar workers occupying higher space within the hierarchies. Indeed, eventually under Soviet power, it would become expedient and sometimes necessary for

[22] Ibid.

[23] In a telling comment Bazilevich notes that from the perspective of the 1920s, it was extremely difficult to clarify the exact social composition of the congress because all former rank and office holders (*chiny*) and other occupations are "now listed under the label sluzhashchii." This serves as one more warning to those who insist on accepting the standard Soviet social categorizations at face value.

[24] This expansion in positions would, of course, be realized under the Soviet regime during the Civil War when the apparatus was flooded with types marginally from the lower middle strata, who were looking for survival. How to shrink the *shtaty* was first on the agenda of the Soviet unions and bureaucracy during the first months of NEP. See the articles in *Golos rabotnika*, no. 204 (1921). This was the paper of the national union of Soviet rabotniki, or employees, the new centralized umbrella union for so many employees from the lower middle strata discussed here.

[25] One delegate complained that at the current tempo, the work would not be complete for four hundred days. Ibid., 77.

[26] As it was the congress began late and hardly mustered a quorum because only about 60 percent of the delegates appeared in Moscow.

the state and unions to restore many kinds of differentials in the white-collar workplace.

On the material question, an ideal was introduced that would also have resonance throughout the white-collar movement in 1917 and under the Soviet regime as well, namely the necessity of new wage scales that placed white-collar workers on a par with industrial workers. In this case the call was for wages throughout the ministry equal to those at goverment factories and enterprises. The congress also called for the eight-hour day and new rules for twenty-four-hour shifts. Local committees were to use this as the basis for creating new tables of organization that would include a 10 percent reserve cadre. The problem for the union leadership and the provisional government was implementing the program before rank-and-file radicalism would mock the notion that the lower middle strata might serve as a social base for the provisional government. Here, as with other major white-collar unions, the record was only one of disappointed hopes and disaffection.

The reorganization of the union according to the June congress principles was not difficult. The spring committees were adapted, and labels changed, though most units did elect new committees. This reorganization was complete by the time of the second Postal Regional Congress in August and September.[27] The central committee took on wide powers and legislative work on relations with the ministry apparatus, salaries, and the eight-hour day. This central committee had been reelected in July to square off with Minister of Post and Telegraph Tseretelli and his successor, Nikitin. Both men stood for the noninterference of the union in ministry operations and the reduction of the union to a purely advisory role. Employees according to Tseretelli had to be fully subordinate to their service chiefs in all business matters. He also prohibited union or political meetings on service time. This angered many in the union movement, as reflected in the post and telegraph press and at general meetings, and it provided a confrontational background to the new central committee's negotiations with the ministry. The Union Central Committee spent the next four months engaged in large and small conflicts with the ministry.

In September one of the sharpest conflicts occurred over the railroad strike. When the Railroad Workers' Union announced the strike, the central committee took a neutral position and issued orders to send both the telegrams of the government ministries and the railway workers. Nikitin, however, ordered the central committee to stop the Union of Railway Workers' telegrams. He threatened those who assisted in these communications with inclusion among the strike participants. The government considered the Union of Post and Telegraph Employees as part of the antigovernment movement, and the ministry would break all relations with the union thereby depriving it of representation

---

[27] Ibid., 87–88.

on mixed government commissions.[28] At the central committee, talk began of a postal strike, but the committee decided that the time was not yet ripe. The Moscow Union, also against a strike, changed its position two weeks later when the ministry dismissed some employees in the Moscow Post Office; the Muscovites approved a strike in principle as a legitimate form of economic struggle.

During the Kornilov Affair, the central committee quickly moved to install telegraph specialists on permanent duty watching over the Petrograd telegraph network.[29] Union officials were to establish surveillance over all correspondence, and the committee sent telegrams to all postal region organizations to do the same. Nikitin blocked these communications for twenty-four hours. Union officials on duty at the Petrograd office were opposed by administrators and even some employees. The central committee then issued instructions to create union commissars in charge of all post and telegraph institutions. The ministry sent this out over the signatures of both Nikitin and Kerensky. Within twenty-four hours, the instructions were cancelled in the face of protest resignations of key postal administrators. The union had taken the first large step toward claiming power over the post and telegraph apparatus, and the provisional government had shown an intransigence similar to that of other employers on the Petrograd labor relations scene.

Significant developments took place at the level of the workplace committee, where the lower middle strata staked its practical claim to power or to administrative control over functions and the right to make and enforce a broad range of decisions that filled the void left by an inactive and unresponsive ministry. The committees attempted to implement certain congressional decisions from below. For example, some committees shortened business hours of telegraph service, changed working hours on holidays, instituted days of rest, cancelled home delivery of packages, and dealt with various personnel matters (hirings, dismissals, and conflicts).

This transformation of regional union organizations into de facto sectors of a new emerging state mechanism replicates in microcosm the role of the lower-middle-strata infrastructure in revolutionary state building. Before even becoming proper trade unions, the emerging organizations had moved into the entirely uncharted waters of administrative units and arbiters of "production"—exactly where they would find themselves within the post-October Soviet regime. In part this was desired by the union leadership, but it was even more a response to pressure from the rank-and-file employees who pressed their union organizations to assume full administrative authority while transforming power relations within the ministry structures. One could hear frequent resolutions from the regional meetings calling for a "transfer of power

[28] Ibid., 90.
[29] Ibid., 91.

from ministerial officialdom to the elected organs of union employees.''[30] This dimension of democratization, of course, was the lower employees' move to replace the higher rank-holders within the committees.

The economic struggle propelled forward conflicts within the union and those between the union and the provisional government. Until the postal congress in June, these issues turned on the March 28 law that mandated salary increases only for certain employee categories—mid- and lower-ranking officials, postmen, messengers, and watchmen.[31] The law satisfied few and led to a struggle for the best positions.

The ministry and the central committee did little to make the new wage scales workable, given the tremendous rise in prices between early summer and September. More than anything this radicalized the rank-and-file and turned them against union leadership and provisional government alike. By early July Petrograd post office employees were ready to strike over the government's delays in paying the promised increases. The employees stepped up their demands for a one-time cost-of-living increase and for ministry approval of their elected post office director. At a June 26 general meeting at the Petrograd Post Office, ministry officials faced two groups hostile to each other: one comprised a portion of the rank-holders; the other consisted of mail carriers and other lower employees.

The strike began on July 3, led by freight haulers but followed quickly by mailcarriers and then the entire post office. Union leadership did not control the situation. At the opening meeting of the Central Petrograd Trade Union Council, only those strongly hostile to the ministry were allowed to speak. Critics of the ministry prevailed and organized a strike committee that set a deadline of twenty-four hours (July 4, 8 P.M.) for realization of strike demands. The strike committee consisted of thirteen to fifteen persons, only one or two of which were members of the official Post Office Union Committee.

The strike committee itself had no definite plan in mind. It developed a set of demands to carry to the Soviet of Workers' and Soldiers' Deputies, but on the way it ran into the armed struggle engendered by the July Days.[32] The executive committee of the Soviet advised the postal union to continue work with the promise that it would raise their demands at the imminent meeting of a joint commission of the Central Council of Trade Unions.

The commission met on July 4. Assistant Minister of Post and Telegraph

[30] Taken from the second congress of plenipotentiaries of the Moscow Postal Region. Quoted in ibid., 100.

[31] Ibid., 107. In addition, these changes were earmarked only for employees of certain sectors of the post and telegraph apparatus.

[32] These demands included abolition of the Tseretelli decree, implementation of the congress decisions, immediate payment of the sixty-ruble supplements, extension of the March 28 law to other employee categories, placement of women into table-of-organization positions, and the like. Ibid., 110.

Rozhkov acceded to several union demands and claimed that he had received funds from the Ministry of Finance for a sixty-ruble supplement. There was, however, no agreement on other issues. Rozhkov agreed to further discussions at another joint meeting of the Central Trade Union Council and the Soviet Executive Committee. He pointed to the window, beyond which massive street demonstrations were under way, and muttered, "And tomorrow, perhaps you and we will alike be gone."[33] The union agreed to this plan and also decided to include the freight haulers as recipients of the supplement and push for personnel increases. In this manner, the confusion of the July Days and timely government concessions resulted in keeping the postal employees at work.

This could not last, however, given the worsening economic situation and the very real threat of starvation among the lower-level employees in September and October. Reports of famine conditions flowed into the central committee. Post and Telegraph employees were losing patience with their union leadership. In Smolensk, telegraph employees had already gone on strike independently of other union members.[34] In Penza, employees threatened to close all facilities if food was not forthcoming. In mid-September, the Moscow employees began to apply pressure to win the remaining congress demands. Apparently the railroad strike and the radical demands of the railway workers were important models.

At the end of September, a general meeting in Moscow produced demands for a one-time 200-ruble supplement to buy winter clothing, in addition to implementing the congress program. By mid-October, there were again desperate demands from below. In Petrograd, employees demanded from the provisional government 300 rubles for clothing, 150 rubles per month extra, plus the right to buy from military warehouses at fixed prices. Rank-and-file union members believed also that the only solution to the food problem was collective requisitioning. These demands took the central committee by surprise, as did a supporting vote of postal plenipotentiaries. This body chose a five-person committee, opposed by the central committee, to negotiate with the ministry. In talks with Assistant Minister Miliantovich the employees received nothing concrete.

The delegates returned to Moscow and appeared before the Union Committee of the Central Post Office. Both the central committee and the main post office committee were opposed to a strike, but employee pressure forced the union officials to permit discussion of a strike in the lower-level committees. Here distinctions among the employees again came into play. Office workers, cashiers, and the like tended to support the central committee and opposed the

---

[33] Ibid., 111.

[34] See, for example, *Golos rabotnika*, the organ of the All-Russian Union of Employees of Soviet and Societal Institutions and Enterprises, which began publication in 1919.

strike, whereas some neighborhood committees argued for forming a strike committee.

At an October 23 meeting of the Moscow post office committee and its section (or neighborhood) committees, delegates decided not only to elect new representatives to the central committee but also to extend the strike deadline to November 1. This ended the immediate threat of large-scale strikes before the October Revolution, but the post and telegraph employees would see short-term gains with the advent of Soviet power.

Commercial and Industrial Employees

No group was destined to play as prominent a role in the white-collar movement in 1917 as the commercial and industrial employees. This large group consisted of sales clerks, bookkepers, cashiers, office workers, and lower-level managers and administrators. These employees were spread throughout the lower-middle-strata infrastructure, in private shops and department stores, in the offices of corporations, and in public and state enterprises. They and their post-October union would become part of the solid foundation of Soviet power during the civil war and into the 1920s.

The union movement of these employees developed rapidly after February 1917 as organizations sprang up like mushrooms.[35] At first these unions were independent and somewhat isolated as they were organized according to type of work, enterprise, and region. There was little communication, and if members did not like the atmosphere in one organization, they easily started another. The Petrograd Union of Commercial Employees, with strong Bolshevik representation, was among the most powerful and radical of these white-collar unions during 1917. The Mensheviks were stronger in the unions of factory employees. These two major groups split early and fought for the allegiance of cashiers and other occupational groups. No united union was created in 1917; indeed, this goal was primary for union and state officials alike after the Mensheviks and SR's were driven out in the post-October period.

In March and April, there were several attempts to form small district unions in Petrograd, and by May there were ten such district union directorates in operation. Within this structure could be counted sections of employees from book, music, furniture, hat, and shoe stores, cooperative employees, and others. Such sections floated in and out of existence in response to the need for strikes. Paper products, cooperative, and bookstore employees tended to go their own ways and avoided merging with the commercial employees. Because of poor material conditions, the bookstore and cooperative employees appealed to the labor section of the Petrograd Soviet and the new Ministry of Labor in May. The ministry recommended negotiations with the employers,

---

[35] D. Antoshkin, *Professional'noe dvizhenie.*

who rejected the idea. The employees then decided to join the larger commercial employees' union to get the necessary leverage over the storeowners and
"to follow the tactics and methods of struggle of the entire proletariat."[36]
According to *Bor'ba*, the official newspaper of the Union of Commercial Employees, paper goods and tavern employees also were involved in the spring-
time strikes, but the rank-and-file were "sold out" by self-centered union
leaders who pushed the strike only far enough to satisfy their personal interests.[37] Employees of the Singer Company met on March 29 and voted to enter
the Union of Commercial Employees, but soon thereafter they shifted to a
newly organized union of company employees.[38] Despite fits and starts, the
commercial and industrial employees managed to absorb many smaller organizations. By early July, the union boasted more than twenty-five thousand
members and a number of significant strike victories.

The economic struggle of the white-collar commercial and industrial employees falls into two phases. The first, up to the July Days, was marked by
the first bloom of union organization and a series of successful strikes; there
was little time for organizational or cultural work. The period after the July
Days was defined by growing hostility between the employers and employees,
stiff employer resistance to union demands, often with the aid of the provisional government militia and ministries, and an apparent decline in employee
interest in their unions. Although all components of the union were motivated
by economic needs and formulated economic demands, mainly the commercial employees took to the picket lines during 1917. Again, the driving force
was the ever-worsening economic situation brought about by the war.

Once again, the provisional government cast itself in the role of defender of
property; in this case of the shopowners, the government became an obstacle
to further economic gains or even one's daily bread. The indifference or hostility of this white-collar mass could not possibly benefit the provisional government in the coming showdown over power.

In July the Fifth All-Russian Congress of Commercial and Industrial Employees met in Moscow. The congress opened with 220 delegates representing
141 organizations. The participants resolved that employees were part of the
proletariat within the capitalist structure in which both blue- and white-collar
workers labored. The "commercial and industrial employees proletariat" was
to organize in a manner most effective in the battle for improving the economic and legal position of the employees. Unions were to be organized according to the principle of "democratic centralism," a phrase that carried mo-
mentous implications during the post-October period.

[36] Ibid., 15.
[37] *Bor'ba*, May 2, 1917.
[38] Antoshkin, *Professional'noe dvizhenie*, 16.

On the subject of cultural work, the resolution again adopted a proletarian line:

The force and strength of the unions depends upon the class consciousness of their members, but contemporary scholarship and art bear a clear bourgeois class character. On the other hand the specific milieu of commercial and industrial employees makes them more receptive to bourgeois (more accurately lower middle class—*meshchanskoi*) ideology. The task of the unions is to give full attention to the spread of socialist ideas among their members, and in that task to work hand-in-hand with other working-class unions in constructing joint cultural and educational commissions and workers' clubs where union members may hold forth.[39]

The congress's economic section worked on liquidating commercial enterprise and state intervention in marketing manufactured goods. Hanging over all employees was the threat of factory closings, unemployment, and resulting impoverishment. The resolution approved government intervention in the economy and called for the obligatory syndication of distribution and marketing of manufactured goods. Furthermore, the resolution demanded immediate implementation of unemployment insurance.

The congress attacked the bourgeoisie for its egotism and its failure to agree quickly on forming a new coalition government, though it approved the July 8 provisional government's program and claimed that this rump cabinet should be termed a "government to save the revolution." The resolution called on all employees to support that savior government and the Soviet of Workers', Soldiers', and Peasants' Deputies. Here was tenuous support at best for the provisional government.

During the revolution's early months, the commercial employees were able to achieve the eight-hour day and defined rest days without resorting to strikes. The first reported strike occurred on April 11 at the Kazakov Store.[40] Here the strikers, mainly women, wanted raises from sixty to eighty rubles a month and a percentage of the yearly profit paid monthly; the owners objected to the demands, and we have no information on the outcome. The first large-scale strikes began on May 1 in thirty-four ready-made dress shops in the Apraksin and Mariinskii markets.[41] The strikers' demands raised issues common to the 1917 movement. They included reduction of the workday to six hours, retroactive wage raises, severance pay in the case of firings or liquidation of the firm, three-month sick leave, an end to the humiliation of standing in front of the store to call in customers, and compulsory arbitration of disputes.

---

[39] *5-yi Vserossiiskii s''ezd organizatsii torgovo-promyshlennikh sluzhashchikh. Resoliutsii priniatsia na zasedaniiakh 15–21 iiulia 1917 g. s predisloviem ispolnitel'nogo komiteta Vserossiiskogo soveta* (Moscow, 1917), 5–6.

[40] *Pervyi Vserossiiskii s''ezd sluzhashchikh kreditnykh uchrezhdenii 28 maia-4 iuniia 1917 goda* (Petrograd, 1917), 60–61.

[41] These were reported in *Bor'ba*, May 1, 1917.

At the first meeting of the negotiating commission, the owners rejected these demands, and negotiations broke down. On May 1, employees showed up for work but did nothing on the job.[42] When the owners tried to sell goods themselves, the employees successfully convinced customers not to buy. The owners then began to break ranks, with some offering concession apart from their negotiating organization. The rest began to capitulate quickly. Six firms gave in on May 7, and by May 12, thirty-one firms had reached an agreement.[43] Two other firms held out for several days and a third for several weeks. The strike effectively shut down the latter (Markov and Sons), and by the end of June the store was liquidated.

On May 9, two hundred employees of the Petrograd hat and shoe stores went on strike with demands almost identical to those of the clothing store employees. Here five firms caved in on the first day, and within several days all owners gave in to all the demands. Two strikes began on May 17 led by employees of confection, ready-made womens' apparel, and linen stores.[44] Strike activity encompassed the entire city but was centered on the Gostinyi Dvor, Passazh, and Apraksin markets. Commerce was halted in more than five hundred shops, and between three and four thousand employees supported the strike. The majority of owners voted for a lockout, but there was significant dissent, and the owners were poorly organized. On the first day, several owners satisfied the strikers' demands; by May 30, the employees could claim full victory. The union of store owners was broken.

In early May, sales personnel of shoestores requested membership in the Union of Commercial and Industrial Employees. They claimed that owners were illegally raising prices. On May 24–25, the shoestore employees launched an ill-prepared strike. One owner of several stores answered with a lockout and a proposal to employees to accept dismissal with three-months pay. Approximately one-third (twenty people) took this route, while the others waivered. Employees organized a boycott, but the strike stretched over time with few employee gains.[45]

More than five hundred employees of Petrograd's furniture and glass stores launched a strike on June 16 that embraced two hundred stores. Storeowners quickly satisfied most demands, and this process of white-collar strikes and owner concessions was repeated in other kinds of retail and wholesale establishments. In May and June there were also numerous strikes in the food stores. Here union leaders wanted to avoid a major strike that would harm the already undernourished population. In mid-June a large general meeting and strike committee representing various food store employees authorized negotiations with intransigent employers. The Union of Commercial and Industrial

---

[42] Antoshkin, *Professional'noe dvizhenie*, 63.

[43] Ibid.

[44] The movement also took in the seamstresses (tailors) who worked in the shops.

[45] Antoshkin, *Professional'noe dvizhenie*, 68.

Employees and the owners then agreed to arbitration by the Ministry of Labor. This went back and forth in July and August as the owners wavered in their commitment to negotiate.[46]

Another major strand of strike activity for the Petrograd union began in late May among the factory white-collar employees. Prior to autumn of 1917, leadership there was in the hands of Elders of Factory and Enterprise Employees, which worked along with the Councils of Elders of the factories. This group formulated demands for and negotiated with the Petrograd Society of Factory Owners. These negotiations began in April with the owners resisting basic demands regarding legal rights and material improvements.[47] They rejected four-week leaves, parity on joint commissions, 150-ruble-per-month wage minimum for adult employees. They agreed only to a six-hour workday. On May 7, a citywide meeting of industrial employees noted the owners' opposition. Three days later, talks were shut down.

On May 16 a conference of the Councils of Elders issued an ultimatum for May 20, with a strike to begin May 23 if there should be no response. With no answer forthcoming, the strike, announced for May 23, aimed at private and public enterprises, banks, insurance companies, and even some government and social institutions.[48] Gvozdev at the Ministry of Labor tried to get the arbitration commission back in session, but the owners resisted. At this point Minister of Labor Skobelev, at the request of the Petrograd Soviet, intervened, and along with his fellow Menshevik Bogdanov, entered into talks with the owners. Enough of them were ready for concession, and with these promises the strike committee halted proceedings. It is significant that the white-collar workers were supported in this instance by numerous workers in the factories as well as the unions of metal and textile workers.

After the Fifth Congress of Organizations of Commercial and Industrial Employees in June, we have reports of scattered strikes in individual firms during the summer and autumn.[49] For example, strikes were reported in August at the Putilov Factory in Petrograd, the Nobel Oil Storage facilities, and among Moscow enterprises of the All-Russian Union of Zemstvos. Of 393 conflicts reported between May 1 and November 1, 25.45 percent were resolved in favor of the employees, and 60.5 percent were unsuccessful.[50] To be

---

[46] Ibid., 69.

[47] Ibid., 83–84.

[48] Notable exceptions were the railroads and such public utilities as trams, water, and electricity. The strikers also meant to keep open hospitals and other health-related facilities. Ibid., 84.

[49] The congress, called by employees in the wake of the Third All-Russian Trade Union Congress, was dominated (at least in terms of those who declared a party affiliation) by Mensheviks with sixty-six representatives as opposed to twenty-four Bolsheviks, fifteen SRs, sixteen Popular Socialists, three Trudoviki, fourteen members of the Bund, eight Edinstvo, and only four Kadets. They represented 103 unions and 29 mutual aid societies in addition to a few clubs, soviets of employees, and the like. Ibid., 94.

[50] Antoshkin, *O professional'nom dvizhenii sluzhashchikh* (Moscow, 1925), 77–79.

sure these are approved Soviet statistics that reflect a period during which the owners of private enterprises had little power in the face of demands from below. But the fact remains that successful resolution of conflict, something the provisional government was unable to promote or deliver, and its apparent disappearance during the early months of Soviet power, might well have eased employee acceptance of the Bolshevik regime.

The white-collar and lower-middle-strata trade unions were front-line participants in the events of 1917 and the process of revolutionary state building. Their strikes contributed to the growing mood of crisis, the sense of provisional government weakness, and even opposition to the aspirations and concrete economic demands of the lower orders. It is important to remember, however, the fissures within the lower-middle-strata movement. Unions consisting of the lower-level employees with a weakly defined professional sense tended to identify most clearly with the proletarian cause. Commercial and industrial employees, railroad and postal employees, pharmacy employees and lower-ranking medical personnel, for example, were direct participants in the October events, often on the Bolshevik side. Teachers and other professionals as well as some public institution and state employees, however, formed unions whose leadership was opposed to the Bolsheviks in October. Many participated in anti-Bolshevik strikes in November and December. It would take some time for union careerists backed by Soviet power to push the 1917 leadership out of office.

The occupations and state-building skills represented by all the white-collar unions were part of the fabric of revolutionary politics. This was masked by apparent splits within the white-collar movement and its inability to take power in the name of democracy during the autumn of 1917. They remained a reservoir of a certain kind of power, however, and the provisional government's demise had as much to do with its failed relationship among these lower-middle-strata institutions as with its similar failure among Russia's workers and peasants.

PART SEVEN

New Social Sensibilities in the Arts

Chapter 17

SOCIAL DISCOURSE IN THE MOSCOW ART THEATER

Edith W. Clowes

As new industrial and cultural groups evolved from the middling estates (*sosloviia*) of Russian society in the late nineteenth century, they began to express new forms of social consciousness that had little to do with traditional estate consciousness. Although after 1905 the press, professional unions, and political parties predominated as vehicles for formulating social identity, they had important precursors in the cultural media, architecture, theater, painting, and fiction. The stage of the Moscow Art Theater provided just such a medium for dialogue, both deliberate and inadvertant, about the issue of changing social self-perception.

In times of grand social and political transformations, such as the late eighteenth or the early twentieth centuries, the theater stage can provide a metaphor for social change, and the behavior of the actor can become a model for shifting and experimenting with one's own social persona in "real" life. For example, as Iury Lotman writes in his essay, "Theater and Theatricality," in the early nineteenth century "the dividing line between art and the everyday behavior of the audience was expunged. The theater invaded life and actively restructured everyday behavior. . . . What shortly before had seemed pompous and comic, since it was ascribed only to the domain of theatrical space, became the norm of everyday speech and everyday behavior. The people of the Revolution behave in life as upon a stage."[1] In the Moscow Art Theater we find a tendency to identify actors' behavior—specifically their professionalism and their serious attempts to "become" the personae being played—with appropriate social behavior, to merge the life of the stage with the life of the street, and even, in a few cases, to realize the ideological challenges cast down on the stage in actual political events; in short, the theater transfigures a purely cultural-artistic persona into a social-political identity willing to assert itself in the political arena.

The research for this chapter was done with the generous support of the University of Illinois Slavic Summer Research Laboratory and an XL Summer Grant from the Purdue Research Foundation.
[1] Jurij M. Lotman, "The Theater and Theatricality as Components of Early Nineteenth-Century Culture," in Ju. M. Lotman and B. A. Uspenskij, *The Semiotics of Russian Culture*, ed. A. Shukman (Ann Arbor: Michigan Slavic Contributions, 1984), 145. For more on the social functions of theater in Russia of the early twentieth century, see essays by Mary Louise Loe and James M. Curtis in this volume.

The expressions of cultural and social identity to which the Art Theater gave rise represented a significant departure from traditional forms of self-perception, one that for the Russian context may be called "middle-class." When the theater opened its doors in 1898, most theater directors, actors, and repertory writers treated the issue of social selfhood in a most ambiguous way: they identified themselves with neither their traditional sosloviia nor any emerging social group.[2] A brief description of the participants in the Art Theater shows a broad diversity of people from educated urban society. The Art Theater was founded and directed by Konstantin Alekseev-Stanislavsky, a textile manufacturer, and Vladimir Nemirovich-Danchenko, a writer and theater director of gentry origin but now professional and urban in orientation. Although its main patron was a leading textile magnate, Savva Morozov, stock in the theater was owned by people from a wide range of groups, including aristocrats, entrepreneurs, and *meshchane*. Its actors came from many different spheres—professional, *kupechestvo*, and *meshchanstvo*, as well as gentry. Its principal repertory writers, Anton Chekhov and Maksim Gorky, were both from provincial meshchanstvo families. And the audience was meant to

---

[2] Particularly members of the *kupechestvo*, such as Stanislavsky and Morozov, and of the *meshchanstvo*, such as Chekhov and Gorky, used all kinds of social guises to escape their *soslovie* identity. Although Gorky in 1889 signed a letter to L. Tolstoi, "Nizhny Novgorod *meshchanin*," by the turn of the century he was dressing himself in the cape, peasant shirt, and high boots of a wanderer and working as a journalist. A. M. Gor'kii, *Sobranie sochinenii v 30-tomakh* (Moscow: GIKhL, 1954), 28: 6. In addition, Gorky could be very hostile to critics and journalists who were too diligent in researching his social background; see Edith W. Clowes, "Introduction," *Maksim Gorky: A Reference Guide* (Boston: G. K. Hall, 1987), xi–xii.

In Stanislavsky and Morozov can be found much the same weakness of social identity. For a supremely self-confident actor, and for the member of a new elite seemingly growing in power, Stanislavsky could exhibit at key moments surprising lack of assurance toward his own social group. In many plays, in which a merchant played a major role, he unconsciously subverted the authority of that character. For example, in staging *The Merchant of Venice* he insisted on having Shylock speak with a Yiddish accent, thus drawing too much attention to the specificities of his Jewishness and detracting from the universal interest of his predicament. Although earlier in the 1890s at The Society for Arts and Literature Stanislavsky had great success playing Ostrovskian merchants, he consistently avoided taking such roles at the Art Theater, claiming rather disingenuously that he had never had much luck playing merchant characters; see Chekhov, *Polnoe sobranie sochinenii i pisem* (Moscow: Nauka, 1977), 7: 267; hereafter PSS. Not only did Stanislavsky avoid merchant roles, but he actively sought aristocratic and gentry roles, thus symbolically following the paths by which earlier merchants had achieved social dignity; see A. J. Rieber, *Merchants and Entrepreneurs in Imperial Russia* (Chapel Hill: University of North Carolina Press, 1982), xxi. Morozov was drawn in the opposite direction, becoming militantly and self-destructively allied with the lower reaches of urban society. Earlier, against his mother's wishes, Morozov had married a worker. At the turn of the century, he was open to suggestions for improvement of working conditions at his factories. Although he served as a director of the Art Theater, his greatest love was to immerse himself backstage in work on sets and lighting. Around 1902 he became sympathetic to the cause of radical social change and helped finance the Russian Social Democratic party. His political activities ended with his dismissal from the family business and possibly promoted his eventual suicide.

be, and indeed was, a cross-section of educated society—students, profession-als, intellectuals, business people (*kuptsy*).

In cultural terms, as well, the founding of the Art Theater represented a departure from tradition. A private institution, the theater was conceived as an alternative to government-run theaters, which were top-heavy with bureau-cracy and short on innovative spirit and professional seriousness. As Nemi-rovich put it in a moment of frustration with Morozov, he preferred private theater because an officious merchant stockholder was still "easier to neutral-ize" than an officious bureaucrat.[3] The goals of the theater's founders were implicitly middle-class: to foster an educated society by bringing enlighten-ment and cultivation to everyone, rich and poor, highly refined and semiliter-ate alike. Stanislavsky and Nemirovich also wanted to reach urban audiences beyond St. Petersburg and Moscow and provide cultural education to the pro-vincial populace, thus potentially cultivating middling society throughout the empire.

Still more important, the Art Theater embodied a phenomenon that helps to define middle-class culture specifically for the Russian case. In the Art Theater converged two socioliterary trends that developed as Russian society's middle levels gained in prominence: first-rate literary talent from the meshchanstvo and the organization of new cultural institutions within the upper levels of the kupechestvo, particularly the Moscow kupechestvo. For the first time in Rus-sian history, writers and readers were emerging from the families of small shopkeepers, artisans, and trading peasants, as well as lower-level function-aries and semiprofessionals. As Jeffrey Brooks has shown, these develop-ments were closely linked to the impressive growth of literacy at the turn of the century.[4] In these groups, learning to read and write was accompanied by a potentially explosive change of values: the business sector, which had al-ways held the most dogmatic religious views and harbored a deep suspicion of secular culture, was itself becoming secularized. The steep rise in level of education from one generation to the next gave rise to a cultural gap between old and young, especially where books and reading were concerned. The great publishing tycoon, Ivan Sytin, remembered that his employers among the ku-pechestvo thought of books as "dung."[5] In his autobiography Gorky de-scribed being taunted and slapped for reading novels.[6] The would-be writers

[3] Vladimir Nemirovich-Danchenko, *Izbrannye pis'ma v 2-kh tomakh* (Moscow: Iskusstvo, 1979), 1: 352.

[4] See Jeffrey Brooks, *When Russia Learned to Read* (Princeton: Princeton University Press, 1985), 59. On the social background of prominent young "realist" writers, see M. L. Loe's chapter in this volume.

[5] Ivan Sytin, *Zhizn' dlia knigi* (Moscow: GIPL, 1962), 25. Sytin uses the word, "der'mo."

[6] Maksim Gorky, *My Apprenticeship*, trans. R. Wilks (Harmondsworth: Penguin, 1977), 154. See also Nikolai Teleshov, *Zapiski pisatelia* (Moscow: Moskovskii rabochii, 1958), 169; Ivan Belousov, *Literturnaia Moskva* (Moscow: Glavlit, 1926), 3–5.

and literary entrepreneurs—among them the merchants Nikolai Leikin and Nikolai Teleshov, the tailor Ivan Belousov, as well as Gorky and Chekhov—
rejected the narrow-mindedness and petty tyranny of their native backgrounds.
Some, like Gorky, dissociated themselves from family and soslovie as they
sought intellectually more fulfilling company. They experienced a traumatic
disjunction of social identity as they crossed from the small-business milieu to
the world of populist literary circles filled with lively social and moral debate
and reform-oriented journals. Contributing to their sense of deracination was
the fact that these new writers were sometimes as misunderstood in these circles as they were at home, welcomed condescendingly as "writers from the
people." It was not long before the young wearied of being the "mascots" of
what they perceived as an aloof intelligentsia. As "populist" didactics gave
way to truly "popular" fiction, they reoriented themselves, finding themselves at the center of new and burgeoning networks of readers, publishers,
and booksellers.

While this ferment developed in the lower parts of the commercial sector, a
tiny segment of the Moscow business elite was becoming a guiding force in
cultural life. If their elders had merely financed cultural ventures, a younger
generation of merchants produced among the most potent creative talents of
the age.[7] This change is particularly noticeable in literature, which until the
1880s had been anathema even for the highest reaches of the merchantry. As
at the bottom of urban society, here too belles lettres had long been reviled as
the vehicle of dangerous radical demagoguery that threatened merchants' traditional religious piety and political arch-conservatism. Literary activity,
which had earlier been reason enough to ostracize a talented young merchant,
now became more acceptable with the broadening of secular education. Valery
Briusov, whose poetically inclined grandfather had been shunned as the black
sheep of the Moscow merchant community, wrote a new kind of "decadent"
poetry and edited a prominent early modernist journal. Aleksei Remizov experimented boldly in "ornamental" prose. Margarita Morozova organized an
important literary salon. Especially significant is the rise, following the decree
of 1882, of private theaters owned and run by merchants. Still bearing the
disapproval of their elders, the children of merchants, such as Stanislavsky,
Ivan Moskvin, and Maria Lilina, leavened a life in the business world with
hobbies in theater; in turn, they gradually attracted to themselves acting, directing, and playwriting talent. By the late 1890s these people and others were
forming the nuclei of fresh literary networks.

There was a palpable difference in the social self-perception of the young
writers from the bottom of urban society and the poets and artists from the

___

[7] Jo Ann Ruckman, *The Moscow Business Elite* (DeKalb: Northern Illinois University Press,
1985), 155–63. See also essays in this volume by John O. Norman and John Bowlt on art patronage.

high Moscow merchantry. The meshchanstvo writers who had been radically alienated from their native social background tended to acquire during their sojourns in populist circles a radical social outlook to match. But their literary styles tended to be conservative and aesthetically uninteresting. By contrast, literary talents from the somewhat more lenient Moscow merchant milieu welcomed aesthetic but generally disliked political radicalism. As a group they tended to embody what Chekhov termed a "cross between cultivation [kul' turnost'] and patriarchy [patriarkhal' nost']."[8] Their typically complacent sociopolitical attitudes grated on the nerves of their confreres from the lower reaches of society.

The tensions between the socially disgruntled meshchanstvo writers and the culturally adept but still socially passive elite were palpable in theater ritual. In the process of writing, staging, and attending plays the outlines of a new social consciousness emerged. The theater and its audience participated in a larger cultural system, what Lotman has called a "semiosphere."[9] Writers, directors, audience, and actors evaluated the remarkable social changes going on around them by means of commonly held and understood mechanisms of interpretation; they established social scenarios, symbols, and stereotypes. For example, in the 1890s when the Art Theater was founded, the great transformations that Russia was undergoing were generally understood in terms of traditional notions of the "right" social order and personal status, that is, through deeply embedded cultural "scripts" that preconditioned expectations and modes of evaluation. The two canonically Russian scripts that set the terms of social discourse in the early twentieth century were conservative, inherited from an era now past. They were the tragic conflict of "fathers and sons" and the sentimental idyll of the "nest of gentry" with its strong sense of belonging to a clearly definable time and place. How these stereotypes and scripts were manipulated in works of art and interpreted by actors and viewers can show us something of the process of altering social consciousness. As realized on the Art Theater stage, the Russian semiosphere's significance was its extreme disjunction, indeed its state of crisis. Familiar stereotypes and scenarios would be evaluated in widely differing ways that revealed the deep rifts at the heart of Russia's social middle. As one mode of social discourse took the upper hand, attitudes toward self and social change solidified that are still recognizable in Russian urban society of the late twentieth century.

The need to rethink social identity was forced on the personnel and audience of the Art Theater by the meshchanstvo writers Chekhov and Gorky. Each writer in his own way had shed the traditionalism typical of his estate and had acquired a more modern, fluid sense of social selfhood during a difficult apprenticeship in populist circles. These writers were attracted to the promising

[8] A. P. Chekhov, PSS, 5: 179.

[9] Lotman and Uspenskij, The Semiotics of Russian Culture, xii.

milieu of the young industrial elite where they were viewed not as plebeians and inferiors, but as exciting, new voices in the otherwise bleak sociocultural landscape of the late 1880s and early 1890s. Both writers challenged conventional systems of social signification. Sometimes subtly, sometimes brutally, they shifted the terms of social discourse by taking and distorting the scripts basic to the long predominant gentry culture. Particular objects of their attack were the social traditionalism and political acquiescence of the merchantry. However, although each writer in his own way was pushing both acting troupe and audience to think of themselves in a new way, only the rare listener or reader really grasped the authors' intentions. A consideration of how each author manipulated existing social stereotypes and scripts in his plays and how these were interpreted and enacted opens to view hidden and inadvertant aspects of social self-image.

The two deep scripts that informed social views both on and off the stage at the Art Theater originated in the gentry culture of Turgenev and the Tolstois and were passed on in the 1890s through minor writers; significantly, all were from the gentry. The first builds on the Turgenevian nest-of-gentry idyll and responds in an artistic evaluation to its actual historical demise in the 1890s. In this scenario, power is transferred from a "languishing" gentry to a "calculating" merchantry. The businessman buys out the landowner and thus manifests his raw financial might. The new power is then reinforced through marriage between the estates: the merchant weds the landowner's daughter or in some variants the daughter of an intellectual. In the 1890s this script provided a basis for several popular satires. It is significant that Stanislavsky's partner, Nemirovich-Danchenko, himself a member of the gentry, inaugurated the mini-genre in 1890 with his play, *The New Enterprise* (Novoe delo). Here an estate, about to be lost to foreigners, is purchased by a wealthy but despised merchant son-in-law. A satire by Prince Sumbatov-Iuzhin, *The Gentleman* (Dzhentel'men, 1897), makes fun of the new predominance of pretentious merchant patrons. Another example, Petr Boborykin's *The Scum* (Nakip', 1899) also satirized nouveau-riche merchants and set them apart from the "true" social elite, the gentry. Although on the surface this script seemed to draw attention to the shift of power to a new elite, its deeper evaluative structure undermines such a change. In all three plays the acts of purchase and intermarriage are implicitly evaluated as acts of usurpation. The interaction between social strata appears inevitable but absurd and distasteful. Thus, the social message of this type of drama is conservative: to discredit social evolution as degeneration and mourn for the past.

Despite their prejudicial slant, such plays helped reinforce in the public mind the merchantry's imminent economic power.[10] They—and other artistic

[10] Two different views of interelite relations are given in Stanislavsky, *My Life in Art* (New

reformulations of the nest-of-gentry script, particularly best-selling novels of Boborykin, such as *Vasilii Terkin* (1893) or *The Pass* (Pereval, 1893) and stories of Chekhov, such as "Three Years" (Tri goda, 1895)—made contact and interaction between estates more thinkable. The very founding of the Art Theater in 1898 was predicated to some extent upon acceptance of the merchantry. A member of the gentry, Nemirovich actually took the initiative to propose partnership with a merchant. Although members of the Art Theater complained audibly about Stanislavsky's dictatorial behavior, they nevertheless accepted his authority in artistic matters.[11] The possibility of such cooperation represented a considerable step forward from the 1860s, from Dobroliubov's demonized view of the merchantry as nothing more than an isolated "dark kingdom."

The narrative of the declining nest of gentry with its traditional evaluations was most significantly addressed in Chekhov's *The Cherry Orchard* and Gorky's *Summerfolk* (Dachniki, 1904). In *The Cherry Orchard*, it can be argued that Chekhov, as a writer of nongentry origin, was trying to displace the social and cultural authority of the gentry implicit in the traditional nest-of-gentlefolk idyll. His strategy was to introduce a new mood. While Nemirovich and other gentry playwrights often favored a sentimental tone for their gentry protagonists and reserved sharp, satiric treatment for merchant antiheroes, Chekhov now treated gentry characters with a subtle irony. In general, the sentimental pull so often noted in Chekhov's play is consistently undermined by the absurdity of the world portrayed. The logic of feelings and conversations is disjointed. The apparent depth of suffering is belied by the speed with which characters recover and forget.[12]

Chekhov presents his merchant character, Ermolai Lopakhin, in a wholly new light, implicitly changing him from antagonist to protagonist. Here he creates a character who seems able to offer an alternative to the stereotype of the cultivated but socially insensitive merchant. Chekhov permits his merchant figure an appealing self-awareness. Although Lopakhin knows that he does not fill the patriarchal mold, he is conscious and proud of the unprecedented social achievement that his life represents: by purchasing the estate, he has taken an important step toward freeing himself of his family's serf heritage. In addition, a refreshing self-irony (for example, describing his cultural ineptitude, he compares himself to a pig in a pastry shop) saves Lopakhin from

York: Theatre Arts Books, 1952), 22; Nemirovich-Danchenko, *My Life in the Russian Theater* (New York: Theatre Arts Books, 1968), 125.

[11] See *O Stanislavskom: sbornik vospominanii, 1863–1938*, ed. L. Ia. Gurevich (Moscow: VTO, 1948), 224. See also Nemirovich-Danchenko, *My Life in the Russian Theater*, 98. On occasion, Stanislavsky would declare "martial law" to intensify actors' discipline and concentration.

[12] Much has been written about this subject. One of the best recent treatments is Richard Peace, *Chekhov: A Study of the Four Major Plays* (New Haven: Yale University Press, 1983), 145.

the obtuseness usual in merchant stereotypes and adds to him a dimension lacking in the other characters. Ironically, Chekhov's gentry figures are in some sense more blindly and negatively bourgeois than Lopakhin. Ranevskaia, who is so adverse to Lopakhin's plan to build dachas, fondly remembers her own dacha near Menton. Furthermore, this landowner is strictly urban in her tastes, milking the estate to finance her life in the city. Her brother Gaev, surprisingly unperturbed by the sale of the estate, is perfectly content to continue his life working in the typically bourgeois banking profession.

Despite Lopakhin's personal triumph of overcoming the serf in himself, his purchase of the land is thoroughly discredited as a symbolic way of "saving" Russian society or gaining authority as a member of the new elite. The sale of property is less a solution than part of the picture of social disintegration. Lopakhin's vision of a country cottage for every citizen is useless because it does not provide a principle of social renewal. It is important to note, however, that the ideal of "freezing" Russia as the Turgenevian rural "nest" is also discredited in the figure of the absurdly deaf servant Firs. Marriage is even more strongly subverted as a ritual of renewal. Ranevskaia is determined in a kindly way to marry her stepdaughter Varia to Lopakhin. As Richard Peace has pointed out, a marriage arranged by his former owner is unendurable on a subconscious level to Lopakhin.[13] Such an agreement tacitly acknowledges the authority that a landowner enjoyed over the lives of her serfs. To Lopakhin, Ranevskaia's encouragement to marry Varia is subconsciously associated with his brutal early life as a serf boy when his father beat him and Ranevskaia comforted him with the condescending remark: "Don't cry, little peasant, . . . you'll heal before your wedding day." Involuntarily Lopakhin evades the subject of marriage even though consciously he likes Varia and supposes he will marry her.

Thus, in *The Cherry Orchard* Chekhov unmasked the real meaning of the narrative of the declining nest of gentry: it was more about entropy than evolution, about a growing social vacuum; it did not discuss new power and legitimacy. Educated society's unwillingness to confront the need to change, he implied, would spell its downfall.[14]

In this, his final play, Chekhov was most concerned to create a sense of urgency, to unsettle his audience, to shake loose standard stereotypes, and, above all, to undermine the nostalgic hold of the past. Nothing in the play, however, suggests an attempt to create new social myth that would provide a usable sense of place, time, and personal fate. Chekhov's consciousness is

[13] Ibid., 149.

[14] Sergei Mamontov, "Desiatiletie 'Vishnevogo sada'," *Russkoe slovo* 14 (1914): 7. The same strong sense of social malaise was conveyed in a comment to Mamontov, a merchant acquaintance, during the summer of 1903 when Chekhov was finishing *The Cherry Orchard*: "We need to hurry and write, write plays, for soon such times will come when people will have more on their minds than theater."

"modernist" in its parodic, myth-breaking tone. Indeed, in Trofimov, the intelligent but ineffectual ideologue of the play, he satirized his one serious literary rival, Maksim Gorky, whom he perceived as the one potential myth-making talent in contemporary Russian letters. As he put it in a private letter, he could not "bear to see [Gorky] appear on the pulpit like a clergyman and read his apostolic letters to his congregation in a churchy manner."[15] Trofimov mimics this preachiness. For example, parodying Satin's famous soliloquy in *The Lower Depths*, he heralds the coming of the "proud man" [*gordyi chelovek*].[16] This monologue is absurdly deflated by Lopakhin's clumsy enthusiasm (he asserts that people "really should be giants"), Ranevskaia's dismissal of Lopakhin's image (she says that giants are nice in fairytales, but scary in reality), and the incongruously noisy entrance onto the scene of a minor character, the clerk Epikhodov with his guitar and squeaky boots. Chekhov has brought us from the Promethean dreams, so loved by Gorky, back to an absurd actuality.

Although *The Cherry Orchard* became a mainstay in the repertoire of the Art Theater, it is important to note that the Art Theater production failed to convey Chekhov's purpose. Chekhov's insistence that his play was a comedy confused both Nemirovich and Stanislavsky, who interpreted it in the old way as a sentimental melodrama mourning the passing of the gentry. Far from enabling the displacement of an outlived script, their production helped reinforce that script. It led to a gross misinterpretation that only deepened the audience's nostalgia for the Turgenevian nest of gentlefolk. When the play was first read to the troupe, the actors cried. No one was prepared to part with the mystique of rural Russia. The casting for the play reveals the social standards and aspirations of directors and actors. The absurdist tone of the play was altered by Stanislavsky's insistence on playing the gentlemen Gaev instead of Lopakhin, as Chekhov had requested, and by the decision to give Lopakhin to the actor Leonidov. A picture of Leonidov-as-Lopakhin reinforces old stereotypes of the merchant, showing a fat, somewhat sloppy-looking man in checkered trousers. He hardly has the elegance or gentle natural spirit of Lopakhin.[17] Moreover, Leonidov apparently overacted the part, speaking too loudly and flailing with his arms.[18] All in all, the character did not fit the ideal of civility and enlightenment sought by Stanislavsky and his troupe.

The ultimate trivialization of the scenario of the nest of gentry in decline came in Gorky's *Summer Folk*. Although the play was written for the Art Theater, Nemirovich refused to stage it, largely because of its very brusque,

[15] Quoted in Stanislavsky, *My Life in Art*, 394.

[16] Compare to A. M. Gor'kii, *Polnoe sobranie sochinenii* (Moscow: Nauka, 1970), 7: 177 (hereafter PSS).

[17] See N. Efros, *Vyshnevyi sad: p'esa A.P. Chekhova v postanovke Moskovskogo Khudozhest-vennogo teatra* (Petersburg: Solntse Rossii, 1919), 33.

[18] Exter, Review of "Vyshnevyi sad," *Moskovskie vedomosti* 38 (Feb. 7, 1904): 4.

even harsh call to social change. Through a crude travesty of Chekhovian types it forces on its audience the crucial issue of the self-consciousness of the new elite and its role in coming social change.[19]

In *Summer Folk* the gentry exists no longer. The play is built on the premise of Lopakhin's plan to build country cottages for vacationing city dwellers. It is peopled with vacuous professionals, the deracinated sons and daughters of the meshchanstvo. The summer folk live isolated, each in a private mindless sphere, bemoaning an empty, boring fate. In Gorky's view, they have no perception of their social role as a new elite. The play's ideologue, the doctor Maria Lvovna, urges upon these people the importance of their new station and their social responsibilities: they should understand their future as leaders of society and should strive to set an example of inspired vision and useful work for those lower on the social scale.[20] Despite the canonized Soviet view of Gorky as "proto-proletarian" writer, in this and others of his early works Gorky was trying openly to challenge precisely the fragmented middle of society, to compel it to envision itself as the elite at the head of a new hierarchy.[21] The directors of the Art Theater disliked Gorky's abrasive style, however, and felt that his social activism was at odds with their own more moderate ideals. They preferred what they saw as the melancholic refinement of Chekhovian drama.

The response to these plays shows the strong hold that gentry myth still had on the imagination, and it suggests an intellectual unwillingness at least in the pre-1905 period—among merchants, professionals, and gentry alike—to grapple with the necessity of change. In fact, both Chekhov and Gorky, the two most famous and popular writers of the day, possessed social sensibility that was considerably more sophisticated than that of either their coworkers or their audiences; they were raising issues that others were simply not prepared to confront.

The second script that Chekhov and Gorky used to consider patriarchal attitudes was the conflict of "fathers and sons." In this narrative, the young struggle against the entrenched authority of the old in order to establish their own legitimacy. Crucial to the struggle between gentry and *raznochinets* cultures of earlier decades, this narrative had long since become a myth of promised but failed change. In major novels and plays of the 1860s and 1870s— *Fathers and Sons*, *War and Peace*, *Tsar Fedor*, and *Brothers Karamazov*— change was conceived not as gradual, peaceful evolution but as a sharp rejection of tradition. This conception was tragic in its implications: inevitably the

---

[19] See, for example, Gor'kii, PSS, 7: 207–8, 288. Gorky parodies *The Seagull*, Nemirovich's greatest triumph with Chekhov; in particular, he criticizes Nina Zarechnaia's performance in Treplev's play and Treplev's off-stage attempt at suicide.

[20] Ibid., 278. For more detail, see M. Louise Loe's chapter in this volume.

[21] For more detail on this point, see Edith W. Clowes, "The Implied Reader in the Early Novels of Maksim Gorky," *Russian Literature* 14, no. 4 (1988): 485–502.

old, patriarchal authority reasserted itself. The choices available to the young were too narrow: either to acquiesce or to submit to self-destruction. Chekhov and particularly Gorky made an effort to reimagine change as a productive force.

While almost all the Russian repertoire used in the Art Theater dealt with the struggle of generations, most plots resolved themselves along traditional lines. For example, in Aleksei Tolstoi's *Tsar Fedor*, which enjoyed special significance as the theater's first production in 1898, Fedor is unable to cope with rival factions in his court. He ends up appealing to the memory of his father, Ivan the Terrible, and resorting to his father's violent and ruinous solutions. The aging Lev Tolstoi, who by now had assumed the role of literary "father" to a new generation of Russian writers, raised the issue in a play written for the Art Theater, *The Power of Darkness* (Vlast't'my, 1902). Here Tolstoi's express purpose was to reassert in mythical terms the moral authority of the fathers over the children. Chekhov's plays—*The Seagull*, *Three Sisters*, and *The Cherry Orchard*—all in some way address the conflict of generations. As James Curtis has shown, *The Seagull* deals with Treplev's and Nina Zarechnaia's (and ultimately Chekhov's) dilemma in establishing their legitimacy before their elders, Trigorin and Arkadina (and Turgenev).[22] In *Three Sisters*, none of the children can find the courage to initiate anything individually. They have become too used to their deceased father's authority. Of all Chekhov's characters, Lopakhin is the exception that proves the rule. He has outwardly overcome the oppressive serf's life of his fathers. But significantly, his victory is not shared by anyone else. With this exception Chekhov forces the question as to whether anyone really is committed to overcoming the past and finding a mechanism for change.[23]

The generational script acquires an incendiary quality in Gorky's two first plays, *The Petit Bourgeois* (Meshchane, 1902) and *The Lower Depths* (Na dne, 1903). Gorky brings out the anarchistic implications of this script. In a tradition in which the fathers hold power if not legitimacy, the young people who do succeed in breaking away do so decisively, cutting all the ties that link them to the past. It is significant that Gorky uses unusual kinship relations as a metaphor for successful social change. Like their counterparts in more traditional plays, sons and daughters remain ineffectual. The people who enforce change in Gorky's world are its outcasts: orphans, stepchildren, outsiders, social déclassés. In *The Petit Bourgeois* a tyrannical Ostrovskian father challenges his meditative, Chekhovian children—stereotypically an aging student and an unhappy schoolteacher—to define their life goals and stop wasting their energies on an unproductive life. They are unable to answer the challenge, and

[22] James M. Curtis, "Ephebes and Precursors in Chekhov's *The Seagull*," *Slavic Review* 44, no. 3 (1985): 423–37.
[23] Chekhov, PSS, 13: 502. At least one student wrote to Chekhov applauding Lopakhin and Trofimov as models of "change from below."

at the end of the play they are in much the same state as they began it. By contrast, the merchant's stepson, Nil, heir to the family business, has made a clear transition from a semimedieval meshchanstvo life to the modern industrial age by "dropping out" of the middle of society. He abandons the traditions of commerce, becomes politically radical, and greets the new era not as entrepreneur but as the head of the newly forming ranks of a worker elite. Symbolically, this (step)son rebels against his (step)father by choosing the life of a worker, a life of lower social status, over one in small business; then he marries a lowly worker without his stepfather's consent. He becomes a locomotive driver who organizes political meetings and encourages his fellow laborers to read and discuss forbidden literature. His life is dedicated to the struggle for the rights of the downtrodden against all father-oppressors— his actual stepfather, his boss on the railroad, or, implicitly, the government with its network of censors.[24] Thus, by focusing on the outcasts from the middle and by heroizing working-class ways of life, Gorky points out and exacerbates in the strongest possible terms the existing vertical fragmentation that threatened the middle of society.

In *The Lower Depths*, Gorky disputes the legitimacy of his own literary and ideological "father," Lev Tolstoi, in the character of the kind, old wanderer Luka.[25] To everyone he meets, Luka preaches a morality of resignation. He comforts the people around him and urges them to accept their suffering. Gorky's "ideologue," the outcast Satin, challenges Luka's philosophy as a lie that condones acquiescence in the face of social injustice. In its place Satin puts a faith in "Man," the idea that people possess dignity, strength, creativity, and the power to overthrow their oppressors if only they would believe in themselves.

Contrary to Chekhov's perception that Gorky was imposing on his audience new social myth, in neither *The Petit Bourgeois* nor *The Lower Depths* did the self-appointed social firebrand outline a real scenario justifying an emerging social order. Like Chekhov, he in his own way was affected by the "modernist," myth-breaking spirit of the day. As with his earlier works, his plays always urged opposition to authority, but not to preach a new ideology. Only in the least interesting of his early plays, *Summer Folk*, did he actually venture some sort of positive concept of a new social hierarchy.

The generational script, as treated in Gorky's work, aroused considerable debate in Art Theater circles. While viewers could ignore the subtle gestures made in Chekhov's plays, they were forced to take sides as Gorky's ideologues harrassed them from the stage. Many, though by no means all, viewers

[24] Gor'kii, PSS, 7: 75.

[25] R. Christian, *Tolstoy: A Critical Introduction* (Cambridge: Cambridge University Press, 1969), 256.

sided with tradition and the "fathers."[26] Although fairly moderate, both Stanislavsky and his gentry partner Nemirovich tended toward this patriarchal view, reproaching Gorky and his crowd for "rocking the boat."[27] But students in the audience were excited by Gorky's anarchistic spirit. The stage production of *The Petit Bourgeois* was tightly controlled by censorship, a condition that added to its *succés de scandal*, particularly among the young.[28]

Gorky's rebellion against elders enacted on the stage had some significant repercussions in political life. How one responded to Gorky the public figure and his writings had by this time become something of a litmus test for where one stood on the issue of social reform. By 1904 his rabble-rousing led to a breach in the Art Theater network, a breach that in microcosm anticipated the political polarization of the middle class during 1905. Tension had been building for a long time because of his attempts to turn the theater into a forum for political and social debate. Savva Morozov, who had become a devoted admirer of Gorky, the actress Maria Andreeva, and a few others left when *Summer Folk* was rejected. They founded their own theater with the express purpose of rousing the public to political action. Nonetheless, even after the breach and much to the dismay of its directors, the public associated the Art Theater with and tended to censure the theater for Gorky's radicalism.

The unusual, isolated phenomenon of Morozov deserves comment. Here was one merchant in whose life the messages of Chekhov's and Gorky's plays resonated. He clearly saw his times in a way that set him well apart from most of the young entrepreneurial elite. Apparently his interest in the Art Theater was predicated on an attraction to the social and political symbology represented on its stage. He perceived the new plays much as their authors meant them. According to Gorky's 1923 sketch of him, Morozov was one of the few to agree that Chekhov's plays indeed must be staged as comedies. He was drawn to Gorky by the writer's "relevance" and appeal to the "element of human will."[29] He was taken with the notion of social-political change from below. According to Gorky, Morozov put no stock by the Romanov dynasty and felt that revolution was the only way to modernize and "Europeanize" Russia.[30]

Thus, Morozov's involvement with the Art Theater may well have been a

[26] See P. A. Buryshkin, *Moskva kupecheskaia* (New York: Izd. Chekhova, 1954), 37; A. M. Gor'kii, "Bugrov," PSS, 17: 102; Exter, Review of "Na dne," *Moskovskie vedomosti* 349 (Dec. 19, 1902), 5.

[27] Stanislavskii, *Sobranie sochinenii v 8-i tomakh* (Moscow: GIIsk, 1961), 5: 221; hereafter, SS8. It is interesting, however, that Stanislavsky used Gorky's mannerisms, movements, and intonations as a model for his ideal of the intelligent, dedicated social reformer, Dr. Stockman in Ibsen's *The Enemy of the People*. See *O Stanislavskom*, 235.

[28] See Gor'kii, PSS, 7: 588–90.

[29] Ibid., 16: 500.

[30] Ibid., 16: 503.

stepping-stone to political activism.[31] In 1902 he harbored the radical engineering student Bauman and started to contribute generously to the Social
Democratic party. His breach with the Art Theater in 1904 and transfer of
funds and loyalty from a cultural to a political organization suggests an attempt
completely to shed the social stereotype of the cultivated but socially and politically hidebound merchant. His sympathy for radical causes soon brought
about a family breach; as a result, his mother fired him from the company
board. Like so many nineteenth-century literary protagonists, once he had
crossed the boundary from intellectual-cultural assertions of self to sociopolitical ones, Morozov was ostracized. He had no inner resources to survive and
no place in a patriarchal society where a politically minded person, let alone a
merchant, was continually frustrated in his search for a constructive political
alternative. Like Gorky's superhumanly self-reliant protagonists, he had become an outsider, but the isolation that literary characters seemed to survive
was too much for a mere mortal to bear. It is all too tempting to say that in
pre-1905 Russian society Morozov's eventual suicide was prescribed by the
existing semiosphere, by available cultural narratives that preordained the social rebel's self-destruction as the only imaginable alternative to submission.[32]
Social consciousness—the awareness of possible options in social and political life—seemed in this particular case to follow a definite script to which art
had already given full tragic expression.

The deep social discourse implied in Art Theater life reveals a fundamental
inability to deal with the crisis of identity that faced urban society, to conceive
of self, even when urged to do so, as part of a new social nucleus, and in short
to find a mechanism of change. It is also clear that people like Chekhov, Morozov, and Gorky were a tiny minority who felt compelled to seek, at least in
the language of artistic ritual, strategies of change and possible new ways of
looking at the social role of educated society. Other repertory writers who
filled the gap left by Chekhov's death in 1904 and Gorky's break with the
theater—among them Sergei Naidenov and Evgeny Chirikov—wrote old-
fashioned plays that reasserted established scripts. Nemirovich reverted to
producing gentry classics such as Turgenev's *Month in the Country* and excerpts from Dostoevsky's *Devils* and *Brothers Karamazov*. Meanwhile Stanislavsky limited himself to training actors and finding new acting techniques.
Although their productions were aesthetically bold and innovative, in the
years after 1905 the directors of the Art Theater merely supported existing
social values.

---

[31] An interesting source for information on Morozov is Aleksandr Serebrov, *Vremia i liudi:
vospominaniia, 1898–1905* (Moscow: GIKhL, 1955), 169–212. Serebrov is one person who followed when Gorky left the Art Theater.

[32] Serebrov, 212. Serebrov claims that Morozov became something of a folk hero after 1905.
According to legend, his life turned out in a yet a different way: he did not commit suicide but
was arrested by the police and was serving time in prison for revolutionary activities.

We have examined the conflicted social imagination that underlay the wonderful resurgence of theater culture in Russia at the turn of the century. However, our picture of the social discourse of this milieu would not be complete if we concluded here. The Art Theater's directors certainly meant their theater to serve a social function, if not exactly a monumental restructuring of social myth. Their goals were more modest, personal, and concrete—thus ultimately of a piece with other expressions of self-image in educated society.[33] Although neither Nemirovich nor Stanislavsky was interested in turning their stage into a podium for a narrow political education, they did encourage in their actors and their audiences an attitude of general social and cultural self-awareness.[34] The theater was intended to give all who participated in it a liberal, Schillerian "aesthetic education," to allow them to achieve a broad perspective on their spiritual, social, and political condition, and to inculcate both civility and cultural refinement. The politically vague nature of this focus is well illustrated in Stanislavsky's treatment of one of his favorite roles, the social activitist Dr. Stockman in Ibsen's *An Enemy of the People*.[35] He viewed Stockman as "a man of ideals, the true friend of his country and his people." The inner, enlightened attitude rather than the resolve to take concrete social measures drew Stanislavsky to this otherwise unlikely model of self.

Stanislavsky also held professional achievement and dignity as a central value—and in this orientation he shared much in common with other groups in the Russian middle class. He was acutely aware of the low status of actors and was indignant that they were typically treated as the dregs of society, as "servants," "prostitutes," and "burglars."[36] He resented the ignominy that actors suffered in the imperial theaters and was determined that actors improve their social stature. Professionalism (*professional'nost'*) became for him the signal of greater social dignity.[37] He was very strict with all members of the Art Theater, demanding from them exemplary behavior in their private lives as well as on the stage. A teetotaler himself, he did not tolerate any drunkenness either on or off the job. He abhorred the usual bohemian atmosphere that pervaded the theater world and encouraged marriage between actors as a way to strengthen the theater troupe. The actor, in Stanislavsky's view, would win respect only if he did more than excel in his trade: he must be an "advocate of beauty and truth" and must "stand above the crowd" on the stage and in his

---

[33] See essays by Harley Balzer, Christine Ruane and Ben Eklof, and William Brumfield in this volume.

[34] See, for example, Nemirovich-Danchenko, *Izbrannye pis'ma* 1: 284, 287; also Konstantin Stanislavsky, *My Life in Art*, 379–80.

[35] See Stanislavsky, *My Life in Art*, 404. See also *O Stanislavskom*, 235.

[36] Stanislavsky, *My Life in Art*, 249. See also Prince Sumbatov-Iuzhin's comments on the acting profession in *Zapisi. Stat'i. Pis'ma* (Moscow: Iskusstvo, 1951), 148, 228–31.

[37] It is interesting to note that after 1917 Proletcult would attack precisely this aspect of the theater's social and ideological profile, professionalism, as being "bourgeois." See, for example, *M. F. Andreeva. Perepiska. Vospominaniia. Stat'i Dokumenty* (Moscow: Iskusstvo, 1961), 415.

daily life.[38] In other words, in the substitute religion that theater was for Stanislavsky, the actor must be an acolyte in a ritual of personal and professional self-perfection. It is important to note that these concrete processes of civil education of actor and audience did have a significant impact both before and after the revolution. Viewers immediately recognized that they were confronted with a new kind of actor, no longer merely an entertainer, but, indeed, an intelligent specialist who served as a general model of professional dignity.[39]

Although Stanislavsky and Nemirovich conceived of the social goals of their theater far more modestly than their repertory writers, they nonetheless had the ambition to spread their vision of theater beyond the bounds of the Moscow audience, to enlighten audiences throughout the empire. In this pursuit they were sorely hampered by the government and its web of censorships. Soon after it opened its doors in 1898 as the "Moscow Generally Accessible (*Obshchedostupnyi*) Art Theater," the theater was compelled either to change its socially provocative repertory or to take the "generally accessible" out of its title, thus limiting the category of citizen who could attend the theater to the wealthy, titled, or highly educated. Moreover, a 1904 plan to establish branch theaters around the country aroused interest within theater circles but never came to fruition.[40] Experience in provincial cities had shown that the police, often the only institution in town, could abuse, delay, and block any activity at will.[41] Soon after 1905, with its Moscow audience alienated and its finances in shambles, the theater went in the opposite direction: it abandoned efforts to broaden its impact at home and went abroad where it quickly rose to the heights of international acclaim.

In conclusion, the Moscow Art Theater exhibited the weak and deeply ambivalent social self-image of a diverse and conflicted middle of society, of people who neither belonged to neat soslovie categories nor defined themselves in other recognizable ways—neither gentry or bureaucrat nor worker or peasant. Quite the contrary, we encounter here a lack of will to strive for coherent social identity in the emerging cultural elite. The process of stage production revealed what was certainly lacking throughout the middle of society: a sociocultural myth that would lend legitimacy to the new predominance of the middle. The middle of Russian society, in its symbolic, theatrical representation, had no strong protagonist, such as a Faust or Robinson Crusoe, who legitimately and productively transformed the terms of the present and created an imaginable future or who challenged the limitations of existing social structures. And it had nothing like the nest-of-gentlefolk or the Prome-

[38] Stanislavskii, SS8, 7: 207.

[39] See A. P. Chekhov, PSS, 7: 288, 303.

[40] Stanislavskii, "Proekt organizatsii 'Aktsionernogo obshchestva provintsial'nykh teatrov'," SS8, 5: 207–10; "O tsenzure," 275–83.

[41] Ibid., 282–83.

thean scripts that respectively gave a high profile to the rural tsarist elite and the new Soviet order.

Nor for the middle was there a sense of present to which they belonged. Time was split between a sorely missed past and a fervently awaited future. Social space, as defined for them by external forces, was limited to their own private holdings and a few major cities, especially Moscow. Russia, as a sociomythic entity, was not allowed to belong to them. In the deep social script they could not enforce their hegemony over the capital, the province, or the countryside; their space remained to a large degree religious, private, isolated, not social, public, national.

Finally, sense of selfhood was generally validated not by grand political or economic projects but rather by personal ideals of individual cultivation and professional perfection. The social image of the middle that remained at least in the symbolic construct of the Art Theater was negative, contained in the word meshchanstvo. It implied the officious nastiness of Natasha (*Three Sisters*), the ignorance and tyranny of the Bessemenovs (*The Petit Bourgeois*), the narrowness of Varia (*The Cherry Orchard*), and the emptiness of the summer folk in Gorky's play.

As in the experience of other elites in post-Petrine Russian history, it was almost impossible for this one to leap from cultural selfhood to an active sociopolitical identity. Moreover, it is possible to speculate that the rapid industrialization and modernization Russian society underwent in the few decades before 1918 left unbridgeable rifts in the middle layers of society, in the life of the imagination as well as in the social fabric. Although the experience of the Art Theater shows the first workings of a new social imagination, there was little time, much inertia, and too much entropic pressure for the middle possibly to conceive the social script in which they would be the heroes.

Chapter 18

REDEFINING THE INTELLECTUAL'S ROLE: MAKSIM GORKY AND THE *SREDA* CIRCLE

MARY LOUISE LOE

CIRCLES HAVE PLAYED a significant role in the history of the Russian intelligentsia since the early nineteenth century, but they achieved their greatest prominence during the years 1890–1917, a period of rapid change in every sphere of Russian life. Because educational and political institutions and the press did not provide a free forum for the exchange of ideas, the circle had evolved as a social institution within which intellectuals could express their feelings and ideas, develop a sense of identity, and achieve a sense of belonging. The circle provided many intellectuals with group support during the transitional period after they had left home and before they had fully developed their own views. The growing number of educated people, the rise in the number and variety of publications, and the dissemination of a wider spectrum of ideas created an intense intellectual and literary life between 1890 and 1917. The growth of an increasingly complex and diversified middle class made the quest for a social identity even more problematic for the generation reaching maturity at the turn of the century. Students, writers, artists, and social activists who wanted to be identified with the intelligentsia sought personal support and greater self-awareness within the closed structure of the circle.

This chapter discusses one of these groups—the literary circle *Sreda* (Wednesdays)—and the writers' attempt to define their social role and portray social reality during the period of the revolution of 1905 (Fig. 12).[1] The original Sreda circle had been formed in 1899 by Nikolai Teleshov and Ivan and Iuly Bunin, among others. Several months later, Maksim Gorky was invited to join, and he soon introduced his discoveries, Leonid Andreev and Skitalets (Stepan Petrov). Andreev introduced other writers, and an inner circle of Sreda soon emerged with Gorky as its leader. While the original circle continued to hold its regular weekly meetings, the inner circle, which developed into a closely knit group under Gorky's direction, included Leonid Andreev, Ivan Bunin, Evgeny Chirikov, Nikolai Garin-Mikhailovsky, Aleksandr Kuprin,

---

[1] See Mary Louise Loe, "Maksim Gor'kii and the *Sreda* Circle: 1899–1905," *Slavic Review* 44, no. 1 (1985): 49–66, for my study of the psychology and structure of the circle, which I briefly summarize here.

Fig. 12. The literary circle *Sreda*, Moscow. Seated, left to right: L. Andreev, F. Shaliapin, I. Bunin, N. Teleshov, E. Chirikov. Standing: Skitalets (S. Petrov), M. Gorky (1902).

Aleksandr Serafimovich, Skitalets, Teleshov, and Vikenty Verasaev (V. V. Smidovich).[2]

Although the writers of this circle were not the most talented, they became extremely popular from 1899 to 1905 because their realistic descriptions of Russia's social conflicts provided the educated public with a current, albeit journalistic, dramatization of what was going on in social spheres other than their own. Their plays, short stories, and novels honestly and vividly portrayed the ambivalent feelings, tensions, and hatreds between the lower classes and those above them and analyzed the dilemma of the intellectual who found himself caught between the two. Their portrayal of workers, peasants, students, hoboes, and criminals offered the reading public vivid subject matter for their debate on Russia's social problems; journals and newspapers were filled with critical reviews of their work, and the performances of their plays often became political events. Yet the writers were not simply interested in documenting the lives of others and heightening the social consciousness of the middle class; they identified with the outsiders and intellectuals portrayed in their work and hoped that in the process of describing their hopes, illusions, and failures, they could find answers to the questions that disturbed them. Who were they, and what was their relationship to the poor, the middle class, and the state? Did they have the ability and courage to pursue their overwhelming desire for autonomy, or would they compromise and accept the traditional obligation of the Russian intelligentsia to help the poor? The need to answer these questions became more insistent as Russia moved toward a revolutionary situation. Because of their own deep feelings of social alienation, the writers, with the exception of Gorky, feared that most Russian intellectuals would not be effective participants in the ensuing struggle, as either mediators or revolutionaries. This chapter explores the dialogue between these writers by concentrating on their collective portrayal of the intellectual.

Nineteenth-century Russian intellectuals generally saw themselves as voices for the oppressed and inarticulate lower classes: they were determined to become their leaders and rescue them from the landlords, the bureaucrats, and the state. Conservative Slavophiles and radical Westernizers, though opposed in their interpretations of the past and their solutions for the future, nonetheless agreed that Russian intellectuals had to help the *narod*. Yet as Russia industrialized and thousands of peasants migrated into its urban centers, the intelligentsia felt the need to redefine its former role. The Populist ethic, with its idealized image of the peasantry, no longer seemed adequate, and in the 1890s large numbers of intellectuals turned to Marxism because it apparently accounted for the surrounding economic and technological changes. But Marxism offered the individual a diminished and less crucial role in the historical

---

[2] Iulii Bunin, ''Doklady i kratkii otchet o deiatelnosti, tseliakh i zadachakh Kruzhka 'Sreda','' TsGALI SSSR, Moscow, f. 1292, o. 2, d. 2.

process: the socialist revolution would occur whether the intellectual participated or not. Although many intellectuals became Marxists, many also resisted, finding it too deterministic and positivistic. Those who rejected Populism and Marxism looked to the Europeans and the movement known as
Modernism. From Paris to Berlin artists and intellectuals were attempting in
the 1890s to create new philosophies, aesthetics, and ethics, and whether they
considered themselves Decadents, Symbolists, Mystics, or Aesthetes, they rejected nineteenth-century positivism, materialism, and naturalism. Caught between two classes—the affluent bourgeoisie and the working masses—which
seemed to be reproducing at a rapid rate and with whom they had little in
common, these young intellectuals wanted to define a unique role for their
generation as they stood at the dawn of the new century. The works of Baude-
laire, Wilde, Nietzsche, Maeterlinck, Ibsen, and Strindberg expressed the
thoughts and sentiments of many Russian writers and gave them a sense of
belonging to this European vanguard. But Russia's historical backwardness
posed special problems for adopting modernist ideas. Unlike Western Europe,
Russia had neither a large nor a cohesive middle class, and Russian intellectuals retained earlier generations' deep hostility toward the bourgeoisie. By
the late 1890s there were large numbers of professionals, bureaucrats, and
entrepreneurs; they shared the intellectuals' contempt for the state and their
desire for modernization and change, but most young intellectuals looked
upon these members of the middle class as their enemy, as selfish opportunists
dedicated to materialistic values. Having rejected revolutionary politics as un-
inspiring and bourgeois conformity as spiritual death, they saw themselves as
independent of all classes and sought to define a role to set them apart from
the older generation of the intelligentsia as well as those of their contemporaries who did not share their vision.

In their search for a new identity, Russia's leading artistic and literary intellectuals were rejecting the utilitarian approach to literature—the view popular since the 1840s that art had to serve a social purpose—and looking for a
new aesthetics. The symbolist, Dmitry Merezhkovsky, who with his wife Zinaida Gippius organized the circle at the Dom Marusi, called on young artists
to search for the universal, eternal truths hidden beneath the world of appearances and argued that artists could create a new national Symbolist literature
that would uncover the collective mind of the Russian people. Sergei Diaghilev's World of Art circle, whose motto was "Art is free, life is paralyzed"
pursued aesthetic and sensual experiences in the unusual and exotic and created new forms in painting, music, and dance. The head of the Symbolist
circle centered around the *Vesy* (Balances) review; Valery Briusov, believing
in the autonomy of art, placed his emphasis on technique and craftsmanship.
Within the lush, decadent, exotic, and refined atmosphere of these literary
salons of the 1890s and 1900s, the poets, artists, and philosophers of Russia's
Silver Age were nourished: Briusov, Belyi, Blok, Balmont, Sologub, and oth-

ers. But these writers who dared to break with tradition by affirming an individualistic, elitist ethic could only speak to a relatively small number of readers who were also highly educated and cultivated.

Because of their social background, education, and interests, the Sreda writers did not feel comfortable among these groups. At the time they came together as a circle in 1899 in Moscow, they were all starting out on their literary careers and had not yet clearly developed their views. Like other circles, Sreda became much more to its members than simply a literary or professional association. Within the circle, the men developed their literary styles and artistic craft, formed professional ties in the publishing world, and most important learned about themselves—what they thought about society and their role in it.

At the time the circle was formed, Gorky was the only one who had already achieved fame as a writer. His three volumes of collected stories, published in 1898 and 1899, had created unprecedented controversy and debate, making him the most talked-about writer in Russia. Gorky's popularity derived largely from his image as a self-made man from the lower classes who had an intimate knowledge of the urban and rural poor. After his father's death when Gorky was only three, he was raised by his maternal grandparents who owned a small dye shop in Nizhny Novgorod. His grandfather had worked his way up out of poverty but remained a violent and tyrannical man. He rejected and abused the young Gorky and forced him out of his house at the age of eleven. Gorky spent years working among the migrants, drifters, and assorted unskilled laborers he later portrayed in his early work. He obtained his education by reading voraciously and mixing in intellectual circles in the provincial cities of Nizhny Novgorod, Samara, and Kazan.[3] The violent experiences of his childhood had alienated him so completely from the lower middle-class merchants, shopkeepers, and former peasants among whom he was raised that he sought total escape from their world. Shifting between the two worlds of the lower classes and the provincial intelligentsia, he struggled to support himself in odd jobs while maintaining his intellectual vitality. Finally Gorky decided to become a writer, a decision based on his firm belief that writers could transform society through literature by creating the image of the new man that would inspire others. Even though he believed that Russian intellectuals had lost touch with reality and were too involved in the world of ideas, he nonetheless was convinced that they alone had the moral commitment and intellectual capacity to induce the total transformation Russia needed. In his view, the problems of Russia did not derive primarily from class exploitation or government repression, though he condemned them as well, but from a deeper, more profound source: the nature of the Russian character exemplified by the peasant

---

[3] Gor'kii, "Avtobiograficheskaia zametka 1897 goda," in S. A. Vengerov, "M. Gor'kii," *Russkaia literatura XX veka, 1890–1910*, 3 vols. (Moscow, 1914–1916), 1: 190–92.

whom Gorky saw as weak, cowardly, lazy, greedy, submissive, intolerant, irrational, and violent.

In his stories, through the voice of the *bosiak* (hobo), he argued that Russian intellectuals should stop trying to help the lower classes, whom they did not understand anyway, and should first try to help themselves by becoming strong, fearless, and independent. Only after they had thrown off the ideological baggage imposed on them by earlier generations of intellectuals, their duty to help the oppressed, could they reach their own potential and become the leaders of society. Gorky's attack on Russian society, influenced strongly by Nietzsche,[4] left no social group untouched, and his denial of social commitment and call for selfish individualism was very appealing to young men looking for a "new" role, distinct from that of their elders.[5] Virtually overnight, Gorky became a culture hero for Russian youth. His rough bohemian looks— long hair, a peasant tunic, cape, high boots—dramatic mannerisms and gestures, and knowledge of the underworld of outsiders and rebels led the young to idolize him, while the older generation generally tolerated his youthful defiance because he was a self-made man.

The writers who became members of Gorky's inner circle were attracted by the same elements that had made him popular. They joined him for personal, ideological, and professional reasons; they shared his hostility to the middle class and the intellectual elite, but they needed his professional support, as well. In 1899 Gorky, then the literary editor of the Marxist journal *Zhizn'* (Life), promised to publish their work and give them complete artistic freedom.[6] In the years of their association, Gorky's talents and skills as an editor and publisher served these writers well.

The writers shared similar social backgrounds. A review of their familial and socioeconomic roots elucidates the reasons for their mutual attraction and social views. Their families were not members of the urban intelligentsia, but belonged to the provincial bureaucracy, military, and impoverished nobility. Although not fully sharing Gorky's view of the writer's role in society, they too believed that their understanding of the lower middle class and the poor distinguished them from other writers. They were not as familiar as was Gorky with the violence of this world, but they were not far removed from it either.

With few exceptions, the writers' insecurity about being provincial *raznochintsy* (commoners) had been intensified by the fact that they had either weak

[4] Mary Louise Loe, "Gorky and Nietzsche: The Quest for a Russian Superman," in *Nietzsche in Russia*, ed. Bernice Glatzer Rosenthal (Princeton, 1986), 251–74.

[5] Ivan Bunin, "Gor'kii, otryvki iz vospominanii," *Don* 3 (1968): 169–70, quoted in Aleksandr Ninov, *M. Gor'kii i Iv. Bunin* (Leningrad, 1973), 44; Chekhov to Aleksandr Sumbatov-Iuzhin, Feb. 26, 1903, Gor'kii and Anton Chekhov, *Sbornik materialov; Perepiska, stat'i, vyskazyvaniia* (Moscow, 1951), 202.

[6] Gor'kii to Veresaev, Sept. 1900, Gor'kii, *Polnoe sobranie sochinenii v tridtsati tomakh* (Moscow, 1959–1965), 28: 128–29; hereafter *PSS30*.

or no relationships with their fathers, due to their fathers' alcoholism, early death, or absence from home. Most writers portrayed their fathers as unhappy and unsuccessful men with little direct influence on their lives. Their lack of a strong paternal figure certainly contributed to their feelings of social deracination. Not surprisingly Teleshov and Veresaev, the two writers who described positive relationships with their fathers, would have greater self-confidence. Their mothers, in contrast, apparently had a much stronger influence on the writers. These women were frustrated and disappointed in their husbands and with their own lives, and they strongly encouraged their sons, many of whom were only or first-born sons, to develop their intellectual and artistic abilities and to escape the dull provincial world that had trapped them.

All the writers were dissatisfied with the formal education they received in the gymnasium in the 1880s. Ivan Bunin and Skitalets were the only ones to enroll in universities, but only Teleshov, Andreev, and Veresaev, and Garin-Mikhailovsky actually graduated and attained the necessary credentials to pursue professional careers. Iuly Bunin, Chirikov, and Serafimovich were dismissed from the university for political activities, and even though their political involvement was neither serious nor long-lasting, it effectively barred them from professional careers. Kuprin completed his military training, but then resigned from the military after a dispute with his superiors. Teleshov was the only writer from a capital city—his father was a Moscow merchant—and the only one who had the financial independence to begin his literary career upon graduation.

Like Gorky, though to a lesser degree, these writers reached early manhood with very weak family support and sense of social status. They decided to become writers because they believed that writing offered them the greatest independence and easiest escape from the banality and boredom of provincial Russia. Because they needed to support themselves, and in several cases their widowed mothers and families, they took jobs as reporters on provincial newspapers until they could earn enough money as independent writers. Veresaev, Andreev, and Garin-Mikhailovsky worked as professionals first—doctor, legal clerk, and engineer—before they devoted themselves to writing. Reporting the lives and problems of the provincial lower and middle strata not only deepened the writers' knowledge and understanding of these people, but it also guaranteed that they would not entertain the kind of romanticized views of the poor held by members of the urban educated elite.

Most of the writers seem to have had a passing involvement with Populist ideas during their early twenties. While a medical student, Veresaev participated in the famine and cholera relief; Gorky worked with some older Populists spreading propaganda among the peasants; Bunin participated in distributing Populist literature and belonged to a Tolstoian colony; and Garin-Mikhailovsky interrupted his engineering career to set up a farm with a school for peasants. Their various experiences with the Populist or Tolstoian move-

ment reflected youthful searching rather than profound, long-term philosophical and ideological interest. These writers had not attended the best universities or art academies and lacked the broad humanistic, artistic, and ideological
background that children who came from the educated elite gained from their
parents, education, and social milieu. And for all these reasons, as well as
their individual personalities, they never developed the kind of intense interest
in either abstract ideas that characterized earlier generations of raznochintsy
intellectuals or the aesthetic quest for beauty of their contemporaries.[7]

The writers worked with Gorky because he gave them emotional support,
personal encouragement, and professional leadership. He served as a father
figure to some, scolding them for being lazy or drinking too much, always
demanding more work. Not surprisingly, he often referred to them as "children," stood in as their father at two of their weddings, and was named god-
father to Andreev's son.[8] In the press, the critics repeatedly satirized the writers, especially Andreev, Skitalets, and Bunin, for imitating Gorky's dress,
mannerisms, and style. Their numerous cartoons depicted the writers as stars
in the constellation of Big Gorky and called them *podmaksimki*, a type of
mushroom that would grow under a "maksim" tree.[9] The writers' need for
identification with Gorky evidently derived from their lack of self-confidence;
in support of one another they each had special nicknames, associated with
their work, personality, or appearance. Gorky, for example, was called
"Crooks' Den" after the Moscow slum inhabited by hoboes, thieves, and
prostitutes.[10] Gorky could be very severe and demanding when it came to their
work, insisting that his followers submit their manuscripts first to him for publication and that they take a combative approach toward those writers whose
views he condemned. Nonetheless, he also was very supportive, encouraging
the members in his group to believe in themselves, praising their talent, abil-

[7] See the autobiographical sketches of the writers in Vengerov, ed., *Russkaia literatura*, vols.
1–3; Vasilii Brusianin, *Leonid Andreev: Zhizn' i tvorchestvo* (Moscow, 1912); Pavel Berkov,
Aleksandr Ivanovich Kuprin (Moscow, 1956); Vera Muromtseva-Bunina, *Zhizn' Bunina 1870–
1906* (Paris, 1958); Mariia Kuprina-Iordanskaia, *Gody molodosti* (Moscow, 1966); Vikentii Veresaev (Smidovich), "Vospominaniia," Veresaev, *Sobranie sochinenii v piati tomakh* (Moscow,
1961), vol. 5; Aleksandr Baboreko, *I. A. Bunin, Materialy dlia biografii* (Mosocw, 1967); Ivan
Bunin, "Kuprin," *Sobranie sochinenii v deviati tomakh* (Moscow, 1965–1967), vol. 9; James
Woodward, *Leonid Andreyev* (Oxford, 1969); Alexander Kaun, *Leonid Andreyev* (New York,
1970).

[8] Gor'kii to Andreev, Dec. 26–27, 1902, *Literaturnoe nasledstvo, vol. 72: Gor'kii i Leonid
Andreev, neizdannaia perepiska* (Moscow, 1965), 166; Andreev to Gor'kii, Dec. 26–28, 1902,
Literaturnoe nasledstvo, 168. Gor'kii to Piatnitskii, Dec. 25, 1902, *Arkhiv A. M. Gor'kogo, vol.
4: Pis'ma k K. P. Piatnitskomu* (Moscow, 1954), 108. Gor'kii to Piatnitskii, before Feb. 11, 1903,
Arkhiv, 118–19.

[9] Kok (N. I. Fidel), "Podmaksimovki," *Iskra* 5 (1903), reprinted in *Literaturnoe nasledstvo*,
72: 199. Re-mi (N. V. Remizov), "Gor'kii i ego ten'," *Strekoza* 41 (1905), reprinted in *Literaturnoe nasledstvo*, 72: 211.

[10] Nikolai Teleshov, *Zapiski pisatelia* (Moscow, 1957), 52.

ities, and intelligence as far superior to his own. Although the writers were often irritated by Gorky's many demands, questioning his sincerity and his increasing intolerance for other groups, they needed him at this time in their lives because he viewed the world in much more simple, less ambiguous terms. Because he saw Russian intellectuals as excessively cerebral and passive, he wanted his followers to be tough and fearless literary warriors.[11] This aggressive masculine role appealed to these men because they recognized their own vulnerability and were deeply disturbed by the violence of the lower classes. The role of warrior provided a vehicle for their feelings of social alienation and hostility, but when Gorky demanded in 1905 that they go beyond literary attacks and participate in the social struggle themselves they were forced to question this assumed identity.

Within the circle, the writers helped one another improve their literary skills. They devoted their literary meetings solely to presenting and analyzing unpublished manuscripts and forbade the intrusion of political or ideological debates. This was quite different from other literary circles, where politics and current events were frequently discussed. Because they were just beginning their literary careers, they sought a place where they could present their works to their peers for criticism and prohibited literary critics or outsiders from attending. As a consequence, a person could attend a Sreda meeting only by invitation and was admitted as a regular member only after he had been carefully "looked over" and approved of by other members. However, the writers occasionally invited a wide selection of literati, artists, and musicians to attend when the most popular writers, such as Gorky and Andreev, were presenting their works.

When the writers were first developing their own literary styles, they generally followed the realist and naturalist traditions. Although they did not share the aesthetic views of the decadents and symbolists, they generally were open regarding style and tried to judge each work individually. They occasionally invited the modernists to their meetings. Chekhov also attended when he was in Moscow, eventually exerting a strong literary influence on all the writers.[12]

Outside the formal literary meetings, however, the writers cooperated in numerous political activities, for example, holding public readings to raise funds for needy groups or writing and signing petitions and manifestoes. After the Russian-Japanese War began in 1904, the Sreda meetings were devoted to political affairs, and throughout 1904 and 1905 the foremost issues in their discussions were war and revolution.[13]

Also in 1904 Gorky began issuing the *Anthologies of the Znanie [Knowledge] Cooperative* which contained the stories, novels, and poems of the writ-

---

[11] Loe, "Maksim Gor'kii," 56–62.

[12] Teleshov, *Zapiski*, 38–71; Iu. Bunin, "Doklady," 5–6, 21–28.

[13] Leonid Andreev to Veresaev, Feb. 6, 1905, *Literaturnoe nasledstvo*, 72: 512.

ers in the Sreda circle as well as newcomers and foreign writers who shared their views. The success of these volumes was immediate, providing Gorky and the others with a wide audience and greater financial independence. They were soon called the Znanie writers. Their stories reflected the increasing tension, social conflict, and violence occurring in Russia and the impact of the war and revolution of 1905. As in the past, the writers concentrated on the specific social groups they knew best: Bunin, the nobility and peasantry; Kuprin, the military and urban drifters and outsiders; Andreev, the lower middle class; Skitalets, the peasant intelligentsia; Veresaev, the medical profession and the radical intelligentsia; Gusev-Orenburgsky, the priesthood; Garin-Mikhailovsky, engineers; Serafimovich, the workers. Jewish writers, such as Semen Iushkevich, David Aizman, and Shalom Asch, also published in *Znanie*, depicting pogroms against the Jews and the conflict between Zionists and assimilationists. Writing about the world in which they had grown up helped them clarify and define their social identity. Many stories focused on the generational conflict within social classes and groups that was intensified by the demographic shift from countryside to city: sons against fathers; priests against the church; soldiers against the military. But as the Revolution of 1905 approached, the writers indicated that this generational conflict was complicated by the larger social conflicts: the growing antagonism between state and society, between rich and poor, between educated and uneducated, between factory owner and worker, between landlord and peasant. The general picture that emerged from the stories was of a society in disintegration, with no class or group possessing the ability to resolve its many problems.

From the beginning of their association, the writers disagreed with Gorky on the intellectual's role. Because he believed that intellectuals had the obligation to transform Russia, Gorky was extremely critical of them, condemning liberals, Godseekers, mystics, and decadents as ineffective, escapist, cowardly, and effeminate.[14] In spite of his attack on intellectuals, he himself was praised and accepted by the intelligentsia because they viewed him as a person of moral authority. Nevertheless, critics from both the left and the right condemned his Nietzschean individualism, accusing him of advocating an amoral, selfish, "master-slave" philosophy, and of rejecting the Judeo-Christian tradition and egalitarianism inherent in Populist and Marxist views.[15] Gorky heeded this criticism, in spite of his public stance of defiance, especially because the Marxists had given him much financial and professional

[14] Gor'kii to Posse, before Aug. 10, 1901, *PSS30*, 28: 170; Gor'kii to Andreev, Sept. 21–22, 1904, *Literaturnoe nasledstvo*, 72: 223.

[15] See A. Andreevich (E. A. Solov'ev), "Ocherki tekushchei russkoi literatury," *Zhizn'*, no. 4 (1900): 311; N. K. Mikhailovskii, "Literatura i zhizn'; O g. Mak. Gor'kom i ego geroiakh," *Russkoe bogatstvo* 9 (1898): 55–75; Mikhailovskii, "Literatura i zhizn'; Eshche o Maksim Gor'kom i ego geroiakh," *Russkoe bogatstvo* 10 (1898): 61–93.

support.[16] And while he continued to believe in the intellectual's role, he began modifying his uncompromising individualism and called for political engagement instead.

By 1900 Gorky began writing plays because he believed, as Edith Clowes shows in this volume, that the theater was a better means for reaching the public. His plays were performed by the Moscow Art Theater and always created controversy, even though most critics found them little more than tendentious morality plays, weak and superficial imitations of Chekhov. It is not surprising that the only play to win critical acclaim, *The Lower Depths* (Na dne, 1902), portrayed the outcasts, hoboes, and criminals Gorky knew well and had portrayed earlier. But his plays *The Petit Bourgeois* (Meshchane, 1902), *Summer Folk* (Dachniki, 1904), and *Children of the Sun* (Deti solntsa, 1905) were far less well received because they were polemical attacks against the middle class and the intelligentsia. Members of the Russian middle class who appear in these plays are self-centered, spoiled, and pathetic people who have no concern for anyone but themselves and who fail to recognize what Gorky considered their responsibilities to the masses.[17] The only heroic figure appears in *The Petit Bourgeois*; the worker Nil is the revolutionary of the future, a potential Nietzschean superman in working-class garb. Nil believes that life can be "corrected" and "transformed by his will."[18] As an anti-intellectual he condemns the spoiled children of the middle-class family with whom he lives because they philosophize too much and lack determination, strength, and courage. Nil is convinced that he and others like him have the power to create a new world.

Drawn by the controversy brewing in the press over Gorky's plays, the educated public flocked to the theater to hear this pariah insult and warn them that time was running out. In his play *Summer Folk*, first performed in Moscow in October 1904, Gorky portrayed a group of raznochinets intellectuals, "standing alone," as he described them, "between the people and the bourgeoisie, without any influence on life, without any strength, and with fear." They cannot find "spiritual kinship in bourgeois and bureaucratic society," and yet they cannot return to their past.[19] They live like summer visitors, foreigners in their own land, unable to help the lower classes in their struggle for freedom; and yet they are entirely responsible for the tragedy unfolding before them: the violent uprising of the poor.[20]

[16] See Vladimir Posse, *Moi zhiznennyi put'* (Moscow, 1929), 116, 143, 151, 222–23.

[17] N. Mikhailovskii, "Literatura i zhizn'," *Russkoe bogatstvo* 4 (1902): 59. A. Chekhov to A. I. Sumbatov-Iuzhin, Feb. 26, 1903, *M. Gor'kii i A. Chekhov: perepiska, stat'i, vyskazyvaniia* (Moscow, 1951), 202.

[18] Gor'kii to K. S. Stanislavskii, Jan. 1902, *PSS30*, 28: 219.

[19] Gor'kii to M. Reinhardt, Dec. 1904, *PSS30*, 345.

[20] Gor'kii, "Dachniki," *Polnoe sobranie sochinenii v dvadtsati piati tomakh* (Moscow, 1968–1976), 7: 278; hereafter PSS25.

The public reacted this time with anger. On opening night members of the audience hissed, yelled, and walked out in protest. The critic Filosofov wrote that Gorky's attack on intellectuals in *Summer Folk* was not only unjustified but also "confused, coarse, and philistine." He argued that one could sympathize with Gorky as long as he "protested and challenged society" and "scorned the power of the satiated bourgeois crowd" but that he failed when he attempted to create a "positive social type." Gorky had set up a "cherished shrine to man with a capital M," but in doing so he denied the heritage of cultural values of the past and consequently "offered nothing beyond the goals of material well-being."[21] To be sure, Gorky's critics were correct: his extraordinary popularity had been based on his bold attack on philistinism, tradition, and authority, and he had never offered a cultural or political program beyond his demand that intellectuals become strong men of action. Nevertheless, Gorky had a firsthand understanding of the hostility of the lower classes toward the intelligentsia and anyone else who was different, and he attacked the weakness, passivity, and self-obsession of intellectuals because he desperately wanted to avert the approaching social tragedy.

The outbreak of revolution in January 1905 confirmed Gorky's worst fears. Gorky had been a member of the delegation that had met with Count Witte on the eve of Bloody Sunday in an attempt to prevent the outbreak of violence the following day. He also witnessed the demonstration at the Winter Palace and remained actively involved in the workers' movement until his arrest. In February 1905, while in prison, he wrote the play *Children of the Sun*, which was recognized as a portrayal of the current conflict, even though it was set during the cholera epidemic of the 1890s. His experience seemed to have taught him that he was being too harsh on the intelligentsia, for he portrayed them more sympathetically, while the rebellious workers were shown as undisciplined, uncontrollable, and violent. The situation in Russia was so tense by October 1905, when the play was first performed, that when angry workers ran onto the stage in the final act and attacked the main character, an intellectual, members of the audience thought the Black Hundreds were interrupting the performance and ran for the exits in terror.[22] The audience was outraged by the play; one critic attacked Gorky for recreating on the stage the kind of "terrifying, inhuman, total horror" people were experiencing in their own lives during the uprisings.[23] Yet Gorky was achieving his objective; he wanted to use the theater and press to shock and frighten the educated public into action. In 1905 he wrote two articles published in the Bolshevik newspaper *Novaia zhizn'* (New Life) blaming the violence on bourgeois selfishness,

[21] D. V. Filosofov, "Zavtrashnee meshchanstvo," *Novyi put'* 11 (1904): 321–32.

[22] V. I. Nemirovich-Danchenko, *Iz proshlogo* (Moscow, 1936), 273–75.

[23] S. V. Iablonskii, *Russkoe slovo*, Oct. 25, 1905, in "Notes," *PSS25*, 7: 658.

greed, hypocrisy, and indifference to the needs of the poor.[24] Although he had witnessed attempts by moderate groups to work with the government to bring about a reasonable solution to the crisis, he condemned the moderates out of hand. The collapse of the revolution in December 1905 convinced him to leave Russia rather than face imprisonment. But Gorky was not a man to admit defeat; what might have appeared to others as simple-minded optimism enabled him to weather this and many future storms. He wrote that he had witnessed the "moral bankruptcy [*krakh*]" of the intelligentsia on Bloody Sunday, but he continued to believe that the revolution could succeed if the intellectuals would act with the personal and moral strength that the times required.[25] They would have to break with the bourgeoisie and form a revolutionary alliance with the workers.[26] By 1905 Gorky had adapted the Bolshevik position to fit his own belief in the intellectual's role. In his view, there must be no compromise between the intellectuals and the middle class. As he wrote to Andreev in 1906, either one was a revolutionary and therefore on the side of the masses, or one was against them.[27] He wanted his followers to accept his rigid definition of their social role, but most found that impossible.

The other writers in the Sreda circle reacted quite differently to the revolutionary violence of 1905: they recoiled in horror and became even more pessimistic than before about their role in society. To be sure, their reactions to the revolution could have been predicted: while they agreed with Gorky that there was a great abyss between the intelligentsia and the people, they did not believe that intellectuals could bridge that abyss. They also portrayed intellectuals as weak, indecisive, and frightened, but they did not share Gorky's belief that intellectuals could transform themselves and lead Russia into a better future. Their literary portrayal of the déclassé intellectual was after all neither a fictional creation nor the portrayal of another class, but a description of their own feelings of social alienation. The main difference between them was that they viewed themselves as "intellectuals," whereas Gorky never admitted to being one.

Not surprisingly, the writers differed from Gorky in their portrayals of both workers and peasants. Especially in his early stories, in which he so greatly emphasized individual will, Gorky either condemned or romanticized the poor but rarely treated them with pity or sentimentality. As a self-made man, he expected everyone to have the strength to rise above his background. The other writers, following in the tradition of the populists of the 1880s, such as Uspensky, often portrayed workers and peasants from the perspective of an educated narrator who viewed them compassionately as victims of their social

[24] Gor'kii, "Zametki o meshchanstve," *PSS30*, 23: 341–67; "Po povodu Moskovskikh sobytii," *PSS30*, 23: 368–69.

[25] Gor'kii to E. M. Peshkova, Jan. 9, 1905, *PSS30*, 28: 346–49.

[26] Gor'kii to I. P. Ladyzhnikov, Jan. 1906, *PSS30*, 28: 405.

[27] Gor'kii to Andreev, March 18, 1906, *Literaturnoe nasledstvo*, 72: 265.

and economic condition. Poverty, ignorance, insecurity, and fear had beaten them, and they seemed incapable of ever gaining control over their own lives. In those stories where both workers and peasants appear for the purpose of contrasting the urban industrial world and the rural, the peasants are always portrayed more positively: they are healthier, livelier, more independent. When peasants appear alone, however, then they too are seen as tragic, passive victims of circumstance. Of course, there are exceptions, but this is the general pattern followed by all the writers, except Ivan Bunin who understood peasants very well and always portrayed them as individuals rather than victims of their social position.

Most stories that portray the relationship between the intelligentsia and the lower classes follow a similar pattern. The narrator feels guilty about his privileged position in society: he wants to do something to help the poor but remains overwhelmed by his own fear, confusion, and insecurity. He is caught between two worlds, just like the characters described by Gorky in *Children of the Sun*. On the one side are peasants and workers who do not accept him and whom he cannot accept, and on the other stands the privileged world of nobles, capitalists, and bureaucrats. Although he comes from this world, he has rejected it and never thinks of working within established institutions to correct inhumane conditions. Although he initially wants to identify with the workers, he realizes that he cannot become one of them and help them. Moreover, he is repelled by their weakness, which he sees in himself. In Kuprin's story, "Moloch" (Molokh, 1899), the engineer Bobrov, working in a mining complex in the Donets region, feels great sympathy for the workers, tending the furnaces like anonymous silent gnomes. He feels completely hostile to the members of his own class: the factory managers and owners, living secure and content alongside the oppressed workers. As the engineer's isolation intensifies, he takes morphine to escape. But the workers are not as passive as he believes and eventually rebel, though they are weak, disorganized, and easily defeated. The engineer attempts to aid them by blowing up the steam boilers, but he too fails and returns to his morphine addiction.[28]

In Serafimovich's story "At the Factory" (Na zavode, 1899), a journalist visiting a steel mill compares the healthy robust peasants just arriving at the plant to the sickly "robotlike" workers who are being devoured by the steel mill, "the voracious monster," "the god of fire and iron" that daily devours its "bloody sacrifices." Like the engineer, the journalist is extremely critical of the factory manager and sees him as an insensitive, cruel exploiter of the workers. The journalist tours the steel mill, where the power of the organized productive plant is so overwhelming in its total energy and strength that he feels drawn to descend into this pit where the workers were "being burned by

---

[28] Aleksandr Kuprin, "Molokh," *Sobranie sochinenii v deviati tomakh* (Moscow, 1959–1960) 1: 428–45; hereafter SS9.

the heat of the flames'' or ''to lie down powerlessly under the oncoming suspended incandescent steel.'' The intellectual's guilt, helplessness, and unfamiliarity with the industrial world make him feel self-destructive.[29]

Repeatedly the typical Sreda narrator tries to help the poor with whom he shares a feeling of powerlessness, but he fails to communicate across the vast social gulf. Moreover, the writers indicate, though often not explicitly, that the closer the intellectual gets to the peasants or workers, the more he fears and dislikes them. In Kuprin's story ''The Swamp'' (Boloto, 1902), a student who considers himself a populist spends the night in a woodsman's hut while working on a forestry project. He is shocked and frightened by the poverty and illness of the woodsman's family. The student naively attempts to advise the woodsman to move away because three of his children have already died of fever, but the woodsman has fatalistically accepted his situation as foreordained.[30]

The differences between the educated narrators and the lower classes go beyond social or economic considerations; they are based on mutual misunderstanding, fear, and mistrust. In Serafimovich's story ''On the Road'' (V puti, 1904), a student bicycling outside the city accepts a ride from a peasant with a cart but barely listens to the peasant's complaints. When the peasant finds out the price of his bicycle, he attacks the student with a stick, and the student shoots and kills him in self-defense.[31] As a Marxist, Serafimovich attributed most social problems to class differences, but he also recognized the complex emotional tension existing between the intellectual and the worker.

Beginning in 1895 Veresaev wrote a series of short novels on the radical intelligentsia, which describe their experiences in the 1890s and 1900s, particularly their disillusionment with Populist and then Marxist ideas, and their growing belief in individualism. In *No Way Out* (Bez dorogi, 1895), the former populist Dr. Chekhanov returns to help the people once again during the cholera epidemic, even though he has become disillusioned and considers populist views unrealistic, banal, and absurd. Gradually he wins the confidence of some metal workers, but when the death of a patient destroys the little trust he has gained an angry crowd mercilessly beats him to death. As he dies, he expresses his bitterness and despair.[32]

In Veresaev's second novel on the radical intelligentsia, *The Epidemic* (Povetrie, 1898), the disillusioned former Populist Dr. Troitsky condemns the Marxists for blindly declaring ''they know the way'' when in fact ''they do not know anything'' and ''are ready to destroy everything which does not fit

[29] Aleksandr Serafimovich, ''Na zavode,'' *Sobranie sochinenii v semi tomakh* (Moscow, 1959–1960), 1: 428–45; hereafter, SS7.

[30] Kuprin, ''Boloto,'' *SS9*, 3: 103–21.

[31] Serafimovich, ''V puti,'' *SS7*, 2: 166–81.

[32] Vikentii Veresaev, ''Bez dorogi,'' *Sobranie sochinenii v piati tomakh* (Moscow, 1961), 1: 156–57; hereafter SS5.

into their scheme."[33] In each of these novels on the radical intelligentsia, the main character becomes alienated from other radical intellectuals because they are unrealistic, dogmatic, and unwilling to give up their false illusions about the peasants and workers. In *At the Turning Point* (Na povorote, 1902), the former revolutionary Tokarev returns from exile determined to reject the intelligentsia's "cursed obligation to the people." But younger radical students view him as their hero and refuse to leave him alone. He tries to convince them that they will accomplish nothing until they develop themselves as individuals. Only one young intellectual accepts his view; after observing the fawning behavior of the other students before a worker, he proclaims his need to believe in himself as an *intelligent*:

> Today's meeting left me with an awfully foul impression! Can there be anything more repulsive? There he [the worker Baluev] sits—relaxed, confident in himself. And we sit around him—delighted, touched, and fawning. And what is the characteristic attitude on our part: mild condescension from the height of our theoretical greatness and at the same time, purely servile groveling before him. What is this? A void, which is ashamed of itself and yearns for him—the "carrier." Life, it seems, is only over there, and there, you are a stranger, without any organic ties. . . . What garbage! Why can he hold his head so proudly, live with himself, and I only can yearn for and gaze upon him? For in the final conclusion I by myself am an historical fact. I am an *intelligent*. What of it? I don't want to be ashamed of it, I want to recognize myself. He's a fine man, I'm not debating that. I believe in him and respect him. But first of all I want to believe in myself.[34]

In Veresaev's novels, the radical intellectual expresses what many of his contemporaries, including those in the Sreda circle, were feeling: for too long Russian intellectuals have not believed in themselves. Their social and moral concerns have failed to help the people. Their first and most important action is to overcome their self-hatred and develop self-confidence and self-respect. To survive, intellectuals must stop believing that the lower classes are somehow more legitimate than they are.

From 1904 to 1907 the writers published many stories, mostly in the *Znanie* volumes, on revolutionary violence. Gusev-Orenburgsky's "In the Parish" (V prikhode, 1905) and "Country of Fathers" (Strana otsov, 1905), Skitalets's "Shackles" (Kandaly, 1905) and the "The Forest Has Been Set on Fire" (Les razgoralsia, 1905), and Chirikov's play *Peasants* (Muzhiki, 1906) all portray the generational conflict in the countryside. Young peasants are rebelling not only against wealthy landlords but also against their fathers, the peasant traditions, and religious beliefs. In contrast to earlier stories, where peasants and workers were passive, dependent, and submissive, the young

---

[33] Veresaev, "Povetrie," *SS5*, 1: 174.
[34] Veresaev, "Na povorote," *SS5*, 2: 58.

peasants in these stories are more articulate, fearless, and angry, but they refuse to listen to the voice of reason, expressed by the narrator—a teacher, a
priest, or a student—sympathetic to their cause; in their rage they attack anyone deemed their enemy. The landowners, estate managers, nobles, and
wealthy peasants view the poor peasants as mindless "bodies without heads"
and "violent beasts." The educated narrator is caught between two irreconcilable camps, unable to mediate between them.

The portrayal of the behavior of urban workers in 1905 is similar. Serafimovich published five stories on the revolutionary events: "In the Middle of
the Night" (Sredi nochi, 1906); "Funeral March" (Pokhoronnyi marsh,
1906); "On the Square" (Na ploshchadi, 1906); "At Presnia" (Na presne,
1906), "The Dead on the Streets" (Mertvye na ulitsakh, 1907). Other stories
and plays portraying the revolutionary conflict include Andreev's "The Governor" (Gubernator, 1906), Teleshov's "Sedition" (Kramola, 1907), Chirikov's *The Jews* (Evrei, 1904), Iushkevich's "The Jews" (Evrei, 1905), and
Kipen's "In October" (V oktiabre, 1906). In all these stories the workers
behave violently and irrationally. The crowd is a spontaneous, faceless mass,
lacking discipline, direction, and leadership. It is significant that the authors
portrayed not only the Black Hundreds, pogromists, and counter-revolution-
aries as savages but occasionally the revolutionary workers as well. The overwhelming presence in these stories is that of the violent mob; the collective
submissiveness and faith portrayed in earlier works has been replaced by collective hysteria and rage. In Chirikov's *The Jews*, Iushkevich's story by the
same title, and Kipen's "In October" the authors depict the pogromists and
their indiscriminate attacks. In each of these works, the Jewish radical is torn
between his religious-cultural loyalties and his political beliefs. In Chirikov's
work, a Zionist indiscriminately shoots at a group of revolutionary workers
who have come to aid the Jews; and the Christian revolutionary loses his social
identity before the mob which brutally attacks not only Jews but also those
who by their behavior appear to be Jews.[35] The masses are intolerant, irrational, and brutal, and the intellectual is afraid that his ambiguous identity might
lead to his becoming the object of their violence. In Serafimovich's "At Presnia" and "The Dead in the Streets" the narrator describes the terror and fear
of people whose instinctive reaction in the midst of the conflict is to hide and
save their own lives. Corpses lie in the snow, being carted away like dead
cattle, and fathers, out of fear, refuse to identify the bodies of their own sons.[36]
In "In the Middle of the Night" the radical organizer, originally a worker
himself, has lectured to workers for twelve years, and as he argues with them
he feels a "caustic, burning hatred towards this impenetrable, self-devouring
incomprehension and darkness."[37]

---

[35] E. N. Chirikov, "Evrei," *P'esy* (St. Petersburg, 1906), 286–87.

[36] Serafimovich, "Na presne," *SS7*, 2: 308–31; "Mertvye na ulitsakh," *SS7*, 3: 85–93.

[37] Serafimovich, "Sredi nochi," *SS7*, 2: 299.

Although the narrator is often depicted as the one rational person caught between two intractable, hostile groups, he is neither rational nor controlled when alone. In Kuprin's story "River of Life" (Reka zhizni, 1906), a student revolutionary has revealed the names of his associates to the police while being interrogated. As he contemplates suicide, he tries to understand the reason for his weakness and decides that his fear characterizes his entire generation. He realizes that his fear of the violence and brutality of other people has paralyzed him and "the entire young generation of preceding and present times." His generation, he says, "scorned servility but we ourselves grew up to be cowardly slaves."[38]

Andreev also wrote many stories on weak, neurotic intellectuals who experienced the same fear as Kuprin's character. Most of his intellectuals are students and professionals, neither radical nor revolutionary. They feel completely alienated from their middle- or lower-class families. Like the other writers in his circle, Andreev often portrayed the middle and lower middle classes as stereotypes: they are materialistic, insensitive, and hypocritical.[39] The young men of his stories are torn between their moral and rational ideas and their emotional and sexual needs. More than any other writer in the circle, Andreev openly criticized the social consequences of middle-class sexual mores. He created a major scandal when, in his story "The Abyss" (Bezdna, 1901), he portrayed a student raping his female companion immediately after she is raped by some tramps in a city park.[40] Many of his characters are guilt-ridden, tormented men who try to escape into an abstract mental world. Unsuccessful in their quest, they consequently go insane or commit murder or suicide.

Repeatedly, the Sreda writers suggest that intellectuals feel that they do not belong anywhere and seek community, social identity, and personal fulfillment by joining the revolutionary movement, but this solution never works. In Veresaev's novel *To Life* (K zhizni, 1908), the revolutionary Cherdyntsev looks back on the experience of 1905 with great nostalgia as a time when "a hundred thousand people merged into one, . . . private life became nothing; man gave of himself joyfully and simply like a bee or an ant."[41] Now that the revolution is over, the sense of community is gone, and the revolutionary finds the workers dull, insipid, even repulsive. He feels still more isolated than before with his earlier hopes shattered, and he resents the workers for their ability to get along with others and to accept life as it is.

The intellectual who emerges in this literature is a man alone, alienated, and

---

[38] Kuprin, "Reka zhizni," *SS9*, 4: 300.

[39] See, for example, Andreev, "Rasskaz o Sergee Petroviche," "Mysl'," *Povesti i rasskazy v dvukh tomakh* (Moscow, 1971), 1: 157–84, 261–302.

[40] L. Andreev, "Bezdna," *Polnoe sobranie sochinenii*, 8 vols. (St. Petersburg, 1913), 4: 134–35.

[41] Veresaev, *K zhizni*, *SS5*, 4: 43.

frightened. In spite of his idealistic attempts to unite with the lower classes, they do not accept him, and he recognizes that he cannot become one of them. He remains an outsider, refusing to join either the middle class, whose lives he views as shallow, materialistic, and meaningless, or the revolutionaries whose ideological solutions are unacceptable. Although the writers repeatedly express their belief, though not as explicitly as Gorky, that the Russian intellectual has to develop self-respect, confidence, and courage, they also convey a fear that this generation of intellectuals is unable to change. They saw the relationship of the intelligentsia to all groups in society as problematic, based on a complex of anxieties, illusions, and misunderstandings. Unlike those of their contemporaries who found satisfaction in the aesthetic or spiritual world or in the revolution, the writers in the Sreda circle were primarily interested in social reality. Confronted with revolution, they were overwhelmed.

Each writer witnessed the violence and chaos of 1905; several were personally threatened by the Black Hundreds because they were considered revolutionaries. Their response to the violence differed from Gorky's, however, for he did not condemn the violence per se, only its chaos and ineffectiveness. The revolution inevitably led to the circle's dissolution, for in the polarized situation that developed the writers realized that they could not assume the role Gorky had prescribed for them as revolutionaries and writer-warriors. They had chosen to be writers, not because they felt a moral calling, as Gorky did and tried to instill in them, but because they wanted to understand their society while still retaining their political independence. Gorky's decision to join the Bolsheviks weakened his moral authority. Only two other members— Veresaev and Serafimovich—were willing to make that commitment.

In the years following 1905 the writers maintained their friendship, but Gorky was living in Italy, and the others spent much time outside of Russia. Inevitably their political differences led to literary disagreements and occasional personal clashes. Gorky attempted to keep his control over *Znanie*, but eventually broke with it in 1911. He also continued to encourage Sreda writers to create positive, socially inspiring literature. He felt that they had become too involved in their own selfish needs and that their literary works were decadent and pornographic.[42] Yet even Gorky's views of the writer's role had changed. Although he still believed writers had to conquer their own fears and become strong social leaders, he was more willing to admit that the role of the writer in Russia was terribly difficult and painful. Nonetheless, he insisted that the abyss between the intelligentsia and the people could be overcome.[43]

Between the Revolutions of 1905 and 1917, the Sreda circle was to meet again. Several former members reorganized Sreda in 1911 to include younger realists. But Gorky's original group of close associates, though preserving

---

[42] Gor'kii to Andreev, Aug. 16–Oct. 8, 1911, *Literaturnoe nasledstvo*, 72: 319.
[43] Ibid.

their ties, had dissolved by the end of 1905. Until the Revolution of 1917, the writers cooperated in several literary ventures as they had in the past. Some of the best writers in the group—Andreev, Bunin, and Kuprin—emigrated after the revolution, feeling that there was no place for them in Soviet society. Gorky, of course, welcomed the revolution as the dawn of the new age, but he too was rapidly disappointed by the Bolsheviks' policies. The Sreda writers keenly felt and depicted the social antagonisms that shattered Russian society from 1917 to 1921, yet they felt powerless to forestall the explosion by promoting mutual trust between obshchestvo and narod. Although few of them ever fully shared Gorky's optimism that they could indeed play a major part in leading the Russian people, they admired and worked with him because he gave them support and confidence and because they wanted to believe that perhaps he was not as naive and simplistic as they thought. However, in seeking their own identity as intellectuals, they inevitably rejected Gorky's definition of their role. When violence actually broke out in 1905, their fears, ambivalent feelings of identity, and sense of powerlessness led them to retreat before the revolutionary commitment that Gorky demanded. The revolution had, in the words of Andreev, "ripped off the masks" and forced the writers to recognize who they really were.[44] Nevertheless, these writers left valuable documents of social consciousness, pictures of the turmoil in both Russian society and their own minds.

[44] L. Andreev to Veresaev, April 1906, in V. V. Veresaev, "Leonid Andreev," *Sobranie sochinenii*, 5 vols. (Moscow, 1961), 5: 407–8.

Chapter 19

BUILDING FOR THE BOURGEOISIE: THE QUEST FOR A MODERN STYLE IN RUSSIAN ARCHITECTURE

WILLIAM C. BRUMFIELD

THE QUESTION of architecture and middle-class identity in turn-of-century Russia involves two separate but closely related topics, each of which has a specific connection to the process of social alignment. The rise of a new sense of professionalism among Russian architects during the latter half of the nineteenth century—the development of architecture institutes, the foundation of professional societies, and the establishment of structures to supervise professional competence—suggests that architects must themselves be placed among the professional groups to be considered in forming a middle class. Beyond this relation between professional and class identity lies the much broader issues of the clientele served by the profession, the social definition of those who commissioned the buildings, and the status of those who lived and worked in them. Ultimately, one might include a broad network of relationships based on the specific social and economic needs that influence the practice of architecture: new building types, technological innovations required for their construction, new means of financing construction.

The challenge presented to architecture by the rapid growth of major Russian cities at the end of the century resulted in building projects whose scale and technical ingenuity were unprecedented. Although their function was not specifically defined by social class, in the majority of cases they were funded by private capital for purposes of financial gain, which in turn required a clientele willing to spend on a scale sufficient to guarantee a profit.[1] (An obvious indication of this mechanism appears in the most common Russian term for "apartment house" during this period: *dokhodnyi dom*, or "profitable house.") The traditional estate division of pre-Reform Russia was of little use in meeting these conditions, based as they were on the presence of an urban population with a reasonably stable level of disposable income.

---

[1] Among numerous studies of housing patterns in St. Petersburg and Moscow at the turn of the century (with references to contemporary census data), see James Bater, *St. Petersburg: Industrialization and Change* (Montreal: Queen's University Press, 1976), 370–79; and Joseph Bradley, *Muzhik and Muscovite: Urbanization in Late Imperial Russia* (Berkeley: University of California Press, 1985), 229–36. Although the data reveal that the nobility comprised a significant part of the population of certain areas, the ability to pay rent, not class status, affected the quality and design of housing during the tremendous expansion of both cities.

To be sure, the growth in urban construction ranged from tenements to dwellings for the very wealthy; but architecture in the usual stylistic sense was directed primarily to that portion of citizens whose income and life-style placed them in a middle category, regardless of their legal status. Indeed, for certain prominent critics of the early twentieth century, architecture acquired a sense of purpose precisely to the extent that it served this group, whose existence—specifically mentioned in the architectural press—was viewed as axiomatic to the growth of the profession. In architectural criticism, building for this class meant building for a future with greater social and economic opportunity.

In examining the relation between architecture and class identity at the turn of the century, we turn to the work of the era's preeminent architect, Fedor Osipovich Shekhtel (1859–1926), whose buildings for bourgeois patrons such as the Riabushinskys represent the highest expression of the uses of private capital in support of a new architectural aesthetic. Quite apart from its stylistic innovations, Shekhtel's work projects in material form aspects of the economic order envisioned by politically active members of the Riabushinsky family—efficiency, practicality, innovation, *delovitost'*. Without the order that the Riabushinskys, above all, so energetically promoted, the prosperity and survival of a middle class would become very dubious propositions, as would the architecture that served them. At the same time Shekhtel's work transcends the limits of class definition, in both its ability to experiment with new forms and its refusal to accept the clichés of "profitable" architecture.

One need not provide a sociological profile of architects to recognize the importance of professionalization to the issue of middle-class identity, not only reflecting a new social alignment, but also expressing the self-image of those entering the profession. The beginnings of such cohesion in Russian architecture date from the 1860s, when architects in both St. Petersburg and Moscow realized the need to create an association that would rise above narrow commercial interests to address problems confronting architects as a group. The reforms of the 1860s not only facilitated the economic development necessary to expand architecture beyond the commissions of state, court, and a few wealthy property owners, but they also created the legal conditions for the foundation of private associations. Although certain St. Petersburg architects had begun to explore the concept of a professional group as early as 1862, Moscow had the first formal organization—the Moscow Architectural Society, chartered in October 1867.[2] From the outset the society served as a clearinghouse for technical information and a center for the establishment of stan-

---

[2] For a detailed survey of the organization and early years of the Russian architectural societies, see Iu. S. Iaralov, ed., *100 let obshchestvennvkh arkhitekturnykh organizatsii v SSSR, 1867–1967* (Moscow: Soiuz arkhitektorov SSSR, 1967), 5–13.

dards in building materials and practices. In addition to its advisory function in technical matters, the society initiated a series of open architectural competitions as early as 1868, thus establishing a precedent to be followed in the award of major building contracts during the latter half of the century. An attempt by the society to sponsor a general conference of architects in 1873 failed for bureaucratic reasons, and not until 1892 did the first Congress of Russian Architects convene.[3]

In the meantime, architects in the capital had obtained imperial approval for founding the Petersburg Society of Architects (October 1870), whose functions paralleled those of the Moscow society. At the beginning of 1872 the St. Petersburg group published the first issue of the journal *Zodchii* (The Architect), which appeared on a monthly—and later weekly—basis through 1917. For forty-five years this authoritative publication both recorded the profession's development throughout Russia and provided a conduit for technical information from Western Europe and the United States. It would be difficult to overestimate the importance of *Zodchii* in its support of professional solidarity among architects and as a platform from which to advance ideas on architecture's mission in creating a new urban environment.[4]

The process of professionalization in architecture signified an increase in the demand for competent professionals who could construct various buildings for a diverse clientele in a way that would be cost-effective and reliable and meet certain aesthetic expectations. Whatever the limitations of tradition and a backward technological base, the architects of this period made considerable progress in meeting the requirements of the post-Reform era, with the construction of educational institutions, shopping arcades, banks and other financial centers, apartment buildings, hospitals, public theaters, exhibit halls, hotels, city administrative buildings, railway and industrial structures, and mansions for the newly wealthy (Figs. 13, 14).

At the same time some factors raised doubts about the goals of the profession, its social standing, and its aesthetic judgment. The profusion of styles characteristic of European eclecticism in general was the subject of ridicule in the Russian press, particularly in commentary on the housing boom in St. Petersburg.[5] Suspended between the commercialism of private enterprise and the public scrutiny of the press, architects were subjected to a plethora of claims and opinions on their performance. The ensuing mood of frustration, if

[3] Ibid., 11–12.

[4] Publication data on this and other prerevolutionary architectural journals can be found in the four volumes of L. N. Beliaeva et al., *Bibliografiia periodicheskikh izdanii Rossii: 1901–1916* (Leningrad: Publichnaia biblioteka imeni M. E. Saltykova-Shchedrina, 1961). See also Iaralov, *100 let obshchestvennvkh*, 103–6.

[5] A notable critical response appeared in Fedor Dostoevsky's extensive digression on architecture in an 1873 issues of "Dnevnik pisatelia." F. M. Dostoevsky, *Polnoe sobranie sochinenii v tridtsati tomakh* (Leningrad: Nauka, 1980), 21: 106–7.

Fig. 13. S. P. Riabushinsky house, Moscow (1900–1902). Architect: Fedor Shekhtel.
Photograph: William Brumfield.

Fig. 14. Riabushinsky house, interior, main stairway (1900–1902). Architect: Fedor Shekhtel. Photograph: William Brumfield.

not self-pity, is expressed by one of *Zodchii*'s architect-critics, V. Kuroedov, writing in 1876 on his impressions of architecture in Berlin. The contrast between the position of the German architect and the Russian does not favor the latter: "In our country an architect is a hireling, obligated for his remuneration to fulfill someone else's will without thinking; in our country, in short, architecture and its practitioners enjoy no respect, rights, or support on a level with other specialists."[6] This observation is particularly interesting as a commentary on the problem of professional identity, with its reference to "other specialists." Just whom Kuroedov had in mind is unclear, but the sense of inferiority in both professional rights and artistic integrity is pointedly noted. The economic mechanism—that is, speculative capitalism—that had created a new professional basis for architecture had also become, in the view of many observers, the bane of the profession's existence. In the search for a solution beyond rampant eclecticism, critics, historians, and architects made claims for a "rational" or "national" style or some combination of both, thus placing upon architecture the additional role as interpreter of the nation's history (for example, Vladimir Shervud's Historical Museum, 1874–1883).[7] New technological methods and economic demands, however, led to a greater emphasis on engineering in ways that ran counter to the advocacy of historicism and nationalism.

Although the profession as a whole remained largely untouched by the debates on stylistic questions that dominated the two architectural congresses in 1892 and 1895, the architectural societies and professional journals maintained a sense of confraternity among architects and engineers. In this they were supported by the expansion of architectural schools such as the Academy of Arts, which simplified its designation of graduates to "architect-artists" and "artist-architects," with the former more qualified in architecture.[8] St. Petersburg's other major institution for architectural education, the Institute of Civil Engineering, experienced especially rapid growth: in 1892 it enrolled 222 students, while the total number of its graduates in the preceding fifty years was only 1,020. Those whose professional training came from the Academy, the Institute of Civil Engineering, or the Moscow School of Painting, Sculpture, and Architecture were among the elite of the profession; and yet graduation from these and other institutions of higher technical education was

[6] V. Kuroedov, "Berlinskaia arkhitektura. Putevye zametki," *Zodchii* 7 (1876): 79.

[7] See N. V. Sultanov, "Odna iz zadach stroitel'nogo uchilishcha," *Zodchii* 5 (1882): 71; A. L. Punin, "Idei ratsionalizma v russkoi arkhitekture vtoroi poloviny XIX veka," in *Arkhitektura SSSR* 11 (1962): 55–58. E. A. Borisova devotes much attention to the "national/rational" question in her book *Russkaia arkhitektura vtoroi poloviny XIX veka* (Moscow: Nauka, 1979), particularly chaps. 4 and 5.

[8] V. G. Isachenko et al., *Arkhitektory-stroiteli Peterburga-Petrograda nachala XX veka* (Leningrad: Vserossiiskoe obshchestvo okhrany pamiatnikov istorii i kul'tury, 1982), 4–5.

not an absolute requirement for success in architectural practice, as the career of Fedor Shekhtel demonstrates.

The coexistence in architecture of art and engineering occasionally created a sense of divergent interests, noticeable at architectural congresses. By the turn of the century, however, it appeared that the profession had entered a phase of confidence in its position—at least to judge by the profusion of architectural publications that joined *Zodchii* in conveying to the public developments in contemporary Russian architecture.[9] Lavishly illustrated with photographs of recently completed buildings, drawings from project competitions, and on occasion student work, these journals publicized, as never before, the accomplishments of members of the various architectural societies.

In surveying the architectural journals one gains the impression that Russia was indeed moving toward integration with bourgeois Europe, with tangible evidence in the form of a rapidly changing cityscape, created by and for the institutions of capitalism. Perhaps by the very nature of their content, most publications studiously avoided political or social commentary, even during the revolutionary years of 1905–1906; and there is little reason to suppose that architects were involved in these events. A notable exception was Aleksandr Glebovich Uspensky, son of the prominent populist writer and graduate of the Institute of Civil Engineering. Uspensky is said to have supported the uprising, and his death at age thirty-three in 1907 elicited an impassioned commentary on architecture and social justice.[10]

If one reads those few critics who commented in the professional press on the social ramifications of architecture, however, a curious, at times contradictory, picture emerges—one that leads to the issue of architecture as a bearer of bourgeois culture. An early, rather crude statement of the profession's priorities in building for a middle class appeared in a presentation at the Second Congress of Russian Architects (1895), which addressed the need for improved apartment housing. Of the four categories of apartment listed—luxury, mid-level (or *srednei ruki*), low-cost, and substandard—only the second offered the possiblity for realistic improvement. The creation of adequate housing for the lower classes was viewed by the speaker as desirable for humanitarian reasons, but impractical (i.e., unprofitable) from an economic standpoint.[11] Given the lack of a coordinated housing policy on the part of city government, the speaker simply stated the obvious: the economic future for

---

[9] Among the most comprehensive in terms of photographic documentation are *Ezhegodnik Obshchestva Arkhitektorov-khudozhnikov* (based in Petersburg) and *Ezhegodnik Moskovskogo Arkhitekturnogo Obshchestva* (Moscow).

[10] P. M[akar]ov, "Aleksandr Glebovich Uspenskii, kak zodchii i khudozhnik," in *Izvestiia obshestva grazhdanskikh inzhenerov* 4 (1907): 110–11.

[11] S. Ia. Timokhovich, "Proekt blagoustroennikh kvartir v gigienicheskom i sanitarnom otnosheniiakh," in *Trudy II s''ezda russkikh zodchikh v Moskve* (Moscow: Izdanie moskovskogo arkhitekturnogo obshchestva, 1899), 179–85.

~~architects in housing construction lay not with the very rich or the poor,~~ but
with those in the middle.

By the turn of the century, this statement of economic reality began to acquire positive significance in the writings of Pavel Makarov, a graduate of the
Institute of Civil Engineering and a prominent critic for *Zodchii* between 1900
and 1910. Makarov was first and foremost an advocate of the "new style," or
the *style moderne*, which was related to movements in contemporary design
such as Art Nouveau and the Vienna Secession. For him the advent of the new
style was so natural and inevitable a phenomenon that anyone who opposed it
on aesthetic or other grounds was doomed to failure in the attempt to contain
Russia within a "Chinese wall." Therefore the creative person should not fear
"to rush to that principle which nature and the history of civilization demonstrate almost every day [!], namely to the eternal change of one order by another, i.e. to evolution."[12]

To Makarov's considerable indignation, some "Mandarins" rejected the
rush toward progress. Of their number, he chose to attack Aleksandr Benois
in the March 1902 issue of *Zodchii*. The pretext for the attack was Benois's
defense—a defense that Makarov endorsed in principle—of St. Petersburg's
architectural heritage in the January issue of *Mir iskusstva*. The thrust of the
polemic, which would continue throughout the decade in St. Petersburg, derived not from a disavowal of the city's monuments, but from what Makarov
saw as Benois's "aristocratic aestheticism," his disdain for all forms of modern architecture, and his refusal to comprehend the demands placed on architecture by contemporary urban development: "From the heights of aristocratic
aestheticism—acknowledging and respecting only that which was created not
less than a century ago, that which is not besmirched by contemporary materialism, and not vulgarized by the lack of taste of today's bourgeoisie—Mr.
Benois points, not without haughty irony, at that undesirable metamorphosis
that Petersburg is going through now."[13] With his democratic ideal of art and
architecture for the people, Makarov issued the challenge of social responsibility: "If mankind, by the will of fate, must now clamber up five or six stories, then art should hustle up there after them, if only so that the people there
do not die from vulgarity. This is what the goal of a true and free art should
be, to ennoble and beautify life everywhere—for the poor as well as for the
rich."[14]

Already there is considerable confusion in the use of terms, for the "poor"
mentioned in the preceding passage were not likely to be the tenants in the
style moderne apartment buildings that were transforming certain areas of St.
Petersburg and Moscow. Nor would the poor be included among "today's

[12] P. Makarov, "Novyi stil' i dekadenstvo," *Zodchii* 9 (1902): 105.

[13] "Arkhitekturnye mechtaniia," *Zodchii* 13 (1902): 160.

[14] Ibid., 161.

bourgeoisie," toward whom Makarov considers Benois unnecessarily condescending. Whether the issue is democratic art for the poor or contemporary
design for the bourgeoisie, there is an unmistakable tone of class antagonism
in his article, not only in the reference to "aristocratic aestheticism" but also
in his frequent, derogatory references to the nobility (in Russia, "a genuine
noble class never existed," he says at one point).

The term "bourgeois" reappeared in *Zodchii* at the end of 1902 with a
vagueness of usage similar to Makarov's. On this occasion, Evgeny Baumgarten, an adherent of the style moderne and frequent contributor to architectural journals, strongly criticized the recently published third edition of Otto
Wagner's major treatise, *Moderne Architektur*. His objection was directed primarily to Wagner's famous dictum: "Nothing that is not practical can be beautiful," a phrase construed by Baumgarten as nothing less than the destruction
of aesthetics: "Under the guise of responsiveness to contemporary needs, the
theory of Professor Wagner proposes aesthetic suicide. Of course it is necessary to build houses solidly, cheaply, quickly, and conveniently; but the
beauty of a house has no relation to the technique of construction."[15]

For Baumgarten the fault of *Moderne Architektur* lies in its replacing of
eternal values with what he calls the "fleeting views of bourgeois contemporaneity." Quite apart from the highly debatable critical assumptions, which
have little to do with Wagner's grandiose claims for modern architecture,
Baumgarten's repeated use of the term "bourgeois contemporaneity" again
demonstrates a confusion in cultural interpretation. For both Makarov and
Baumgarten, bourgeois had acquired negative connotations, yet both were
dedicated to an aesthetics applicable to the modern world. In point of fact no
Russian architect of the prerevolutionary period achieved the radical break
with tradition advocated by Wagner and practised by Adolf Loos. The concern
with beauty, as traditionally interpreted by Baumgarten, continued to play a
major role in the design of buildngs ranging from commercial structures to
apartment houses: virtually all were intended precisely for the "bourgeoisie."

In view of the importance of the style moderne in creating a new environment for the middle class, there is an odd pathos in statements by critics supporting the moderne as an expression of revolutionary development. While
Makarov wrote of the new style as part of the eternal and inevitable principle
of evolution, his radical colleague Ivan Volodikhin, writing in the journal *Arkhitekturnyi muzei* (Architectural Museum), described the style in maximalist
terms: "The stormy bursts of innovation in architecture, unfortunately manifesting their activities in often rude and thoughtless forms, represent as it were
the beginnings of an uprising, the toppling of power based on an outmoded
system that could not revive itself in time."[16] The subtext is inescapable, and

[15] "Sovremennaia arkhitektura," *Zodchii* 50 (1902): 571.
[16] "Zadachi arkhitekturnoi estetike," *Arkhitekturnyi muzei* 1 (1902): 3.

Volodikhin's extended metaphor of revolution appears throughout the concluding passage, rife with words such as "struggle," "reaction," and "revolution." While the old order may still view the Young pretenders with arrogance, the fatal decline has already begun, according to Volodikhin. Should his readers miss the message, he concludes: "As in the living world, so in architecture there is a struggle between the old and the new."[17]

Does such rhetoric suggest a significant voice among the professions, the middle class, that extolled modernism as part of a democratic movement casting aside the old order? Volodikhin apologizes for the "rude and thoughtless forms" of the "uprising." Yet what type of uprising did he envision—a bourgeois revolution? His aesthetic views were hardly revolutionary in any sense; but with such thirst for change, any innovation might portend the coming of the new order. Even so knowledgeable an architect-critic as Vladimir Apyshkov, whose *The Rational in the Latest Architecture* (1905) was the first successful attempt to assess the Russian *moderne* within the European context, expressed a belief in architectural aesthetics as a regenerative force in society. Less strident than Makarov and Volodikhin, Apyshkov welcomed the changes in the built environment and even the commercialism that they signified. Yet he, too, in the conclusion to this thoughtful work, adopts an extremist view of the moderne: "Not one person who values art is in a position to oppose this movement, whose force is not in the subjective views of individuals, but in a deep and solid bond with our culture, with our technology, with the best democratic aspirations of our century, and with the nascent demands of the truly beautiful."[18]

In retrospect one strains to understand how the style moderne could have represented a radical cultural phenomenon. The situation is complicated further by recent Soviet scholarship, which asserts that the style is profoundly antibourgeois. Evgeniia Kirichenko, a leading interpreter of the *moderne*, has written: "The life-building illusions of the moderne are firmly rooted in its aestheticism, in an aesthetic rejection of *burzhuaznost'* and capitalism just as emphatic as its rejection of revolution. Bourgeois reality repulses by its lack of spirituality, its complacency, mediocrity, and fear of the bright, the strong."[19] From a broad cultural perspective of Russia during the Silver Age, there is much to support this position, particularly in view of the contradictory elements contained within the moderne: rational use of new technology and

---

[17] Ibid., 3 (1902): 23. The conclusion to Volodikhin's article was never published "for reasons not of the editorial board's making." Kazhdan suggests that Volodikhin's revolutionary rhetoric may have been cut by the censor. T. P. Kazhdan, "Arkhitektura i arkhitekturnaia zhizn' Rossii kontsa XIX-nachala XX veka," in *Russkaia khudozhestvennaia kul'tura kontsa XIX-nachala XX veka (1895–1907)* (Moscow: Nauka, 1969), 2: 275, fn. 1.

[18] *Ratsional'noe v noveishei arkhitekture* (Petersburg: T-vo khudozhestvennoi pechati, 1905), 65.

[19] *Russkaia arkhitektura 1830–1910-kh godov* (Moscow: Iskusstvo, 1978), 284.

materials on one hand, and on the other a tendency toward a flamboyant expression of form and decoration. While exploiting functional approaches to the construction of apartment buildings and commercial structures, the moderne retained a romantic, aesthetic impulse that would indeed appear to contradict the conformity and alienation of the urban environment. Although these contradictions were justified in the critical excerpts quoted above as part of the democratization of art, they might just as easily have served as devices to increase the visibility—and therefore economic value—of buildings in a speculative market.

This duality of economic concerns and aestheticism is typical of twentieth-century architecture, but the intensity with which Russian architectural critics debated the proper relation between style, money, and urban development in the two decades before 1917 suggests a deeper polarization in society and culture. Indeed, the work of Fedor Shekhtel illustrates not only the creative blending of functionalism and decorative aestheticism but also the ultimate failure of the new style to survive in the rapidly expanding commercial environment of Moscow and St. Petersburg. Shekhtel's close working relations with members of Moscow's entrepreneurial elite—the Morozovs, Riabushinskys, Kuznetsovs, and others—convey the impression of an architect committed to the economic and cultural milieu of a developing bourgeois society in Russia.[20] Yet aspects of Shekhtel's career suggest something more complex than a remarkable talent in service to the marketplace, and the complexity increases as Shekhtel's career evolves. Its beginning stages—from the mid-1880s to the mid-1890s—are devoted to building or remodeling mansions and dachas, usually in some flamboyant, eclectic style. Although not equal to the tastelessness achieved by many of his contemporaries, this is still the architecture of conspicuous consumption, cheerfully indulged by a young artist with a taste for the theatrical.

During the mid-1890s the flamboyance was still present (for example, in the mansion for Savva and Zinaida Morozov) but subsumed within a tectonic and spatial system of increasing sophistication. At the turn of the century Shekhtel created his most distinctive houses, for Stepan Pavlovich Riabushinsky (1900–1902, Figs. 15, 16) and Aleksandra Derozhinskaia (1901). The design of the former, with its chapel isolated from the luxuriant moderne decor of the rest of the house, demonstrates with remarkable clarity a tension between the Old Believer traditions of the Riabushinsky family and the desire to express a cultural identity representative of the wealth and aspirations of a new bour-

---

[20] The primary authority on the work of Shekhtel is E. I. Kirichenko, author of the monograph *Fedor Shekhtel* (Moscow: Stroiizdat, 1973) and numerous articles on the architect. In English the best survey is by Catherine Cooke, ''Fedor Osipovich Shekhtel: An Architect and His Clients in Turn-of-century Moscow,'' *Architectural Association Files* (London), 5–6 (1984): 5–31.

Fig. 15. Riabushinsky house, main stairway (1900–1902). Architect: Fedor Shekhtel.
Photograph: William Brumfield.

geois elite.[21] During the course of the decade, however, the focus of Shekhtel's work shifted to commercial buildings in a more functional style and to
museums, churches and social institutions. Between 1910 and 1916 most of
his projects remained unbuilt: few had any connection with his former patrons.

The English architectural historian Catherine Cooke has stated that Shekhtel's work projected a "conception of a bourgeois-industrial Russia, and a
corresponding culture, through the medium of architecture."[22] Like Kirichenko's treatment of the moderne as an antibourgeois phenomenon, this view
has much to recommend it: yet both dramatize the situation. Shekhtel's architecture must indeed have represented the aspirations of certain of his bourgeois patrons, but it differs in significant ways from the work of other well-
established architects in Moscow at the beginning of the century. He did not
use an indiscriminate stylistic repertoire to cater to the demands of fashion—
a practice common among many successful designers of speculative apartment buildings. Although his career spanned several styles, his mature

[21] James West discusses the political views of the Riabushinsky circle in "The Rjabusinskij
Circle: Russian Industrialists in Search of a Bourgeoisie, 1909–1914," *Jahrbücher für Geschichte
Osteuropas* 32 (1984): 358–77. For an analysis of the S. P. Riabushinsky house, see William
Brumfield, "The Decorative Arts in Russian Architecture: 1900–1907," *Journal of Decorative
and Propaganda Arts* 5 (1987): 23–26.
[22] Cooke, "Shekhtel," 27.

Fig. 16. Riabushinsky house, interior, stained glass window (1900–1902). Architect: Fedor Shekhtel. Photograph: William Brumfield.

work showed a logic that would not be deflected by purely commercial considerations.

Furthermore, Shekhtel's use of the style moderne moved rapidly toward a rationalist interpretation of design, as in his Riabushinsky bank (1903) and *Utro Rossii* printing works (1907, Fig. 17), and his building for the Moscow Merchants Society (1909). This entailed a diminished emphasis on the decorative elements and, correspondingly, showed an indifference to the aestheti-

Fig. 17. Utro Rossii printing office, Moscow (1907). Architect: Fedor Shekhtel. *Ezhegodnik moskovskogo arkhitekturnogo obshchestva* (Annual of the Moscow Architectural Society), 1909.

cism associated with visions of a new architecture for the middle class. To be sure, Shekhtel produced at least one apartment building (for the Stroganov School, in 1904) that combined brilliantly both the aesthetic and the functional: yet his Shamshin apartment house of 1909 is almost totally lacking in "beautifying elements," apart from a cornice frieze. Here, as in his commercial buildings, the structure creates its own, rational form of aesthetics (Fig. 18).

At the end of the 1900s, Shekhtel experimented with the neoclassical revival for his own house (1909) on Bol'shaia Sadovaia, and he also designed a number of projects in a "neo-Russian" style. Yet the fact that he built little in the 1910s indicates a cultural impasse, a loss of the moderne aesthetic in an era of large commercial structures (Fig. 19). The rapid decline of the style moderne toward the end of the first decade suggests that the pronounced dualism between functionalism and romantic aestheticism—with its emphasis on the individual character of each project—could not be reconciled, despite expectations of new forms capable of transforming the urban environment.

In the years immediately preceding the outbreak of war, the style moderne aesthetic had been largely discarded by architects as well as architectural critics; and in its wake there appeared retrospective styles such as the neoclassical revival, which had its moments of brilliance in both Moscow and St. Petersburg. In the latter, some welcomed the demise of modernity and a return to a style more compatible with the St. Petersburg ensemble, without realizing the extent to which concepts underlying the moderne had penetrated all styles, particularly in large-scale commercial projects. A number of architects turned to city planning, which emphasized a regulated, instead of idiosyncratic, approach to style; and others looked to the New World and the American skyscraper as a model for the future.[23]

Yet the rejection of the moderne involved not simply a change of styles on a common technical base, but an opposition to all that the new style represented on a social and cultural level for critics such as Makarov and Apyshkov. There could be no clearer statement of this opposition than Georgy Lukomsky's article "New Petersburg," in a 1913 issue of *Apollon*. Taking a frankly monarchist position in the year of the Romanov tercentenary, this devotee of Russia's artistic heritage insisted that great architecture derives from the power of the state and church: "Therefore, all efforts to present New Petersburg only on the basis of proposed conditions in economy and hygiene can

---

[23] In addition to frequent articles on aspects of city planning in architectural journals at the beginning of the century, a number of books on urban planning and garden cities appeared between 1910 and 1916. Reports on American skyscrapers were also prominently featured in journals such as *Zodchii*; see, for example, N. Lakhtin's article in *Zodchii* 18 (1913): 203–11. See William Brumfield, "Russian Perceptions of American Architecture, 1870–1917," *Architecture and the New Urban Environment: Western Influences on Modernism in Russia and the USSR* (Washington, D.C.: Kennan Institute, 1988), 51–70.

Fig. 18. Shamshin apartment house, Moscow (1909). Architect: Fedor Shekhtel. *Ezhe-godnik moskovskogo arkhitekturnogo obshchestva*, 1910–1911.

Fig. 19. "Delovoi dvor" office complex, Moscow (1912–1913). Architect: Ivan Kuznetsov. *Ezhegodnik obshchestva arkhitektorov-khudozhnikov*, 1913.

lead to nothing other than pale, gray facades. For just this reason, the entire epoch of bourgeois and democratic modernism has given Petersburg *nothing*."[24] However contentious these views, they were widely held by architects and critics in both major cities—hence the rise of retrospectivism advocated by Lukomsky. The process of privately funded urban development would continue in Russia (for two more years), but the ideal of a new architecture expressive of the democratic ethos of the bourgeoisie had long since vanished.

[24] "Novyi Peterburg (Mysli o sovremennom stroitel'stve)," *Apollon* 2 (1913): 10. Lukomskii was to expand on these views in his survey of the neoclassical revival, *Sovremennyi Petrograd* (Petrograd: Svobodnoe Iskusstvo, 1916). By that time Ivan Fomin had already designed his neoclassical development "New Petersburg," intended for Golodai Island.

Chapter 20

A PLACE FOR US: *EMBOURGEOISEMENT* AND THE ART OF KONSTANTIN KOROVIN

JAMES M. CURTIS

No ISSUE has caused more debate in Russian culture than that of the relationship between art and society—or, to formulate it more appropriately, the relationship between creativity and the society in which it arises. For more than a century now, various forms of the romantic assumption that we can best understand art if we study the artist's conscious intentions, ideology, and state of mind have predominated in this debate. However, autobiographical and ideological interpretations do not work well with artists such as the Impressionist painter Konstantin Korovin (1861–1939). A representative figure of late nineteenth-century aestheticism, and an inarticulate one at that, Korovin had no known social "views" and took no interest in what Russians call *obshchestvennaia zhizn'*. Korovin painted for the joy of it and would not have known how to define, much less use, the word "ideology."

It might appear, then, that Korovin's work has little to offer a discussion of middle-class consciousness in the last years of the Russian empire. Yet art styles often express a response to social processes without seeming to do so, and they often express this response most completely when the artists create without a conscious desire to give their work social significance. So one can ask whether Impressionism in Russia—and specifically Korovin's work—is also related to Russian middle-class consciousness, and if so, how. I believe not only that it is but also that Korovin's paintings can help us understand something important about the social processes of late nineteenth-century Russia, especially when we consider them in their European context.

It is useful to begin by characterizing, however briefly, the differences between the social structures of Russia and France at the time. Various contributors to this volume mention that Russia, unlike France and England, did not have a middle class with its own institutions and power bases, and thus we cannot use such terms as "middle class" or "bourgeoisie" without awkward qualifications. Yet how do we describe the appearance of railroad firms, banking comglomerates, and art patronage in post-Emancipation Russia? How do we discuss the substantial geographical and social mobility that undoubtedly occurred?

We can obviate such difficulties by following up Abbott Gleason's comment that the Russian revolution was not a single dramatic event that occurred in 1917 but a process of modernization that lasted for about a hundred years, from the end of the Crimean War in 1855 to the death of Stalin in 1953. Analogously, we may say that while no coherent, self-conscious middle class existed at a given moment in tsarist Russia, such a class was in the process of being formed. We can therefore use the French term *embourgeoisement* (German *Verbürgerlichung*) to refer to this process, which includes such general trends as industrialization, secularization, and urbanization. Overall such trends produce a society that allowed for greater social mobility, often at the price of a coherent personal identity.

Although these trends were occurring in Russian society, they had not reached a stage of development comparable to that in France. As it happens, a number of art historians, most notably T. J. Clark in *The Painting of Modern Life*,[1] have made various connections between embourgeoisement in France and the Impressionist painters whose work greatly affected Korovin. Thus, a chronological survey of his career, with particular attention to his reception and use of Impressionist techniques and subject matter, can help us understand embourgeoisement in Russia.

In relating individual identity, social structure, and art in Korovin's life, two important biographical facts about his father have great signficance: his religious identity and his profession. First, he was an Old Believer, like the powerful Morozovs and the Riabushinskys whom James West discusses. While the association between Protestants in Europe and Old Believers in Russia is general, one requiring various qualifications, it nevertheless has a certain suggestive quality because a number of important entrepreneurs were Old Believers. Korovin's evolution from the ethos of the Old Believer to the ethos of the artistic free spirit is less startling than it might appear, since artists, like Old Believers, had only a tenuous link to society as a whole. In the terminology of Michel Foucault, which Clark has adopted, both groups existed on "the margins" of society, and Foucault has argued that we find the genesis of the modern sensibility there.

The second significant fact about Korovin's father is that he owned a livery stable. When we recall the railroad boom that began to restructure the Russian economy in the 1860s and 1870s, we realize that industrialization endangered the elder Korovin's livelihood; in fact, his livery business eventually dwindled to nothing because of competition from the railroads. Unable to deal with this trauma, he committed suicide.[2]

There is no obvious relationship between Korovin's artistic career and his father's suicide because none of his paintings even hint at darker emotions. Thus, we are not dealing here with simple autobiographical references.

---

[1] See T. J. Clark, *The Painting of Modern Life* (New York: Alfred A. Knopf, 1985).

[2] On Korovin's father, see Dora Kogan, *Konstantin Korovin* (Moscow: Iskusstvo, 1964), 14.

Rather, this is a matter of the psychology of creativity, the branch of psychology that studies patterns in the life cycle of artists without interpreting their works. To comprehend the significance of Korovin's father's suicide, we need to relate this isolated fact to the conclusions of numerous studies of the careers of Western artists. Before we can do so, however, we must acknowledge the validity of working with Russian material through reasoning by analogy with the far better investigated and documented material from the lives of Western artists. Second, and more vital, we must acknowledge that scholarship on that much-debated issue can legitimately draw on the conclusions of the social sciences. Korovin may be used as a test case in applying the psychology of creativity to the career of a Russian artist.

In this matter, as in several others in this essay, the crucial issue is the meaning of patterns in the lives and works of artists. A substantial body of literature on the psychology of creativity shows a definite correlation between an impaired relationship with the father and the formation of an artistic personality.[3] Some commentators have speculated that a father who dies at a relatively young age, who is frequently absent, or who does not play a substantial role in the family (e.g., he fails to support the family, as Korovin's father did) gives rise to both female and male identity and that such an androgynous personality structure fosters creativity.[4] In this context, the unstable economic climate in post-Emancipation Russia seems related to the appearance of artists from the families of nonaristocrats. We notice a similar pattern in the lives of writer Anton Chekhov and painter Isaac Levitan, whose fathers also went bankrupt, although they did not commit suicide.

As luck would have it, Korovin found a surrogate father figure in the artist Vasily Polenov, who gave the younger man much-needed support and encouragement. At the same time, Russia's greatest nineteenth-century painter, Ilia Repin, was acting as a similar father figure to the young Valentin Serov, whose own father, the composer Anatoly Serov, died when his son was three years old. Such quasi-familial relationships between the generations of Russian painters created a continuity lacking in France at that time. Whereas in France the presence of a powerful academy, a well-defined art public, and influential art critics forced the Impressionists to look to each other for help and support, the very absence of institutions in Russia was conducive to closeness between the generations.

When Korovin began his first serious paintings in the late 1880s, Impressionism was coming to an end as a coherent movement in France. The eighth

---

[3] See, for instance, J. Marvin Eisenstadt, "Parental Loss and Genius," *American Psychologist* 32 (March 1978): 211–22.

[4] See Robert S. Albert, "Cognitive Development and Parental Loss among the Gifted, the Exceptionally Gifted and the Creative," *Psychological Reports* 29 (1971): 19–26; and Colin Martindale, "Father absence, psychopathology, and poetic eminence," *Psychological Reports* 31 (1972): 843–47.

and last Impressionist exhibit took place in 1886, and such major Post-Impressionist painters as Paul Gauguin, Odilon Redon, and Georges Seurat exhibited at it. Phoebe Pool says that, ''In the early 1860s each of the great Impressionists became obsessed with problems of style and went through a process of doubt.''[5] In particular, Renoir went to Italy in 1881, and the art he saw there made him decide that he needed to return to firmer handling of masses and more classical modeling. Renoir, born in 1840, was a recognized master by the time Korovin, twenty-one years his junior, and thus a contemporary of Seurat, was a beginning art student. Dmitry Sarabianov has made such matters of chronology the determining factor in the reception of Impressionism in Russia.[6] Chronology is indeed important, but not quite in the way Sarabianov thinks.

It is convenient to date the beginning of Post-Impressionism as a self-conscious movement in 1889, when Felix Fenelon coined the term ''art de synthese,'' in opposition to what one might call the Impressionists' ''art de Antithese.''[7] Art historian Werner Hoffman rightly refers to this term in characterizing much of modern painting as ''the crisis of the easel picture.'' Thus, he comments that, ''Gauguin, for instance, carves a folding screen and a walking stick; his potteries include plates, vases, and a tobacco jar.''[8] In the spirit of Art Nouveau, not of Impressionism, which was interested only in *plein air* easel painting, Korovin applied his talent to whatever came to hand. In addition to his easel paintings, he created set designs, stage costumes, furniture, and what we would nowadays call ''installations'' in the Pavilion of the Far North at the Nizhny Novgorod Exhibition in 1896 and in the Russian Pavilion at the Paris exposition of 1900. Like that of his friend and contemporary, Fyodor Shekhtel, Korovin's career exhibits many varieties of artistic expression. Thus, we can think of Korovin's career as a lengthy search for an artistic identity. His challenge was to develop his own talent by reworking Impressionism, but it was a style of painting that had arisen in response to a set of historical conditions nonexistent in Russia.

What Korovin, as well as his contemporaries such as Isaac Levitan and Valentin Serov, did take from French Impressionism is easy enough to see: plein-air painting, loose brush strokes, pastel colors, and atmospheric effects. However, what they did not take is as important as what they did take; this corresponds to what Roland Barthes has called ''the zero degree of writing''—the absence of something that is as significant as the presence of something.

---

[5] Phoebe Pool, *Impressionism* (New York: Frederick Praeger, 1969), 216.

[6] See Sarabyanov's remarks on Korovin, for instance, in ''K voprosu o spetsifike russkogo impressionizma,'' in D. B. Sarabyanov, *Russkaia zhovopis' XIX veka sredi evropeiskikh shkol* (Moscow: Sovetskii khudozhnik, 1980), 172.

[7] See Werner Hofmann, *Turning Points in Twentieth-Century Art: 1890–1917*, trans. Charles Kessler (New York: George Braziller, n.d.), 20.

[8] Ibid., 23.

As often happens, the specific features of Russian culture become distinct only in contrast to those of other cultures. In the case of Korovin and his contemporaries, only a series of references to the principal features of French Impressionism can provide the missing term of comparison.

We can see Korovin's ambiguous response to Impressionism in *Girl at the Threshold* (1880s), where the glorious handling of the light makes the girl so radiant. Yet this girl holds a lyre—no mortal woman, she is the painter's Muse. Nothing was more foreign to the Impressionists than such mythological references, recalled the academic painting they detested. As art historian Richard Shiff has said, "The impressionist sought a technique or means of expression that would convey his own spontaneity, orginality, and sincerity; above all he wished to avoid traditional academic conventions because they would link his art to a communal school rather than to a unique temperament."[9] Thus, *Girl at the Threshold* both is, and is not, an Impressionist painting.

Korovin's most ambitious painting of the 1880s, *At the Tea Table* (1888), depicts various members of the Polenov family seated around the table on the veranda at Zhukovka, their estate where Korovin spent that summer. The picture may well represent Korovin's response to Impressionist paintings because there is some evidence that he made a quick trip to Paris in 1887. Certainly many elements of the painting—the loosely painted foliage, the off-center composition, the sense of the moment, and the chair in the lower right-hand corner pulled back as if to invite the viewer to join the group—recall Impressionism. In particular, the vantage point of *At the Tea Table* is the same as that of Renoir's *Un Dejeuner de Bougival* (1880–1881), now known as *The Luncheon of the Boating Party*; there are also similarities in the renderings of the glassware and table linen. Yet Renoir's painting exhibits feathery brush strokes that create what Shiff has called the "integration of perceiving subject and preceived object."[10] These brush strokes are essentially the same over the entire surface of the painting. Korovin, however, uses loose brush strokes for the foliage at the top of the painting but delineates the faces and bodies of the people more distinctly than Renoir, and he thereby retains a more distinct sense of interaction among them. The similarities in the overall composition point up the differences between both the settings of the two paintings and more generally the ways French and Russian painters represented their societies' organized cultural environments.

Whereas *The Luncheon of the Boating Party* shows a group of people in a public place, a restaurant, *At the Tea Table* shows people in a private place, the veranda of an estate. By contrast, some of the most famous paintings of

---

[9] Richard Shiff, "The End of Impressionism," in *The New Painting: Impressionism, 1874–1886*, ed, Charles S. Moffet et al. (San Fransicso: Fine Art Museum, 1986), 83.

[10] Ibid., 74.

the Impressionist era, such as Manet's *The Bar of the Folies Bergère* (1867), Renoir's *The Ball at the Moulin de la Galette* (1876); and Seurat's *Sunday Afternoon on the Island of Grande-Jatte* (1884–1886), all depict people in contemporary clothing in public places that were familiar to the paintings' viewers. When the artists created such works, they were, among other things, responding to the new social organization of space created by the principal agent of change in the nineteenth century, the railroads. Clark has pointed out that "the railroad lines laid down since 1850, especially those to the west of the city, had quite abruptly rendered the countryside available to Paris, as part of weekend or even a work day."[11] As technological change made new places of leisure accessible to the bourgeoisie, the Impressionists' paintings began legitimizing their presence there by depicting them in great works of art.

Despite the importance of railroads in Russia at the time, no Russian artist depicted people enjoying themselves in well-known public places. Despite the importance of Moscow industrialists as art patrons, we have no paintings of Russian factories from this period—no Russian equivalents of Pissarro's *Factory near Pontoise* (1873), for example. Moreover, no Russian artist depicted the new urban enrivonment, as Monet did, for instance, in his series of paintings of Gare St. Lazare in Paris during the 1870s. It is most significant that in this period all the important paintings of public places in Moscow—such as Andrei Riabushkin's *Wedding Procession in Moscow (Seventeenth Century)* (1901) and Apollinary Vasnetsov's *Moscow at the End of the Seventeenth Century* (1900), both of which use a quasi-Impressionist style—are set in the distant, almost fairy-tale past. This contrast between the subject matter of Russian and French paintings in the late nineteenth century is apparent to anyone who studies the paintings in question. What is less apparent is the social meaing of this contrast, or even that there can *be* any social meaning at all.

Those who adhere to the nineteenth-century belief that art has only the meaning of which the artists were conscious while they were painting are in effect espousing a behavioristic model of human activity. While the appeal of behaviorism is such that people will continue to believe in it, the interrelated work of neurologists and linguists makes it apparent that much goes on in the human psyche to which we have no conscious, verbal access. Assuming that this is the case, I conclude that art can have a general meaning for the society as a whole—even the artist has no conscious intention of creating that meaning—and that that meaning will appear in the larger patterns of the artist's oeuvre, rather than in isolated works.

Let us now consider the meaning of the complete absence of contemporary urban spaces in late nineteenth-century Russian paintings. This absence is all the more striking because of the numerous models offered by French Impressionism. Korovin took up Pissarro's and Monet's palette and brush strokes,

---

[11] Clark, *Painting of Modern Life*, 149.

but what kept him from painting contemporary Moscow, as they had painted contemporary Paris? Assuming that patterns in art history have social significance, I conclude that Korovin and his contemporaries did not do so because little had changed in the symbolic landscape of Russia's quasi-feudal social structure: there was a place for the tsar, the aristocrat, the priest, and the peasant, but there was no place for the nonaristocrat on the way to becoming a bourgeois and creating an urban, secular culture.

The absence of such a symbolic place has a corollary in the absence of national organizations for the fascinating array of private societies that Joseph Bradley discusses in "Civic Moscow." It appears that they represented only an initial stage of embourgeoisement in Russia. The bicycle clubs and other interest groups had managed neither to achieve a social identity for themselves nor to claim public space as their own. Therefore, public space did not appear in the painting of the time.

To return to Korovin from these more general matters, we realize that the absence of Russian urban life in his work did not necessarily make the depiction of Russian country life any easier. As a matter of fact, we find in his *Nasturtiums* (Fig. 20), also from the summer of 1888, a quandary whose resolution changed the course of his career. Like *At the Tea Table*, *Nasturtiums* depicts the veranda at Zhukovka, but this time the vantage point is from the yard. While Korovin's treatment of light and color has a distinctly Impression-

Fig. 20. Konstantin Korovin, *Nasturtiums* (1888). Moscow, V. D. Polenov Museum.

ist quality—it is difficult to believe that he had never seen a painting by Monet—his composition does not.

In *Nasturtiums*, a woman stands at the bottom of the steps and rests her arm on the railing so that she is directing her attention to a man who is standing on the veranda and looking out over the yard. Her gesture implies a certain interaction between them, yet the painting gives us no iconographic clues, such as the lyre in *Girl at the Threshold*, that might enable us to understand what is happening. Like the short stories Chekhov was writing at the time, *Nasturtiums* suggests, but does not resolve, a human drama.

Still another painting from the productive summer of 1888, *In the Boat* (Fig. 21), has a similar composition. A woman sits in a rowboat and looks at a man who has turned away from her. There is a certain tension between them, but we do not and cannot know what it is. Although there are many late nineteenth-century paintings of people in boats, only the people in Korovin's *In the Boat* have such an enigmatic interaction. It thus contrasts strikingly with its probable model, Manet's *Boating*(1874), which also depicts a couple in a boat. In the Manet, however, the man at the rudder looks ahead, and the woman, half-reclining, looks to the side. In *Boating*, as in so many Impressionist paintings, the people's lack of interaction is most striking.

I have emphasized the interaction between people in *Nasturtiums* and *In the Boat* because this is exactly the quality Impressionism frequently eliminated. Monet in particular tended to merge the human figure into the landscape as merely another element in a dazzling color field. This is what Cezanne's famous statement, "Monet is nothing but an eye, but my God what an eye!" means. But this feature, too, is generally absent from Russian painting. Soviet art historian Vasily Fillipov commented: "Only in a few works is the complete 'dissolution' of the person in the environment, the reduction of the role of the person to a spot on a painting observed."[12] The hint of frustration in Fillipov's remark implies that Russians needed something more definite in their paintings. Late nineteenth-century Russians needed what today we call role models, and the painter who provided them, Valentin Serov, became Russia's best-loved artist and the one whom Russians most deeply mourned when he died.

Korovin spent much of 1892 and 1893 in Paris, where he saw a lot of Impressionist painting. At first, it had a paralyzing effect on him, and the early 1890s mark a break in his artistic evolution. In February 1893 he wrote to Apollinary Vasnetsov, "The technique [of the Impressionists] is mighty poisonous—you can't paint anything afterwards."[13] That is to say, you can't paint original motifs. In the early 1890s Korovin suffered from a bad case of what Harold Bloom would call "the anxiety of influence" and painted a num-

[12] Vasily Fillipov, "K voprosu o sud'bakh russkogo impressionizma. Russkii impressionizm kak istoriko-khudozhestvennaia problema," *Sovetskoe iskusstvovedenie* 2 (1981): 196.

[13] Quoted in R. I. Vlasova, *Konstantin Korovin, Tvorchestvo* (Leningrad, 1969), 63.

Fig. 21. Konstantin Korovin, *In the Boat* (1888). Moscow, Tretiakov Gallery.

ber of Impressionist subjects in an Impressionist style. The Impressionists had
often taken the new streets and squares of Paris as their subject matter, so he
could paint some lovely exercises such as *Paris Cafe* (1890s) and *Paris After
the Rain* (1900). Like virtually every Impressionist painter, he painted a *Venice* (1900s), which is related to his *The Port at Marseille* (1890s). His most
imitative Impressionist painting, *Paris. Boulevard des Capucines*, dates from
1906, almost thirty years after Monet painted the same street in the same style.
Still, Korovin never painted any comparable views of Moscow, which he
knew so well. (The departure from Impressionist practice by Russian painters
becomes all the more striking when we consider that painters outside of France

did follow it, at least in the beginning; see Edvard Munch's *A Spring Day on Karl Johan Street*, 1890.)

Korovin could not find an urban space for people, or any clearly defined space for them at all. Virtually all his paintings that depict people place them in transitional space. This pattern begins with the aptly named *Girl at the Threshold* and *At the Balcony* (1886) and continues with *At the Tea Table*, *Nasturtiums*, his portrait of opera star Tatiana Liubatovich (also from the 1880s), *Paper Lanterns* (1895), and concludes typically with *On the Terrace* (1910). All these paintings show people in the transitional spaces of porches and balconies; they are never clearly inside or clearly outside.

Here we have another pattern in Korovin's work, one that has as much significance as the absence of paintings of contemporary street life. If Korovin had painted only one figure in transitional space, his *Girl on the Threshold*, say, then it would remain an isolated instance, and we could not draw any conclusions from it. However, one has only to flip through an album of Korovin's easel paintings and notice their titles to convince oneself that he places virtually all his figures in transitional spaces such as balconies, thresholds, and verandas. I conclude from this pattern that it conveys Korovin's unconscious awareness that Russian nonaristocrats were experiencing a transition. Although they had not yet claimed public space and thus social legitimacy for themselves, they were moving toward it. T. S. Eliot would surely have called these ambiguous spaces, in which Korovin's people perch uncertainly, an "objective correlative" for a social group in the process of change.

Korovin's treatment of both space and the interaction of people within that space contrasts strikingly with the practice of the Impressionists. For them, transitional spaces such as balconies belong in an urban, not pastoral, setting because they serve as something like a stage for the spectacle of Parisian life. Late nineteenth-century French painting offers a number of such paintings, such as Manet's *The Balcony* (1867) and Gustave Caillebotte's *A Balcony. Boulevard Haussmann* (1880).

Korovin's difficulty in finding appropriate space for his subjects corresponds to the more general difficulty that Hoffman characterized as "the crisis of easel painting." His friendship with a key figure in late nineteenth-century Russian art, the railroad magnate and art patron extraordinaire Savva Mamontov, provided a resolution of the whole conundrum and dramatically altered the course of his career.[14]

Korovin met Mamontov in 1885, and Mamontov in his generous fashion took him to Italy with him in 1888 and again in 1889. Mamontov was interested in the economic development of the Far North, and in 1894 he sent

[14] On Mamontov, see Stuart Grover, *Savva Mamontov and the Mamontov Circle, 1870–1905. Art Patronage and the Rise of Nationalism in Russian Art* (Ph.D., diss., University of Wisconsin, 1971); and Mark Kopshitser's brilliant biography, *Savva Mamontov* (Moscow: Iskusstvo, 1974).

Korovin and Serov on a trip to explore the area, with the understanding that he could use some of their paintings and drawings for publicity purposes. One major painting, *Hammerfest, Aurora Borealis* (1894), resulted from this trip. At this time Korovin also began working on the decorative panels he created for the Pavilion of the Far North, which Mamontov had built for the Nizhny Novgorod Fair of 1896.

Before discussing Mamontov's effect on Korovin's work, let us pause for a moment to consider briefly Mamontov's significance as an art patron in late nineteenth-century Europe. Although Harrison White and Cynthia White have shown that the Impressionists' financial difficulties have been exaggerated in the interests of romanticizing them as social outcasts, they did suffer from real, if sporadic, deprivation.[15] They experienced financial problems primarily when the one dealer who believed in them, Paul Durand-Ruel, was out of the country or experiencing his own financial problems. The tightly organized French art world offered artists few choices between the propriety of the salons and the uncertainties of bohemia.

In effect, Mamontov offered Russian artists a third possibility. Mamontov had immense resources, and, unlike Pavel Tretiakov, he combined the sensibility of a bohemian with the organizational skills of a manager. Mamontov provides a key to embourgeoisement in late nineteenth-century Russia, as he began to create the elements of a secular, nonaristocratic culture. In 1870 he bought Abramtsevo, the estate of the Aksakovs, a Slavophile family, and turned it into an art center. It is no exaggeration to say that Mamontov bought works from every significant artist in turn-of-the-century Russia; he literally saved the greatest painter of the period, Mikhail Vrubel, from starvation. In a sense, then, he resembles his contemporary, Pontus Fuerstenberg, a Swedish art patron who also had cosmopolitan tastes and bought the paintings of his fellow Swedes.[16] Just as Korovin's work differs distinctively from that of the French Impressionists, so Mamontov's patronage activity differs from that of Fuerstenberg and the American Havermeyer family, which bought a number of Impressionist masterpieces.[17] Unlike these patrons in countries with prominent, well-established middle classes, Mamontov was fascinated—not to say obsessed—with the performing arts.

After the government ended the imperial monopoly on opera in 1882, he formed the Private Opera, a company that derived from the amateur theatricals he, his family, and his artist friends put on during the holiday season at

---

[15] Harrison White and Cynthia White, "The Sociology of the Art Market," in *Impressionism in Perspective*, ed. Barbara Ehrlich White (Englewood Cliffs, N.J.: Prentice-Hall, 1973), 73–92.

[16] On Pontus Fuerstenberg, see Tone Skedsmo, "Patronage and Patrimony," in *Northern Light: Realism and Symbolism in Scandinavian Painting, 1880–1910* (New York: Brooklyn Museum, 1982), 43–52.

[17] See Frances Weitzenhoffer, *The Havemeyers. Impressionism Comes to America* (New York: Harry N. Abrams, 1986).

Abramtsevo. When Mamontov met Korovin, he drew him into the fascination with the performing arts that prevailed in the Mamontov circle. Korovin painted his first set for Nikolai's *The Merry Wives of Windsor* in January 1885. Later that same year he worked on productions of Rossini's *Oratorio*, Verdi's *Aida*, and Donizetti's *Linda*. As these names indicate, the repertoire of the Private Opera derived from Mamontov's own love of Italian opera; he had earlier studied voice in Milan when he was supposed to be learning the textile business. In all, Korovin worked on seven different productions during that first year in show business, and it changed his life.[18]

In the 1890s Korovin became Mamontov's principal designer. His sets for the epoch-making Private Opera production of Rimsky-Korsakov's *Sadko* in 1898, for example, created a sensation. During Korovin's career in the theater, he designed more than 125 major opera productions. Like so many members of his generation in Russia, Korovin both loved, and emotionally needed the performing arts; when Mamontov first induced him to work on stage sets for *Aida*, he found it so fascinating that he could not tear himself away.

Before discussing Mamontov's and Korovin's work in the performing arts, I wish to note, however briefly, the exceptional importance of theatricality in general, for a study of embourgeoisement in Europe because it evokes so distinctly the contrast in sensibilities betwen the nobility and the middle class. While eighteenth-century aristocrats certainly enjoyed the theater, they did so rather as people enjoy television today—as a form of entertainment in which they had no thought of participating.

In his provocative book *The Anti-Theatrical Prejudice*, Jonas Barish cites the relevance of the amateur theatricals in Jane Austen's novel *Mansfield Park*. The action of the novel takes place on the estate of Sir Thomas Bertram, and in his absence the people there decide to put on amateur theatricals. However, when he returns, he strongly denounces the theater, and the abashed would-be performers abandon their plans. Lionel Trilling was the first to sense the psychological and social implications of Bertram's attitude, and Barish quotes Trilling on the incident: "His [Bertram's] own self is an integer and he instinctively resists the diversification of the self that is implied by the assumption of roles."[19] Trilling's point is that to act is to impersonate, to take on the identity of another. While European aristocrats allowed their inferiors to impersonate others for their own amusement, they would have put at risk the security of their own class identities, and thus of the social order itself, if they themselves had appeared on the stage.

In the aftermath of the French revolution, however, this is precisely what

[18] I take all the information about Korovin's work for the Private Opera from Vera Rossikhina, *Opernyi teatr S. Mamontova* (Moscow: Muzyka, 1985).

[19] Quoted in Jonas Barish, *The Antitheatrical Prejudice* (Berkeley: University of California Press, 1981), 305. For more on theater and obshchestvennost', see essays by Edith W. Clowes and Mary Louise Loe in this volume.

the bourgeoisie did, as Roger Shattuck has astutely shown in his essay, "The Prince, the Actor, and I: The Histrionic Sensibility." He notes that in the aftermath of the French revolution, people needed a personal identity to compensate for the loss of the older fixed social order; our habit of referring to social roles makes explicit the incorporation of theatricality into everyday experience. Shattuck explains, "In the absence of station and self assigned by mere birth, it is as if playacting offered a means of forging a self and constituting a community."[20] Shattuck's comments on the legitimization of acting and role playing suggest that in nineteenth-century France the secular, urban self had reached an advanced stage of development. Moreover, in *Impressionism: Art, Leisure, and Parisian Society*, Robert L. Herbert adduces much indirect evidence that theater functioned as a metaphor for widely diffused role playing and posing on the boulevards of Paris. Thus, he says of Manet that "Paris itself became his theater."[21] Although the Impressionists loved the theater and painted both playgoers and performers, none of them worked in the theater.

This contrast between French and Russian aesthetes is especially instructive. If we assume that by the turn of the century embourgeoisement in Russia had begun but had not sufficiently progressed to allow the diffused role playing that characterized the Parisian bourgeoisie, then it explains the theater mania that gripped Moscow in the 1880s and 1890s, of which Mamontov and Korovin were both symptom and product. For Russian turn-of-the-century aesthetes, theatricality meant literal performances in the theater, and they concentrated their artistic energies on the productions of the Private Opera, which Mamontov founded, and the Moscow Art Theater, which Mamontov's protégé Konstantin Stanislavsky cofounded. In the quality of their performances, the range of their repertoires, and their lack of governmental support these institutions were unique in Europe.

In the Private Opera and the Moscow Art Theater, gifted nonaristocrats created a legitimate space for themselves that was neither public nor private. In a sense, these theaters were the secular equivalents of monasteries, and in fact Stanislavsky's writings on the theater and on acting abound in religious metaphors. We may also hypothesize that because of their concentration on theater as theater, the Russians were able to produce a world-class playwright, Anton Chekhov, whereas the comparable figure in France is George Feydeaux, the author of charming but superficial bedroom farces.

And what of Korovin's theater work? Freed from the necessity to relate figure to environment, Korovin showed great variety of style and treatment in his sets. In his design for Anton Rubenstein's arch-romantic opera *The Demon*

[20] Roger Shattuck, "The Prince, the Actor, and the I: The Histrionic Sensibility," in *The Innocent Eye: On Modern Literature and the Arts* (New York: Farrar Straus Giroux, 1984), 118.

[21] Robert L. Herbert, *Impressionism. Art, Leisure, and Parisian Society* (New Haven: Yale University Press, 1988), 96.

(1902, Fig. 22), he blends the figures of the Georgian women into the overall scheme of things in the best Impressionist fashion. However, only four years later, in his set for Rimsky-Korsakov's fairy tale *The Legend of the Invisible City of Kitezh* (1906), he shows something like a Fauvist sensibility, with great blocks of strong colors. This versatility made him a favorite of designers not only in Moscow and St. Petersburg but also in Paris, Milan, and London. He may justly be considered one of the premier theater designers of the early twentieth century.

Oddly enough, Korovin's tendency to place human figures in ambiguous, transitional spaces in his easel painting helps explain his success as a set designer. He lacked Serov's genius for psychological portraiture, yet he also found the Impressionist manner of merging the figure into the landscape unacceptable. His solution, in effect, was to expel the human figure from the canvas and onto the stage in front of it. As a set designer, he could do what he did with such success in creating Mamontov's Pavilion of the Far North at the 1896 Nizhny Novgorod Fair and the Russian Pavilion at the Paris exhibition of 1900—he could design environments without any responsibility for how the people related themselves to that environment. The costumes he designed for the great bass Fedor Shaliapin functioned in the same way; Shaliapin's stage persona had such power that it created a deeply emotional relationship between character and environment.

Fig. 22. Konstantin Korovin, Set for Act 2 of Nikolai Rubenstein's opera *The Demon* (1902). Moscow, Bakhrushin Theatrical Museum.

In conclusion, we may think of Korovin's career as one more stage in the ongoing assimilation of Western art styles by Russians. Because art styles arise in the context of a particular social process, artists in another country can successfully take them over only if they themselves are experiencing a similar social process. Thus, the Baroque churches of Italy arose as part of the Counter-Reformation, yet there was nothing comparable in eighteenth-century Russian society; Rastrelli's Baroque masterpieces in St. Petersburg remained isolated examples of imperial whim. A more complex and more productive example occurred when Tolstoi brought an embattled aristocratic sensibility to a middle-class form, the novel.

Consider, then, the nature of the process in which Impressionism arose. The combinations of Haussman's boulevards and the new railroad system tended to break down the older, quasi-medieval system of *quartiers* and bring the bourgeoisie into the open, so to speak.[22] This process, a process of growing self-consciousness through the legitimization of a social identity and thus the right to public space, did not occur in Russia. Although Russians such as Mamontov did build railroads, Russians often used them to go on pilgrimages to the Trinity-Sergey Monastery, not simply for pleasure outings.

Therefore, the capacity to merge the human figure into the landscape, which came so easily to Monet and Renoir, posed severe difficulties for Korovin, as his paintings of the 1880s show. In the 1890s, he both imitated the Impressionists and radically departed from them altogether, with easel paintings of familiar motifs on one hand and innovative stage designs on the other. By the early twentieth century, his theater work had brought him sufficient recognition that he could use Impressionist styles and motifs without feeling threatened. In this respect, his work chronicles the progress of embourgoisement in Russia, a movement about to reach a critical mass when World War I and the Revolution of 1917 intervened.

[22] On this process, see Clark's chapter, "The View from Notre Dame," in *Painting of Modern Life*, 23–78.

PART EIGHT

Conclusions

Chapter 21

THE SEDIMENTARY SOCIETY

Alfred J. Rieber

THE GREAT HISTORIAN V. O. Kliuchevskii found the key to Russian society in the relative simplicity of its social forms in comparison with Western Europe. But in writing his magisterial history of Russia he revealed a degree of complexity that belied his disarming formula. The apparent contradiction stems from the standard of comparison. Some elements of complexity in Russian society had no counterparts in the experience of the West. Moreover, the definition of society in nineteenth-century social history may have been too confining. If we make the effort to explore the unique features of Russian history and at the same time expand the boundaries of social history, we may arrive at a more comprehensive picture of Russia's social structure on the eve of revolution.

Boundaries and Boundary Crossings

Social history ought to resemble a mobilization center for intellectual forces on the march rather than a field so narrowly defined that it discourages boundary crossings. At its core lie questions about the definition, function, cohesion, collective action, and interaction of human conglomerations assembled into classes, estates, elites, status, and interest groups. But social historians ought not restrict themselves to examining the activity of those groups solely within the socioeconomic sphere. The dynamics of social groups penetrate political institutions, for example, filling them with social content, profoundly affecting their formal, legal-administrative structures, and often transforming them beyond the intentions of their original architects.

To be sure, social groups are not impervious to changes in their encounters with institutions; there is always a reciprocal though rarely equal influence of one upon the other. In Imperial Russia the institutional structures outside the rulership itself, that is, the autocratic power, tended to be fragile and vulnerable to social pressures over long periods of time. Most administrative departments were short-lived or changed their functions. After a hundred years of experience with collegial rule, colleges gave way to ministries. The nature of

This is a much expanded version of a paper delivered at the World Congress of Slavists in Washington, D.C., October 1985. The author wishes to thank Alan Wildman and Abbott Gleason for their stimulating comments and suggestions which greatly assisted in the revision.

ministries changed radically over the following hundred years gradually accumulating most if not all the trappings of modern bureaucracies. The senate changed from the highest administrative to the highest judicial body. The powers of governors-general waxed and waned. Constitutional experiments proliferated in the borderlands: the Kingdom of Poland, the Grand Duchy of Finland, the Baltic provinces, the Viceroyalty of the Caucasus, the Siberian Committee, protectorates in Central Asia. Overall the empire was a hodgepodge of conflicting jurisdictions distinguished by no guiding principle of government. Rather, the ruling elite responded reluctantly and sluggishly to acute social problems as they accumulated. The social ferment from below seemed to run its own course, regardless of state officials' attempts to control and direct it. Yet there was a marked contrast between the accelerating pace of changes in urban, educated Russia and the much slower but stronger pressures exerted on the body politic from the countryside. The small elites were forming new groups and combinations while the overwhelming mass of peasants were becoming more resistant to change. Yet the action of both forced the state to respond in its erratic fashion. To many the perspective of social movements molding state institutions is still heretical. But the heresy is becoming orthodoxy.

Over the past decade studies have challenged the once prevailing view that endowed the state with awesome power and self-awareness as it shaped and reshaped society much as a sculptor might pummel an inert lump of clay into a pleasing form. It is now clear that throughout the nineteenth century extensive changes in the top strata of society profoundly altered the institutions of government. The changing social composition and educational level of personnel within the central administrative organs had far-reaching effects on the attitudes, values, and behavioral patterns of officials and on the formation of policy as well. The middle and upper ranks of the bureaucracy, both civil and—by the end of the century—military, were shedding their aristocratic cast and acquiring a more plebian outlook. Traditional forms of politics based on court factions and clientele networks were giving way to occupational and opinion interest groups. The growth of literacy and the emergence of a mass press in midcentury further broke down the artificial wall between the state and society. There was a two-way flow of information and influence. But the heavier volume of ideas was surely coming into the government from the outside.

The professions—especially law, medicine, and engineering—in their struggle to free themselves from state tutelage, began to acquire some attributes of autonomy by the second half of the nineteenth century. The ethos of state service was powerful, but there were signs that a different loyalty, equally demanding and involving greater self-sacrifice, was taking its place: service to the *narod*. The growth of new economic interests clustered around more vigorous capitalist enterprises produced another kind of social group. As

the government relied more and more on their entrepreneurial skills to stimulate productivity and mobilize foreign capital, it was obliged to surrender some
of its control over the economy. By the end of the century the interpenetration
of capitalist entrepreneurs and the financial bureaucracy engendered ambiguous loyalties. At least in the economics ministries, it became difficult to determine whether state policies were shaping social values or vice versa. In
light of the crosscurrents within the bureaucracy and external social pressures
upon it, to what extent can we speak of the state as a cohesive organism with
a unified outlook by the end of the imperial period?

The state had legislated for centuries to define a social organization for the
peasantry, but it was dealing with an elusive substance. Konstantin Kavelin
described it as "Kaluga dough," malleable enough in form but possessing its
own weight, texture, mass, and resistance—above all resistance.[1] Composed
of elements that do not change readily under pressure alone, Kaluga dough
can be shaped and molded but it also seeps through cracks or spills over edges
or simply bursts out of confining partitions. No society is a water-tight con-
tainer, least of all one spread out "over the thinly settled Russian plain."[2] The
state had virtually no effect on peasant culture; it left intact peasant customary
law, right down to the end of the Old Régime; it did not attempt to run the
skhody, the rough and ready assemblies that settled internal peasant affairs.
The state fixed the amount of taxes and the number of recruits that the peasants
apportioned and gathered for it. It punished disobedience and rebellion. Beyond that the state had little to do with the peasants in ordinary times; it was a
kind of absentee government.

Despite the legislation that constrained peasant movements both before and
after Emancipation, there were always large numbers of peasants on the move.
There were wanderers and pilgrims, *otkhody* seeking work, colonists, both
legal and illegal. Even before the abolition of serfdom, small but significant
numbers drifted into the cities and penetrated other social categories, the
meshchanstvo, the merchantry, and the working class. The government did
not encourage these movements; to an extent they even feared them as signs
of erosion within the peasant commune. But it could not stop them. As the
government struggled to increase peasant productivity while maintaining stability, it conceded more and more to the egalitarian and collectivist features of
peasant life. In the end the state appeared to have been more arbitrary than
powerful, as even historians of the state school admitted. Early in his distinguished career, Paul Miliukov described the Russian state as having "an enormous influence on social organization" so that, in contrast with the West,

[1] D. A. Korsakov, "Pervye gody moego znakomstva s K. D. Kavelinym, 1861–1864 gg.,"
Vestnik Evropy 10 (1886): 745–46.

[2] The phrase and the concept, both enormously influential in Russian historiography, belong to
S. M. Solov'ev. See especially his *Istoriia Rossii s drevneishikh vremen*, 2d ed. (St. Petersburg,
n.d.), 762–91.

"Russian history was locked in by a strong state power." After the revolution, a sadder and wiser man, he lamented in his postmortem of the Old Regime that on "the plasma-like quality of the people the marks of history are only weakly and fragmentarily printed."[3]

If social historians are bold enough to cross boundaries into institutional and legal history they should also march in the opposite direction toward culture defined in its broadest anthropological sense to include institutional norms and material artifacts as well as values, belief systems, and attitudes. The social historian has two objectives here: first to analyze the ideology of the specific reference group, that is, class, estate, elite, and so on; the second, to identify those common elements of a national culture that transcend social divisions and provide a network of shared social values. Until recently, historians of Imperial and early Soviet Russia permitted the Russian intelligentsia to speak for the nation and also, to the limited extent that they were permitted to speak at all, the non-Russian intelligentsia to speak for their separate peoples. But the voices of the inarticulate are beginning to be heard. It is becoming clear that numerous subcultures in Russian life associated first with the soslovie but also with certain regions and the religious sectarians. The formal organization of the soslovie was a creation of the state; but their soslovie culture content preceded structure and evolved autonomously. This was true of the peasantry above all. Peasant monarchism, popular religion, customary law, and the entire elusive peasant mentality frustrated and bewildered officials and intellectuals alike. Perhaps the artists came closest to understanding, but they too translated the peasant culture into their own aesthetic vocabulary. The peasantry was not simply a primitive society awaiting enlightenment, but a complex culture with a self-awareness of its interests that shaped attitudes toward God, nature, authority, land use, and education.

This is not to argue that the peasants possessed a uniform, monolithic culture. There were striking regional and ethnic differences. There was, for example, a very distinctive regional culture of the north where in the absence of serfdom and large estates strong local traditions survive into the late twentieth century. Here much of the ancient, oral culture of the peasantry survived as exemplified by the byliny of Onega Province; here wooden architecture flourished with its challenge to official Orthodoxy (as in the fantastic multidomes Cathedral of the Intercession of Kizhi). The North was a great refuge of the Old Belief; it produced many of the original colonists of Siberia who, transplanted to their new homes, carried on the independent traditions of their ancestral lands.[4]

---

[3] P. N. Miliukov, *Ocherki po istorii russkoi kul'tury*, 5th ed. (St. Petersburg, 1904), 1: 133–34; Miliukov, *Istoriia vtoroi russkoi revoliutsii* (Sofia, 1921), 1: 12–17.

[4] Yanni Kotsonis, "Regionalism and Revolution in North Russia, 1917–1918" (M.A. thesis, Columbia University, 1988), 4–10; A. F. Gilferding, *Onezhskie byliny* (St. Petersburg, 1871),

In the cities and provincial towns a variety of subcultures clustered around the merchantry, meshchanstvo, and the emerging proletariat that had no soslovie tradition behind it. The insular life of the merchantry with its partriarchal family structure, traditional religious outlook, and conservative business methods was only beginning to break down at the end of the imperial period, and then only among a few elite families. The meshchanstvo remains a mysterious urban subculture, barely explored, but surprising in its association with the radical left in the revolutionary years of the twentieth century. Surprising in the sense that its counterparts in Western Europe were associating with more movements of the radical right during the same period. The rediscovery of the worker-intellectuals and the many shades of cultural difference among the workers, distinctions of craft, skills, life-styles, introduce large and important differences of outlook and values into an urban landscape that has been for far too long rendered flat and featureless.[5]

The relationship between the subcultures of groups and soslovie and the national culture is bound to be complex. At each level one cluster of values is conscious and codified, while another cluster remains unconscious, inarticulate but deeply imbedded in the behavior of individuals and collectives. In exploring the dimensions of subcultures and national culture the social historian must overcome the temptation of drawing too sharp a line between high culture or "the great tradition" and popular culture or "the little tradition." In Russian society the constant interpenetration of the two kinds of cultural expression makes such a radical distinction highly arbitrary and misleading. The social distance between the upper classes and the peasant masses was never so great in Russia as in Western Europe.

At all periods in Russian history mediators abounded between the two cultures. Up to the sixteenth century the wandering minstrels (skomorokhi) mediated. Household serfs on rural estates and even in town houses played a remarkably consistent role in transmitting the tales and songs of peasant Russia to their young charges—from Pushkin to Vladimir Nabokov and Glinka to Stravinsky. In the nineteenth century the "natural amateur" (samorodok) could be met in all walks of life in the towns, performing for friends, occasionally making a career in the theater, but always mediating between popular and high culture, between the peasants and lower-class urban masses. Critics noted the subtle gradations of mixed styles in choral music from the oral tradition throughout the accompanied folk song, the romance, the art song with folk overtones to the conservatory culture. Similarly, gradations could be found in architecture. In all forms of cultural expression the exchange of influences was reciprocal. High culture penetrated into the world of the folk

---

xi–xiii, xviii, xxiii, xlii; I. Bartenev and B. Fedorov, *Arkhitekturnye pamiatniki russkogo severa* (Leningrad-Moscow, 1968).

[5] A vivid portrait of these differences emerges in Reginald E. Zelnik, ed., *A Radical Worker in Tsarist Russia: The Autobiography of Semen Ivanovich Kanatchikov* (Stanford, 1986).

song and epic, even into the design of the peasant wooden hut (*izba*). The idea
that peasant culture was "horizontal" needs to be seriously reconsidered.[6]

ELEMENTS OF COHESION IN THE NATIONAL CULTURE

Once these interactions have been clarified, the social historian faces additional tasks in evaluating the relative strength of subcultures and the national
culture as a measure of social cohesion and social fragmentation. Three powerful strands in the culture of the dominant elites percolated down irregularly
and unevenly into the mass of the population: the imperial idea, the ethic of
social service, and the commitment to industrialization. They constitute what
might be called the Petrine legacy. First, *Rossiiskaia imperiia*, the unique imperial idea, combined three interrelated imperatives: in order to be a great
power, Russia had to be a multicultural power; the Russians had a civilizing
mission in Asia similar to that of Western Europe but one that accepted the
mingling of races; the dominant Great Russian culture had to tolerate a degree
of cultural pluralism under the umbrella of Orthodoxy but occasionally outside
it, as in the case of the Lutheran Baltic Germans, Jews, and some Muslim
people of the Caucasus and Central Asia.

The idea of the multicultural empire was rooted in the early history of the
Muscovite state, the legacy of steppe politics, and the struggle for succesion
over the Mongol Empire. Without abandoning this tradition, Peter reoriented
its main thrust to the West. Absorption of the Baltic territories and domination
of Poland became cardinal principles of state policy that acquired a mass base
in the nineteenth century during the surge of Great Russian nationalism that
confronted the Polish rising in 1863. It acquired a popular literary veneer in
the works of Dostoevsky. The belief that the loss of any significant part of the
empire would precede dismemberment and dwindling power status was widespread among the ruling elites and the nationalist right. It is difficult to esti-
mate how deeply this attitude seeped into the popular consciousness. Yet the
opposition to a separate peace in the spring and summer of 1917 by the liberals
and most of the socialist left is eloquent testimony to the persistence of the
imperial idea even among self-appointed and elected representatives of the
majority of the population.

The Russian civilizing mission in Asia was first popularized by the old Caucasus hands in the first half of the nineteenth century and carried on by the

---

[6] E. A. Borisova and T. P. Kazhdan, *Russkaia arkhitektura kontsa XIX–nachala XX vek*a (Moscow, 1971), 29–30, 102–3; A. I. Nekrasov, *Russkoe narodnoe iskusstvo* (Moscow, 1924); B. V.
Astaf'ev (Igor' Glebov), *Russian Music from the Beginning of the Nineteenth Century* (1930),
trans. Alfred Swann (Ann Arbor, 1955), 78. Apollon Grigor'ev, "Russie narodnye pesni s ikh
poeticheskoi i muzykal'noi storony," *Sochineniia* (Villanova, 1970), 1: 359–64; Anthony Netting, "Images and Ideas in Russian Peasant Art," *Slavic Review* 35, no. 1 (1976): 52; cf. Wla-
dimir Weidle, *Russia Absent and Present* (New York, 1961), 20–21.

proconsuls in Central Asia in the second half of the century. Russia's imperial heroes—Ermolaev, Bariatinsky, Chernaev, and Skobolev—never quite attained the celebrity of their British counterparts, but they were certainly more than a match in fame and flamboyance for their counterparts in France and the rest of the continent. The civilizing mission was taken up by the Russian officer corps and celebrated in the mass press and popular literature in the second half of the nineteenth century. Russian belles lettres was enormously influential in capturing the mystery and excitement of imperial expansion into the Caucasus. They virtually apotheosized the spectacular beauty of the region. Pushkin, Lermontov, Tolstoy, and lesser figures like Bestuzhev-Marlinsky treated the conquest ambiguously. They sympathetically portrayed the resistance of the wild mountaineers, the noble savage, against the civilized Russian. But the overall effect of their work was to enshrine the Caucasus in the popular imagination as part of the imperial heritage.[7] In central Asia the descriptive medium was more prosaic. For the most part interest in the region was spread through the travel literature of the explorers and adventurers like M. N. Przhevalsky and Petr Semenov-Tian-Shansky. But the stirring realistic painting of Vereshchagin, the Russian Remington, especially the more than one hundred paintings in his Turkestan series, created a sensation among the Russian public. But two military figures captured popular enthusiasm—"the Lion of Tashkent," General Chernaev, and the white General M. D. Skobelev, whose achievements were memorialized in popular songs. Under the influence of European models and in rivalry with Great Britain, Russian army officers in Central Asia like General M. T. Veniukov offered a more systematic rationale for their mission in the East that somehow managed to accommodate Social Darwinism and racial tolerance.[8]

The attraction in the opposite direction, of subject peoples who took advantage of opportunities to assimilate and rise in the tsarist service, is largely an unexplored subject in the modern period. The cooptation of native elites into the Russian nobility in the early years of conquest is the best known part of the story. Beginning with the acceptance of Tatar princes into the highest ranks of the nobility in the fifteenth and sixteenth centuries the process was extended to the Cossack starshina in the seventeenth century, the Baltic nobility in the

[7] Paul M. Austin, "The Exotic Prisoner in Russian Romanticism," *Russian Literature* 16 (1984): 217–74; Susan Layton, "The Creation of an Imaginative Caucasian Geography," *Slavic Review* 45, no. 3 (1986), 470–85; Thomas M. Barrett, "The Limits of Radicalism: Imperialism, National Identity and the Journalism of the Left under Alexander II" (Paper delivered at conference on premodern and modern national identity, University of London, 1988).

[8] L. V. Evdokimov, "Belyi general M. D. Skobelev v narodnykh skazaniiakh," *Voennoistoricheskii sbornik*, 2 (1911): 33–60; David MacKenzie, *The Lion of Tashkent* (Athens, Ga., 1974), 240. Donald Rayfield, *The Dream of Lhasa: The Life of Nikolai Przhevalsky (1839–1888), Explorer of Central Asia* (London, 1976) is popular biography but captures the imperialist flavor; W. Bruce Lincoln, *Petr Petrovich Semenov Tian-Shanskii: The Life of a Russian Geographer* (Newtonville, Mass., 1980), esp. 24–27.

eighteenth, the Georgian, Armenian nobles, and the Kazakh-Kirghis khans in the nineteenth. In Late Imperial Russia there was never a large number of non-Russians in the army, but in the eighteenth century Kalmyk and Bashkir cavalry units were used as irregular troops. In times of crisis special units were raised from the tribes (*inorodtsy*); Caucasian tribesmen were particularly valued. During the Russo-Turkish War the creation of new formations increased their number to twenty-four thousand. Although concerns over internal security discouraged recruitment of draftees from Central Asia into regular army units, individual cases of Kirghiz and Kazakh entered the military and served with distinction. The Omsk Cadet Corps, for example, was an important source of russification and education for sons of Siberian and Central Asian khans and begs. The most famous graduate from the tribes was the distinguished explorer, naturalist, and military officer Ch. Valikhanov, son of a Kirghiz khan who sought to combine elements of European (Russian) civilization with the preservation of his own culture.[9] By the turn of the twentieth century these fragile ties had begun to fray, and then in 1905 most of them snapped under the pressure of anti-Russian urban movements led by native intelligentsia. But it is well to recall that the policy of co-opting non-Russian elites probably delayed the emergence of ethnic consciousness and then restricted it mainly to the cities with the result that autonomous movements in 1905 and again during the Russian civil war found little resonance, and then mainly outside the urban centers.

A second theme of the Petrine legacy may be called the imperative of social service. Repeated efforts by the state to reconstruct political and social institutions, a veritable tradition of reform, alternated with repression and rebellion in the political culture of Imperial Russia. Initially the Petrine concept of service was resolutely tied to the state as opposed to society. Yet there were latent possibilities for the evolution of this relationship toward broader social aims. Although Peter's views on education were primarily practical, even technological, in orientation, he was also concerned with manners and attitudes, dress and deportment, thus opening the way for penetrating into the mentality of the educated elite of a nonmaterial culture from the West. Western thought introduced secular ideas of ethical restraint on arbitrariness to replace the weakened moral authority of the Orthodox Church. Peter's administrative scheme also combined hierarchy and mobility. The social system of service classes and the Table of Ranks favored the social and political hegemony of the dvorianstvo, but it did not exclude other social groups from acquiring education, rank, and status.

A great political struggle over access to service and education lasted

[9] D. A. Skalon, ed., *Stoletie voennago ministerstva, 1802–1902: Konspekty istoricheskikh ocherkov* (St. Petersburg, 1906), 964; A. Margulan, "Ocherk zhizni i deiatel'nosti Ch. Ch. Valikhanova," in Ch. Ch. Valikhanov, *Sobranie sochinenii v piati tomakh* (Alma Ata, 1984), 1: 22–24, 29, 72–76.

throughout the life of the monarchy. In the nineteenth century, for example, the educational reforms of 1803–1809 oscillated between greater social openness favored by reformers like Speransky and a socially restrictive system of education and state service favored by the aristocracy. In the 1840s Nicholas virtually militarized the institutions of higher learning and the bureaucracy. But the Great Reforms opened up both. In the post-Reform decades conflicts continued over classical versus real schools, Sunday schools for the lower classes, technical education and the relative importance of knowledge and skill as opposed to seniority as the basis for promotion in the bureaucracy. The main result of this see-saw contest was the slow, uneven but inevitable penetration of humanistic ideals, a scientific outlook, and various social types into the bureaucratic ethos. As early as the mid-eighteenth century a "raznochintsy intelligentsia" flourished briefly in the face of a noble reaction.[10] After the church school reforms in 1808 a steady stream of sons of clergy entered the secular world of the universities and state service. Formal schooling assumed greater importance than private tutoring among the landless nobles' sons who began to enter state service in increasing numbers in the early decades of the nineteenth century.

By the 1860s the Russian education system was unusual if not unique in Europe. Although it may be going too far to call it, as Leikina-Sverskaia does, "democratic" and "impoverished," the university student body was, nevertheless, more critical in its attitudes toward authority and the social order and more socially variegated than anywhere else on the continent.[11] In this way Russian universities resembled those of the Third World in the second half of the twentieth century rather than the elite class institutions of nineteenth-century Europe. In the Russian lycees and gymnasiums, in the universities and higher technical schools, future bureaucrats and radicals rubbed shoulders. It would be a mistake to perceive them as representing two sharply defined antagonistic camps. Only a few dared to cross the line dividing them, and there were many gradations of belief between one pole and the other. They were exposed to the ideas of the same teachers, and the professoriate itself was scarcely uniform in its ideological composition, although the spectrum of belief was assuredly more narrow than that of their students. Students of different or as yet unformed beliefs gathered in the scores of kruzhki that offered an informal but passionate setting for the free exchange of ideas and the reading of illegal literature.

How many bureaucrats concealed a radical past, or who at the very least harbored sympathies for ideas they had absorbed as youths? Three dramatic examples come to mind. Count S. S. Lanskoi, Alexander II's minister of in-

---

[10] M. M. Shtrange, *Demokraticheskaia intelligentsia Rossii v XVIII veke* (Moscow, 1965).

[11] V. P. Leikina-Svirskaia, *Intelligentsiia v Rossii vo vtoroi polovine XIX veka* (Moscow, 1971), 27ff.

terior who helped prepare the Emancipation, had been an ardent Mason and a member of the Union of Welfare, although he quit before it plotted the Decembrist uprising. The military reformer and chief of staff and of the army, General N. N. Obruchev was an associate of Nikolai Chernyshevsky on the editorial board of *Voennyi sbornik*, a fact that probably prevented him from ever becoming minister of war. V. I. Kovalevsky, Witte's deputy minister of finance, had been arrested as a student for having harbored, albeit unwittingly, the terrorist Nechaev.[12]

Socially mixed, Russian educated society was also among the most cosmopolitan in Europe, if only because it was multilingual. Lacking strong secular tradition in the arts and sciences before the early nineteenth century, Russian culture relied heavily in its formative period on European models or rather on adapting them to the needs of Russian life. The role of the English nanny, the French governess, and the German tutor in the upbringing of the Russian nobility had no precedent in Europe. Exposure to European belles lettres and technical literature in the original languages penetrated deeply into the consciousness of educated society. With the exception of the Emancipation, no major reform in Russia was undertaken, no important technological innovation launched without a thorough, often exhaustive investigation of the European (and even American) experience. This may have delayed at times the process of borrowing. Whatever the case, Russian xenophobia was always tempered and often balanced, at least in the imperial period, by the influences of European culture.

In this socially and culturally diverse society imbued with a strong service ethic, elements of the educated elite were able to sustain the reforming impulse even in periods of repression. During the early 1830s and 1840s the first generation of "enlightened bureaucrats" began to move up the service ladder into the middle ranks of the state administration. They were the main architects of the Great Reforms of the 1860s. By adopting a more distinctive ethos and setting their own professional standards, the reformers displayed their own form of moral, if paternalistic, earnestness toward the people. It would not be an exaggeration to speak of a bureaucratic populism lurking behind the mask of *opeka*. The official defense of the peasant commune reflected not simply the fiscal, military, and internal security needs of the state but also a moral concern over the fate of the peasantry exposed to the ravages of individualism, the free market, and proletarianization. Similarly, the concern of the local and central governments over the education of the peasantry, though also shot through with misguided paternalism, was profoundly informed by ethical concerns.[13]

[12] "S. S. Lanskoi," *Russkii biograficheskii slovar'* (St. Petersburg, 1914), 10: 71; E. M. Feoktistov, Za kulissami politiki i literatury, 1848–1896 (Leningrad, 1929), 358, n.13; S. Iu. Witte, *Vospominaniia* (Moscow, 1960), 1: 211.

[13] David Macey, *Government and Peasant in Russia, 1861–1906* (DeKalb, 1987); Ben Eklof,

If the service ethic was pronounced among bureaucrats, how much more deeply did it sink into the mentality of the professions? The emergence of the legal, medical, and engineering professions as autonomous bodies standing outside the bureaucratic hierarchy was a slow and gradual process that only began in the second half of the nineteenth century. But by the end of the century the professions represented an intermediate strata between the radical intelligentsia and the bureaucracy, blurring the edges of its boundaries with both groups. They shared the same social and educational origins, the same cultural and intellectual heritage. The history of their dedication to social service particularly in local government still lies buried in the massive documentation of the local and provincial zemstvos. But their political activism clothed in moral outrage during the early months of the Revolution of 1905 demonstrated a deep commitment to social justice. The willingness of Russian professional organizations to take a strong political stance in 1905 was not confined to lawyers and teachers but included doctors and engineers as well.[14] Their association with radical social causes provides a striking contrast with their Western European counterparts in the same period.

The third strand in the Petrine legacy was state intervention in economic development. Peter's massive and ruthless mobilization of human and material resources in order to bring Russia into the European great power system built on an earlier tradition of state intervention in the economy. His efforts were more comprehensive, purposeful, and effective. Following his death the crisis atmosphere evaporated and the forced pace diminished, but the state maintained its direct interest in and control over key sectors of the economy— in particular mining, metallurgy, and woolen cloth, all connected with the army. A parallel growth of private industry by merchants, nobles, and peasant entrepreneurs gained ground particularly under the reign of Catherine II. Yet the vigorous participation and common interest of these groups in private enterprise never overcame their profound social differences. They failed to unify in defense of their common interests, and none of them was sufficiently strong to overcome the competition from the other. Moreover, the state economic bureaucracy was unwilling to surrender the economy into private hands. A middle class that in the Western European sense unified the propertied, edu-

---

Russian Peasant Schools: Officialdom, Village Culture, and Popular Pedagogy, 1861–1914 (Berkeley, 1986), esp. chap. 5.

[14] The attitudes of professional groups can best be savored in the petitions published by the liberal law journal, *Pravo*, in the first half of 1905. For physicians, see Nancy M. Frieden, *Russian Physicians in an Era of Reform and Revolution* (Princeton, 1981); for the technical intelligentsia, see Kendall Bailes, *Technology and Society under Lenin and Stalin: Origins of the Soviet Technical Intelligentsia, 1917–1941* (Princeton, 1978), chap. 1; N. M. Pirumova, *Zemskaia intelligentsia i ee rol' v obshchestvennoi bor'be* (Moscow, 1986); and the studies in Harley M. Balzer, ed., *Professions in Russia at the End of the Old Regime* (Ithaca, 1990).

cated society never materialized in Russia. A capitalist economy under state tutelage did.

In the first decade of the nineteenth century tsarist officials engaged in the first of many great industrialization debates that occurred throughout modern Russian history. It was ignited by Russian domestic problems combined with transformations in the global economy. Beginning with Catherine a fiscal crisis caused by excessive printing of paper money (assignats) and the pressures of the steam and mechanical revolution in manufacturing taking place in the West seriously threatened Russia's economic well-being. The debate over industrialization centered on two questions: First, should Russia seek to industrialize at all or remain basically an agricultural country? And second, what should be the role of the state in promoting, encouraging, and actively developing industry? A secondary economic issue, but one of cardinal political importance, questioned which government agency would preside over an industrial policy if it were to be approved and implemented. The debate was interrupted by the war of the Third Coalition against Napoleon, the wave of postwar xenophobia that attacked Western ideas and innovations and the shock of the Decembrist uprising. During most of Nicholas's reign the government adopted a policy of drift, presided over by Count E. F. Kankrin, minister of finance, who worried about the socially disruptive effects of industrialization. The state ownership of industry in the pre-Reform period declined to a small share of the total productive forces, and it was confined mainly to stagnant metallurgical and woolen industries for armaments and uniforms. Yet the state revived the building of canals, financed and built the first railroad trunk line between Moscow and St. Petersburg, and maintained a supervisory role over the organization and development of private industry.[15]

A second major industrialization debate opened up in the 1860s over similar sets of questions. By this time the supporters of a more vigorous state-directed industrial policy within the bureaucracy had substantially increased; the lesson of the Crimean defeat was too sobering to ignore. The major opponents of industrialization among the landed nobility could no longer block changes required by the financial and military stability of the state, although from their entrenched position within the bureaucracy they could delay them. But the proponents of industrialization could not agree on the means. Interest groups, centered on competing ministries of state, had independently evolved distinctive ideological positions. The economists in the Ministry of Finance favored a mixed economy in which the government and private entrepreneurs would share risks and apportion functions to achieve fiscal and budgetary stability; the engineers in the Ministry of Transportation supported state investment and

[15] A. V. Predtechenskii, *Ocherki obshchestvenno-politicheskoi istorii Rossii v pervoi chetverti XIX veka* (Moscow-Leningrad, 1957), chap. 8; N. S. Kiniapina, *Politika russkogo samoderzhaviia v oblasti promyshlennosti (20–50-e gody XIX v.)* (Moscow, 1968); Walter M. Pintner, *Russian Economic Policy Under Nicholas I* (Ithaca, 1967).

organization of the economy for developmental aims; the military bureaucrats also favored state control of industry mainly for strategic aims. The lack of coordination among state agencies imposed a stop-and-start pattern of industrialization, but the government persisted in its efforts to avoid falling too far behind the West. It possessed several powerful instruments to promote this progress, including the creation of a central state bank, the control over railroad concessions, subsidies, state orders for armaments, and a gradually rising protective tariff.[16]

Sergei Witte was able to build on the policy of his predecessors Reitern, Bunge, and Vyshnegradsky in Finance and the engineers in Transportation; in his hands the various threads of fiscal, tariff, and railroad policy merged to draft a comprehensive industrial policy. Yet there is now evidence that Russia's industrial growth in the 1890s was as much a continuation of previous trends in both its aims and pace as a radical departure from the past. Interrupted by the Russo-Japanese War, Revolution of 1905, and depression, industrial growth revived after 1909 and expanded rapidly after 1912 until the eve of World War I. Toward the end of Witte's tenure a third industrialization debate broke out. The landed interests mobilized for the last time to decry the effects of forced industrialization on the agricultural sector. Witte fell victim to political opposition within the bureaucracy and among the provincial nobles. But his policies were carried on by his successors, and the government's commitment to industrial growth was never in serious doubt.

The industrialization of Russia carried out in an unfavorable geographical environment by a relatively poor country with underdeveloped infrastructure on the periphery of the main global trade routes was, for all its fits and starts, a remarkable achievement. The successors of Peter were not, with a few exceptions, particularly intelligent or perceptive. Yet all of them recognized in one fashion or another that Peter's vision of Russia as a great power was inextricably linked to Russia's sustained economic growth and that, in the face of its peculiar social structure, the state had to accept prime responsibility for that undertaking. Dedication to that vision held together the most progressive elements of the bureaucracy, army, and commercial and industrial groups. Financial stability and military parity with the most advanced countries were the only guarantees against economic subjugation or political subordination in an age of imperialism. The examples of China and the Ottoman Empire were evident for all who wished to see.

So the Petrine legacy of the imperial idea, the ethic of social service, and the commitment to industrialization provided the mainstay of the dominant political culture that held the empire together as long as it did. At certain crit-

---

[16] I. F. Gindin and L. E. Shepelev each in his own way have stressed the continuity of economic policy and industrial growth since the 1860s. See Gindin, *Gosudarstvennyi bank i ekonomicheskaia politika tsarskogo pravitel'stva (1861–1892 gody)* (Moscow, 1960) and Shepelev, *Tsarizm i burzhuaziia vo vtoroi polovine XIX veka* (Leningrad, 1981).

ical or symbolic moments these shared beliefs and values provided a valuable social cement binding the various groups and classes together, if only briefly. Such moments at the end of the imperial period included the Russo-Turkish War, response to the famine of 1891, the death of Lev Tolstoy, and the outbreak of the First World War. But clearly the cohesive power of these combined elements was insufficient in the long run to survive the strains of social conflict and external war.

Elements of Social Fragmentation

The countervailing trends of social fragmentation were growing stronger within Russian society at the end of the imperial period. The particularism of the peasantry had not been overcome; its desire for the land was unsatisfied, and its integration into civic society was incomplete. The proletariat had developed a particularism of its own; it had never been accepted as a distinctive social group, never even recognized as a soslovie; it was deprived of the most fundamental right to organize. The vast splintered middle of Russian society—merchants, professionals, clerks, petty shopkeepers, and artisans had no sense of class consciousness and no ability to unify politically. The nobility was steadily losing its landed properties as well as its domination of the higher ranks in the civil and military bureaucracies. Perhaps even more ominous for the stability of the empire, the very top stratum of Russian society—Tsar Nicholas II, the imperial family, and elements of the court and church hierarchy—were turning away from the Petrine legacy. They were looking back toward the seventeenth century, readapting rituals and symbols in which to clothe the monarchy that represented a social, cultural, and psychological rejection of the modern, secular state.[17]

Older forms of social identification such as estates (soslovie), status (sostoianie), and rank (chin) were growing weaker among broad sections of the population, yet they had by no means disappeared. There were in fact belated attempts to revive them. More important, however, they were not entirely replaced by socioeconomic classes. Soslovie forms survived because they performed useful functions for both the state and social groups. Government officials perceived them as valuable self-regulating administrative units in preparing legislation, regulating social mobility, maintaining public order, and apportioning rights and privileges in relationship to state service. In defining the franchise in 1864 and 1870 for local bodies, zemstvos, and town dumas and in 1905 for the proposed consultative (Bulygin) duma, soslovie was employed in combination with property qualification.[18] The uneasy coexistence

---

[17] Richard Wortman, "Invisible Threads: The Historical Imagery of the Romanov Tercentenary" (forthcoming in *Russian History*, nos. 2–4 [1989]).

[18] Gregory L. Freeze, "The Soslovie (Estate) Paradigm and Russian Social History," *Ameri-*

of legal status and wealth as criteria for exercising civil responsibilities demonstrated the ambiguity of social valuation in Imperial Russia.

Beyond administrative convenience soslovie symbolized to its members and supporters an attachment to a particular social order that embodied strong sentiments about the role of social honor and occupational status. There were still vital signs of life within the soslovie organizations themselves. They were not held together merely by the will and determination of the state. Most social life of the merchantry continued to revolve around soslovie organizations. The revival of the landed gentry as a political force in the post-1905 period owed much to its use of soslovie organizations, the assemblies and marshalls of the nobility. There were plenty of signs of socioeconomic decay in peasant soslovie organization even before the Stolypin reforms. But their internal dynamism reemerged with great vigor during the revolution and civil war, sweeping away external influences and reaffirming the self-regulating principles of land usage and customary law.

At the same time it cannot be denied that new social fissures were opening along class lines under the uneven and irregular development of the capitalist sector; uneven not only in Trotsky's meaning of the contrasting dichotomies of conflict within urban and rural Russia but also in terms of the vast regional disparities in economic growth that were often reinforced by ethnic antagonism. The expansion of trade and industry drew more and more peasants, raznochintsy, and nobles into a widening circle of capitalist activities. Merchants joined with entrepreneurs from other social categories in order to found regional associations that acted like pressure groups on the government. But the persistent social and legal distinctions imposed by soslovie, status, regional, and ethnic identities prevented the coalescence of these groups into a self-conscious bourgeois class.

In the second half of the nineteenth century the Russian nobility split into several sections under the impact of the Great Reforms and commercialization of agriculture. Emancipation had proved financially ruinous for many who sold off their land and drifted into the cities. The educational reforms ended their monopoly of state service, which had already been eroded, and the military reforms brought non-nobles into the officer corps in increasing numbers. The distinction between hereditary and personal nobility became more pronounced as the old families attempted to defend their concept of honor and status against upstarts who could not pass their ennobled status to the next generation. Three or four main social groups emerged from the old dvorianstvo: the nobles in government service, mainly landless except at the very top of the service, educated in schools rather than at home, self-identified with the bureaucratic ethos; the professional men who entered law, medicine, engi-

can Historical Review 91 (1986): 11–36; Frank Wcislo, Reforming Rural Russia: State, Local Society, and National Politics, 1855–1914 (Princeton, forthcoming).

neering, and teaching and adapted the particular outlook of their calling; the commerical-industrial entrepreneurs, the wealthiest nobles, who can be subdivided into the passive investors or rentiers with capital placed in private railroads, metallurgical industry in Urals and the south, oil, machinery and shipbuilding, and the landlords who were occupied with distilling, sugar refining, milling, and beer making; and finally the bulk of the landowners who produced grain, cattle, and some industrial crops for the market.

These were not mutually exclusive groups. But the nobles themselves recognized the difficulty of reconciling the distinctive interests and outlook that lodged at the core of each. In 1897 the Novgorod marshall of the nobility admitted that "our Russian nobility includes people of such varied religions, nation, economic and regional character that to unite them at the present time is impossible: the interests of each noble is more fully expressed by the interest of the occupation to which he belongs than to the interests of his estate (soslovie)." The same sentiment was expressed at the Sixth Congress of the United Nobility in 1910 by N. A. Pavlov in his report "Ob ob'edinenii dvorianstva na pochve ekonomicheskoi" (Concerning the unity of the nobility on economic grounds).[19]

The social particularism of these groups is mostly dramatically demonstrated in the coalescence of a provincial landed gentry at the turn of the century. The government's commitment to industrialization and the greater bureaucratic intrusion into the countryside for administrative and fiscal reasons stimulated a strong reaction in the countryside. Drawn back to the land by a dual threat to their financial well-being and their psychological attachment to their estates, the landowners began, in Leopold Haimson's words, "to create for the first time in Russian history a provincial society."[20] At first they accepted the liberal leadership of a minority that acted through the zemstvos to defend the rural way of life against the tax and tariff policies of the bureaucratic industrializers. Then, after the Revolution of 1905 had demonstrated the complete bankruptcy of their paternalistic patronage of the peasantry, they rejected constitutional reform. Turning in on themselves, they became increasingly isolated from the rest of the nobility and indeed from Russian society in general.

The emergence of a bureaucratic ethos based on the professionalization of the civil service did not prevent the appearance of social fissures within this group. All bureaucratic systems exhibit signs of departmental rivalries and infighting. But the absence in Imperial Russia of a cabinet system and a prime

[19] A. P. Karelin, "Dvorianstvo v poslereformennoi Rossii (1861–1904 gg.)," *Istoricheskie zapiski* 87 (1971): 172; A. M. Anfimov, *Krupnoe pomeshchich'e khoziaistvo evropeiskoi Rossii (konets XIX-nachalo XX veka)* (Moscow, 1969), 285.

[20] Leopold H. Haimson, "Conclusion: Observations on the Politics of the Russian Countryside (1905–1914)," in *The Politics of Rural Russia, 1905–1914*, ed. Haimson (Bloomington, 1979), 263.

minister until the last decade of the monarchy intensified the fissiparous tendencies. Each minister enjoyed virtual autonomy under the direct authority and supervision of the tsar. From mid-nineteenth century the individual ministers were no longer drawn from the small elite of court aristocrats and personal favorites of the autocrat; they were, in general, professionally trained and career oriented. They gathered around them similar men whose personal and professional loyalties powerfully reinforced one another. The ministries became the core of bureaucratic interest groups.

The broader the functions of a ministry, the larger its claims of centrality in the administrative machinery, the greater its temptations to set the general tone for state policy. In Late Imperial Russia the main contenders for hegemony in the government were ministries of finance, interior, security services, war, and transportation. In addition to defending their own departmental turf, the ministers attempted to colonize or subordinate lesser ministries or occasionally other major ministries. The most ambitious efforts aimed at nothing less than a de facto unified government dominated by a single energetic minister who had successfully gained ascendancy over all others. Such attempts were made most notably by Petr Shuvalov in the 1860s and 1870s and by Sergei Witte in the 1890s. The intensity of the bureaucratic infighting grew as the field of debate widened into the public arena. The emergence of a mass press in the 1860s, the moderation of censorship, and the growing complexity of issues, particularly in areas like economic development and educational policy, broke down the insularity of government. The wider the debates over state policy were, the greater was the tendency of government officials to argue their case in public.

The autocrat did not discourage bureaucratic infighting, unless it threatened open disruption. Interministerial rivalries kept power in the hands of the tsar. Moreover, the selection of ministers was frequently based, not on ideological considerations, but on personal contact and recommendations, service records, and evidence of loyalty to the throne. The tsar himself did not seek to create a unified government under his own leadership. It was no longer a question of his direct personal rule. The massive flow of state documents—the complexities of administering—had grown far beyond the capacity of one man to manage, let alone understand. Thus, the tsar became an arbiter of the contrasting interests; a managerial tsar, he made no sustained effort to overcome the fragmentation at the very apex of Russian politics.[21]

At the other end of the social spectrum the growth of capitalist relations in the countryside accelerated the economic differentiation among the peasantry. But the extent and meaning of the process was, and remains, a matter of dispute. Despite its many ties to urban and even educated society, the peasantry

[21] This point is elaborated in my forthcoming article, "The Politics of Reform," to be published jointly by Indiana University Press and Moscow State University.

remained strongly particularistic in its outlook and customs. Overall the peasant mentality remained dominated by the land question to the exclusion of larger civil and political issues, although there were regional exceptions, especially in the Baltic littoral and Siberia where peasants began to take a broader view of politics at the end of the imperial period.[22]

There were exceptional reasons for the exceptional conditions: higher literacy and the nationalities question in the Baltic; the absence of a landlord class and the influence of sectarians in Siberia. In the succession of great social crises that shattered Russian society from 1905 through the civil war, the mass of the Great Russian peasantry concentrated in the central agricultural provinces and radiating outward along their lines of migration and settlement consistently ignored the blandishments of the political parties, yet it was totally incapable of forming a party of its own. Unwilling to accept leadership from outside its ranks, it was unable to provide it from within. This was a classic example of Marx's contemptuous description: a sack of potatoes, jumbled together but lacking any real unity.

By contrast, the factory workers undoubtedly constituted the most socially cohesive and highly conscious class in Late Imperial Russia. They had no archaic past to combat; there had never been a workers' soslovie. The older crafts' (*remeslennaia*) tradition, to be sure, had a distinctive social organization dating back to Peter's time and acquired soslovie form from 1802, but this was declining by the end of the nineteenth century. It would be an error, however, to perceive the factory workers as an undifferentiated mass. Differences in skill, education, and ties to the countryside created subgroups among the workers even within some of the largest plants. The more highly skilled, better educated workers, who no longer retained any ties to the countryside, flaunted their own life-style and considered themselves much superior to their less fortunate brethren who worked at unskilled manual labor for smaller wages and kept a peasant passport, send remittances to the village, and still held communal strips. These distinctions showed up dramatically in the greater willingness of the skilled worker to join unions and participate in political or revolutionary activities in the decades preceding the revolutions of 1917.[23] Yet the government did not even try—as in the case of the Stolypin reforms with the peasantry—to take advantage of potential divisions among the working class by extending the basic rights to organize as a means of winning the top strata over to peaceful methods of social action. Forced to legalize unions and strikes in 1905 under revolutionary pressure at a moment of weakness, it diluted and virtually crippled those rights in the years of reaction that followed. Thus, for different reasons the great mass of the Russian population,

---

[22] Eugene D. Vinogradoff, "The Russian Peasantry and the Elections to the Fourth Duma," in *Politics*, ed. Haimson, 245–46.

[23] Victoria Bonnell, *Roots of Rebellion* (Berkeley, 1984); Tim McDaniel, *Autocracy, Capitalism, and Revolution in Russia* (Berkeley, 1988), esp. chaps. 8, 11.

the *nizy* in both the cities and the countryside, were forced into taking more active, coordinated, and violent social action than they might otherwise have done.

It is tempting to tidy up this picture of social fragmentation of Imperial Russia by introducing that delightfully disarming panacea known as the transitional period. The argument here is that Russia was passing through a prolonged phase of a transformation between a traditional to a modern society, or some such variation of that theme. All the contradictions, anomalies, archaisms, and irregularities can thus be explained or explained away as epiphenomena that accompanied the main process of social change or its residue, survivals (*perezhitki*) of a decaying social formation. At this point, however, it is worth exploring whether the transition period was not so prolonged, incomplete, and abortive that it began to acquire qualities of its own, qualities so marked and persistent that they refused to wither. Indeed, they periodically rose to the surface again, particularly at moments of economic decline, political reaction, or social disruption. In other words, there may be conditions in which what appears to be a transition ceases in fact to become an intermediate stage between two well-defined types of society, asserts its own stubborn character, and takes on a life of its own.

THE SEDIMENTARY SOCIETY

Fresh perspectives on the nature of Late Imperial Russian society might gain inspiration from some kind of synthesis between the two major Russian (and Soviet) historical schools, the juridical and the sociological. If the analytical categories of state and society now appear somewhat artificial, then perhaps the choice between the state or society as the major driving force of Russian history might also appear arbitrary. Still, it is necessary to offer more of an explanation than irregular or unpredictable interplay between the two. There was some peculiar historical quality, one hesitates to use the term regularity, in their interrelationship. The state pursued an active interventionist course in its attempts to organize and direct the social groups. It is hardly necessary to rehearse the many major and minor instances of this intervention: Peter's introduction of a wholly new kind of social stratification, Catherine's attempts to create an urban society and to homogenize the administration of a multinational empire, Alexander's emancipation of the serfs, the greatest single peaceful liberation and confiscation of noble property in modern European history, the launching of an industrial revolution from above. In witnessing these great historical moments, it is important to give equal time to what the state did not do, to the resistance it encountered, to the partial changes it affected. Unquestionably, each transformation created new social conditions, but at the same time it did not doom or obliterate the social conditions it was designed to replace. As a result of this process, what might be termed a sedimentary society emerged. Although metaphors in history may be dangerous when abused, they may be highly effective in dramatically shifting perspective. In this case, the image suggests that throughout modern Russian history a successive series of social forms accumulated, each constituting a layer that covered all or most of society without altering the older forms lying under the surface.

The state was constantly attempting, without success, to impose order on the social flux. The territory it governed was too vast, its servitors too few, the opportunities for flight too great, and the differences too numerous to resolve in neat compartments of duties and obligations. Thus, the first major codification, the Ulozhenie of 1649, imposed strict categories on the multiplicity of Muscovite social groupings but left many smaller urban groups, like the iamshchiki and remesleniki, intact with their own particular organs that evolved slowly over the centuries. Peter's service classes provided another overlay, and after his death a privileged social stratum that violated his service ethic, the dvorianstvo, silted in to cover the whole. Yet under the impact of the Emancipation that stratum also broke into smaller components while retaining its soslovie character until the end of the empire. Additional irregular layers took shape. Some emerged from the breakdown of the older structures, like the raznochintsy; others had a special soslovie created for them, like the Cossacks; still others retained their general identification with a soslovie but were given important rights that in fact separated them from it, like the state peasantry. Moreover, the uneven course of capitalism created new fault lines: proto-classes, like the working class, had no place in the older juridical structure of soslovie but were denied any civic standing until 1905. There was no lack of effort to reform the social structure, but the nature of the reforms themselves helped frustrate their intention.

In Russia reforms demanding rapid and radical social change have almost invariably been initiated from above, not below. Reforms, most often in response to a systemic crisis that threatened the body politic, were launched without much preparation and without any consultation with the population. The course of reform was irregular, depending on the unity and determination of the ruling elite, the resistance or indifference of the population, and the distraction of foreign wars or the sudden death of the ruler. Given the arbitrary nature of the autocracy, it was always possible to flood the country with new legislation and advance the most radical kind of innovation. But the very arbitrariness of power deprived the state of a means to make reform permanent—that is, to institutionalize the changes by means of a constitution, rule of law, or even a dominant ideology. Everything that was done could be just as easily undone; or at least it could be hidden. At the same time the population was likely to ignore or evade the changes, accepting their form but not their intention unless the changes corresponded to its immediate needs. In this sit-

uation the impermanence of things prevailed on the surface, and deep continuities lay below it.

Nothing demonstrates more vividly the permanent impermanence of change
in Russia than the drafting of the law codes. To turn once again to the historians of the juridical school for instruction, the law was, in their eyes, the essence of the state principle, the most powerful instrument of social control
wielded by the state in its efforts to tame a restless and often rebellious population. Yet K. V. Kavelin, a leading exponent of the juridical school, presented in his *Nachala russkogo sudoustroistva* an extended argument that the
autonomous development of Muscovite juridical principles stemmed "directly
from popular custom." The first codification of 1649 (Ulozhenie) was simply
a systematic arrangement that Kavelin called "the ancient juridical way of
life" (*byt*)—the customs of those regions that subsequently became a part of
the Great Russian state. According to him these origins explained why the
Ulozhenie and all subsequent Muscovite legislation possessed a "casuistic
character." That is to say, the law code did not explicitly state the juridical
principles upon which the mass of legislation that had been collected and arranged within its pages was based. As social relations governed by civil law
became more complex in the latter half of the seventeenth century, it likewise
became more difficult to apply customary law to individual cases as in the
past. At the same time, the Ulozhenie did not contain a set of abstract legal
definitions upon which individual cases could be adjudicated. The confusion
over the interpretation of the law did not originate with the introduction of
foreign legal principles, as Slavophile publicists insisted. Instead, when customary law was applied to new situations, the results sometimes contradicted
previous decisions. Kavelin maintained, nevertheless, that throughout this
process of resolving conflicts "the entire juridical way of life constituted a
single, organic, harmonious whole." Clearly then, Kavelin concluded, it was
baseless to claim that no abstract concept of the law and no understanding of
rights existed in Russia before Peter the Great and that he bestowed both on
the Russian people.[24]

The idea that the law emanated from society rather than having been imposed upon it from above or outside may sound strange coming from a leading
representative of the juridical school and a notorious "Westerner" to boot, but
there are stranger things to come. In Kavelin's mind Peter's achievements did
not rest upon creating the law or even substituting a new set of juridical principles for an old one. Instead, he extracted concrete legal principles from customary law, gave them explicit expression, and based his legislation upon
them. Although this gave precedence to the letter of the law over its spirit, it

[24] K. D. Kavelin, "Osnovnye nachala russkago sudoustroistva i grazhdanskago sudoustroista
v period vremeni ot Ulozheniia do uchrezhdeniia o guberniiakh," *Sobranie sochinenii. Etnogra-
fiia i pravovedenie* (St. Petersburg, 1900), 4: 209–10, 350–51.

did not significantly weaken the organic, historical development of the law. That is, the law remained responsive to changes in social life. Moreover, although Peter's legislation was characterized by a greater degree of legal precision and self-consciousness, it did not culminate in a comprehensive, systematic digest of laws. Paradoxically, the very absence of an abstract body of legal principles may well have served as the surest guarantee that much of Peter's legislation survived him. For, as Pavlov-Silvansky remarked, the persistence and vitality of Peter's reforms after his death demonstrated the extent to which his reforms embodied and fulfilled the needs of society or at least its ruling stratum. The results would have been different if he had imposed upon that society a set of alien legal norms borrowed from other societies with different historical experiences.[25]

If we pursue this insight of Kavelin's it leads to a remarkable conclusion about the continuity in the relationship between law and society throughout the imperial period and into the early Soviet period. The very persistence of customary law as the basis for legal principles prevented a codification of law as understood in countries whose legal systems were founded on Roman law. The Svod Zakonov of 1832 was much like its predecessor, the Ulozhenie of 1649, a compilation of laws that had not fallen into disuse. Among other things, it clarified and systematized the soslovie system. This had its ironic side. For the code was published just a generation before the Emancipation and Great Reforms fractured the soslovie strata, leaving only a crumbling residue in place. Aside from eliminating repetition and prolixity, the code made no attempt to tamper with the letter of the law. When the codifiers encountered contradictory edicts they simply selected the most recent whether or not it was considered the best. As Richard Wortman has observed, Nicholas I "adopted historical and nationalist views . . . [which] banished the notion that the law had to conform to universal natural norms."[26] The monarch's resistance to a rule of law was a long-standing defense of his monopoly of authority, but, paradoxically, it was also a means of preserving the influence of custom upon law particularly in the largely unexamined mass of petty legislation and regulations that had nothing to do with the direct exercise of power in Imperial Russian society but that profoundly affected the daily life of millions of its inhabitants. At this level, perhaps, it would be most fruitful to begin to study the ways in which customs became legal norms through the state's acceptance of existing social realities rather than to assume that legislation reflected the abstract ideas of order and system that inspired reforming bureaucrats.

The potential usefulness of this method does not end in 1917. E. H. Carr

[25] N. P. Pavlov-Silvanskii, "Mneniia verkhovnikov o reformakh Petra Velikogo," *Sochineniia* (St. Petersburg, 1911), 2: 375–79.
[26] Richard Wortman, *The Development of a Russian Legal Consciousness* (Chicago, 1976), 43; see also Marc Raeff, *Michael Speransky, Statesman of Imperial Russia*, 2d rev. ed. (The Hague, 1969), 324.

was perhaps the first to point out that legal principles did not fare well in the early days of the Soviet regime. Extreme suspicion of any legal system during the civil war yielded to the establishment of law codes in 1922 based mainly on the emerging property relations of the New Economic Policy. In neither period was much attention paid to "the far fetched constructions of intellectuals," in other words to theories of either proletarian or bourgeois law. As a result, gradually prerevolutionary legal norms and practices, which themselves had already grown out of customary law, were reintroduced. One dramatic illustration of this process was the harshness of rural as compared to city courts in dealing with crimes against property and individuals; in these years the peasantry in general shared the view that sentencing was far too lenient.[27] In Soviet as in autocratic Russia the problem was how to instill the values of the dominant culture—these deeper layers of society that rested underneath the accumulation of superficial social and institutional forms erected from above.

Without wishing to force the sedimentary metaphor, it might be taken one step farther by examining a transverse section of the accumulated social layers as they appeared at the end of the monarchy. From this perspective emerges the much larger number of layers that have accumulated within the top strata of society. This concentration may be attributed to the greater vulnerability of the elites to the three major instruments of social change: state legislation, external cultural influences, and market capitalism. The multiplication of social identities was politically debilitating in an autocratic state that was forced to make a rapid transition under the pressure of revolution in 1905 to a parliamentary or constitutional government. The fragmentation of elites was reflected in the proliferation of political parties in 1905 and afterward, their highly unstable character, and the absence of a strong political center on the eve of the revolution.

At the other end of the social spectrum, the peasantry remained relatively more homogenous in its social organization than the elites. There were, as we have seen, regional differences; the impact of a national market and forced industrialization on the dvor, the commune, and the village was highly disruptive; the Stolypin reforms administered another blow to communal life. Yet when the revolution and civil war blew away the fragile state institutions, broke the urban-rural nexus, and wrecked the market economy, the peasantry almost everywhere in the core provinces of the empire reacted against the most recent socioeconomic trends. They plunged back into an archaic social form, redistributed the land according to the oldest customs of social justice, and emerged more homogenous than ever before. It even absorbed much of the urban working class that fled famine and the breakdown of social services in the cities. In the case of the peasantry, the accumulated layer of social changes

---

[27] E. H. Carr, *Socialism in One Country, 1924–1926* (New York, 1958), 1: 78–79.

that affected its fundamental values was much thinner than that of the elites.[28] Thus, the peasantry was spared the excessive fragmentation that weakened and ultimately destroyed the elites in Russia from 1917 to 1920. To transform the peasantry itself required either a long period of gradual absorption into the cultural life and economic system dominated by the cities or a violent, coercive, and sustained attack by the state. This was the choice that the new rulers, like the old, faced in the young Soviet republic.

[28] Moshe Lewin, *The Making of the Soviet System* (New York, 1985), 49–56, 81–87.

Chapter 22

RUSSIA'S UNREALIZED CIVIL SOCIETY

Samuel D. Kassow

If the criterion of middle-class identity is the attainment of common political action, then Russia clearly failed to develop a middle class. The unitary vision of the 1905 Liberation Movement and Riabushinsky's appeal for a new bourgeoisie to assume the mantle of national leadership failed to achieve their goals. Merchants split along regional and ethnic lines, professionals argued over authority and status, writers and intellectuals agonized over where they belonged. Would-be leaders of a new middle class found the right words but emerged with relatively few followers.

In short, those social groups occupying the shifting space between the peasantry and the tiny but still-powerful stratum of the landed nobility failed to find a common political and social identity. But if we look beyond conscious political choices toward more nuanced and complex phenomenons—new ideas of space and time, new attitudes toward the role of law and the possibilities of purposeful individual action, the acceptance of new ways of conceptualizing the place of the individual and society—then we can see that a new public culture was indeed developing in Late Imperial Russia. Indeed, if we accept Eley and Blackbourn's argument that the *Kaiserreich* was a "bourgeois" society or Blumin's "paradox of middle-class development," then one can at least see a strong case for arguing similar developments in Russia. The rise of voluntary societies, the steady if slow development of respect for property rights, the rapid expansion of higher and secondary education, artistic patronage, the growth of professions, the rite of a multilayered press, the emergence of the Duma as a forum for political articulation, the unrelenting assault on the *soslovie* system, philanthropy, new opportunities afforded by municipal government—all pointed toward the creation of what Habermas would call a "public sphere."

But this public sphere developed in a specific context, one far removed from nineteenth-century America or even the Bismarckian Reich. A key determinant of this context was the state. The Liberation Movement had found its voice in appealing to an aroused *obshchestvennost'* to take its place alongside the state as the guardian of the nation's fate, and the pat juxtaposition of a creative public battling an obstructionist state remained a stock theme of certain political discourse until the revolution. But in fact the supposed dichotomy between state and society was insufficient to help maintain a sense of common middle-class identity. First, the state remained the major agent of social transformation. Physicians, professors, schoolteachers, lawyers, and entrepreneurs might resent certain aspects of state policy, but they needed the state to create essential preconditions for purposeful social action. Furthermore, the governmental elite included many hard-working officials who fought for the rule of law, respected individual rights, struggled to expand educational opportunities, and tried to formulate sensible and progressive policies to deal with Russia's enormous problems.

One way of conceptualizing the role of the state in the formation of a public sphere in Late Imperial Russia is to examine the interplay between the emergence of middling elites and a growing internal crisis within the state apparatus. Faced with an enormous peasant problem, an unstable international situation, a tax base of limited options, an administrative system incapable of governing a vast, disparate, multi-ethnic society, many government officials, as Dominick Lieven points out, insisted that the state must hold the fist in reserve. Even moderate liberal demands that stopped short of political democracy, but asked instead for the basic rudiments of a *Rechtstaat*, threatened this vital ultimate weapon—the state's ability to use brute force as the only alternative to national disintegration and chaos. This hard-bitten pessimism, combined with the obvious ambivalence of the tsar to the post-1905 order (and even to key cultural aspects of the Petrine legacy), highlighted the internal disarray of the state and in turn created a crisis of confidence and authority.

The disarray of the state and the ongoing crisis of authority also influenced the process of social self-definition by skewing fundamental patterns of perceiving and legitimizing deference and hierarchy. If one antidote to the nagging political malaise was the call for "democracy," then why not also extend "democracy" to the university, municipal council, zemstvo professional, cultural, or commercial arena? Why should zemstvo employees accept the authority of their superiors, or junior faculty the dictates of professors, or commercial employees the whims of their employers? Thus, the essential differences between the perceived norms governing relationships in the political and civil spheres failed to achieve the recognition in Russia that they did in the West. In short, on the one hand, the crisis of state authority in a time of economic change and growing urbanization fostered a process of social redefinition. On the other hand, that very process indirectly shaped attitudes that complicated the growth of strong civic and professional structures.

One example of a structure clearly affected by this crisis of authority was that basic incubator of key professional elites—the university. The universities had to meet complex, manifold, and contradictory expectations from the government, the professoriate, and the students. Professors called for a "neutral" university and asked students to accept their authority. All too often, students refused, in part because they disagreed with professors on how to protect themselves from state interference, in part because they did not share their professors' confidence that the universities were preparing them for professions and careers that would bring psychological fulfillment. Caught in a transitional space and time, the students rebelled, as much against the assumptions of Russian liberalism as against the state and the political system per se.

The case of the universities illustrates a central issue in the problem of constructing new social identities in Russia: the concept of neutrality. In his essay, "Binary Models in the Dynamics of Russian Culture," Iury Lotman writes that a basic feature of pre-nineteenth-century Russian culture was its essential polarity, "a polarity expressed in the binary nature of its structure." Unlike medieval Western culture, there was no "axiologically neutral zone":

> In the actual life of the medieval West we find a wide band of neutral behavior and there are neutral social institutions which are neither "holy" nor "sinful," neither "state organized" nor "anti-state" they are neither good nor bad. This neutral sphere becomes a structural reserve from which tomorrow's system develops. Since continuity is obvious here, there is no need either to emphasize it structurally or to reestablish it consciously and artificially.[1]

In a very basic sense, the entire theme of this collection of essays has been, to quote Lotman, the examination of the developing of this "structural reserve" in Late Imperial Russia. Can we say that on the eve of the revolution, Russia was witnessing the emergence of an "axiologically neutral zone"?

In Vasily Grossman's masterpiece, *Life and Fate*, the historian Madiarov complains about the way Chekhov, "the first true Russian democrat," has been misunderstood in Russian culture:

> Our Russian humanism has always been cruel, intolerant, sectarian. From Avvakum to Lenin our conception of humanity and freedom has always been partisan and fanatical. It has always mercilessly sacrificed the individual to some abstract idea of humanity. Even Tolstoy, with his doctrine of non-resistance to Evil, is intolerant—and his point of departure is not man but God. He wants the idea of goodness to triumph. True believers always want to bring God to man by force; and in Russia they stop at nothing—even murder—to achieve this.
>
> Chekhov said: let's put God—and all these grand progressive ideas—to one side. Let's begin with man; let's be kind and attentive to the individual man—whether he's a bishop, a peasant, an industrial magnate, a convict in the Sakhalin Islands, or a waiter in a restaurant. Let's begin with respect, compassion, and love for the individual—or we'll never get anywhere. That's democracy, the still *unrealized* democracy of the Russian people.
>
> The Russians have seen everything during the past thousand years—grandeur

---

[1] Jurij Lotman and Boris Uspenskii, *The Semiotics of Russian Culture*, ed. A. Shukman (Ann Arbor: Ardis, 1984), 4.

and supergrandeur; but what they have never seen is democracy. [emphasis added][2]

Of course, Madiarov clearly reveals his own values: a preference for the "unrealized democracy of the Russian people." But implicit in Grossman's argument here is the realization that democracy is more than a political stance: it is a way of perceiving human relationships within specific social contexts and without moral or ideological prejudice.

On the one hand, that sounds self-evident, simplistic, and banal; on the other hand, that might be the very point. That "still unrealized democracy" of the Russian people did not soar to a vision that would have stirred a Dostoevsky, Tolstoi, or Lenin. But for all its vagueness, it comes closest to what obshchestvennost' was all about. Implicit in the concept was the inherent tension between the structured authority in professional and economic relationships and the basic equality and respect arising from the human condition. Such a tension could only be worked out in "neutral zones," but such refuges had a difficult time taking root in the political conditions of Late Imperial Russia. Nevertheless, the process had begun.

The introduction to this volume employed many terminologies: *obshchestvo*, obshchestvennost', *burzhuaziia*, "middle class," and "civil society." These words reflect a search for new identities that might have attenuated the personal and social tensions generated in Late Imperial Russia. This search proceeded in intermediate places: the space between state and society, the moving ground between the ruling elites and the peasant masses.

It goes without saying that these antinomies fail to capture the complex reality of a rapidly changing society that masked, as Al Rieber points out, deep perceptual and social continuities. Does one consign all educated *chinovniki* to the ranks of the state, all literate peasants to the ranks of the *narod*? Of course not. The work of Walter Pintner, William Wagner, Richard Wortman, Dominick Lieven, and others clearly shows how misleading it was to draw too sharp a line between the *chinovniki* and educated society. And at the other end of the social spectrum, Jeffrey Brooks shows that there was no iron curtain marking off the cultural perceptions of the peasant masses from the literate urban culture.

Yet in the end, there *was* a state *regarded* as repressive. There were peasant masses whose "moral indignation" (to borrow Moshe Lewin's term) against the state *and tsenzovaia Rossiia* (yet another new term) was all too real.

The key question, therefore, is the extent to which a public sphere and a civil society could develop in a country where fear of violence—from either the state or the masses—lurked in the wings. Solving problems by dialogue, process, law, and debate requires certain shared beliefs that did not flourish in

---

[2] Vasily Grossman, *Life and Fate*, trans. Robert Chandler (New York: Harper & Row, 1985), 283.

an atmosphere of suspicion and mistrust. Yet there can be no doubt that a public sphere was developing. It was neither rooted enough nor powerful enough to overcome the crises that called forth the ultimate resort to repression and violence. But it did create a new sense of possibility and suggestive elements of a "usable past" that contemporary Soviet leaders like Gorbachev so desperately need.

LIST OF CONTRIBUTORS

Harley Balzer
Russian and East European Institute
Georgetown University
Washington, D.C.

John E. Bowlt
Department of Slavic Languages and
    Literatures
University of Southern California
Los Angeles, California

Joseph Bradley
Department of History
University of Tulsa
Tulsa, Oklahoma

William C. Brumfield
Department of German and Russian
Tulane University
New Orleans, Louisiana

Edith W. Clowes
Department of Foreign Languages and
    Literatures
Purdue University
West Lafayette, Indiana

James M. Curtis
Department of German and Russian
University of Missouri
Columbia, Missouri

Ben Eklof
Department of History
Ballantine Hall
Indiana University
Bloomington, Indiana

Gregory L. Freeze
Department of History
Brandeis University
Waltham, Massachusetts

Abbott Gleason
Department of History
Brown University
Providence, Rhode Island

Samuel D. Kassow
Department of History
Trinity College
Hartford, Connecticut

Mary Louise Loe
Department of History
James Madison University
Harrisonburg, Virginia

Louise McReynolds
Department of History
Sakamaki Hall A203
University of Hawaii at Manoa
Honolulu, Hawaii

Sidney Monas
Department of Slavic Languages and
    Literatures
University of Texas
Austin, Texas

John O. Norman
Department of History
Western Michigan University
Kalamazoo, Michigan

Daniel T. Orlovsky
Department of History
Southern Methodist University
Dallas, Texas

Thomas C. Owen
Department of History
Louisiana State University
Baton Rouge, Louisiana

Alfred Rieber
Department of History
University of Pennsylvania
Philadelphia, Pennsylvania

Bernice G. Rosenthal
Department of History
Fordham University
Bronx, New York

Christine Ruane
Department of History
Washington University
St. Louis, Missouri

Charles E. Timberlake
Department of History
University of Missouri
Columbia, Missouri

William Wagner
Department of History
Williams College
Williamstown, Massachusetts

James L. West
Department of History
Trinity College
Hartford, Connecticut

INDEX